Macmillan Illustrated
ALMANAC For KIDS

Ann Elwood
Carol Orsag
Sidney Solomon

MAC

10.⁹⁵

Macmillan Illustrated ALMANAC For KIDS

Text: Ann Elwood and Carol Orsag
Design and Artistic Direction: Sidney Solomon
Drawings: Lindsay Barrett

Aladdin Books • Macmillan Publishing Company • New York
Collier Macmillan Publishers • London

The information given in this book is intended solely as a guide of broad general usefulness, but it is sold with the understanding that the Publisher is not engaged in rendering a legal, medical, educational, psychological, or other professional service. Those wishing further information should consult the organizations listed in this book and/or the educational, religious, medical, and legal advisers in their area. The information this book contains is as accurate and up to date as possible, and has been carefully checked by the authors. Nevertheless, the Publisher hereby disclaims responsibility for the accuracy of the text.

Raymond Solomon: Principal picture researcher and associate art director

Florence Lazerson: Assistant picture researcher

Annette Blackwell and Linnea Johnson: Administrative assistants

J. Frances Tindall: Production associate

Jane Sufian: Legal Consultant

Jim Natal: Sports Consultant

Steven Bryant and Ronald Brook Madigan: Science Consultants

Micheline Karas: Editoral Assistant

Aladdin Books
Macmillan Publishing Company
866 Third Avenue, New York, NY 10022
Collier Macmillan Canada, Inc.
Macmillan Illustrated Almanac For Kids is also published in a hardcover edition by Macmillan Publishing Company.
First Aladdin edition 1986

Printed in the United States of America

10 9 8 7 6 5 4 3

Library of Congress Cataloging in Publication Data
Elwood, Ann.
   Macmillan illustrated almanac for kids.
   Includes index.
   Summary: A reference book with twelve chapters on subjects of particular interest to children: what kids think, problems, odd facts, law, people, body and mind, sports, money and work, animals, science, arts, and communication.
   1. Almanacs, Children's.   [1. Almanacs] I. Orsag, Carol.   II. Solomon, Sidney.
III. Barrett, Lindsay, ill.   IV. Macmillan Publishing Company.   V. Title.
AY81.J8E45   1984   051   83-26296
ISBN 0-02-043100-7 (pbk.)

Contents

Photograph Credits

We are gratefully indebted to the many suppliers of the photographs reproduced in this book. Without their cooperation and suggestions, this almanac would not have been possible. Every effort has been made to credit each photograph properly, where it appears in the book, with the names of the photographer and supplier. These credits appear in parentheses at the end of each caption accompanying the photograph. Any omissions or errors are unintentional and will be immediately corrected by the authors and Publisher, upon notification by any of the involved parties. We highlight here the names of all suppliers of photographs, with deeply felt thanks for their assistance.

AIP—Niels Bohr Library; American Cancer Society; American Junior Bowling Congress; American Lung Foundation; American Museum of Natural History; American Pet Motels, Inc.; American Red Cross; Anne Frank House; Bicycle Manufacturers' Association of America, Inc.; Big Brother/Big Sisters of America; Boston Children's Museum; Boy Scouts of America; Burndy Library (AIP); Ming Chen; John Chernoff; Contact; Croaker College; Ted Curson; Selma Curtis; Design Photographers International, Inc.; Paul Duckworth; Eastman Kodak Company; Edumed, Inc; 4 H Clubs; Friends of Animals; Freelance Photographer's Guild; Ewing Galloway; Renato Glasso; Charles Hamilton Galleries; Harvard University Archives; *Holt County Independent;* International Frisbee Disc Association; International Gymnast; International Society for the Protection of Mustangs and Burros; Israeli Consulate (NYC); Jackson Memorial Hospital; Japan National Tourist Organization; Jerusalem Biblical Zoo;

Marlene Karas; Media Factory; MGM, Inc.; NASA; National Commission on Resources for Youth; National Foundation, March of Dimes; National Marine Fisheries Service; National Park Service; National Portrait Gallery, Smithsonian Institution; New York City Ballet; New York City Police Department; New York Public Library; Parker Brothers, Inc.; Photo-Researchers, Inc.; Photoworld/ FPG; Dave Powers; Ringling Brothers Barnum and Bailey Combined Shows, Inc.; Save the Children Federation, Inc.; Scholastic, Inc.; Sequoia National Park; Special Olympics, Inc.; Stock, Boston; Michael D. Sullivan; Tourist Information Service of Hungary; Ukrainian Art Center (LA); Unimation, Inc.; United Nations; U.S. Department of Argiculture; U.S. Department of the Interior; U.S. Figure Skating Association; U.S. Geological Service; U.S. Patent Office; UPI, Inc.; University of Kansas Museum of Natural History; Walt Disney Productions; Doyle Weaver; Wide World Photos; Wild Horses of America Registry, Inc.; Wimbledon Lawn Tennis Museum; Yad Vashem's Martyrs' and Heroes' Remembrance Authority, Israel.

Text Credits

We would also like to acknowledge and thank the following for permission to reprint the written or published material listed below. Numbers in parentheses refer to the pages in the *Almanac* on which the material appears. Any omissions or errors in crediting any copyright holders are unintentional and will be rectified by the authors and Publishers, upon notification.

Academic Therapy Publications, Novato, CA, for excerpts from *The Two-Sided Trick Book* (392–395). Avon Books, New York, from *How Children See Our World*, collected and edited by Jella Lepman, the poems "Lonely Old Man" and "When . . ." (403), translation copyright © 1975 by Avon Books, reprinted by permission of the publisher. Mr. and Mrs. Carpenter, Gainseville, FL, for "Here Lies Nicole" (82). Center for Science in the Public Interest (membership available for $15 per year), 1755 S. Street, N.W., Washington, D.C. 20009, for the chart "Added Sugar in Processed Foods" (191), August 1979, *Nutrition Action*. Crown Publishers, Inc., New York, NY, for material adapted from *Our Gang: The Life and Times of the Little Rascals*, by Leonard Maltin and Richard W. Bann (409–413), copyright © 1977 by Leonard Maltin and Richard W. Bann, by permission of the publisher. Curriculum Concepts, Inc., New York, NY, for "Jazz Is . . ." by Marge Curson (389–391), *Scoop*, 11/10/79, copyright © 1979 by Curriculum Concepts, Inc. "Dear Abby," "*Dos and Don'ts for Parents*" (16–17), with permission of Abigail Van Buren. Doubleday & Company, Inc., New York, NY, for excerpts from "Calendar for Beginners" (302), from *Sylvia Porter's Money Book*, copyright © 1975 by Sylvia Porter, reprinted by permission of the publisher. Mr. and Mrs. Hogue for "My Great Uncle Bob" (34–35), by Don Hogue. Methuen Inc., New York, NY, from *Dear World: How I'd Put the World Right, by the Children of Over 50 Nations*, Richard and Helen Exley, eds., two poems, "If your friend . . ." (405) and "If I could rule . . ." (404), copyright © 1978 Exley Publications Ltd., published by Methuen Inc., by permission of the publisher. The *New York Times*, for "Children Predict" (18–19), copyright © 1967 by The New York Times Company, reprinted by permission. Save the Children, 1981, for "Kids Write to Save the Children" (12–16). Simon & Schuster, a Division of Gulf and Western Corp., from *There Are Two Lives*, by Richard Lewis, translated by Haruna Kimura, the poem "The Land in My Mother" (404), copyright © 1970 by Richard Lewis and Haruna Kimura, reprinted by permission of the publisher.

We would also like to thank the following parents for permission to reprint their kids' entries in the *Almanac*'s contest, "What Will Happen in the Future?" (20–27): Vicki Abernathy; Mr. and Mrs. J. Baltz; Robert Cunningham; Judith and Robert Crumby; Karen Kupper; B. Jennings; Richard and Colleen Hanley; Carol Ann Greene; Carol and John Magyar; Robert Mascaro; Mr. and Mrs. Mays; Sue and Bill Monahan; Ann and John Moriarty; Jerry Osborne; Mrs. Rita Pinhal; Ronald and Dolores Polidora; Kathy Mahoney; G. Rubel; Carol Ann and Thomas Sgroi; Patricia Sova; Florence and K.W. Steinbrecher.

Acknowledgments

To our families, friends, and associates who have given us help and support, with special mention to: Doug Beagle, Mary Ann Berosh, Fern Bryant, Steven Bryant, Ken and Rene Bundy, Ming Chen, Lisa Connelly, Fred Cushing, George Elgin, Scott Englehorn, Diane Fontanazza, Jane Hammoud, Marlene Karas, Micheline Karas, Daniel Lamberti, Karen Lang, Ronald Brook Madigan, Jim Natal, Louis Neiheisel, Betty and John Orsag, John Orsag, Jr., David Raht, John Raht, Susan and Richard Schultz, Jane Sufian, Linda Wood, Bill Worth, John Zebrowski.

And to all those people from organizations and agencies who helped us obtain information, with special thanks to: Yvonne Anderson, Yellow Ball Workshop; Fran Burd, La Habra City School District; Paula C. Domedion, Edmund Scientific Co.; Donald F. Duncan, Duracraft, Inc.; Aalbert Heine, Director of the Corpus Christi Museum; Carol Jordan, U.S. Environmental Protection Agency; Laura Malis, Save the Children; Mary Ann Paris, Eastman Kodak Co.; Mike Roytek, Boy Scouts of America; Florance M. Schook, American Numismatic Assn.; Dr. Dan Shannon and Robert Jones of the San Diego City Schools; Doyle Weaver, Missy Junior Gloves; personnel at the Carlsbad City Library and the Santa Monica Public Library; personnel at the libraries of the University of California, San Diego, and San Diego State University.

We are very grateful to the children and teachers of the fifth and sixth grades at: Ada Harris School, Cardiff-by-the-Sea, California; Ambridge Area Catholic School, Ambridge, Pennsylvania; Clinton Rosette School, DeKalb, Illinois; Holy Rosary School, Nashville, Tennessee; Moseley School, Westfield, Massachusetts; Rutherford School, Monticello, New York; and South Middle School, Westfield, Massachusetts.

In addition, we wish to thank our editor, Charles Levine, of the Macmillan Publishing Company, whose enthusiasm and dedication to this project are deeply appreciated—and his assistant, Glady Villegas.

Ann Elwood

Carol Orsag

* * *

A book covering such a large variety of topics owes a great deal to the support of everyone involved. I would especially like to thank Frederic S. Cushing, former Director of the Glencoe Press in Los Angeles, for putting me in touch with Ann Elwood.

I am grateful for the encouragement and moral support given to this work by my long-time friend and associate Jeremiah Kaplan, Chairman of the Board of Macmillan Publishing Company.

Lindsay Barrett, who did all the original drawings, not only displayed excellent artistic skills and imagination but was a truly fine collaborator, whose helpfulness and good cheer made possible much that would otherwise have seemed impossible.

Norman Fein, president of Trufont Typographers, the company that did the typesetting, was indeed helpful in solving many of the complex typesetting problems.

J. Frances Tindall, my editorial associate on all my complex book projects, lent her unique publishing skills and organizing talents to the job of coordinating text and pictures in the crucial page makeup stage.

Our editor, Charles Levine, was a willing helper, advisor, mediator, decision-maker, and splendid all-around publishing executive. I am also grateful to Glady Villegas, his able assistant, who helped in many of the difficult details and kept the communication lines open.

Raymond Solomon, my son and business partner, pitched in early in the game and took charge of picture research, contributed many of the picture ideas, drafted many of the captions, helped with the organization and the art direction, and all in all played a major role in making this book a reality.

I am deeply indebted to my wonderful wife, Clara Solomon, whose patience, wisdom, good cheer, and never-failing good advice made it possible for me to keep myself working on an even keel.

Sidney Solomon

Introduction

This book is a grab bag of fun and information, for and about kids. Some of the writing is *by* kids, too. The *Almanac* will tell you about a chain of shrews, where to go for help if you have a broken heart, about the laws covering children, how to interview your grandparents to write your family history, and much more.

These days most kids live in families in which both parents work, so kids are on their own a lot of the time. They often don't have immediate help to get into a sport, pursue an interest, or solve a problem. The *Almanac* shows them how by pointing in the right direction. For almost every interest or problem, a network of people is waiting to help. Where would you go to play baseball with a bunch of kids? What group helps with drinking problems? The *Almanac* tells you how to get in touch with those networks. Some-times the book goes further than just pointing. It tells you how to send messages in code, perform animal first aid, set up a garage sale, or ask for a raise in your allowance.

When we wrote the book, we always asked ourselves: Is that fact or story interesting? So expect to have fun reading it. Your parents might even want to sneak a look. They may be as interested as you in some things, for example, in the section "What Life Was Like When Your Parents Were Kids." Did you know that Cinderella's slipper wasn't glass? What is an elephant joke? Will people of the future play aerial football? Will robots flirt with each other? Who was the real Christopher Robin? What American president inspired the teddy bear? What famous general was a poor speller? And how about the baseball player who chewed tobacco and spent most of his childhood in reform school? Meet a six-year-old who played piano for kings, the director of a frog-training college, and Dinosaur Jim—who stows away dinosaur bones under a football stadium. What happens to a raisin in a glass of champagne? What is the world's hardest tongue twister? What does the word yo-yo really mean? Why are little kids sometimes afraid of baths? Meet an attack rabbit, and a tortoise who fell in love with a garbage can lid. Amaze your friends with a magic trick, or pantomime, or facts. What facts? For instance, facts about strange inventions—chicken eyeglasses or the twirling spaghetti fork. Facts about robots, such as the robot mouse and space spider. The story of the exploding apron. The facts about famous volcanoes. The life stories of comic-strip heroes like Spiderman, the Incredible Hulk, and Wonder Woman.

Finding Your Way Around the Book

If you want to find some special thing, look in the table of contents or the index. If it's a problem, it will be listed alphabetically in the contents under Chapter 3 on problems, along with a page number. If it's basketball, look it up in the sports chapter. The chapter headings will give you an idea of what's in the book.

But the *Almanac* is meant for browsing, too. Just leaf through it for entertainment. You might want to keep it beside your bed, or even in the bathroom. But of course there's no law that says you can't read it straight through if you want.

How It's Written

Not all kids are readers. Some like to read all the time, while others don't. The *Almanac* is for both readers and nonreaders. We've kept the writing simple. When only the facts are needed, we present

them bare. Why did we decide to write it this way? A young friend of ours, supposedly a nonreader, was crazy about reading the *Guinness Book of World Records*. In that book, interesting facts are presented in short, fairly easy to read sections. It's a no-nonsense book. It was one of our models. So too was the easy style of *The Book of Lists* and *The People's Almanac*.

Here are a few more questions that will be answered in the *Almanac for Kids*: What sport was first played in church? How can you adopt a wild horse from the government? Who wrote *The Cockroach Ballet* and why? Why do you get dizzy when you spin around? What food would most kids take to a desert island? What can you do about zits? What are the laws about bike riding? How can you make a movie? What are the best sports cards to collect? How can you walk like an Indian, and why is that the best way to hike? What were penny dreadfuls? It's all here in short, entertaining sections.

And . . . One Last Note

Want to get more information on some of the subjects in this book? We have included the names and addresses of many people to contact. When sending a letter, make sure you include your name and address so the person will be able to reply.

Make friends with the librarian at your public library. Librarians are wonderful information sources. They can help you find information in places other than just books.

And always keep a dime in your shoe so you can make a phone call. If you need help, dial "O" for operator.

We hope you like this book. Do you have any ideas you'd like to tell us or other kids about? If you do, please write to us. We really would love to hear from you.

Macmillan Illustrated
ALMANAC
For KIDS

Kids want to be able to share their feelings with others.
(Linda Riley, Big Brothers/Big Sisters of America)

Chapter *1*
WHAT KIDS THINK

The Almanac's Special Survey

To get a firsthand idea of what kids are thinking, we made up a list of questions and sent it to 7 schools. Exactly 310 kids answered—156 boys and 154 girls. Kids didn't have to answer all 25 questions—just the ones they liked. Fifth and sixth graders from these schools took part in the survey:

Ada Harris School
Cardiff-by-the-Sea, California

Ambridge Area Catholic School
Ambridge, Pennsylvania

Clinton Rosette School
DeKalb, Illinois

Holy Rosary School
Nashville, Tennessee

Moseley School
Westfield, Massachusetts

Rutherford School
Monticello, New York

South Middle School
Westfield, Massachusetts

What would you have told us? Here is the questionnaire. Think of your answer for each question. Then turn the page and see what other kids said.

The Almanac Questionnaire

1. What is the perfect age for a person to be? Why?

2. Are kids growing up faster now than they did 10 years ago?

3. At what age should people be allowed to drive cars?

4. At what age should people be allowed to marry?

5. How do your parents treat you? (a) like a baby (b) like someone your age should be treated (c) too much like an adult

6. Are your parents proud of you? (a) yes (b) no (c) I don't know

7. Pretend you could tell all the parents in the world 3 things to help them get along better with their kids. What 3 things would you tell them?

8. If you had a million dollars, what would you do with it?

9. Pretend that you are going to be stranded alone on a desert island. What book would you take with you?

10. What 3 kinds of food would you take with you on the desert island?

11. *For boys only:* If you were talking with your friends (other boys) for an hour, how much time would you spend talking

3

about girls? (*a*) no time (*b*) about 5 minutes (*c*) more than 5 minutes

12. *For girls only:* If you were talking with your friends (other girls) for an hour, how much time would you spend talking about boys? (*a*) no time (*b*) about 5 minutes (*c*) more than 5 minutes

13. If you could have an unusual animal (like a giraffe) for a pet, what animal would you choose?

14. What job would you like to have when you get older?

15. Do you want to go to college?

16. Do you think you will get married when you get older?

17. Name one famous person (living or dead) whom you would like to be like.

18. If you could have one of the following, which would you choose? (*a*) good looks (*b*) great personality (*c*) lots of money

19. How much time do you spend daydreaming? (*a*) a lot of time (*b*) just a little time (*c*) no time at all

20. What worries you the most?

21. What scares you the most?

22. What makes you the angriest?

23. What makes you the happiest?

24. If you could change 2 things about the world, what would they be?

25. What is one question you have wanted to ask, but have been afraid to ask?

EXTRA: Do you have a message for other kids in the world? If so, what is it?

What Kids Had to Say in Response to the Survey

1. *What is the perfect age for a person to be? Why?*

Every age from one to 65 got some votes. The "perfect age" for most kids

The *Almanac* survey showed that kids think a lot about dating.

turned out to be 16. They said things like this:

"You can drive, date, and still have your whole life in front of you."

"So my parents can't boss me around."

"Because everything is waiting for me and my Sweet Sixteen party."

"That's when all the pizzazz comes into your life."

In second place was age 20:

"Because you are young, strong, and smart."

"Because you go out into the world and learn new skills."

"You are not too old and not too young."

In third place was age 18:

"Because you can drive, get a car, and be free."

"Because when you are 18, you've reached your peak."

2. *Are kids growing up faster now than they did 10 years ago?*

Exactly 293 kids answered this question. "Yes, kids are growing up faster," said 227 kids. Only 66 answered "No."

3. *At what age should people be allowed to drive cars?*

The big winner here was age 16.

4. *At what age should people be allowed to marry?*

In first place was age 18; in second place was age 20; in third place was age 19.

5. *How do your parents treat you?* (a) *like a baby* (b) *like someone your age should be treated* (c) *too much like an adult*

All 310 kids answered this question. And 260 of them said that their parents treat them as someone their age should be treated. Thirty said they are treated like babies. Only 20 said they are treated like adults.

6. *Are your parents proud of you?* (a) *yes* (b) *no* (c) *I don't know*

"Yes" got 217 votes. "No" got 6 votes. "I don't know" got 85 votes.

7. *Pretend you could tell all the parents in the world 3 things to help them get along better with their kids. What 3 things would you tell them?*

There were a lot of wonderful answers to this question. Some of the best:

"Be friendly and ask your kids if they had a good day."

"When kids are in a bad mood, leave them alone."

"Teach them to do things. Teachers don't teach *everything*."

"Say what you have to say, but don't holler."

"Don't abuse your children for something that is your own fault."

"Remember that children can't hurt you."

Some children want to be left alone when they are in a bad mood.

"Don't make kids eat what they have tasted and don't like."

"Teach kids the facts of life."

"Don't divorce or you'll make your kid unhappy."

"Believe your kids and give them some space."

"I don't think spanking a child is worthwhile—just ground them."

"Don't give kids jobs that are too big for them."

"Try to remember what it was like to be a kid."

"Love—just love your kids."

"Don't make your kid take out the rubbish twice a day. Especially, don't make enough rubbish for us to have to do it twice."

"Don't jump to conclusions."

"Don't let younger brothers and sisters get away with bad things."

"Act like a parent."

"Treat your child like a friend."

"Don't fight with your husband or wife."

"Parents should stop fighting about money."

"Don't embarrass kids."

"Treat children with proudness."

8. *If you had a million dollars, what would you do with it?*

Most kids would put some of the million dollars in the bank for the future; but many of them would share the money with their families and help the poor. Some would save money for college. Trips (or vacations) got many votes. The 2 most popular things to buy were houses and cars (Trans Ams and Corvettes were the favorite cars). Other things to buy: animals (especially horses), swimming pools, toys, clothes, and bikes.

A million dollars? One kid would buy a car, go to New York, and buy 10 pairs of sneakers.

Here are some of the unusual or funny answers:

"Buy a car with Olivia Newton-John in the back seat!"

"Buy a new car, go to New York, and buy 10 pairs of sneakers."

"Buy my mother a driver's license!"

"I'd put it in the bank with lots of guards around it."

9. *Pretend that you are going to be stranded alone on a desert island. What book would you take with you?*

The favorite was *How to Survive on a Desert Island*—not even a real book! Of the real books, the Bible got the most votes. In second place was *Are You There God? It's Me, Margaret*. There was a big tie for third place: an atlas, a cookbook, a book of jokes and riddles, *Blubber*, *Treasure Island*, and *Robinson Crusoe*. Everybody had a lot of fun with this question. Some of the make-believe titles were:

Stranded? The favorite book to read—*How to Survive on a Desert Island* (not a real book)!

How to Get a Nice and Even Tan
How to Make Contact with Other
Islands
How to Make Food from Coconuts
How to Signal Planes and Boats
Things to Do All by Yourself
How to Build a Boat
How to Get Off a Desert Island
Prisoner with a Problem

Some kids didn't care what books they read—just so they were "long ones!"

10. *What 3 kinds of food would you take with you on the desert island?*

Pizza got the greatest number of votes. Next came meat (mostly steak and hamburgers). In third place was fruit (mostly apples and bananas). Other popular choices: spaghetti, vegetables, ice cream, bread, and milk. Some answers featured pretty wild combinations:

"Meatballs, bananas, and milk."

"Pizza, caviar, and corn."

"Ice cream, noodles, and peanut butter sandwiches."

"Marshmallows, vegetables, and Twinkies."

Food to take to a desert island? Most kids chose pizza.

A few kids figured out just how much of each food they would need:

"400 packs of Doritos, 500 pizzas, and 3,000 McDonald's milkshakes."

"16 steaks, 10 gallons of milk, and 3 boxes of Potato Buds."

11. For boys only: *If you were talking with your friends (other boys) for an hour, how much time would you spend talking about girls?* (a) *no time* (b) *about 5 minutes* (c) *more than 5 minutes*

All 156 boys answered this one.
Here is how they voted:
"No time," said 20. "About 5 minutes," said 25. "More than 5 minutes," said 111.

12. For girls only: *If you were talking with your friends (other girls) for an hour, how much time would you spend talking about boys?* (a) *no time* (b) *about 5 minutes* (c) *more than 5 minutes*

Like the boys, all the girls (154 of them) marked in an answer:
"No time," 14 said. "About 5 minutes," 37 said. "More than 5 minutes," 103 said.

Girls spend a lot of time talking about boys.

13. *If you could have an unusual animal (like a giraffe) for a pet, what animal would you choose?*

The Number One choice was the monkey, which won by many votes. Number Two choice was the lion. Number Three choice was a tie—the elephant and the tiger. More than 60 animals were named, including a hyena, an alligator, a shark, and a skunk.

14. *What job would you like to have when you get older?*

Kids wrote in 95 different jobs. The favorites:
1. Teacher
2. Doctor
3. Veterinarian
4. Football player
5. Nurse
6. Secretary
7. Policeman

15. *Do you want to go to college?*

Yes: 257
No: 43

16. *Do you think you will get married when you get older?*

Yes: 268
No: 36

17. *Name one famous person (living or dead) whom you would like to be like.*

Exactly 110 famous people were picked. Here are the top 5:
1. Elvis Presley
2. Cheryl Ladd
3. Olivia Newton-John
4. Cheryl Tiegs
5. No one. I like being myself!

The lion was named as one of the unusual animals kids would like as a pet.

18. *If you could have only one of the following, which would you choose?* (a) *good looks* (b) *great personality* (c) *lots of money*

This was a close race. "Great personality" won with 110 votes. Then came "good looks," with 104 votes. Finally, "lots of money" got 83 votes.

19. *How much time do you spend daydreaming?* (a) *a lot of time* (b) *just a little time* (c) *no time at all*

This was a popular question and 302 kids answered:
A lot of time, 88; just a little time, 174; no time at all, 40.

20. *What worries you the most?*

Kids worry most about school—especially tests, bad grades, and not getting homework done on time. The second-biggest worry is death. Many kids are worried about dying themselves or about someone in their families dying.

21. *What scares you the most?*

Here are the top 5 answers:
 1. Scary movies
 2. Death
 3. The dark
 4. Being alone
 5. Noises, when you don't know what they are

22. *What makes you the angriest?*

The top 4 answers:
 1. Brothers (or sisters)
 2. Being called a name
 3. Being teased
 4. Being blamed for something you didn't do

23. *What makes you the happiest?*

The top 5 answers:
 1. Being with my friends
 2. My family

Children do not like being blamed for things they did not do.

3. When school is out
4. Christmas
5. My mother

24. *If you could change 2 things about the world, what would they be?*

Many ideas went something like these: "End poverty and prejudice." "Turn meanness into friendship." "Clean up the world." "We must feed, shelter, and clothe the poor." "No more killing—peace everywhere."

And, of course, there were some silly answers: "Let my mom marry Robert Redford." "Money should grow on trees." "Kids shouldn't go to school; parents should."

Parents—instead of kids—going to school was an idea to improve the world.

25. *What is one question you have wanted to ask, but have been afraid to ask?*

Some of the best questions:
"What do you do on a date?"
"Am I ugly?"
"How many kids get expelled from school for having sex?"
"Why was I born?"
"Would you go out with me tonight?"
"Do you like me?"
"What does our teacher do after school?"
"Will we kids be able to grow up with all the nuclear war stuff?"
"What happens when you die?"
"Why did my parents get divorced?"
"How long do my mom and dad have to live?"
"Why do mothers get to tell you what to do?"

EXT RA: *Do you have a message for other kids in the world? If so, what is it?*

Here are just some of the many messages:

"I hope that none of you are sick, and dying, and starving. I hope you all get a chance to go to school and grow up the right way."
"Don't be afraid to stand up to people. Don't be shy—speak up for yourself."
"Don't get interested in drugs, drinking, smoking, and war."
"Kids have rights, too—just like adults. Don't ever be afraid to ask questions. Who cares if people laugh? Be honest and remember that kids are people, too."
"I just want to wish everyone good luck."
"When your parents get mad, it's because they love you. My mom says that it

is hard to be a mother. So respect your parents."

"Move to America—it's Number One."

"Late to bed and late to rise makes a man sick, poor, and stupid."

"Whatever you do, don't get your older brother mad."

"Watch out for mean teachers—that's all."

TV? Kids Give Their Ideas

For years, grown-ups have been arguing about what kids' television should be like. The Federal Communications Commission, which sets TV standards, asked the young people themselves. Here are some of their answers:

"I am a person who watches television a lot, but there are too many commercials. And one more thing, the amount of reruns these days is ridiculous. I've practically seen all of them. I'm a 10½-year-old girl in the fifth grade and I'm not complaining about much."

—*Denise Kupperman, Chatsworth, California*

"I like a couple of commercials because you have time to go to the bathroom and get something to eat."

—*Sherry Sharpe, Newark, New Jersey*

Everyone is watching more and more TV these days, especially with video cassettes and video discs on sale. But kids think there's a lot of room for improvement in TV.

"TV is too violent now. You should make TV calmer. You should remember that children get too excited by violent shows."

—Michael Craig, Palisades Park, New Jersey

"Most of the shows we watch are phony. You should show things that really happen in people's lives."

—Kelly White, Parlin, New Jersey

"I like most of the shows but my brother watches "Mighty Mouse" and there is a lot of punching and it gives him the wrong idea of life. Every time he sees a kid he wants to punch him."

—April Brockman, South Portland, Maine

"I don't believe in showing more educational shows. If a kid has to go to school 6 hours a day, 5 days a week, then he really doesn't want to see the same boring stuff. I believe that school is for working, and home is for fun and entertainment, which includes television."

—Elizabeth Breen, Lawrence Harbor, New Jersey

"I'm 11 years old and I think TV for kids today is just about the pits. The national networks have to shape up."

—Uzra Zeya, Winston-Salem, North Carolina

"I think there should be more children's shows on TV. Saturday morning is all we have and grown-up shows are on all week. It just isn't fair. Children are people, too."

—No name, Midwest

Kids Write to Save the Children

Save the Children is a group that works to help children throughout the world. Every year, the group asks children to send in letters about a specific subject. Then, on May 1, which is Save the Children Day, some of the letters are presented by children to a group of senators in Washington, D.C. An agenda, which is a summary of the letters, is also read. In one year Save the Children received 8,000 letters. The stack was 4 feet high. In the letters, the children wrote to the president about their hopes for a better world. Here are some of the children's letters:

"If adults keep wasting energy there won't be any fuel for us kids when we grow up. So I suggest you kind of hide some fuel in the ground someplace. Then before another president comes along . . . you can tell him about it."

—Steve (fifth grade), Sharon, Massachusetts

"I have bad dreams that we are going to have a war again—World War Three. I have heard that on the news and in the newspaper and it will ruin our future when we kids grow up."

—Vicki (second grade), Ullaha, California

"Children are worrying about things like their parents getting a divorce. . . . Well, maybe this has nothing to do with saving the children. But I think it has something to do with children's hearts."

—Heather (sixth grade), Novato, California

A child writes a letter about an important issue to the Save the Children Campaign. *(Renkel, courtesy Save the Children)*

Kids worry about another war—even one in the future fought in outer space.

"The cost of living is high and my mom's paycheck is low. I think they should go together."

—*Steve (fifth grade), Wolcott, Connecticut*

"I'm okay, but I've heard of a lot of kids that aren't. There are children in many parts of the U.S. that are sick, homeless, and starving. They need help from you and many other Americans! Stop wasting money on luxury. Start giving more to charity. Without you, we can do nothing to save the millions of people who live in ghettos and countless more who are falling into poverty each day. Please help the children!"

—*Nicole (sixth grade), Vienna, Virginia*

"I think there should be no smoking in this country. There is too much pollution in this country. Please help us. There is too much junk food for kids. Commercials on TV are bad for kids, like cereal and toy commercials. Things that you buy don't work as good as they do on the commercials."

—*Jenny (second grade), Little Chute, Wisconsin*

"I have made a plan how to save energy and this is what I have. Turn old cars into bicycles because bikes don't use gasoline. Make the bike faster by putting a battery in it and safer by getting all the safety rules with it. Take out some roads and make paths in place of them, then put them all over the world."

—*Billy, Southport, Ohio*

"Kentucky has a lot of coal. Our coal has a big problem. It costs too much to take it out. Coal mines don't want to spend a lot of money on it. People then won't buy it. I want a cheaper way to get sulphur out so it won't go to waste. Also, so our state will be popular for something.

"I live beside a coal mine. They help our water stay clean. It used to be red and have iron in it. It is not bad for drinking water. It just killed the fish in the creek, beavers, maybe deer. I am glad they cleaned it.

"At our house, people go out in our cornfield to hunt. They kill a lot of animals. If they are shooting a particular way, they might shoot our horses. They just don't seem to care."

—*John (fourth grade), Beboe, Kentucky*

"I wish my mom would stop smoking. Her lungs will turn black and I do not want that to happen. Can you make the prices of cigarettes go up so she will not buy them?"

—*Heidi (fourth grade), Wisconsin*

"A better world. I would like to live in better conditions than I live in now. I live in an area where most people are black or Puerto Rican. I don't mind that at all.

Many kids think everyone should stop smoking, because it's unhealthy.

Some people call this place slums; others call it the ghetto. But I call it a bad place to live.

"I would like to live in good conditions, not somewhere where you see a roach every 10 or 15 minutes, where the parks are ragged and the grass barely turns green. . . .

"One thing we need, and the only thing we need to make this world a better place, is love. Don't forget that word because some people do. I feel this is the only thing that can change our world is that word."

—*Crystal (seventh grade), Brooklyn, New York*

In another year Save the Children asked kids to write about, "If I were elected President, this is how I would change the world for children." They responded with 20,000 letters. On May 1, some of them dragged five mail bags, each four feet high, into a hearing room and dumped them at the senators' feet.

Here are some of their letters:

"Do you know the saying 'all men are created equal'? Does that include kids? We do not have the right to vote, pass bills, take jobs, and become President. You also say we have freedom of speech. Not true. If we have ideas . . . we have no way of getting them to Congress or expressing them.

"What grown-ups do not understand is that these decisions will affect children more than adults, so we want to help.

"If I were President, I would make a special congress for kids to help adults. Some people do not understand that we hear enough about each subject to think about them. Our ideas are good."

—*Kelly (sixth grade), Boulder, Colorado*

"If I were elected President, this is how I would help children. I would help children by sending food and doctors to the children. The doctors would be to help the sick children, because they are weak and hungry and cannot fight off germs. The food would be to make them strong so they can defend themselves from germs and to nourish them.

"P.S.—Young people are starving all over the world and they need our help. That is bad enough, but when we can help them and we do not, that is even worse."

—*Joseph (sixth grade), Pass Christian, Mississippi*

If this girl were someday elected president, she would change the world for children.

"If I were elected President, this is how I would help children. I would try to see to it that the children 11 and older could get fairly easy jobs. I have found that when some kids around 11 or older want jobs, it is very hard for them to find them. Sometimes kids would like to get jobs to help themselves get things that they want. It seems more rewarding for you to buy something with your own money, or even save it for something you want later. Some kids are really responsible enough."

—*Jill (sixth grade), Devault, Pennsylvania*

"Some people think we children are things that do not break, but we are not. We are just as good as them. But we really can get hurt. If I was elected President, I would put a stop to all that. I even heard about some dying. I am sure glad my parents are not like that.

"We are people too, but smaller and not as smart. We can do some things that they cannot. But when we did it better, they get mad and hit and slap us around. I feel sorry for kids with parents like that. I think it is unfair. But I wish the people who do that would stop and think how much they are hurting us. If we did that to them, they would not like it."

    —Luanne (fourth grade), Ridgeway,
      Pennsylvania

"We have more than a hundred health societies in the United States. We even have doctors to help us live our lives better. I hope that I have made it clear that the United States cares about my health and about everybody else's—well, almost everybody else's.

"Have we ever thought about caring for other people, such as the children all over the world? Children are dying all over the world because of malnutrition, not enough food, shelter, and clothing.

"We are one of the richest countries in the world, and the only thing we care about is showing movies about how poor countries are. Tell me, is there something wrong with that? Yes. It goes to prove that the United States only cares about showing disaster films. The children in these films hope that the people watching will do something to help them so that they will live a better life, but we just watch and feel pity for them, and that is all.

"If I were elected President, I would stop the films and start with the action. That is what these kids need—more action. Even a loaf of stale bread will make them happy. What we need is more community work. If any adults care enough to help these kids, please do, because remember this world will be in our hands like it is in yours."

    —Cecilia (fifth grade), New Rochelle,
      New York

"I am concerned about every child. I feel that every child should have a home, a place to live. What do you think? Do you care?"

    —Brooke (third grade), Chautauqua,
      New York

Dos and Don'ts for Parents

The following, by a 14-year-old girl, was printed in the *Dear Abby* column of August 5, 1979:

Don't ever search your kid's room while he is at school, work, etc.

Don't choose their friends for them.

Don't read their diary or personal letters, etc.

Don't give your child's things to another child without checking with the owner first.

If you're divorced, don't ask your child why they love the other parent, or try to talk him out of loving the other one.

Don't ever tell your kid that if he's not satisfied with the situation at home, he can pack his bags and go.

If your child is adopted, don't tell him that if he doesn't behave, you will send him back.

Don't always make them bring a "tag-along" (younger brother or sister) wherever they go.

Don't embarrass them by putting them down in public or in front of friends.

Don't keep telling them how hard things were when you were a kid.

Don't call them names. That really hurts a kid.

Don't yell at a smaller kid, or hit him because he dropped, spilled, or broke something. Nine times out of 10 it was an accident and he's already sorry for doing it.

If you're having an argument, let your kid talk, too.

DO tell them you are sorry, or that you make a mistake once in a while. (Nobody's perfect. Not even parents.)

DO hug your kid and tell him in words that you love him.

Kids Predict the Future

Children are creative in predicting the future. Here are some examples:

1944 The comic book *Captain Midnight* requested readers to send in their ideas for inventions. Some replies were clever, but probably won't work:

Bulletproof paint

A see-through plastic plane that couldn't be spotted by the enemy

A parachute that would turn into a tent on the ground

An "iron man" that could carry 1,000 soldiers, plus guns and tanks

Other suggestions were of things that were to be invented later, like a long-distance rocket-driven bomb.

1953 A teacher asked his fifth-grade class to make predictions about what the world would be like 25 years later. He put their answers in a time capsule and opened it in 1978. The children had correctly predicted:

Men wearing skirts? One kid thinks they will in the future.

Planes that carried people across the country in 3 hours

Touch-button phones

Computers being used a great deal

Travel in space

1967 New York 5-year-olds had some ideas about the future:

"All the cities will be different colors. New York will be pale blue. The whole world is gonna be projects. The houses are gonna be 103 feet long."

"There will be no stairs cuz everyone will press a button in their shoe that will make them go up or down."

"The men are gonna wear skirts and everybody is gonna wear cloaks."

"The TV sets will be so cheap there will be no more poor people. The sets will cost about 25¢."

"There will be no doctors when you get sick. You'll take a whiff of a special gas that a machine shoves out and you'll be better."

"Everyone will have a robot maid."

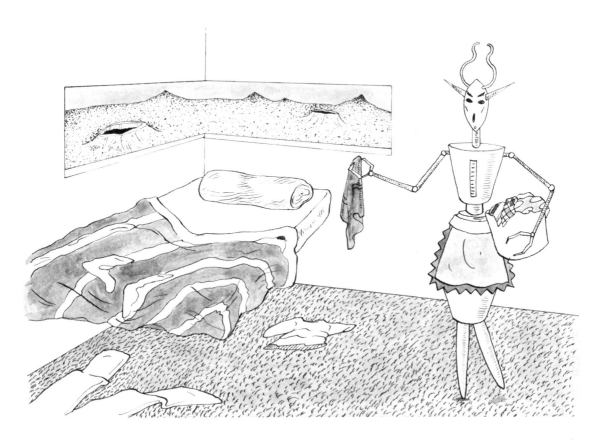

In the future everyone may have a robot maid to do all their tasks.

"We'll have books that move. As they tell the story, they'll show."

"Powerful vacuum cleaners are going to pull up the dirt. Gee, I hope they don't pull up the people, too."

"People are going to fly in balloons and speed jets. They are going to have electric toothpaste. Everyone is going to wear a motor thing on their backs so they can fly. No one will be walking. Sidewalks will die out."

"They will put wires around your head that will play into a big machine. When they turn the machine on, you will learn everything in the whole world. You'll be in college when you are in kindergarten."

"In 20 years there won't be anything to do, so people will just sit and stare at things. It will be real nice."

"In 20 years the world is going to look real old and it's going to end."

The *Weekly Reader* sponsored a project called "Letters to Our Children's Children." Kids wrote in, and their letters were put in a time capsule to be opened in the year 2029. Some of their predictions about their grandchildren's world are:

Kids as young as 6 would be driving cars.

Electric motors would power surfboards.

People would get around in motorized chairs or by flying with a jet pack.

People might be able to appear and disappear at the touch of a button.

There would be space colonies and lunar colonies.

Some homes would be underwater.

In the year 2029 people may get around by flying with a jet pack.

1980 A group of fifth graders in Rhode Island predicted these inventions:

Houses that shrink so they can be easily moved.

Stereos with memory computers. Call out the name of a song and it starts playing.

Shows that would be staged in space.

"Smart" footballs that go where the quarterback tells them to.

Pens that write automatically as you speak.

No more schools, but video robot teachers instead for learning at home.

The Almanac's "Children Predict the Future" Contest

While we were writing this book, we asked young people in 7 schools to enter a contest on the subject of "What Will Happen in the Future?" To enter, kids gave their ideas on what the world would be like in the year 2000. Here are our winners:

First Prize: Kara Moriarty, Westfield, Massachusetts, age 11

"THE FUTURE OF THE WORLD"

Schools are scarce, one per city,
The population has decreased,
School vacations are in winter,
We spend summer in our seats.
We must conserve energy.

The food is delicious and nutritious,
Keeps you running and ambitious,
Some is sweet, some is sour,
Filled with vitamins for power.
It comes in tubes.

The houses in the year 2000
Use sun, coal and electricity,
The houses are square and very bare,
A heating stove is always there.
All the trees are gone.

Free time is very exciting,
You can play with your robot or dance
  with your dolls,
Play your glass records and
Study with your talking computer.
Everything is electronic now.

Monorails are now in fashion,
Riding high above the street.
Electric cars plugged into sockets,
Costing less for the pocket.
Gas is now $10 a gallon.

The president is talking to us
About inflation and high prices,
Energy, wages, and equal rights,
Taxes will take bigger slices.
The president is a lady.

An electric-powered car for the year 2000—that's not too far away for quiet, pollution-free automobiles.

Robots flirting? Why not!

Second Prize: Michelle Sova, Ambridge, Pennsylvania, age 11

"DEAR DIARY"

January 1, 2000

Dear Diary:

Today nothing much happened. Wait a minute. Something did happen. We got a new electric-powered car. Of course, it won't be the same as our deutronium-powered space ship, but Mom and Dad said we should start acting like a family and not as hoodlums.

January 2, 2000

Dear Diary:

Hi, it's me again. Today we went to Africa to see the new mall. When the atomic-powered submarine went on the fritz, everyone had to use the portable, electric-charged mini-spaceship.

January 30, 2000

Dear Diary:

I'm sorry for not writing to you, but with these new robot maids you can never find anything. Well, I didn't have any school today. Our electric television wasn't working so I decided to skip it, and I can catch up later.

January 31, 2000

Dear Diary:

Today we got rid of our old maid. Mom said she is too much trouble, having to be repaired a lot. So we got a new maid. Her name is Lola, but Mom is on the verge of getting rid of her. Yesterday Mom caught her flirting with the man robot next door. The neighbor keeps complaining how much money it is to keep fixing his blown-out circuits.

February 13, 2000

Dear Diary:

The reason that I have not been writing to you is that we were on vacation. We went to the moon. It took us only 45 minutes to get there. You know how it is with those new rockets, it only takes a few minutes. But the trip wasn't very interesting. There weren't any plants, animals, or people. We were the only ones there. Everyone was going to Mars, Saturn, and places like that.

February 14, 2000

Dear Diary:

I am going to cut these messages short. Nothing has been going on around here. Well, today we went to Mars on the tour. We also went to Venus Fly Trap's lunar drive-in. Then we went to eat at Al's Launching Pad. The food there wasn't very good.

March 1, 2000

Dear Diary:

Nothing is happening around here. But my brother fell in love with Miss Lunar Landing of the Year. Of course, I don't think she is that great. I prefer Mr. Lunar Launching of the Year.

June 3, 2000

Dear Diary:

I couldn't find you; somehow you managed to get stuck in the garbage disposal. You're pretty messed up, but you're okay. I'm putting you in a special place because we are going to another galaxy and I'm going to be put in a time capsule. So I hope you won't get tired. We're all packed and ready to go. Nothing happened when you were lost, so don't worry. Well, I guess that's all until I wake up. Good night, Diary.

Third Prize (Tie): Jim Steinbrecher, Nashville, Tennessee, age 12

Dear Steve,

Yesterday I went into the future to the year 2000. It was really exciting. I'm not really sure how I got there, but I did. The last thing I remember was going into a telephone booth and dialing a phone number. That is all I can remember.

Well, Steve, I guess you're wondering what it is going to be like in the year 2000. I'll tell you now. The transportation isn't going to be in a car or bus on the road; it's going to be in the air. They will have jet cars that fly, run on water, and do not pollute the air.

You will not believe the number of electronic games, calculators, and watches. All the TV sets will have remote control and touch tuning.

The advances of medical science are going to be great. They will have found a cure for the common cold. They will have spare parts for the human being that look real and do the same things that the real parts do. And get this, Steve, the life span for a normal human will be 120 years.

But there is a bad side to the twenty-first century. Even though the jet cars don't pollute the air, cars of the late twentieth century already have. The water and land pollution is very serious, too. Some of the world's natural beauty will be destroyed. Countless trees will be cut down for buildings and roadways. Many of the animals will be on the Endangered Species list. And the animals on it now will be gone forever. Jobs will be hard to get, but pay will be good. Inflation will have made the dollar worth about 5¢, and a nickel won't be worth anything at all.

A lot of people, including myself, are looking toward the future. But if it's going to be like that, I would rather go back in time than go forward.

Third Prize (Tie): Danny Rubel, of DeKalb, Illinois, age 12

"MY SCHEDULE 2000"

When I grow up, if technology is far advanced and I become an engineer, this is how my life might be:

6:00—I wake up, get out of my water bed, and press a button which automatically straightens the covers and pulls the bed up into the wall. Then I get into my sweat suit.

6:05—I step into a pneumatic tube which whisks me to the top of my apartment building into the gym. I step on a conveyor belt and jog 4 miles, then I lift weights and go downstairs.

6:40—I go to my automatic closet which has already picked out an outfit for me and take the clothes into the shower room, where I take an automatic shower. All you have to do is stand—it washes your hair, brushes your teeth, cleans you, shaves you, dries you, grooms you, then gives you your clothes. Then I dress and go into the kitchen.

7:00—My breakfast is 2 fried eggs, 2 strips of bacon, juice, milk, toast, and a high-nutrition pill.

7:15—When I'm done with breakfast, I grab my briefcase and step into a pneumatic tube and go down to the monorail station.

7:20—The monorail is on time, so I board and take a seat. I have to commute every day from Fort Collins to Denver by monorail. It takes around 30 minutes, so I read the morning paper.

7:50—Remarkable. The monorail arrives in Denver on time, so I step on the escalator and go down to street level and step onto a hovercraft which takes me to my building.

7:56—I get off the hovercraft in front of my building, Lockheed Aeronautics International. I walk into the lobby and step into a pneumatic tube and go up to the twelfth floor.

8:00—I punch the time clock just in time, then walk into my office and work on plans for a new space shuttle until lunch.

12:00—My electronic secretary, a little

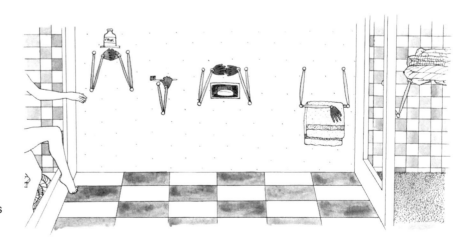

An automatic shower would make mornings easier.

computer that sits on my desk, tells me it's time for lunch. I walk over to a pneumatic tube and go to the top of my building, the ninety-fourth floor, and into the restaurant. I take a tray and punch a code into a computer—the codes for the lunch I want. Then it comes out of a little machine. I sit down with some friends and eat.

12:27—I finish with 33 minutes left, so I go into the game room and play some electronic games.

12:56—My lunch hour is almost over, so I go down to my office where I get a cup of coffee. Just as I sit down, my electronic secretary tells me to start working.

5:00—My electronic secretary tells me it's quitting time, so I punch my time clock and step into a pneumatic tube. When I get into the lobby, I walk outside and just barely make the 5:00 hovercraft.

5:08—I step off the hovercraft and take the escalator up to the monorail station to wait for the 5:15 monorail.

5:13—I step on the monorail and read. The ride usually takes longer during the rush hour.

5:50—I leave the monorail and go down the escalator. I step into a pneumatic tube and go up to my apartment.

5:54—I take off my suit coat and program my computer oven to make my dinner—a steak, some corn, a baked potato, chocolate mousse, and a drink.

6:00—I sit in front of the television and watch the news.

6:48—I eat.

7:18—I watch television.

10:30—I go to bed.

It's a Push-Button World

Most kids felt there would be a good deal of automatic living in the future.

Honorable mention: Patty Baltz, Lebanon, Tennessee, age 11

"The houses in the future will have push-button maids, push-button vacuum cleaners, push-button beds, push-button stairs, push-button tables and chairs, and push-button dog walkers."

Honorable mention: Robert Mascaro, Westfield, Massachusetts, age 10

In the morning you would wake up with a robot. While it would shake you, it would say, 'Time to get up.'"

Honorable mention: Denise Osborne, Nashville, Tennessee, age 11

". . . if you spilt a glass of water on the floor, all you would have to do is push a button and out comes a mop and cleans up the mess. You wouldn't even have to move."

Honorable mention: Teresa Magyar, Nashville, Tennessee, age 11

"We might even have push-button eating! In 2000 every house would have a machine that said 'Food.' The 3 sizes would be small, medium, and large. Suppose you wanted a large-size pizza pill. You would push a button that said 'Pizza, Large.' Then you would have it."

Sports in the Year 2000

The sports world might see lots of changes, according to our winners:

Honorable mention: Richard Hanley, Hermitage, Tennessee, age 12

"Enjoyment would probably be terrific. I can imagine playing golf in the air. Football and baseball would probably be played in the air. The referees might be robots. It would be fun to watch football with people flying around or being socked in the air.

"They might have weird games like

One kid can imagine playing golf in the air in the year 2000.

strategy games played with computers or obstacle courses in spaceships. There would be all kinds of races.

"The Olympics would be about 30 times bigger. They would have people from all over the galaxy. . . ."

Honorable mention: Joey Pinhal, Nashville, Tennessee, age 11

"In baseball . . . in the year 2000, the ball will be a push-button ball for curve, slider, fast, slow, change-up, and backward curve. The bat will probably have push buttons on it, to hit over the fence on a double, triple, or single. The gloves will be very different—like guns, to intercept the ball as it is coming.

"Football will have shoulder pads that come down to your stomach. They will have shoes where you can jump 20 feet to catch the ball or block a pass from the quarterback to the receiver. The field will be made of one foot of rubber, and the yard line will be lit, and it will be a bubble like a baseball field. The ball will have a push button for long pass, short pass, quick pass, and stuff like that."

Flying Beds, Rubber Cars, Et Cetera

Think of what you might be able to buy in 2000! The winners did, and came up with some interesting products.

Honorable mention: Melissa DiSpirito, Rock Hill, New York, age 10

"Rise and shine. As a matter of fact, don't rise. You're on your flying bed. How do you get out? Jump! Boy, is it comfortable. Oh, I forgot to tell you, don't leave your door open on a windy night—you might find yourself outside in the morning."

Honorable mention: Stefanie Cunningham, Nashville, Tennessee, age 11

"Tonight I have to go get a new diary out of my Diary-Maker machine. That's a new machine they came up with in 1989. It works like this—push button for start, pick the design you want, put one cup of water in. In 20 seconds out comes the diary. Neat, isn't it?

"I'm going to tell you all of the nice gifts I got and who they were from. . . .

"'Party in a Box' from Martin, Susan Leanne, and Steve Donying, and Tony, Marty, Nancy, and Scotty Phillips. Open the box up, press one button for start, it goes around the room putting decorations up, putting food on tables, and playing music."

Honorable mention: Teresa Magyar, Nashville, Tennessee, age 11

"In 2000 there will be a lot more jobs than there are now. There will be many factories in the year 2000. Among the things made in these factories will be food pills, electric erasers, rubber cars, waterproof books, and bendable steel that can be bent by the human hand!"

No More Teachers? They're Different, Anyway!

School in the year 2000? Here are some predictions:

Honorable mention: John Sgroi, Westfield, Massachusetts, age 10

"Let your fingers do the walking. What I mean is, everything is done with the fingers with the new Home Box Office for students. No walking to school or bus rides. You stay home and learn everything you normally would. Each morning turn on the computer. Find your station, teacher, and level. You'll learn a different thing each day. At the end of a 2-hour class, you take a test. The teacher (a robot) corrects your test. The next morning, press a button labeled TR (Test Results) and your marks will appear on the screen."

Honorable mention: Renée Maines, Freedom, Pennsylvania, age 11½

"And for the child in the family, a Home Teaching System where you put a tape of your choice into it and push 'Start,' and it teaches your child at his or her speed. To do your child's homework is an Automatic Homework Machine which is simple to operate. All you have to do is put in the problem and it solves it."

Honorable mention: Nancy Mays, De Kalb, Illinois, age 11

"Those darn electronic teachers. All they do all day is tell you your assignment and sleep. One of my friends tried to wake up our teacher, Mrs. Electrifi, and she got bopped on the head. When we have to create a story we never have to write it, we only have to think it and push buttons."

Energy and Pollution — Where Are We Headed?

Most kids were gloomy in their predictions about energy and pollution, but not all.

Honorable mention: Zöe Abernathy, Cardiff-by-the-Sea, California, age 10½

"A scientist just invented a new device—all the dirty air from cigarettes, cigars, and machines goes into a big jar and is disposed of every year. Astronauts fly it to an inactive galaxy and release the dirty air."

Honorable mention: Sean Monahan, Nashville, Tennessee, age 12

"The water would be different, too. You would be able to buy the elements and make the water yourself. The clean water will be almost gone, and it might be worth more than oil."

Honorable mention: Tom Jennings, De Kalb, Illinois, age 11

"How we got rid of waste collected from 1986 to the year 2000: After we colonized the moon, we had an easy, inexpensive way to get rid of atomic waste. Since the moon has less gravity power, we are able to launch successfully a series of rockets full of atomic waste to the sun. The sun will then burn them up without harm to us. . . ."

"When we colonized the moon in 1983, it was a good place to put safe nuclear power plants. There are still some power plants upon the earth but they're only used on private property. On the moon it is much safer, for if a blow-out does occur, it will be sucked out into space and away from the moon and earth. . . . One-fourth of the newly created power is used on the moon. The remaining 75 percent is transported to earth by laser. . . ."

And a Way of Life for 2000

Will people be the same or different? Richer or poorer? Some answers from the winners:

Honorable mention: Lisa Polidora, Ambridge, Pennsylvania, age 10

"The rich people's cars will fly and get them anywhere in a minute. . . . The people who are poor will have the slowest

Sending all the dirty air into deep space and disposing of it there would be one kid's way to solve the pollution of the future.

cars that will get them to where they're going in 10 to 20 minutes. The average people will have cars that will get them to work or school in 2 to 4 minutes. The businessmen and businesswomen will have cars like the rich people, but they will be limousines that fly and get them to work in one minute."

Honorable mention: Kristine Prezkuta, Monticello, New York, age 11

"Dear Kathy,

"Hi, how are you? . . . I heard you got a new house. How is it? Mine is fine. I had to clean my room today because my friends came over, and they got their feet marks all over my ceiling."

Honorable mention: Kathy Crumby, Nashville, Tennessee, age 11

"Since the food in 20 years is all good for you, the people will be very healthy. They will wear white, tight suits and real way-out hairstyles. Almost everyone is good-looking, and no one is real ugly. The people of 2000 will like to keep in shape. The law will be to exercise every day. The people of this day will all be very well off."

Honorable mention: John Sgroi, Westfield, Massachusetts, age 10

"Portable roofs? It's possible, and it's only one of many new features of a 2000 home.

"In the summer, when it's not raining, you can push a button, and your roof will slide down tracks inside your walls. Taking the place of your roof will be a plastic dome that will let in any heat needed. . . ."

People in the future may wear white, tight suits and way-out hairstyles. People in the year 2000 will probably like to keep in shape.

Chapter 2
THE PAST

Making a Family Tree

*W*ant to know how all of your family members are related to each other? Make a family tree. It's easy to do. Just follow the steps given below. Before you start, remember these rules:

    1. Use a circle (○) to show the males in your family.

    2. Use a triangle (△) or a square (□) to show the females in your family.

    3. Use a double line (=) to show when people are married.

Turn the page to see a sample family tree.

Search for Your "Roots": Interviewing Your Grandparents

What were your grandparents like as children and teenagers? What did they daydream about? What did they look like? What problems did they have? What was their life like when they grew up?

Most young people know very little about the history of their families. There are many unanswered questions about the past. A science called "genealogy" can help you to discover your "roots." However, genealogy can be pretty confusing. It takes a lot of time and work to trace the complete history of your family. But there is an easy way to get many of the more interesting facts—though a branch of genealogy called "oral history."

That means interviewing older members of your family.

The best people to interview are your grandparents, and the easiest way to do an interview is with a tape recorder. If you don't have one, try to borrow one. If you can't get a tape recorder, you will have to take good notes throughout the interview. The interview will still work but it will take longer.

Pick *one* grandparent to begin with, for interviews should always be done one at a time. If you enjoy the interview, you might want to go on and do more of them. But what if all of your grandparents live too far away? In that case, you will have

Making a Family Tree

1. Put yourself in the middle

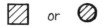

2. Add your parents

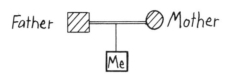

3. Brothers and sisters

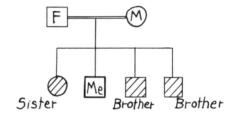

4. Aunts and uncles

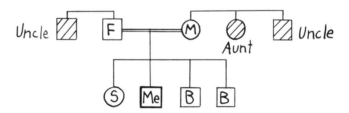

5. Grandparents, cousins, and so on...

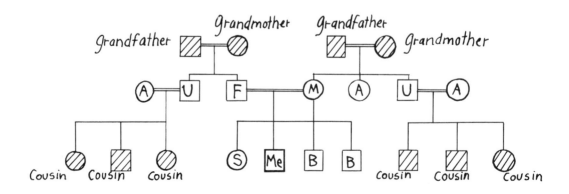

to pick another relative. Choose one of the family's best storytellers, but—*and this is important*—be sure to pick someone who is old enough to have had a different lifestyle than your own.

Here are suggestions to help you get ready for the big interview. Though they are written for an interview with a grandfather, the same suggestions will work for an equally good interview with a grandmother. Be prepared, because you want to be as much of a "pro" as possible.

Getting Ready for the Interview

1. Like any good reporter, you should do a little "advance" work. Get some facts about your grandfather before the interview. Talk to your parents, and ask them what they know about his past. These "leads" will help you to make up a list of good questions.

2. Be sure your tape recorder is working. Most tape recorders today use cassettes and are easy to operate. Ask a friend or a relative to help you test it. If it is run by batteries, put new ones in before you start. Know how far away you have to be to pick up voices clearly. It would be horrible to get to the end of a terrific interview and find out that the recorder was not working.

Tips on Being a Good Reporter

1. Try to limit the interview to one hour. This means you can't ask too many questions, so choose your questions carefully.

Interviewing your grandparents will help you trace your "roots." They are a living link with the past.

2. Ask short questions. Start with easy ones to make your grandfather feel at ease.

3. Ask only one question at a time.

4. Be a good listener. You won't get any facts if you do all the talking!

5. Be alone with your grandfather. Having other people around might make you or him feel self-conscious. Also, you do not want any other relatives butting into the conversation.

6. You want your grandfather to be relaxed, so do the interview in his favorite part of the house, where he'll be comfortable.

7. Get rid of as much noise as possible. Turn off radios and televisions.

8. Remember to check on the tape recorder. Do a short test. Don't forget to turn the cassette over after you have used up the first side. (Wear a watch to help you judge the time.)

9. Take a few notes during the interview, especially about the spellings of some places and people you may not be sure of. You will spoil the "flow" of the interview if you interrupt, so wait until the interview is over, and then get the spellings right.

10. Your grandfather may not want to answer some of your questions. Or he may not know the answers. Don't pressure him. Move on to other ones.

Questions

IMPORTANT: Prepare your list of questions in advance. Have them in front of you at the interview.

Be sure to ask interesting questions. You don't want your grandfather to answer only yes or no. For instance, you may ask, "Were you a soldier in World War Two?" But follow it up with "What are the 3 things you remember most about the war?"

Here is a list of sample questions to give you a head start. You will probably want to use some of them. Don't try to ask every one; otherwise, you and your grandfather will be up all night!

Childhood

1. When and where were you born?

2. What did your parents (my great-grandparents) look like? Where were they born? What did they do for a living?

3. Who was the most unusual relative you can remember? Why?

4. How many brothers and sisters did you have? Were you a close family?

5. At what age did your family consider a person grown up?

6. What kind of chores did you have to do as a child?

7. What can you remember about your early days in school?

8. What was the biggest holiday that your family celebrated? How did you celebrate?

9. How did your family survive the Great Depression?

Teenage Years

1. What did you look like as a teenager?

2. Who was your best friend? What was he or she like? Did you have a lot of friends?

3. Tell me about high school. Why did you or didn't you like it? What kind of grades did you get?

4. Did you have a job when you were a teenager? What did you do?

5. What is the funniest thing you can remember about high school?

6. What kinds of clubs and sports groups did you belong to?

7. What did your clothes look like?

8. Can you remember your first date? Where did you go and what did you do?

Military Life

1. Were you in the service? When? Army? Navy? Air Force? Marines?

2. What did you think of military life?

3. What are the 3 things you remember most about World War Two?

Marriage and Family

1. Where and how did you and Grandmother meet?

2. What was the first thing you noticed about her?

3. How long did you know her before you got married? What did your parents think about the marriage?

4. What was your wedding like?

5. What did your house or apartment look like?

6. How many children did you have? What was the hardest thing about being a father?

Work and Money

1. How many different jobs have you had? Which one did you like the most?

2. If you could have picked a "dream job," what would you have picked?

3. Any great stories in the family about how someone *almost* got rich?

Wrap-up Questions

1. What was the best moment in your life?

2. If you could change one big decision in your life, what would it be?

3. What *one* piece of advice would you like to give to children today?

Writing the Article from the Tape

1. Play back the tape. Take notes on what you think are the most interesting parts of the interview. You may have to play the tape a few times.

2. Organize your notes and write the article.

3. Make sure you have the right spellings for names and places.

Here are two interview articles. The first is by one of the authors of this book, written when she was 14 years old. The other is by Don Hogue (age 13), an eighth-grade student at La Habra City School District in La Habra, California.

MY GRANDFATHER
by Carol Orsag (age 14)

Peter Wanchik, my grandfather, like many men before him, left Europe in 1906 and came to America in search of a better way of life. For 18 years he had lived on a small farm in Czechoslovakia. He had nothing to take with him to America but $150 which he had saved. Although Peter was leaving most of his family in Czechoslovakia, he had 4 brothers waiting for him in Patton, Pennsylvania. He went through Poland by train. Upon arrival in Hamburg, Germany, he spent all but $64 of his savings for a boat ticket to New York. There were 4,000 people on board. They met with no major problems at sea except for a dense fog that stopped the voyage for 3 days. Peter arrived in New York, bought a train ticket to Patton, and set out with a total of $4 to his name.

When he arrived in Patton, he found his brothers and got a job in the coal mines. This was a very hard job, and the pay was not good. Although a man might work from 8 to 16 hours a day, his pay was decided by the amount of coal that he dug. The pay was 47¢

per ton of coal. The average amount for a day was 3 or 4 tons. Since the mining company controlled everything in the town, it subtracted all the rents on company boarding houses and any other amounts owed to the company before the paychecks were issued. The paychecks were often very small. My grandfather can remember receiving 10 paychecks in a row, each check being less than $1.00. For 20 years he worked in the mines. It was during his second year in Punxsutawney, a nearby mining town, that he met my grandmother, Anna Tacak.

On a cold, wet day in February 1908, they were married in a little church in Punxsutawney. My grandmother was 16 years old, and my grandfather was 20. The entire bridal party, including the groom, rode to the church in a small wagon, commonly called a hack. Their friends who attended the ceremony had to walk a distance of 6 miles to the church. Upon returning to the house, the guests made themselves at home and had quite a good time. The good time lasted for 4 days! The guests drank 400 gallons of beer. A band of traveling Gypsies from Europe entertained the guests. They, too, stayed for 4 days. However, there was one catastrophe in the wedding celebration. Because she did not want to ruin her blue silk wedding dress, my grandmother had changed into another dress. She left her wedding dress in her room. One of my grandfather's old girl friends sneaked into the room and took the wedding dress. The old girl friend then used the dress to wipe up the dirty floors, which were wet and sloppy. Despite this, everyone had a good time. My grandparents had a total of $40 with which to begin their new life.

Lack of money was not their only difficulty. They made their own clothes. They grew most of their vegetables and raised pigs, cows, and chickens. They made their own butter and buttermilk and peddled milk for 5¢ a quart. Of course, there were no electric appliances. This meant no refrigerators, and meat was kept cold by placing it between the kitchen door and the screen door. There were no stoves, no furnaces, no sinks, and no light bulbs. To get drinking water, they had to use a pump which usually served every two houses. To get light, they had to use kerosene lamps.

They faced many hardships, including a great flu epidemic that hit the town.

Many people died in the epidemic. There were very few doctors. People did not have money to pay doctor bills. My grandmother, Anna, was very sick. The doctor said it was a miracle that she lived. The Wanchik's oldest daughter, Margaret, fell out of bed and lay on the floor for 2 days because everyone else in the house was too sick to notice her. Whole families died within weeks. The Wanchiks were lucky and lost none of their family. However, they were left penniless after paying the doctor bills.

During their first years in America, Peter and Anna did not have an easy life. My grandfather had to work very hard to keep his family together and happy. Altogether the Wanchiks had 10 children. They ended up in a place called Ambridge, Pennsylvania. My grandfather got a new job in a steel mill. He worked there for many years. Now he is retired.

MY GRANDFATHER'S YOUNGER BROTHER
by Don Hogue (age 13)

My great uncle Bob was born Robert Melville Ferguson McLachlan at 12:30 A.M. on July 8, 1900, in Leith, Edinburgh, Scotland. His father, Peter McLachlan, was an "agriculturer" and later became a warehouse man in a whiskey distillery. His mother, Elizabeth Fair Ferguson, worked in a bakery shop before her marriage and, naturally, became a housewife afterwards.

Robert had 4 brothers and 3 sisters in his family. He can vividly remember gathering around the piano and singing at night with the rest of the family. He preferred singing to the chores that he and the other children had to do. One thing he really liked was going to Cook's Circus every Christmas as a child.

In earlier times there were no supermarkets and people had to travel all over town to get whatever goods they needed that day. One item Uncle Bob often had to buy was eggs that came in a very thin paper sack. He would have to carry the eggs home (about a 2-mile trip) with his hand always on the bottom of the sack, or his family would end up with scrambled eggs whether they liked them or not.

Soon Robert became ready for school at age 5. His older brother, Peter (my grandfather), was a grade higher, so when they got to school Bob cried because he couldn't be with his brother. The teacher sent for Peter to calm down Robert. Peter looked at Robert and started to cry, too! Both cried all day until school was over. Robert finally took a liking to school and became a good student.

Uncle Bob spent 6 years in his first school and enjoyed going there; but what he really liked was going on vacation every summer. The whole family would cross the Firth of Forth to Burnt Island to spend a 6-week vacation by the beach. Robert's father still had to go to work, so he would leave in the morning and return at night to be with his family. Robert enjoyed his vacations and could tell story upon story of his adventures.

Robert went to a school much like a junior high school for 3 years. When he finished that school, he continued on to a night school that was just what today's high schools are like. He was very athletic and participated in such sports as soccer, gymnastics, track, wrestling, and boxing.

At age 15½, Bob began his apprenticeship as an accountant. He studied for 3 years until he enlisted in the Highland Light Infantry to fight in World War One. He was put in the armored transport division and learned to drive the big trucks that transported supplies. Robert was discharged when the war was over.

Soccer is a big sport in Britain, and Robert started playing semiprofessional soccer soon after the war. He continued playing soccer in Honolulu after arriving there in 1927, bringing my grandmother over for her wedding to my grandfather. He played for 25 years altogether and also had a job as an accountant.

When he was about 40 years old, he met Louise Cook. The first thing he noticed about her was her beauty. He fell in love with her and a year later, in October 1941, he married her. But soon World War Two broke out in the Pacific and Robert and Louise's marriage ended as quickly as it had begun. She returned to her Canadian home and they divorced shortly after.

Robert, known to family and friends as "Uncle Bob," is still an accountant (and he'll celebrate his eightieth birthday this year!). He lives in the same house that he bought in 1941. He enjoys having visitors and receiving and writing letters. He has problems with his legs and back and has to have them "dressed" regularly by Tamar Robinson, who is the best friend and neighbor anyone could have, according to Uncle Bob.

Ellis Island: Great Gateway and Island of Tears

"Quick! Hurry up!" the voices echoed in the huge, 2-story hall. They spoke in different languages, but the message was the same. Confused people from the ships were herded into aisles marked with metal rails. They were scared but, at the same time, they were hopeful. If the doctors found them healthy and if they gave the right answers to questions, they would get through and be allowed into the United States.

The hall is a building on Ellis Island, facing the jagged skyline of New York City across the harbor. From 1892 until 1924, 16 million people from other countries came ashore at Ellis Island. Almost half the people in the United States today have a parent, grandparent, or great-grandparent who passed through Ellis Island.

The people who arrived at Ellis Island all rode in their ships' steerage section. Steerage was the cheapest way to come and often meant having makeshift ac-

Steerage passengers hoping to live in the United States pass the Statue of Liberty in New York Harbor. *(Leslie's Weekly, 1887/New York Public Library Picture collection)*

commodations on the deck or in the hold of a ship. It cost about $34 from Europe to the United States in 1903.

Morris Raphael Cohen, now a philosopher, came to the United States in steerage with his family when he was only a boy. He and his mother and sister slept in bunks. The food was bad. Morris was afraid the ship would hit another ship and sink; when he heard a fog horn, he was sure of it. But not all was terrible on the ship. People played music and danced, and they practiced their English for the New World.

Once on the island, in the hall, the people lined up for doctors' examinations. All parts of the body were checked. One doctor flipped up the eyelid on each person, looking for eye disease. If a person had anything wrong with his or her body, a letter was chalked on the coat. *H* meant heart disease, for instance, and the per-

son whose coat was marked with *H* might not be allowed into the United States because of this.

Children were asked questions to make sure they could hear and speak. Adults were questioned, too. They worried about giving the wrong answers.

Anyone who didn't pass the exams was held at Ellis Island, some for months. They still had a chance of getting through, but they could also be sent back to the country they came from. For them Ellis became the Island of Tears. But those who passed the exams were on their way to a new life in a new country! They piled onto the ferries, eager to reach New York and start anew.

In 1965 Ellis Island was made part of the Statue of Liberty National Monument. Tours are conducted from late spring through the fall.

What Was It Like When Your Parents Were Kids? When Your Grandparents Were Kids?

To find out when your parents were kids, ask how old they are now. Subtracting that number from this year's date will give you the year they were born. If you want to know the year when they were 10, add 10 to their birth year.

Example:

1984 (year now)
−27 (Mom's age in 1984)
_____
1957 (year Mom was born)
+10
_____
1967 (year Mom was 10)

Then look on the following pages for the 1960s. You'll find some stories and facts about that 10-year period (decade) that can lead to some fun. For instance, you might want to ask your mother and father to sing their favorite television kid-show song from their childhood.

Follow the same steps to find the decade in which your grandparents were kids. (Sometimes you'll need to look in 2 decades. For instance, 1929 was more like 1930 than 1920.)

If your parents or grandparents lived in other countries as children, this information may not be right for them. But you can always ask.

From 1910 to 1919 — The Olden Days?

Though some families had electric light, most didn't. They lit their houses with gas light or kerosene lamps. Food was kept cold in iceboxes, not refrigerators. Inside the icebox was a big block of ice delivered by a wagon. The ice wagon followed a route from house to house. At each stop, the man driving the wagon would bring in a heavy block of ice, using giant tongs to carry it.

Many families didn't have water piped into the house. Instead, they had to carry water in from a well, in a bucket. The bathroom was an outhouse—a tiny building separate from the house. Inside, a hole cut in a wooden board was a toilet seat. Some people had a half moon☽ cut in the door of the outhouse for ventilation and fun.

Cars had been invented and some people had them. Most were started by turning a crank, though by 1913, half of the new cars had self-starters. A comic strip called "Gasoline Alley" was popular because it featured the new cars.

An outhouse, an outdoor toilet without a flush, was common in olden days.

What There Wasn't

There were no electric irons, electric vacuum cleaners, electric toasters, electric washing machines, jet engine planes, plastics, computers . . .

What Kids Wore

Boys dressed in short pants until they left grade school, then they were allowed to wear long pants. Girls' dresses got shorter during this time, and they wore big ribbons in their hair.

Toys and Games

Toys were made of metal and wood. Teddy bears and crayons had come into being only a few years before 1910. A bicycle was called a "wheel." Kids didn't "ride bikes"—they went "wheeling." In 1919 the pogo stick was patented. Soon thousands of children were jumping up and down on their pogo sticks. In winter, they rode on their Flexible Flyer sleds.

In 1911 over half the arrests of children in New York were for playing games in the street.

Raggedy Ann. When John Gruelle found an old rag doll in his attic, he gave it to his daughter Marcella, who was very sick. Together they named the doll "Raggedy Ann"—from 2 famous poems written by their neighbor, James Whitcomb Riley—"Little Orphant Annie" and "The Raggedy Man." Then Gruelle made up stories based on Marcella's doll, which the little girl was holding when she died in 1916. But the stories were published and became so popular that Gruelle went on to write 25 Raggedy Ann books. And the Raggedy Ann doll became a favorite toy.

Movies and Crystal Sets

Movies were very short, black-and-white, without sound. As a movie was shown in the theater, someone played background music on a piano. If the action was fast, the person played fast. If it was romantic, a love song was played. The first movie serial was *The Adventures of Kathlyn,* but the serial most people remember is *The Perils of Pauline,* which began in 1914. Pauline was always getting into dangerous places—on the wing of a flying plane or tied to the railroad tracks when a train was coming. Other movies of the time were *Tarzan of the Apes,* and *Sleeping Beauty.*

Radio had been invented, but radio programs were few and far between. Some people made crystal sets—crude radios. In 1917 someone suggested making a "radio music box," but nothing much came of that suggestion for several years.

Odd and Wonderful Facts

The "I-Scream" Bar was invented in 1919. It was a chocolate-covered ice-cream stick and led to Good Humor bars and Eskimo Pies.

Children's shoes cost less than $1 a pair.

Animated cartoons were invented.

This decade saw the first Boy Scouts, Girl Scouts, and Campfire Girls of America.

Some popular songs were "He'll Get Out and Get Under, Get Out and Get Under" (which had to do with a car breaking down); "Kitchy-Koo"; "K-K-K-Katy"; "Alexander's Ragtime Band"; and "Oh, How I Hate to Get Up in the Morning."

Very straitlaced folks were shocked by

some of the new dances, among which were the One-Step, the Turkey Trot, the Grizzly Bear, and the Bunny Hug.

"Over There"—
World War One, 1917—1919

Late in the decade, the United States joined other countries in a war against Germany. Boy Scouts and schoolchildren sold war saving stamps, with the money raised going toward the war effort. (After the war was over, people traded in the stamps and got their money back.) Children collected peach pits to burn to make charcoal for gas masks for the soldiers; the charcoal trapped the gas before it could get into the soldiers' lungs. (World War One may have been the only war in which gas was used as a weapon.)

Families gave up eating pork and wheat 3 days a week. Some nights were "lightless." In those ways, food and energy were saved for the war.

Because the Germans were our enemies, many schools stopped teaching

During World War I, this Belgian refugee boy (right) was adopted by the 125th Company. He would often join the bugler in sounding meal times. *(Photoworld/FPG)*

the German language. And since "sauer-kraut" was a German word, the food was renamed "liberty cabbage." These were hard times for German-Americans.

The German army had invaded France, and when American soldiers arrived to help drive the Germans out, the French people cheered them. An American magazine of the time printed some essays French children wrote about the American soldiers. Here are a couple of examples:

"I saw the American soldiers at their meals. It is very funny. They stand in a long line and laugh aloud. When their meal is over, they start singing." (*Pierre Loupien*)

"They are all fine men, large shoulders. I know one, a big fellow. He has a scar on his right cheek, which was made by a horse kick. He has a rosy face, long hair, carefully arranged. . . . He is gay. He is good. He eats chocolate and sweets. Next Sunday I was playing at spinning-top with my friends. He was looking at us. My small brother had no spinning top. He gave him 2¢ to buy one. The Americans are polite. When they shake hands, they bow down their head a little. . . . They are more daring than we are; they do not fear expense." (*Jean Laberiote*)

At home, in the United States, everyone was overjoyed when the war ended. To celebrate, they snake-danced and blew tin horns and marched in parades.

Teachers

The following were the rules for teachers in 1915 in a town in West Virginia. They were not unusual. Most teachers had to follow rules like these in those days.

RULES OF CONDUCT
FOR TEACHERS

1. You will not marry during the term of your contract.

2. You are not to keep company with men. That means no dating.

3. You must be home between the hours of 8 P.M. and 6 A.M. unless attending a school function.

4. You may not loiter downtown in ice-cream stores.

5. You may not travel beyond the city limits unless you have the permission of the chairman of the board.

6. You may not ride in a carriage or automobile with any man unless he is your father or brother.

7. You may not smoke cigarettes.

8. You may not dress in bright colors.

9. You may under no circumstances dye your hair.

10. You must wear at least 2 petticoats.

11. Your dresses must not be any shorter than 2 inches above the ankle.

12. To keep the schoolroom neat and clean, you must: sweep the floor at least once daily; scrub the floor at least once a week with hot, soapy water, clean the blackboards at least once a day; and start the fire at 7 A.M. so the room will be warm by 8 A.M.

Working Kids

"'Work fast! Work fast!' our parents cry. . . ."

Many children were working at hard jobs for long hours. In Boston, "bag boys" searched through markets for castoff food. Others picked over dumps looking for things to sell. Kids worked from sunup to sundown ("can see" to "can't see") on farms.

Child actors were making pretty good money for the time—from $1.50 to $3.00 a day. (Remember, things cost much less in those days.) But their work was often dangerous and scary. Some told of playing scenes in ice cold water, when they had to pretend to be drowning. In another scene, a kid's crib was set on fire.

A 1915 poem was:

THE TOILING CHILDREN

We never see the big blue sky
From out some country lane—
We never watch the clouds sail by
Above the waving grain.
We never hear at close of day
The birds grow quiet in sleep,
We never run, we never play—
We only toil and weep. . . .
"Work, fast! Work fast!" our parents cry,
And, though our tears flow free,
We choke them back, for if we cry
Our task we cannot see.

A real tear-jerker, yes; but it was based on the truth. Laws to protect children were passed by the states. Most said that children under a certain age could not work for pay. They specified the number of hours children could work, and prevented children from doing dangerous jobs. Still, child labor was a scandal, for employers disobeyed the laws. A national child labor law—the Owen-Keating Act—

In the past, many kids worked very hard from sunup to sundown on farms. (Paul Thompson, Photoworld/FPG)

passed Congress in 1916. However, it was declared unconstitutional 2 years later.

Kids in the News

Henry Chambers was made organist at Leeds Cathedral in England in 1913. He was 11 years old.

The 1920s — They Roared

This decade was called the "Roaring Twenties." Why? World War One had ended and many people had more money than they had ever had before. So they had fun. Young people in their teens were acting wild. Their dances were daring. Bold teenage girls and women bobbed their hair (cut it short). Girls' and women's dresses were short—they actually showed the knees!

Sound: Movies and Radio

Movies with sound tracks were show-

Mickey Mouse in his first film, *Steamboat Willie*. (©*Walt Disney Productions*)

ing in theaters by 1926. *Steamboat Willie* (1928), by Walt Disney, was the first cartoon with a sound track. It featured a newcomer—Mickey Mouse. Some other movies kids liked were *Peck's Bad Boy,* with child star Jackie Coogan (1921); *Little Lord Fauntleroy,* with Mary Pickford (1921), and *Son of Zorro,* with Douglas Fairbanks (1925). People were still in-

Pearl White and William Nally appear in the popular 1923 movie *Plunder*. (*A&C Archives*)

terested in the movies of Pearl White, who had become famous in the serial *The Perils of Pauline.*

Radio was coming in. Late in the decade a show called "Barn Dance" was broadcast. In 1927 it was renamed "Grand Ole Opry." Some of the country-music stars on the show were the Fruit Jar Drinkers and the Gully Jumpers. Later radio programs were "Amos and Andy" and "The National Farm and Home Hour." Mostly, people listened to music on the radio.

Television had been invented, but not much was broadcast. It was not until the late 1940's and early 1950's that television became really popular.

The first all-electric jukeboxes were blasting music in 1928.

Some Fascinating 1920s Facts

Earl Wise had too many potatoes in his restaurant. So he peeled them, sliced them with a cabbage cutter, and fried them. What did he have? You guessed it—the first potato chips! He sold the first ones in brown paper bags.

Model-T Fords were selling fast and accounted for half the cars sold in 1920. Two million were sold in 1923, and another 2 million in 1924.

One in every 3 Americans lived on a farm.

The Baby Ruth candy bar was created, named after the daughter of President Grover Cleveland. It was made of fudge, caramel, and peanuts. The price was 5¢. To advertise it, the company that made Baby Ruths dropped them by parachute from an airplane. They fell on the streets of Pittsburgh, and when people rushed into the street to pick them up, traffic jams occurred.

Thomas Edison sits in a Model-T while Henry Ford looks on. *(Burndy-AIP Niels Bohr Library)*

In 1924 the first Macy's Thanksgiving Day Parade was held.

Emmett Kelly started his career as a clown in his famous role of Weary Willie.

Broccoli was introduced to the United States. A cartoon in *The New Yorker* magazine showed a kid refusing to eat broccoli. The kid was saying, "I say it's spinach, and I say the hell with it."

In 1926 Robert Goddard launched the first liquid-fuel rocket. He sent it up from his Aunt Eppie's farm in Massachusetts. It was in the air 2½ seconds and didn't fly very fast or far. Most experts didn't think rockets would ever make it. One newspaper article in 1921 claimed they couldn't fly in outer space.

Also in 1926, Harry Houdini, the magician and escape artist, stayed under water for 91 minutes. He had enough air to last an ordinary person 5 or 6 minutes. He died a couple of months later.

A lemonade salesman, Frank Epperson, left a glass of lemonade on a window sill overnight. In the glass was a spoon. The weather was cold, and the next morning the lemonade was found frozen around the spoon. Epperson replaced the spoon with a stick and called his creation an "Epsicle." Only later was his "invention" renamed the Popsicle.

In 1927 it was found that 343,000 women in the United States had been married between the ages of 11 and 15.

Some magazine article titles: "Curing Queerness in Children"; "When Miss Fourteen Entertains"; and "Little Liars and How They Grow."

Popular dances were the Charleston and the Varsity Drag. Older people were shocked when young people did these dances. It would lead to trouble, they said.

Some popular songs were "Ain't We Got Fun"; "When the Red, Red Robin Comes Bob, Bob, Bobbin' Along"; "Let a Smile Be Your Umbrella"; "Makin' Whoopee"; and "Yes, We Have No Bananas."

Some new things: Scotch tape, penicillin, Band-Aids, the autogyro (a kind of helicopter), and Yankee Stadium.

New cartoon characters were Popeye and Little Orphan Annie.

Some wonderful children's books were published in those years. Among them: *When We Were Very Young, Winnie the Pooh, The House at Pooh Corner, The Little Engine That Could, Millions of Cats,* and *The Voyages of Dr. Doolittle*

In England, A. S. Neill and his wife started Summerhill School. The school was run by a student government and discipline was up to the students. Kids chose what they wanted to learn. Some other schools followed Summerhill School's lead, but it was considered revolutionary for the times.

"Jes' Like a Dog"

Kids were still working in great numbers—one million in 1923. Some children in New York tenements (apartments) made tin toys and doll clothes, which were sold to the parents of rich kids.

In the fields of Michigan, children worked pulling beets. A reporter wrote that "much of the time they are crawling on all-fours, 'jes like a dog,' their knees sore, their wrists swollen, their faces scorched . . . and this posture they [keep] almost steadily for three to six weeks, six or seven days a week, and twelve to fifteen hours a day."

Mother Jones, a labor leader, asked a boy of 10 why he wasn't in school. "I ain't lost no leg," he said, meaning that kids went to school only when they had been hurt in the mines or the mills.

Children working on canal boats sometimes were drowned or kicked by mules.

In 1924 a child-labor amendment to the Constitution was proposed but failed to pass.

Kids in the News

In the Soviet Union kids by the thousands roamed the streets. A writer told of how they took baths in puddles and smoked cigarette butts people had thrown away. At night they slept in railroad cars.

In 1925 Nathalia Crane, 12, published "The Janitor's Boy," a poem, in newspapers.

A boy was found in a cave in India in 1927. He could not walk or speak. Some people thought he had been brought up by wolves, and called him a "wolf boy."

In August 1929, kids in Baltimore were hit by a flagpole-sitting craze. It started with Avon ("Azie") Foreman, a boy who sat for several days on a platform atop a pole. Jimmy Jones, 12, beat Azie's record by lasting 250 hours, 10 minutes, and 11 seconds on his pole. It became an official contest on the day the local newspaper reported 25 kids sitting on poles. The mayor said they had "pioneer spirit." Ruth McCruden, 10, climbed a 25-foot pole. "Everything is pip," she said. She had ice cream and an electric light with her, and her boy friends spent nights sleeping in a tent at the foot of her pole. Only thunderstorms frightened her. Dorothy Staylor, 13, had cushions and a radio while she sat on her 17-foot pole. Ruth McCruden's mother thought it wasn't fair that Dorothy had so many luxuries.

The 1930s — "Brother, Can You Spare a Dime?"

The Great Depression began in 1929 and lasted all through the 1930s. Millions could find no work, and hungry people stood in lines to get free soup and bread. Families were evicted (thrown out of their homes) when they couldn't pay the rent. Little girls played a doll game called Eviction.

In the middle part of the United States, dust storms raged. They were so bad that lights had to be left on in the daytime. This part of the United States became known as the Dust Bowl. Nothing would grow there anymore, and some farmers left and headed west, where they thought things might be better.

Thousands of children were on the road; they had no homes and no jobs. They hitched rides on freight trains to go to new places, hoping to find work. There was little money for schools. Desks were set up in the halls of school buildings, and some classes were held in tin shacks. An article in a magazine asked, "Can We Afford Children?" In a mining town a teacher told a hungry girl to go home and eat. "I can't," the girl replied. "It's my sister's day to eat."

Fortunately, however, government programs were started for people who were out of work. Things *were* being done.

Toys, Games, and Pastimes

In 1933, the Dy-Dee-Doll was created. The doll drank from a bottle, then wet its diapers. It was a smash success.

Kids made scooters out of orange crates, scrap lumber, and roller skate wheels. Some kids called them "jitney buses." Races were held downhill.

On Sundays families that had cars often went for drives in the country. On the way they sometimes saw Burma Shave signs posted in a row on the edge of the road. Put together, they made up a rhyme. One example:

Bearded Lady
tried a jar.

She's now a famous
movie star.

Burma Shave

Some Interesting Facts

Babysitting paid from 15¢ to 25¢ an hour. Kids mowed lawns for 25¢.

Hostess Twinkies first came out in 1930.

Scientist Robert Goddard talked about

sending rockets to the moon. Most people thought he was a dreamer.

Knock, knock jokes were popular. Example:

First person: Knock, knock.
Second Person: Who's there?
First person: Boo.
Second person: Boo who?
First person: What are you crying for?

"Handies" were jokes that had to be acted out. Try to act out one of the favorites, an Indian driving a Ford V-8.

Some popular songs were "The Music Goes Round and Round"; "Flat Foot Floogie with the Floy Floy"; and "Three Little Fishies," in which the chorus went "Boop, boop, dittem dattem wattem chu."

Big-band swing music was in, and the "King of Swing" was Benny Goodman. Stiff-necked grown-ups were sure that swing would make young people go bad. And if not swing, then some of the dances—the Susie Q, the Jitterbug, and Peckin' the Shag.

In 1930 Harriet Adams wrote the first Nancy Drew mystery novel. In 1938 *Man of Bronze*, a Doc Savage adventure novel, came out. Other newcomers in the 1930s were Flash Gordon, Mary Poppins, and the Dr. Seuss books for little children.

Famous Funnies, the first comic book, began in 1934.

Two high school boys, Jerry Seigel and Joseph Schuster, created Superman while still in high school. Superman became the rage when the first *Superman* comic book was issued in 1938. Men joined Superman clubs and one little boy put on a cape and tried to fly off the roof of a 5-story building. He broke some bones, but lived. The local papers called him Superman Jr.

"A Cloud of Dust, and a Hearty 'Hi-Yo, Silver. . . .'"

Kids came home from school and listened to the radio the way kids look at television today. They would gather around the big wooden radio with its fancy dial to listen to serials like "Jack Armstrong, the All-American Boy" and "Tom Mix." Sponsors of the shows would invite kids to send in boxtops from cereal packages for prizes.

"The Lone Ranger" was a favorite radio show. It featured the masked cowboy and his Indian sidekick Tonto. It began: "Hi-Yo, Silver. A fiery horse with the speed of light, a cloud of dust, and a hearty 'Hi-yo, Silver. . . .'"

And there were "Little Orphan Annie," "The Singing Lady," and "Death Valley Days." "The Shadow," a scary program, began with, "Who knows what evil lurks in the hearts of men? The Shadow knows!" And Lamont Cranston (The Shadow) was off to catch another criminal.

At night, grown-ups listened, too. Some programs featured comedians like George Burns. A favorite was Edgar Bergen, with his ventriloquist's dummy, Charlie McCarthy. Of course, since it was radio, no one could watch Bergen to see if his lips moved. But it didn't matter. People liked hearing smart-mouth Charlie talk back to Bergen, and kids asked for Charlie McCarthy dolls. A string opened and shut the doll's mouth. He wore a monocle in his eye.

By 1938 parents were worried about what the radio was doing to kids. They thought it was too violent. In the broadcasting studio, a melon would be smashed as a sound effect for a head being bashed in. Some said that kids had become nervous, that they were biting their nails more than usual, and that it was all because of the "blood-curdling bunk" of radio.

A Quarter Bought a Feature, a Serial, a Cartoon, and a Couple of Candy Bars

An afternoon movie for kids cost a dime in the 1930s. For that, kids got a serial which ended in a cliff-hanger (so they would come back the next Saturday), a cartoon, a newsreel, and short subjects. And they got a full-length movie. The 1930s was the time of the child stars. Shirley Temple, who made 2 million dollars between her fifth and twelfth birthdays, was the biggest star. In 1939 Judy Garland appeared in *The Wizard of Oz*.

Walt Disney brought out *Snow White and the Seven Dwarfs*—the first full-length animated cartoon. The names of the dwarfs? Doc, Grumpy, Happy, Sleepy, Dopey, Sneezy, and Bashful.

The *Our Gang Comedies* also were popular in the 1930s. They're now shown on television as "The Little Rascals."

Snow White and the Seven Dwarfs first appeared in 1939. Can you name each dwarf?
(© *Walt Disney Productions*)

The New York World's Fair of 1939

The 1939 World's Fair, held on Long Island, New York, cost $157 million. Children under 12 got in for 50¢. A popular feature was Futurama, in which people sat in chairs that moved over a landscape of the future, as experts thought it might be in 1960. The people who built Futurama did *not* predict SSTs, space flights, or atomic energy. They said there would be cars with air-conditioning (correct) and throw-away houses (incorrect).

The most popular attraction at the Fair was the 250-foot-high Parachute Jump. More than 500,000 people paid to drop off it and be scared.

The Trylon tower and Perisphere were symbols of the 1939 World's Fair, which was optimistic about the future—but war was closing in. *(Photoworld/FPG)*

Working Kids

Two million kids between 5 and 17 years of age were working during the Depression. Children were cheap labor. Some kids worked over 80 hours a week, even though it was against the law. Three-year-olds in New York City were making fake flowers. Girls in Pennsylvania went on strike. One of these "baby-sitters," as they were called, 15-year-old Mildred Sweeney, told of supporting her whole family of 10 on what she earned. And she didn't make much.

Kids in the News

David ("Dudy") Davis, 6, was famous for playing the violin. His parents fed him raw vegetables and believed in going naked. Dudy went to school wrapped in a big cape. Then he took it off. All he had on underneath was a little loincloth, which is what he wore when he practiced his violin. Even so, he complained, "I'm sweating bullets."

William Marsh, 11, a Connecticut kid, published a biography of President Herbert Hoover in 1930. "When I grow up, I want to be a self-made man," he said. "I myself would rather be an honest working man than a society bug. . . . I think some of them act and talk so foolish."

Margaret Heifetz, 9, of the Soviet Union, conducted the Moscow Philharmonic Orchestra in 1933. The program included 2 symphonies. Her government let her conduct only twice a year.

Ananda Mahidol, 10, had to leave his school in Switzerland in 1934 to go home. His home was Bangkok. The reason? He had been made king of Siam.

In 1934 the Dionne quintuplets were born in Canada. Their names were

Emilie, Yvonne, Cecile, Marie and Annette.

Arthur Greenwood, 7½, also of New York, had a flash of fame in 1934. He was very, very smart: his I.Q. was said to be 230. "I consider it utterly silly and in bad taste for a person to desire to see his name in public print," he said. He didn't see it much after that.

Charles Louis Fuchs, 3, of New York, was featured in a magazine article. He was so strong he could lift a 45-pound barbell. Once he threw a china closet at his sister. His parents called him Cyclone and said he was comical. "He defaces the walls," they said. "He breaks the furni-ture. . . . Once he dug a hole in the wall with a coat hanger. Charlie does the funniest things." His father was responsible for Charlie's strength. He started training the boy when he was only 6 months old.

Marjorie Gestring, 13, won a gold medal in the 1936 Olympic Games in the springboard event.

Alfred Cohen, 8, had 40 of his paintings on display in 1938, and the newspapers publicized the exhibit. One painting showed a devil with white horns, a red body, and wearing black tights. When Alfred was asked why the horns were white, he said, "Maybe he fell in the snow."

The Dionne quintuplets celebrate their seventh birthday. They made quite a stir when they were born in Canada in 1934. *(Photoworld/FPG)*

The 1940s —
"There's a War On"

The United States fought World War Two from 1941 to 1945. The mainland of the United States was not attacked by its enemies—Germany and Japan—but people weren't sure that it wouldn't be. Air raid drills were held. Black curtains were draped over windows so enemy bombers couldn't spot towns by their lights. Mothers worked outside the home and school kids who had working mothers wore their house keys around their necks, so they could let themselves into their homes after school. They were called "doorkey children."

Sugar, coffee, meat, fat, cheese, gasoline, and other things were rationed.

The government decided each person's share of rationed items and issued ration stamps in a little book which could be traded for goods. Each person got 2 pairs of shoes a year. Sneakers weren't available and kids' shoes left black marks on school gym floors.

People saved kitchen fat in tin cans. They started Victory Gardens to grow food in vacant lots, backyards, zoos, and playgrounds. Children helped the war effort by collecting rubber, waste paper, aluminum, tin cans, and tinfoil from cigarette packs. These were recycled because materials were scarce.

During the war, 32,000 British kids were sent to the United States to keep them safe from German bombing. Many people were getting killed in Europe. In

The Nazis deported Jewish kids to concentration camps, where almost all of them were killed—a terrible tragedy for these helpless children. *(Courtesy Yad Vashem Martyrs' and Heroes' Remembrance Authority, Israel)*

Luckier children in America contributed to the war effort. *(Arthur Wolff, Freelance Photographer's Guild)*

1944, when the British children went home, they had habits that seemed strange in Great Britain. They chewed gum and wore makeup, and their table manners were different.

Millions of kids were killed in gas chambers by the Nazi Germans, and many more lost their parents and couldn't find them. Some kids were orphaned.

Germany took over many countries in Europe. Groups were formed in these countries to fight the Germans in sneaky ways. This was called the "underground." Kids were in the underground, too. Examples:

Denmark. Children put acid from chemistry labs in water pistols and then sprayed the German soldiers' clothes, causing the clothes to dissolve. The Germans tried to take away all the water pistols in Denmark.

Holland. Children wore orange flowers, orange being the national color. When the Germans snatched the flowers off the children, they were cut with razor blades hidden among the petals. Children painted an orange *W*—for Queen Wilhelmina of Holland—on the backs of German army cars.

Poland. When the Germans tried to invade the city of Warsaw, children helped fight to save it. Besides the Boys' Rifle Brigade there were Boy Scouts and Girl Scouts. They dug trenches, carried messages, and took wounded people to the hospital.

Some Interesting Facts

Teenage became part of the language. For the first time, children 13 to 19 years old were considered a special group.

Babysitting paid 25¢ an hour.

Girls wore their hair long in a pageboy style, with the ends turned under, while boys' hair was short. Some kids wore bangs.

Huge "sloppy Joe" sweaters and saddle shoes were popular with girls. They wore short socks called "bobbysox," and teenage girls were called "bobbysoxers." In the late 1940s girls also wore blue jeans and men's shirts.

Some inventions of the 1940s were nylon and Dacron, helicopters, 33⅓ rpm records, and ballpoint pens.

"Kilroy was here" was a World War Two slogan written everywhere. Soldiers wrote it behind the German lines.

"V for Victory," a popular hand gesture during the war, was done with the first 2 fingers on the right hand. Also, some restaurants arranged knives and forks in a V shape. The Morse code for *V* is dot-dot-dot-dash; a victory door knock was 3 fast knocks, a pause, and then a final knock.

"The Voice" was Frank Sinatra, a skinny young singer. In 1942 girls swooned over him; when he sang, they screamed and fainted. A newspaper called him (along with the Lone Ranger) a bad influence on kids.

Some expressions were *What's cookin', good-lookin'?; Hubba-hubba; Long time no see; Get lost* and *Drop dead;* and *moolah* (money). A snappy dresser looked "sharp" or "nifty" or "cute"

In 1946 Dr. Benjamin Spock's book, *Baby and Child Care,* was published. It changed the way parents treated their kids.

Silly Putty was created in 1949, when a smart advertising man saw what some "useless" stuff thrown out by the General Electric Company could do. It could be molded, stretched, and bounced. So he bought a batch for $147, hired someone to package it in plastic—and a fad was born.

"Mairzy Doats"?

People sang "Open the Door, Richard" and "Nature Boy" and "One Meat Ball." They also loved a song called "Mairzy Doats," which went like this:

"Mairzy doats and dozy doats and lid-dle lamzy divey
A kiddledy divey too, wouldn't you?"

It's not just nonsense. If you say it enough times, you may hear what the words really are.

In 1949 a composer named Johnny Marks found an old booklet that was one of 2 million given away free by the Montgomery Ward department store in 1939. It contained a poem with pictures, "Rudolph, the Red-nosed Reindeer." Marks set it to music, then shipped it off to Gene Autry, the cowboy singer, because he thought Autry might want to put it on a record. Autry didn't, but his wife loved the song. To please her, Autry recorded it on the flip side of a record, and it was a hit, a big hit. It sold 11 million copies. Since then, the song has been recorded in many versions. One of the latest is by Paul McCartney's rock group Wings—"Rudolph, the Red-nosed Reggae."

Televison? Never!

In the early 1940s a college professor said he didn't think television would make it. Why? Partly because it "demands constant attention." He was wrong, of course, but television wasn't much in the 1940s. There were television shows, yes—the first western, featuring Hopalong Cassidy, for example; and a roller derby program. If a store turned on a television set in its window, passersby gathered to watch.

In 1949 a school principal in New Jersey said TV watching was the reason kids fell asleep in class and did sloppy homework. A New York teacher replied, "If they weren't looking at television, they would be up late anyhow, maybe out in the streets. My kids are tough. They can take it."

Kids still were listening to the radio programs young people had listened to in the 1930s. Plus some new ones.

And movies were going strong. Walt Disney brought out several full-length animated movies: *Dumbo, Fantasia, Pinocchio,* and *Bambi.* Elizabeth Taylor, 12, starred in *National Velvet,* and Margaret O'Brien, 5, appeared in *Journey for Margaret.*

Laws About Children

In 1943 a state law making kids salute the flag was ruled unconstitutional by the Supreme Court.

In 1946 Congress passed a National School Lunch Act.

The star of the Disney favorite *Bambi*—as a baby.
(© *Walt Disney Productions*)

In 1949 the powerful countries of the world made a promise to kids under 15. The promise was that during war, food, clothes, and other necessary things would not be kept from reaching them.

Kids in the News

Five French school kids found ancient cave paintings in Lascaux, France. When the children told of their find, most people didn't believe them. The paintings became famous.

Quiz Kids. In 1940 a radio program called "The Quiz Kids" was launched. It starred smart kids who answered tough questions. Gerard Darrow, then 8, was good at answering questions about animals. At age 4 he had been able to name 365 birds on sight. The rules of the show were that the top 3 of the 5 kids on the program would be allowed to return and compete again the following week, and 2 new kids would replace the 2 who had been dropped. When Gerard was dropped,

people wrote in. They wanted Gerard to stay. One wrote, "I will buy no more Alka-Seltzer [the sponsor's product] until Gerard comes back." Gerard came back.

Joel Kupperman, 6 when he first appeared on the show, was a math whiz, who could figure out hard problems without pencil and paper. At the age of 4 he had put himself to sleep reciting multiplication tables.

When grown-ups played against the Quiz Kids, they usually lost. Only a group of University of Chicago professors beat them.

Some examples of questions answered correctly by the Quiz Kids (with answers upside down at the bottom of the page):

1. Would a steel ball fall faster through water at 20° Fahrenheit temperature or water at 60° Fahrenheit?

2. What is the only 4-letter word in the English language ending in *-eny*? (One Quiz Kid answered this one in 5 seconds.)

3. When did the American flag have the largest number of stripes?

Child Composer. In 1944, when she was 13, Philippa Schuyler played the piano part for "Manhattan Nocturne," a composition she had written for a 100-piece symphony. She was smart as well as talented. At 2½ she could spell 550 words. One was *rhinoceros*. She started composing at 4, and 2 years later she had written several pieces, including "Cockroach Ballet." The head of her convent school asked why she wrote about cockroaches. Why not angels?

"But, dear mother, I've never seen an angel, and I've seen many cockroaches,"

---

3. From 1795 to 1818.

2. Deny.

1. At 60°. At 20°, the water would be frozen into ice.

Philippa replied. Her mother said the girl was bright because she ate raw food, including uncooked meat. "Genius is only an overdose of energy," she said.

Juvenile Jury. In the late 1940s a radio program called "Juvenile Jury" was popular. Children 5 to 11 years old gave advice about problems. For example, a 5-year-old girl wanted her allowance raised from 10¢ to 12¢ a week.

Robin Morgan, one of the "Jury" members said, "I think 12¢ a week is too much for a 5-year-old girl."

"How old are you, Robin?" asked the host. "Five." "And how much allowance do you get?" "Fifteen cents."

The 1950s —Rock 'n' Roll and Big TV

In 1950 there were about 24 million kids 5 to 15 years old. In 1960 there were more than 35 million of them. Membership in Little League was more than 10 times greater in 1960 than in 1955, and the number of Girl Scouts and Brownies doubled. Kids and their activities became more and more important.

The 1950s was the decade of school desegregation. In 1954 the Supreme Court ruled that schools must be desegregated, that it was illegal to keep students in certain schools according to race. Integration was tough at first on black kids when they entered schools that had been all-white. They were spat upon and jostled. In Little Rock, Arkansas, the Army was sent in to make sure the schools were integrated peacefully.

In the beginning of the 1950s, school was easy. Teachers were told to teach the child, not the subject. Young people were supposed to have fun in school. The idea was to make them "well-rounded," mean-ing they weren't supposed to get hung up on just a few things. Then the Soviet Union sent an artificial satellite, called *Sputnik,* into space. Why was the Soviet Union the first to do this? people asked. And they looked to the schools. Were U.S. kids being prepared to be scientists? No. In the Soviet Union, young people went to school 6 hours a day, 6 days a week, for 213 days a year and they got a heavy dose of math and science. In the United States, kids went to school for fewer hours and days—only 180 days a year. And as for what they were learning . . . In 1958 the government passed a law that promised more money to schools so that they could teach more math and science and foreign languages. School got tougher. The days of easy grades—*S* for Satisfactory and *U* for Unsatisfactory—were over.

"King of the Wild Frontier"

Television came into its own in the 1950s. In the beginning of 1950 there were 3 million television sets in the United States. By the end of the year there were 7 million sets, and by 1960, 50 million sets. In 1951 it was found that some junior high school students were watching television nearly 30 hours a week. The TV dinner was created in 1954.

The Davy Crockett craze hit the kid world in 1954. In December of that year, the first of 3 Disney films about Davy Crockett, a frontiersman, was shown. Kids loved the show's song, "The Ballad of Davy Crockett." They wanted Davy Crockett school lunch boxes, playhouses, and—most of all—coonskin caps. The price of old coonskin coats went from $2 to $10.

Howdy Doody was another favorite.

Howdy was freckle-faced and silly, and his friend Clarabelle the Clown was silly, too. Children loved this TV show; adults hated it. The actor who played Clarabelle later became Captain Kangaroo on another kids' show. "Captain Kangaroo" was a more serious program than "The Howdy Doody Show" and tried to teach kids things. For example, there was this question: What invention permits you to see through a brick building? Answer: A window.

Pinky Lee began his show by singing, "Yoo-hoo, its me. . . ." Then he always burst a balloon. And there was Rootie Kazootie with his puppets El Squeako the mouse and Polka Dottie.

In 1955 the NBC television network's committee on children's programs had something to say about it all. Too many people were getting squirted with seltzer on children's shows. "Playing a trombone with a mouth full of watermelon . . . is more messy than funny," someone said. Howdy Doody and Pinky Lee became less silly.

But even so, experts were worried that children were watching television for too many hours.

The Big Schedule

In the 1950s many families moved to the suburbs, where children often led very scheduled lives. After school they were taken in the family car to piano, dancing or acting lessons. Or to Little League baseball games. Or to play groups. Or to Cub Scouts or Brownies.

They had money to spend but not much time in which to spend it. Kids gave each other going-steady rings at $12.95, paying for them at the rate of 50¢ a week. In California a shopping center for teenagers was built.

Some experts began to think that kids were spoiled. An article in a magazine was titled "Let's Allow Teenagers to Work." The writer, a judge, thought laws should allow more employment for young people. (Remember child labor?)

Et Cetera

The average parent thought a girl should not date until she was 16. Yet girls wore bras at a younger age than ever before. Bras for 12-year-olds had names such as Allowance, Little Angel, and Freshman.

A 1954 survey found that 4 out of 5 kids had complaints about their parents.

Roger Bannister "broke" the 4-minute mile. He ran a mile in 3 minutes, 59.4 seconds in 1954.

Every day in 1957, people in foreign countries drank 50 million bottles of Coca-Cola.

Drag racing with hot-rod cars was very big. Hot rods were called *hacks, stormers,* and *draggin' wagons.* Lowering the roof was called *chopping,* and lowering the front end was known as *raking.* Tires were called *skins;* white-wall tires were called *snowballs.* Riding around was referred to as *bombing* or *spooking.*

People who weren't "with it" were called "squares." To show someone was a square, you drew a square in the air. L 7 also meant square. A cube was a very square square.

When a not-so-funny joke was told, the listener might say "Har-de-har-har."

Other expressions were *That's the way the ball bounces; See you later, alligator; DDT* (drop dead twice); *cool,* and *the end* (good); and *turkeys, nerds,* and *yo-yos* (people who weren't "with it").

New things: electric pencil sharpeners,

Elvis Presley drove the kids wild in the '50s with his songs and gyrations onstage.
(Dwight Ellefsen, Freelance Photographers' Guild)

Disneyland (opened 1955), *Mad* magazine (cost 10¢).

Hula Hoops were a craze in 1958. At first the hoops were wooden; later they were made of plastic. They cost 93¢ each, and tens of millions were sold.

Popular boys' clothes were chino pants, pegged pants, and motorcycle jackets. Many girls wore pedal pushers and short shorts.

Hair: For boys, crew cuts and duck-tail haircuts. For girls, poodle hairstyles.

Rock Around the Clock

In 1956 Elvis Presley, rock 'n' roll star, appeared in the movie *Love Me Tender*. Earlier he'd sung "You Ain't Nothin' But a Hound Dog." On stage, he rolled his hips and played his guitar while girls went crazy over him. Some carved his initials on their arms. He was the biggest of the 1950s rock stars. And rock was big then. In 1958 there was a rock 'n' roll riot in New York.

"Nothin' To Me"

A company talked to 3,620 children aged 6 to 11 about money in 1953. They found that:

About 75 of the kids thought a penny would buy nothing.

About 750 of them thought a penny was worth nothing by itself.

Their allowances ranged from 26¢ to a dollar a week. Most spent their money on junk food.

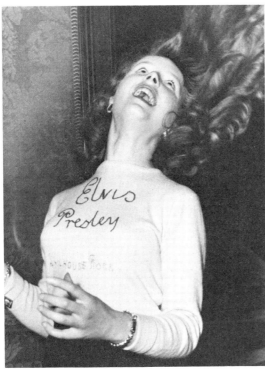

Above, 16-year-old British skating champion Susan Ranm demonstrates on ice the craze of 1958: the hula hoop. Below, a teenager goes crazy over another fad of the times: Elvis Presley (pictured on the opposite page). *(Paul Popper, Photoworld/FPG)*

Gary Thorne, 11, said, "When you only get pennies these days, it's tough."

Eddy Marchak, 7, said, "A penny? Heck, that's like nothin' to me."

Kids in the News

Jimmy Boyd, 12, a freckle-faced kid who had been singing in public since he was 7, made a hit record in 1951 called "I Saw Mommy Kissing Santa Claus." The song brought him $100,000.

Eddie Cates, 13, and his friend, Roy Brousseau, 11, took up a small airplane without permission in 1956. They had seen it sitting on a landing strip with the keys inside, and the temptation was too much. Neither boy knew how to fly, but fly they did—over 60 miles above Long Island. Eddie was spanked by his mother. "He might have killed someone," she said.

Minou Drouet, a little French girl, was 9 when her book of poems was published in 1956. It was called *Tree, My Friend*. When some people claimed it was a fake, several poetry experts asked her to write a poem, in their presence, using one of 2 titles they had made up. She chose "The Skies of Paris" and composed a poem in a very short time while bouncing a ball.

Minou had been adopted at the age of 4. She would eat only food that had been ground up. Her eyes were crossed. It was thought that she was retarded. One day she turned on the radio, and the sound of music changed her completely. She began to talk and laugh—and write. "Death is not the end, but another kind of vibration" was one of her lines.

The millionth refugee to enter the United States was Andres Suritis, 10, who had been living in refugee camps before he was granted permission to emigrate.

The Mouseketeers, on TV's "Mickey Mouse Club," were famous kids. They wore hats with mouse ears. Some of the Mouseketeers were Annette Funicello, Cubby O'Brien, Karen Pendleton, and Cheryl Holdridge. The Mouseketeer song, in part, went like this: "M-I-C. See you real soon. K-E-Y. Why? Because we *like* you. M-O-U-S-E."

Joy Foster, 8 years old, won the international Jamaican singles and mixed doubles table tennis championship in 1958.

The 1960s — The "Now Generation"

In the 1960s, when the older people asked where the action was, kids gave fresh answers. Examples: "Vincent van Gogh-Gogh" or "Long ago-ago." Everything was go-go. Young people were the "Now Generation." They were important people. A popular slogan among the young was "Don't trust anyone over 30."

There were teen magazines and newspaper columns. A book came out called *How to Be a Successful Teen-Ager*. And a movie—*I Was a Teen-Age Frankenstein*.

The hippies, or "flower children," were young people who had their own culture. They wore strange clothes—long dresses, fringed jackets, old jeans. Many took drugs. A good number of the flower children were runaway teenagers.

In 1969, 400,000 people, mostly young, gathered on a New York State dairy farm for a rock festival. The people who managed the festival had figured on 50,000 people coming. The gathering was peaceful and was called the Woodstock Nation. The music went on and on, and the fans listened—in the rain while the ground turned to mud. People were cold and the place was crowded, but the good feelings lasted throughout the event.

During the 1960s:

The Vietnam War was going on.
President John Kennedy was killed.
Men walked on the moon.

The Twist and More Rock Music

In 1960 Chubby Checker, 19, started a dance craze. The dance was called the Twist and was done to the beat of rock music.

Rock groups were popular during the 1960s and 1970s. In 1963 the most fa-

Kids crowd an open field at a rock festival in Sutton, Washington, in 1968. *(Paul Popper, Photoworld, FPG)*

mous group of all, the Beatles, had their first hit, a song called "I Wanna Hold Your Hand." When the Beatles came to the United States, crowds and crowds of young people gathered to hear them play and sing. Girls screamed. They were "in love" with Ringo, the group's drummer, or with Paul or John or George. In the beginning the Beatles' hair was fairly short. Then it got longer and longer as time went on. So did the hair of most kids.

Other groups were the Beach Boys, the Rolling Stones, and the Bee Gees.

Fascinating Facts

The McDonald's slogan in 1960 was "Over Five Billion Served." "Fast food" was part of the scene.

Barbie, the doll, acquired a whole family of friends during the 1960s. Ken joined her in 1961. Then Midge in 1963 and Kristy in 1968.

One of the popular Christmas toys in 1961 was Garloo, a green robot-monster doll. It moved around picking things up and putting them down.

A skateboard meet in California was featured on national television in 1963.

In 1963, 3 out of 4 people lived in the cities or suburbs.

Little girls had Thumbelina and Tiny Tears dolls.

Yo-yos cost from 25¢ to a dollar.

In 1964 a money expert suggested that people planning to have children be required to buy a license first. Of course, nothing was done about this.

The miniskirt was "in," starting in 1965. As time passed, it got shorter.

Some popular expressions were *tough toenails* (too bad), *out of sight* (great),

hairy (difficult), *rat fink* and *triple rat fink* (people you didn't like), *flake out* (relax), and *real blast* (lots of fun).

Elephant jokes were the rage in the early 1960s. Some examples:

Question: How can you tell there's an elephant in your bathtub?

Answer: You can smell the peanuts on his breath.

Question: Why are elephants gray?

Answer: So you can tell them from blueberries.

Question: What did Tarzan say when he saw elephants coming?

Answer: "Here come the elephants."

Question: What did Jane say when she saw the elephants coming?

Answer: "Here come the blueberries." (She was color-blind.)

Question: Why do elephants wear sneakers?

Answer: To creep up on mice.

Question: Why do elephants wear green sneakers?

Answer: To hide in the tall grass.

Question: Why do elephants wear red sneakers?

Answer: The green ones are in the laundry.

"The Bomb"

In the 1960s kids had a fear of the atomic bomb. One ninth grader wrote a very short "poem" called "Ode to the Atom Bomb." It went like this: "Flash . . . Trash." Ten-year-old Deborah Deihl of Connecticut sent a letter to the leader of the Soviet Union. She wrote: "I, and all the children on the 7 continents, should have the right to grow up in a world that is not black with ashes and red with blood."

The Beatles, in Shakespearean costumes, rehearse for a scene from *A Midsummer Night's Dream*. *(Paul Popper, Photoworld/FPG)*

And in School . . .

Communities had been ordered to integrate their schools in the 1950s—to stop setting up schools just for children of one race. To achieve integration kids were bused from their homes to faraway schools. Some people didn't like this and tried to make laws against it. In 1971 the Supreme Court said they couldn't.

During the decade, the Supreme Court ruled that teachers could hit children only under certain conditions. A child who misbehaved had to be warned before being struck, and other disciplinary methods had to be tried first. The teacher could not hit the child too hard.

Pies in the Face

Kids watched more and more television in the 1960s. Their favorites? Soupy Sales, who was silly and had pies thrown in his face to make people laugh. Howdy Doody, whose opening song began: "It's Howdy Doody time, it's Howdy Doody time. Bob Smith and Howdy, too, say howdy-do to you." "Bozo's Big Top," featuring Bozo the Clown.

More? "Winkydink and You," "Lucky Pup," "Life with Snarky Parker," "Captain Video," "Mr. I-magination," "Sky King," "Space Cadet," "Captain Midnight," and "Superman."

In 1967 "Star Trek" began. It went on for 78 shows.

The Children's Television Workshop created "Sesame Street" for little kids in 1969, and the program is still going strong in the 1980s. It is supposed to teach children their letters and numbers, among other things. The characters are Oscar the Grouch, Big Bird, the Cookie Monster . , .

In the same year, "Misterogers' Neigh-borhood" became a nationwide TV program. One of the listeners' favorite songs was "You Can Never Go Down the Drain." Mister Rogers had found that many little kids were afraid of baths because they thought they would be sucked down the drain and so he wrote a song to calm their fears.

Kids in the News

Donna Karpiak, 8, was learning to fly an airplane in 1961. The year before she had asked her parents for a bicycle. Afraid she would get hurt, her parents said she could have anything else. Her answer: "We're getting along in this space business. I think I'll learn to fly." And she did.

Mike Grost, 11, became a freshman at Michigan State University in 1964. He was very smart: When he was 6, he drew a picture of the solar system. But he was still a kid at heart, even in college. He liked Nancy Drew mysteries and Superman. When another student at the college asked him for some notes, Mike said okay. The student asked if he was bothering Mike. "Oh, no," Mike answered, "I was just outside playing with my flying saucer."

Dorothy Straight's book, *How the World Began*, was published in 1964. She was 4 years old.

Janet Lessing, 12, was selling her paintings for $50 to $100 each. Some were shown at a Los Angeles art gallery. Janet was almost blind, and kids in school laughed at her because she was awkward. So she went into other worlds in her imagination. Some of her worlds were Celephonos, Alos, and Biones. She also had a doll called Dirty Mildred.

Designs sewn on cloth by the children

of Chijnaya, Peru, were being shown around the United States. The designs were of llamas, birds, houses, roosters—what the kids knew. Over 200 children from 6 to 16 made the tapestries, a skill they had learned from a craftsman from the United States.

Oliver Knussen, 15, conducted the London Symphony Orchestra in playing his own "Symphony Number One." The Symphony, written the year before, was based on a 12-tone scale. An American conductor said, "I would have taken it to be the work of an adult. The fact that it was written by a boy of 14 is amazing and frightening." The symphony was not Oliver's first work; he had written about 60 pieces for orchestra. "I don't like all this prodigy rubbish," he said in an interview. "I just started early."

Kevin Hooks, 11, starred in a television show as a kid called J.T. who lived in a ghetto. When he wanted to bring home a cat, his mother said, "Only animals they allow in here is rats."

A phonograph record entitled "Kuro Neko No Tango" (Black Cat Tango) sold a million copies. The artist was Osamu Minagawa of Japan, 6 years old.

A 1960s Adventure. In April 1966, Bill Waddell, 13, and David Harvey, 12, set off on an adventure. They took with them 2 bikes, 1 sleeping bag, and $40. When they left Fort Bragg, North Carolina, where they lived, all they knew was that they wanted to travel to South Carolina. In Fayetteville, early in their journey, they spotted a freight car sitting in a railroad yard. Inside were empty and almost-empty beer bottles. It was going to Milwaukee, a worker told them, and the boys decided to go there instead of to South Carolina. They climbed into the car. Later the door slammed shut and they were in the dark. For 3 days the car sat on a siding.

"We tried to break the door down, but we couldn't," Bill said. "We yelled, but nobody came." The freight car finally started moving slowly. It moved for 7 days, then it stopped—for 3 days. They were in the car a total of 13 days. They told jokes and stories to cheer each other up, but they thought they'd die in the car. Bill promised God he would stay out of trouble if they did escape.

All they had to drink was the beer left in the empties, and it kept them alive. Finally a workman opened the door of the car. Out in the light, the boys wobbled and squinted. They'd lost some weight, but they were all right. The beer? "I never want any more of it," Bill said.

This volunteer worker is helping a handicapped child. Kids who have handicaps, with our help and understanding, can learn to lead useful and productive lives. *(The National Foundation, March of Dimes)*

Chapter *3*
PROBLEMS

Part 1: Introduction

This chapter is a serious one, because problems are serious to the people who have them and to their families and friends. You probably won't want to read the pages here for fun. Instead, they should be a source of help and information for you. Not every problem is discussed, but most of the important problems that bother kids in everyday life *are* included. Terrible world problems like the threat of nuclear war have been left out. Why? Because this section deals with the immediate personal problems that *mostly* affect children. If you are concerned about a world problem that affects all of us in more indirect ways, you can do something: Join a group that fights it.

For any personal problem, don't forget your closest sources of help—your parents, teachers, doctor, club leader, minis-

ter, priest or rabbi, and friends. Friends can do a great deal for each other. Just listening is important. As a friend, you can give as well as receive help.

When a problem is too big for you, admit it. The United States has lots of free, low-cost services for kids. There's no reason to suffer because you think no one cares or if you're short of money.

This chapter lists national groups with local branches. Usually you can find the local branch in the white pages of your phone book. A gold mine of agencies can be found in the Yellow Pages under "Clinics," "Social Service and Welfare Organizations," and "Youth Organizations and Centers."

EMERGENCIES: Telephone operators are trained to help people in emergencies. If you have a problem that won't

In an emergency dial "0" for operator, for help in reaching the police, fire department, or doctor.

wait (like a fire, or a person who has passed out, or terrible emotional pain), dial O for operator.

Sometimes local services advertise on television. Clinics often do. Be quick with your pencil to get the phone number. It's never on the screen very long.

The national addresses of groups are given in the following pages so that you can write to find out your nearest local branch or get more information. When you write, mention your age. That way you will get information written at your level. Include a self-addressed, stamped envelope.

Counselors

If you need a counselor to help with a problem, try the Family Services Association or the Mental Health Association. Look in your phone book in the white pages or in the Yellow Pages under "Social Service and Welfare Organizations" or "Mental Health Services."

You can also find help through your church or synagogue. Ministers, priests, and rabbis are usually trained counselors. Your school or club may offer counseling services, too.

Your library may have the *Mental Health Directory,* which lists counseling services in all states. If not, write to:

National Institute of Mental Health
5600 Fishers Lane
Rockville, MD 20857

or Closer Look
1201 16th Street, N.W.
Washington, DC 20036

Part 2: A Dictionary of Problems and Solutions

Abuse. *See* "Child Abuse," page 74.

Accidents and Other Emergencies.

Facts: Accidents are the main cause of death for kids 5 to 14 years old. Accidents kill more kids than the 6 leading diseases *together.* Motor vehicles (cars, motorcycles, trucks, and so on) are the Number One cause of death by accident. Many of these accidents happen when a car hits a kid on a bike. Drowning is second. Fire is third. Others causes of death include guns, falls, choking on food or other objects, and poisoning.

What You Can Do: Learn how to avoid accidents, and be prepared when they do occur. Among the precautions to be taken are the following:

Never point a gun, even an "unloaded" one, at yourself or at other people.

Never ride your bicycle against the traffic. (Know bicycle safety laws (Chapter 5) and obey them.

Have an escape route to use in case of fire.

Don't leave things where people can trip over them.

Turn off any electrical appliances that spark or overheat, and keep electrical appliances and their cords away from water.

Learn how to swim.

Learn how to give basic first aid.

Know the emergency numbers of the services listed below. Many of them are listed on the inside front cover of your phone book. Write these numbers on a card and keep the card next to your telephone.

Doctor
Hospital
Ambulance
Fire Department
Police Department (or Sheriff's Office)
Poison Control Center
Crisis Hotline

Where to Get Help: 1. Your phone book. In addition to the emergency numbers listed on the inside front cover, a Survival Guide is included in the front part of

Children learn first aid at a Red Cross course.
(Rudolf Vetter/American Red Cross)

many phone books. Look for it in the index. The Survival Guide includes things like first aid, what to do in an earthquake, and how to make an emergency phone call.

2. Your doctor.
3. American National Red Cross
   17th and D Streets, N.W.
   Washington, DC 20006

Your local American National Red Cross is probably listed in your phone book. The Red Cross, established in Switzerland in 1863, helps people in big disasters, like earthquakes, and teaches such things as first aid, swimming, and an emergency life-saving measure called cardiopulmonary resuscitation. Here are some Red Cross programs:

Basic Aid Training (BAT)—a 6-hour course in safety and first aid for kids in the fourth grade.

Basic First Aid—a 9-hour course that teaches both adults and young people how to save a life in an emergency.

Cardiopulmonary Resuscitation (CPR)—an 8-hour course for anyone at least 13 years old or finished with seventh grade. It teaches people what to do for someone who has stopped breathing and/or has no heartbeat.

Swimming courses for people of any age.

Basic Water Safety—a 4-hour course that anyone can take.

Basic Rescue—a 10-hour course. You must be 11 or older, must pass a swimming test, and must have taken Basic Water Safety.

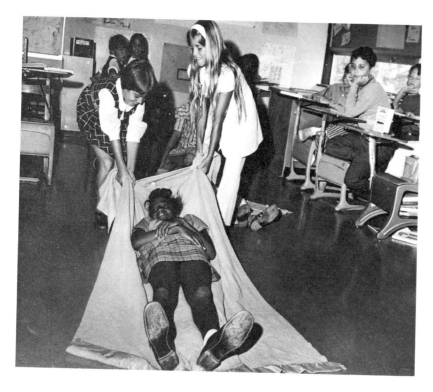

Fifth graders in a first-aid course learn the blanket drag for rescuing someone hurt. *(Jack Shere/American Red Cross)*

Also . . . Courses in how to handle boats safely, in home nursing, and in child care.

4. National Safety Council
   444 North Michigan Avenue
   Chicago, IL 60611

You can write to the Council for easy-to-read pamphlets about safety.

Acne.

Facts: Acne, also called pimples or zits, is the most common skin problem of teenagers. It is so common that only about one out of 4 kids 12 to 17 years old has clear skin. Even so, kids with acne feel ashamed, ugly, and alone. Acne comes from body changes that happen at puberty. Oily skin leads to blackheads, and blackheads lead to zits. The problem can last a year, several years, or longer.

Why do some kids have worse problems with acne than others? The tendency to get acne may be passed on from parent to child. It tends to get worse just before a girl's period. If you get into a nerve-wracking situation, you may have more trouble with acne than before. It's common for zits to show up just before an important date, for instance.

What You Can Do: Washing helps. Wash your skin 2 or 3 times a day. You can follow that with a special lotion or cream for acne. Wash your hair often and use a back brush when you take a shower. Some doctors say that it's a good idea to use a comedo extractor to remove blackheads.

Never pick at pimples with your fingers. If you do, you will leave scars.

The idea that there is a connection between acne and what you eat has not been proved. But you may notice that certain foods, like potato chips, seem to bring it on. If so, it probably would pay not to eat them.

Where to Get Help: If you have a bad acne problem or if it's causing you a lot of grief, see a skin doctor (dermatologist). Acne can be treated.

More Information: Write to:

National Institute of Allergy and Infectious Diseases
9000 Rockville Pike
Bethesda, MD 20205

Ask for the free fact sheet on acne.

See "Looks," page 86.

Alcoholism.

Facts: Alcohol is both a drug and a food. Many people are able to drink some alcohol without problems. Others can't. Drinking is a problem for them. They are alcoholics. Many experts think of alcoholism as a disease with some of these symptoms:

1. Loss of control over drinking.
2. Family or social problems caused by drinking.
3. Job or school or money problems in some way arising from drinking.
4. "Blackouts"—people can't remember what happened when they were drinking.
5. Physical and emotional effects from stopping drinking.
6. A need to drink greater and greater amounts of alcohol to get the same effect.
7. Changes in behavior or in personality when drinking.
8. Getting drunk often.
9. Starting the day with a drink.

Among the people who have had problems with alcohol are actors, writers, factory workers, people in government, truck drivers, housewives, rock super-stars . . . and kids.

Where to Get Help: Alateen is an organization for children of parents who are problem drinkers. The group helps them understand their parents' problems and also helps them deal with the difficulties those problems present. One member said, "I learned I wasn't the problem, and I'm not the solution." You must be 12 or older to join. Look in your phone book for:

Al-Anon Information Service
or
Al-Anon Family Groups

Ask for information about Alateen. You also can write to:

Al-Anon Family Group Headquarters
P.O. Box 182
Madison Square Station
New York, NY 10059

You are not alone.

What You Can Do If Someone Close to You Is an Alcoholic: Talk to the person about it. Encourage him or her to get help.

What You Can Do If You Are an Alcoholic: Talk to someone about your problem. People who might help you are your parents, a teacher, a school counselor, a doctor, a minister, a priest, a rabbi. Children can join Alcoholics Anonymous. Some have been as young as 12. Look in the phone book for the number to call, or write to:

Alcoholics Anonymous
175 Fifth Avenue
Room 219
New York, NY 10010

Alcoholics Anonymous (A.A.) is a group of alcoholic people who want to stop drinking and stay sober. It costs nothing to join and anyone can join. All you need is the wish to stop drinking.

Another source of help is:

National Council on Alcoholism
733 Third Avenue
New York, NY 10017

This group can give you the names of doctors and clinics that treat alcoholism. Some local branches offer counseling and treatment to alcoholics directly.

NOTE: Riding in a car with a driver who has been drinking too much is very dangerous. You might make this pact with your parents:

You: "I will call you to come and get me if I am ever in a situation where a friend whose car I need to get home has had too much to drink."

Parent: "I will come and get you any time, any place, with no questions asked. Or I will pay for a taxi to bring you home."

Anger. *See* "Feelings," pages 82–83.

Anorexia Nervosa.

Facts: One teenage girl out of every 300 in the United States gets this illness, says one psychologist. Boys can get it, too, but few do. It attacks kids from 13 to 19, though some kids get it as young as 11. Young people with anorexia nervosa starve themselves and usually exercise too much. Even though kids with anorexia get very thin, they consider themselves fat. Why do they get this illness? No one knows for certain. If nothing is done the condition gets worse. Girls stop having their periods. Hair thins out. Blood pressure, pulse rate, and temperature drop. Sometimes people with anorexia nervosa become so starved that they can't stand up anymore and end up in the hospital.

What You Can Do: If you know some-one who seems to have anorexia, try to get her to see a doctor. If you have it, *you* see a doctor. There are ways to treat this illness.

Where to Get Help:

1. See your doctor.

2. Go to a counseling center (*see* "Counselors," pages 66–67).

3. Write to:

Anorexia Nervosa Association, Inc.
133 Cedar Lane
Teaneck, NJ 07666

This group may put you in touch with a person who has had anorexia nervosa and gotten well.

Bed-wetting.

Facts: Kids who wet the bed often have what people in the olden days called a "weak bladder." That means that their bladders—organs that hold urine—have not developed as fast as in some other kids. When they are deeply asleep, these kids lose control of their bladders without knowing it. This trait can be passed on from parent to child. Most people out-grow bed-wetting, so if this is your prob-lem, don't despair. Chances are that when you're older the problem will solve itself. And don't feel that you're weird be-cause of it.

What You Can Do: Try not to drink liq-uids in the evening. Go to the bathroom before you go to bed.

Where to Get Help: Your doctor.

Birth Control. *See* "Sex," pages 89–90.

Blindness.

Facts: Stevie Wonder, who writes and

Blind girl from the Colorado School for the Deaf and Blind reading a Braille description of an animal sculpture. *(Myron Wood, Photo Researchers, Inc.)*

sings his own songs and plays the piano, is blind. So was the writer and artist James Thurber. Thurber wasn't born blind. As his eyes gave out, he wrote larger and larger words and drew larger and larger pictures with a thick crayon so he could see them.

Blind people may use a cane as a feeler to help them find their way. The cane is white so that others will know they are blind. That way drivers know to be careful when a blind person with a cane is crossing the street. At 18, a blind person can have a guide dog to serve as his or her eyes.

Braille is a special alphabet system using raised dots. The patterns of the dots stand for letters of the alphabet. By feeling the patterns, blind people read books in Braille.

Sports are *not* impossible for blind people. They play games like soccer with a beeping ball and can even ski. When blind kids go on Easter egg hunts, the eggs are made of plastic and have noisemakers inside.

What You Can Do: If a friend of yours is blind, it's probably better to help only if asked. However, when your blind friend comes into your house, tell him or her where things are. "There's a couch to your right," for example.

Don't shout at a blind person.

To help someone who is blind cross a street, offer your arm. Don't grab a blind person's arm, but say, "Here's my arm," then brush the person's body with your elbow.

Don't pat a blind person's guide dog.

Where to Get Help and More Information: See "Handicaps," pages 83–84.

Talking Books are tape cassettes that blind people can get for free. For information about them, ask the librarian in your local library.

Braces.

Facts: Braces aren't just to improve your looks. Straight teeth last longer. If you need braces, it's best to get them when you're young. Your bones are softer then, and soft bones can be molded more easily than hard ones.

What You Can Do: If you wear braces, brush and floss your teeth often. Avoid sweets, which tend to get stuck in braces and cause cavities. Remember, you won't be wearing braces forever. If you do what your dentist says, you may not have to wear them as long as you would otherwise.

See "Looks," page 86.

Brothers. *See* "Parents and Brothers and Sisters," pages 87–88.

Cancer.

Facts: The causes of childhood cancer are still not clear. We do know that no one "catches" cancer, and that when a person gets the disease it doesn't necessarily mean his or her children will get it. However, heredity may play a role in the tendency to get cancer. So if there is a history of cancer in your family, you should learn more about the disease and its causes.

More and more children who have cancer are being successfully treated. Leukemia, a cancer that affects the blood, is being stopped more and more every year in children who have it.

Where to Get Help: Some local groups of the Candlelighters have clubs for teenage cancer patients and their brothers and sisters. These groups help them cope with their feelings. Some have crisis hotlines. The kids get together for picnics and other activities. A Teens Newsletter is edited by a former teen cancer patient. Their national address is:

WHY START A LIFE UNDER A CLOUD?

Cigarette smoking is perhaps the stupidest habit a kid can take up. It's a terrible way to start out in life. *(American Cancer Society)*

Candlelighters
123 C Street, S.E.
Washington, DC 20003

More Information: To find out about cancer, you can call a toll-free number of the National Cancer Institute: 1 (800) 638–6694. (In Maryland call 1 (800) 492–6600.)

Other groups that offer information are:

1. American Cancer Society
   777 3rd Avenue
   New York, NY 10017

2. Leukemia Society of America
   800 Second Avenue
   New York, NY 10017

Cerebral Palsy.

Facts: Over 2 million kids have this condition. Their nervous systems have been damaged, and as a result they can't control their muscles. Sometimes they shake; sometimes their heads, arms, and

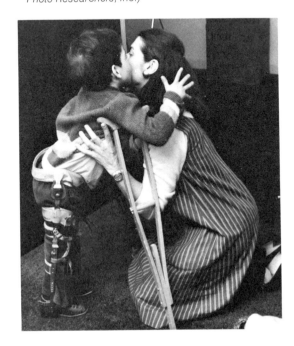

A child with cerebral palsy. *(Hannah W. Schreiber, Photo Researchers, Inc.)*

legs may jerk or be very stiff. There are several kinds of cerebral palsy.

Christopher C. Lee, who has cerebral palsy, writes puppet plays. The hero of his plays is Christopher Puppet, who travels in a wheelchair and has a puppet dog, Gretchen, that pushes him out on stage. One of Lee's plays is called "The Camel Who Wanted to Dump Her Hump."

Where to Get Help and More Information: Call the local branch of the United Cerebral Palsy Association. Or write to:

United Cerebral Palsy Associations, Inc.
66 East 34th Street
New York, NY 10016

See "Handicaps," pages 83–84.

Child Abuse.

Facts: Every year in the United States, about a million cases of child abuse are *reported.* That means someone told a person in authority—a police officer or a social worker—about them. Some experts believe the real number is much higher—that up to 20 million children are abused, but that most cases go *unreported.*

Even experts don't agree on the definition of child abuse. However, if a child is beaten and hurt by an adult, that is child abuse. If an adult does something sexually to a child, or makes a child do something illegal, like steal, that is child abuse. *Child abuse is not the child's fault.*

Parents who abuse their children usually love their kids. Many child abusers were abused by *their* parents and it made them mentally sick. Those parents often can be helped.

If a child is in danger from a parent, the child may be taken away and put in a safe place, such as a foster home or a hospital. However, many experts now think it's best for an abused child to stay at home if at all possible, while counselors help the parent or parents learn to stop hurting the child.

What You Can Do: If you or someone you know is being abused, tell an adult about it—your teacher, doctor, counselor, minister, priest, or rabbi. Don't worry about being loyal to the abuser. You must get outside help before the situation gets out of hand and you or someone you know is hurt badly and permanently. By law, a teacher or a counselor must report a case of child abuse to the police.

Where to Get Help: Parents who abuse their children need help in learning how to stop. They can join:

Parents Anonymous
22330 Hawthorne Boulevard
Suite 208
Torrance, CA 90505

Children who are abused can get help from a counselor. *See* "Counselors," pages 66–67.

Choking.

Posters, teaching slides, and wallet cards that show how to perform the Heimlich Maneuver are now available. For information, send a stamped, self-addressed envelope to:

Edumed
Box 52
Cincinnati, OH 45201

Deafness.

Facts: One American in every 10 has a hearing problem. It is hard for deaf

FOOD CHOKING

Food choking occurs when a piece of food lodges in the throat, blocking the airway. The victim cannot breathe or speak and will die of strangulation in 4 minutes if you do not act to save him or her.

What To Look For

1. Victim cannot speak or breathe.

2. Turns blue. Hand to neck signals "I'm choking!"

3. Collapses and will die if not helped.

HEIMLICH MANEUVER*

Exert pressure on victim's abdomen, forcing up diaphragm and compressing air in lungs: This expels object blocking airway.

Victim standing or seated

- Stand behind. Wrap your arms around his or her waist.
- Place fist (thumb side) against victim's abdomen, above navel, below rib cage.
- Grasp fist with other hand. Quickly press upward into victim's abdomen.
- Repeat if necessary.
- See physician immediately.

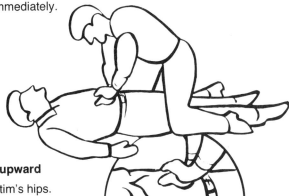

Victim lying, face upward

- Kneel astride victim's hips.
- With one hand on top of the other, place heel of bottom hand on victim's abdomen, above navel, below rib cage.
- Quickly press upward.
- Repeat if necessary.
- See physician immediately.

The Heimlich maneuver is used to save choking victims.

This is a class at the New York School for the Deaf.
(Guy Gillette, Photo Researchers, Inc.)

people to talk because they can't hear themselves, and their speech often sounds strange to hearing people. Deaf people can communicate by using speech, finger spelling, or sign language. Finger spelling is a way of spelling out words letter by letter with hand symbols, while sign language is a method of expressing words or phrases with hand and body signs. When deaf people get together, they may start "talking" excitedly; hands and arms move fast and furiously. They call this "windmilling." Many deaf people "read" oral speech by watching mouths.

Deaf people can tell the phone is ringing by attaching a light to it that flashes when someone calls. They can talk on the phone by using a special teletype machine, which works like a long-distance typewriter: The deaf person types a message, and it is transmitted by phone to a similar machine that types out the words at the other end. Some deaf people have a machine that shakes their beds to tell them it's time to get up.

Composer Ludwig van Beethoven continued to write music after he became deaf. He could hear it in his head. Linda Bove, a deaf actress, played a leading part in an episode of the *Happy Days* TV show. Although Kitty O'Neill, a Hollywood stunt woman, is deaf, she drove a 3-wheel, rocket-powered car at 512.71 miles an hour, breaking the women's speed record on land.

What You Can Do: If you have trouble hearing, see a doctor. If a friend of yours is deaf, try to learn sign language. Your friend may be glad to teach you. When you talk to a deaf person, talk slowly but naturally. To see what it's like to be deaf, turn on the TV with the sound off and try to figure out what people are saying by looking at their mouths.

Where to Get Help: See a doctor.
More Information: Write to:

National Association of the Deaf
814 Thayer Avenue
Silver Spring, MD 20910

Finger Spelling

Deaf people have more than one way to "say" things to each other. American Sign Language (Ameslan), in which each sign stands for something, is one. Another way is finger spelling, in which the letters of the alphabet are shown with the hand as it is held in front of the chest. This chart shows the letters.

Manual Alphabet for the Deaf

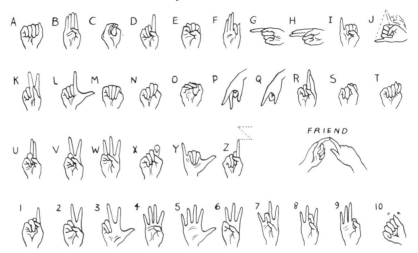

The Manual Alphabet for the Deaf uses hand and finger positions to spell words.

Try spelling out the word *hello.* Can you "read" the word represented in the illustration below? (The answer is at the bottom of the page.*)

See "Handicaps," pages 83–84.

Depression. *See* "Feelings," pages 82–83, and "Suicide," pages 92–94.

Diabetes.

Facts: Diabetes is a disorder in which your body cannot regulate glucose, a kind of sugar, because its production of a substance called insulin is out of whack. Most diabetics take insulin each day, usually in a shot. Some well-known people who have diabetes are baseball player Ron Santo, hockey star Bobby Clarke, actress Mary Tyler Moore, comedian Dan Rowan, and baseball pitcher Catfish Hunter. Jackie Robinson, another baseball player, also had the disease.

In the United States there are one million people with juvenile diabetes—the kind of diabetes that kids can have, although grown-ups can get it, too.

*Thanks

Where to Get Help:

The Juvenile Diabetes Foundation
23 East 26th Street
New York, NY 10010

Send for a booklet written for children with diabetes.

More Information: Read *You Can't Catch Diabetes from a Friend* by Lynne Kipnis and Susan Adler.

Divorce.

Facts: In the United States about 5 million kids have parents who are divorced. Though most live with their mothers, quite a few live with their fathers. Studies show that many (though not all) kids whose parents divorce feel bad about it at first. They may feel depressed and have trouble in school. Lots of kids are angry at the parent who left, and many dream that their parents will get back together. Some are ashamed about the divorce and don't want to discuss it. After time passes, they feel better about it.

A group called Parents Without Partners asked kids aged 12 to 19 from one-parent families about themselves. The kids said they hated to be pitied. The last thing they wanted to hear was "Oh, you poor thing!" Many believed that the divorce made them more grown-up and more responsible.

If their parent got married again, some were confused by it, at least at first. Most were against the idea that parents should stay together for the sake of the children.

What You Can Do: Remember that the divorce is not your fault. Your parents didn't get divorced because you didn't always behave.

If you have questions about your parents' divorce, don't be afraid to ask them about it.

Where to Get Help:

1. Parents Without Partners
   7910 Woodmont Avenue, Suite 1000
   Washington, DC 20014

Check the white pages of your phone book to find the branch of this organization nearest you.

Parents Without Partners was started for single parents who were divorced or never married. Their kids are invited to parties and outings in which they can take part if their parent joins. There are activities such as scavenger hunts, car clinics, biking, fishing, photography, sports, and puppetry classes.

Parents Without Partners now includes 2 groups for kids of divorced parents:

Buddies and Pals, International, for kids 6 to 11 years old, was started by 2 10-year-olds who asked, "Why doesn't Parents Without Partners have something special that we could join?" The group has 2 divisions: Buddies for kids aged 6 to 8, and Pals for kids from 9 to 11. Sometimes they meet together. To join by mail, write to the Parents Without Partners address above, saying you want to join Buddies and Pals. Enclose 25¢ with your letter to get a membership card, a Junior Amigo badge, and the names of 2 pen pals to write to. One pen pal will live close to you. You can also start a group in your area; all you need are 5 kids and an adult leader. At meetings, kids talk about their ideas and they plan things to do and ways to help others. They get involved in projects like collecting money for the March of Dimes and other organizations. The motto of Buddies and Pals is "Doing Something for Somebody Else."

For kids aged 12 to 19 there is the International Youth Council (IYC), open to children of single parents as well as to all other young people in this age group. For kids of divorced parents to be eligible for membership, a local Parents Without Partners group must sponsor them, but their parents do not have to belong to Parents Without Partners. To start an IYC group, all you need are 10 members. Kids in IYC share problems, ideas and companionship, and they become involved in school and community activities. At meetings, they may have speakers or panel discussions. One group went on an all-night bus ride to visit police stations, hospitals, and night court, ending with breakfast as the sun came up. Another went on a week-long canoe trip. IYC groups often visit kids' institutions to put on shows and encourage the kids to play games.

2. Big Brothers/Big Sisters of America
   117 South 17th Street
   Suite 1200
   Philadelphia, PA 19103

A boy and his "Big Brother" working on a car.
(Big Brothers/Big Sisters of America)

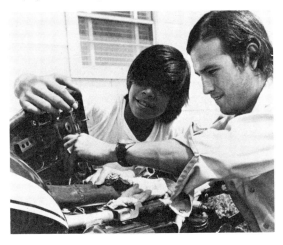

A girl and her "Big Sister" share affection.
(C.D. Sewell, Big Brothers/Big Sisters of America)

If you live with only one parent, you may be able to have a Big Sister (if you are a girl) or a Big Brother (if you are a boy). Big Sisters and Big Brothers are adults who want to be friends with and spend time with young people—about 2 to 5 hours a week. They don't take the place of parents, but help make up for an absent parent by giving kids more of the attention they need. To find out if you qualify, have your parent call the local group.

More Information: A couple of good books are: *How Does It Feel When Your Parents Get Divorced?* by Terry Berger, and *How to Get It Together When Your Parents Are Coming Apart* by Arlene Richards and Irene Willis.

Drugs.

Facts: Drugs can help or hurt people. Any chemical that changes the way the mind or body works is a drug. Coffee contains a drug; so does chocolate. "Drug abuse" means taking a chemical that harms the mind or body or that in some way hurts someone else. After taking a drug for a time, some people develop a need for it. That's "dependence." When a person cannot do without a drug, and becomes sick if the drug is taken away, this strong dependence is called "drug addiction."

Some drugs are legal: It's not against the law to buy and use them. These include alcohol, the nicotine in tobacco, and the caffeine in coffee. Aspirin and other drugs you can buy in the drugstore are also legal. Buying or using alcohol or tobacco is *not* legal for people under a certain age. The age is set by the state in which you live.

If you buy or use illegal drugs, you are breaking the law. These include pot (marijuana), LSD, heroin, angel dust, and speed. Using medicines to get high can also be illegal.

Some drugs are more dangerous than others. Any can be dangerous if taken by the wrong person, in too big a dose, or at the wrong time and place.

Street drugs often are not what the dealers say they are. What a dealer calls THC, for instance, can really be angel dust, a dangerous drug.

These students in a high school in Washington, D.C., are interviewing a local police officer to learn more about preventing drug abuse. *(Michael D. Sullivan)*

What You Can Do: Learn about drugs and what they can do to you. Remember, you have the right to turn down drugs.

If a friend is having trouble with drugs, talk it over and listen. Don't preach. Let your friend know where to get help. If this doesn't work, you may have to get help for him or her yourself.

Where to Get Help: 1. Hotlines, like crisis hotlines and drug hotlines. Look for them on the inside front cover of your phone book.

   2. American National Red Cross.
     17th and D Streets, N.W.
     Washington, DC 20006
Red Cross drug abuse programs are available. Check your phone book.

   3. Boys' Clubs of America
     Project TEAM
     771 First Avenue
     New York, NY 10017
Find the number of your local club in the phone book.

Other sources of help are your doctor or counselor (*see* pages 66–67).

More Information: Write to:

   1. National Institute on Drug Abuse
     Office of Communications and
     Public Affairs
     5600 Fishers Lane
     Rockville, MD 20857
This agency offers an excellent book with straight information written for kids. It's called *This Side Up.*

   2. Do It Now Foundation
     P.O. Box 5115
     Phoenix, AZ 85010
See "Alcoholism," pages 69–70, and "Smoking," pages 91–92.

Dying.

Facts: It is human to be afraid of dying. Death is a fact of life, but our society likes to pretend death is not there. Adults often try to keep children from knowing about it.

Yet children fear dying anyhow. It is normal for a child to be afraid his parents will die. When children hear of another child dying, they fear their own deaths. Pets die, and children grieve. Many people have to face the death of someone close to them by the time they grow up.

Almost all human groups have funeral ceremonies of some kind. Humans who lived more than 35,000 years ago sprinkled flowers on the graves of their dead. (Scientists have found the flower fossils.) The ancient Egyptians made mummies of the bodies of dead people by treating the bodies with chemicals and by drying them so they would last a long time. This was done in the belief that people could live on in a life-after-death world. Many of the mummies, thousands of years old, can be seen today in museums.

Halloween used to be known as All Hallows Eve. The day after, November 1, was called All Hallows' in honor of the saints. November 2 was All Souls Day to honor the souls of the dead. That's why ghosts are part of Halloween.

Many societies have kept death more out in the open and less of a secret than we do. In these cultures, death has been dealt with more realistically than in our own.

What You Can Do: Learn some facts. For example, dying is almost always not painful. It's okay to cry when someone dies or your pet dies. People do better when they face their own sadness about a death.

Some schools teach kids about death and dying, and encourage kids to talk about it so that it isn't so scary and mysterious. Sometimes they visit graveyards and read what the gravestones say, then write their own death notices and epitaphs (words for the stone). Nicole Carpenter of Gainesville, Florida, wrote:

Here lies Nicole
Who fell in a hole.
Without a doubt
She could not get out.

Where to Get Help: You might want to see a counselor if worry about death is keeping you from living your life or if someone you love has died and you feel you can't bear it.

See "Counselors," pages 66–67.

More Information: Read *Learning to Say Good-by* by Eda LeShan.

Dyslexia. *See* "Learning Disabilities," pages 85–86.

Emotions. *See* "Feelings," pages 82–83.

Epilepsy.
Facts: Epilepsy used to be called the "sacred disease," and those who had it were treated as very special people. Some famous epileptics were great military leaders: Julius Caesar, Alexander the Great, Napoleon.

Epilepsy has several causes. An epileptic seizure results when the brain gives off too much electricity. The epileptic's eyelid may twitch and that's all you see, or he or she may fall down and start making jerking motions.

What You Can Do: If someone has an epileptic attack when you are there, don't try to stop it or attempt to hold the person down. If you can, loosen the victim's clothing and put a handkerchief between the teeth to prevent biting of the tongue. Don't put anything hard between the teeth. When the epileptic attack ends, the victim won't remember anything about it.

More Information: Write to:

Epilepsy Foundation of America
4351 Garden City Drive
Landover, MD 20785

The foundation offers booklets about epilepsy written for children.

Family. *See* "Parents and Brothers and Sisters," pages 87–88.

Fat. *See* "Weight," pages 94–95.

Fear. *See* "Feelings," below.

Feelings.
Facts: At all times of life, people have problems with their feelings. The more "changes" they go through, the more problems they seem to have.

It's common for kids in their teens to feel self-hate, and such teenage emotions as jealousy and anger can seem frightening because they are so strong.

What You Can Do: Here are a few rules. You may have heard some of them before, but they often work.

1. Make a list of what you like and don't like about yourself. Can you change what you don't like? How? How can you live with what you don't like and can't change?

2. Face the feelings you don't like and get rid of them in harmless ways. If you're mad at someone, consider punching a pillow or going someplace where you can yell your head off.

3. Talk to someone you trust—a friend, parent, teacher, or counselor.

4. If something you used to enjoy, like basketball, stops being fun, slow down. You're probably overdoing it.

It's good to share your feelings with someone.
(Big Brothers/Big Sisters of America)

5. Set goals for yourself. Do things in steps that you can manage. If your grades are slipping, try to raise them a notch. Don't try to go from a D to an A in a month.

6. Live in the present; don't rake over past mistakes.

7. If you're depressed or bored, try a change of pace by doing something new. Exercise. Try to plan something to look forward to every day.

Where to Get Help: Sometimes problems can be just too much for kids. If this is true of you, talk to a counselor. (*See* "Counselors," pages 66–67.)

The American National Red Cross offers a course called "Good Grooming" that helps people look their best and feel better about themselves. Look in your phone book for the number. Or write to:

American National Red Cross
17th and D Streets, N.W.
Washington, DC 20006

Handicaps.

Facts: Almost all people have things they don't like about themselves. Handicapped people have special difficulties. Some can't see; others can't hear. They may have trouble moving or not be able to move at all. The problem may be not having grown very tall, or learning slowly.

According to the law, handicapped children must be allowed (if they can) to go to regular classrooms to learn. Public buildings must be designed so that handicapped people can get into them.

What You Can Do: If you meet someone who is handicapped, keep these ideas in mind:

1. Remember that a person with a handicap is a *person.*

2. Talk about things you have in common.

3. Offer help if asked or if there is a real need. Don't overdo it. Respect the handicapped person's right to ask for the kind of help needed.

4. Talk about the handicap if it comes up in conversation, but don't pry. Go along with the wishes of the person with the handicap.

5. Appreciate what the person can do. Remember that often the hardest thing handicapped people face is not the handicap, but rather the attitudes of other

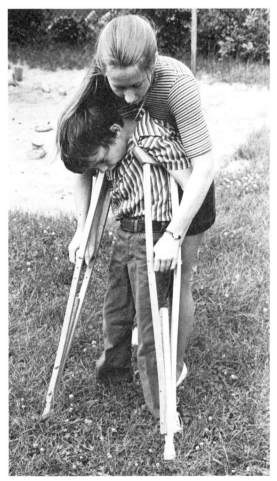

A crippled child is being helped by a college student.
(Christopher Marrow/Photo Researchers Inc.)

9. Don't move a wheelchair or crutches out of the reach of someone who uses them.

10. Before you push the wheelchair of a handicapped person, ask how he or she wants it done.

11. Put yourself in the handicapped person's shoes in order to become more aware of his or her needs.

> Adapted from "Points to Remember," The National Easter Seal Society for Crippled Children and Adults.

Where To Get Help and More Information:

1. Muscular Dystrophy Association
   810 7th Avenue
   New York, NY 10019

2. The National Easter Seal Society for Crippled Children and Adults
   2023 West Ogden Avenue
   Chicago, IL 60612

3. The National Federation/March of Dimes
   1275 Mamaroneck Avenue
   White Plains, NY 10605

4. Clearinghouse on the Handicapped
   Office for Handicapped Individuals
   Department of Education
   400 Maryland Avenue, S.W.
   Room 3106, Switzer Building
   Washington, DC 20202

5. Little People of America
   P.O. Box 126
   Owatonna, MN 55060

6. Closer Look
   1201 16th Street, N.W.
   Washington, DC 20036

people and the ways in which others stop the handicapped from being themselves.

6. Take the extra time to allow handicapped people to get things said or done. Let them set their own pace.

7. Remember that we all have handicaps to one extent or another.

8. Don't talk as if the handicapped person is not there. Speak directly to him or her.

A good book about handicapped kids is *Feeling Free* by Mary Beth Sullivan, Alan J. Brightman, and Joseph Blatt.

Homework.

Facts: Homework is a fact of school life.

Where to Get Help: If you have fallen behind in school, ask your teacher for help. Many schools offer special classes or after-school tutors to kids who are having problems. Find out if your community has a hotline for kids with homework problems. For example, a California school district has a "Homework Hotline," and Philadelphia offers "Dial-a-Teacher." Many clubs give help with homework. And don't forget your parents, brothers and sisters, and friends.

Whatever you do, don't give up!

When you get someone to work with you, take only as much help as you really need. Dont be afraid to ask questions. You won't learn anything by making the same mistake over and over. For instance, if you can't add fractions, get someone to show you how, then do some problems on your own. Sometimes all you need is a hint or two, and it all becomes clear.

Having someone *do* your homework for you won't help in the long run. You don't learn anything from it.

If emotional problems are stopping you from learning, visit a counselor. *See* "Counselors," pages 66–67, and "Learning Disabilities," below.

Jealousy. *See* "Feelings," pages 82–83.

Learning Disabilities.

Facts: Some children who find it hard to learn have special disabilities. One is dyslexia. Kids with this disorder are "word blind"—that is, they may "see" words as upside down or backwards. They may read "was" for "saw," for instance. (At certain stages in learning to read, many children do this. They are not all dyslexics.) Because kids with dyslexia have trouble with reading and spelling, they get frustrated. "I can't do anything right," they say, or, "I'm no good."

In truth, many famous people have been dyslexics. Thomas Edison and General George Patton may have been. Nel-

A tutor can help you with homework.
(Peter Kleinbard/The National Commission on Resources for Youth)

son A. Rockefeller, who was governor of New York, wrote in a diary when he was 11, "engen repar schop." Auguste Rodin, a famous sculptor, was the "worst pupil in school." Olympic champion Bruce Jenner is also a dyslexic.

Four times as many boys as girls are dyslexics.

Kids with dyslexia and other learning disabilities have trouble with spoken and/or written language. However, if you are having such trouble, it doesn't necessarily mean you have such a disability.

What You Can Do: If your friend or brother or sister has a learning disability, try to understand. Don't make fun of such people. Be patient. Kids who have trouble with learning would rather be thought of as "bad" than "dumb," so they tend to act up. And remember, although people with such handicaps may never be crazy about reading, they become doctors and inventors and artists and almost anything you can think of.

Where to Get Help: If you have a learning disability, you can get help, for there are special ways of teaching young people with these problems. For more information, you or your parent can write to:

1. Learning Disabilities Program
   Clearinghouse on the Handicapped
   Department of Education
   3119 Switzer Building
   Washington, DC 20202

2. The Orton Dyslexia Society, Inc.
   724 York Road
   Baltimore, MD 21204

The Orton Society loans out cassette tapes about dyslexia. One is No. 40, "Language Learning Differences in Plain English" by Margaret B. Rawson. The Society also has written information.

Leukemia. *See* "Cancer," pages 72–73.

Looks.

Facts: What don't you like about your looks? Your hair, because it's too curly or too straight? Freckles? Weight? Height? Your shape? The color of your eyes? Most people have a complaint about their appearance. How you feel about how you look has a lot to do with how you feel about life.

What You Can Do: Take a good look at yourself in a mirror. What do you like? What don't you like? Can anything be done about what you don't like? You might be stuck with freckles, for instance. But if you want to be thinner, you can go on a diet.

If you can't change something, you can change how you feel about it. For example, lots of people *like* freckles. Find out about some famous people who have them.

Where to Get Help: Certain groups offer courses in making the most of your looks. One is the American National Red Cross. Look for the number of the local Red Cross group in your phone book. If it's not there, write to:

American National Red Cross
17th and D Streets, N.W.
Washington, DC 20006

See "Acne," page 69, "Braces," page 72, and "Weight," pages 94–95.

Love.

Facts: You can love your mother,

father, sister, brother, teacher, uncle, aunt, grandmother, grandfather, neighbor, friend, boyfriend, girl friend, dog, or cat. You may have feelings of love for a movie star, a character in a book, a child crying in a newsreel. Chances are, the love that causes your problems is "being in love." It can be serious, even if you're only a child when it happens. Love is a problem if it takes up all of your time, if the person you love doesn't love you, or if you break up with the one you love.

What You Can Do: Here's what "This Side Up," a government booklet, says about love:

If you accept yourself as a worthwhile person, other people will be attracted to you. If you have a low opinion of yourself, you'll give off hidden signals and tell other people that you don't think you're okay.

If you can be close to and care for members of your own sex, then you're likely to have a much easier time feeling close to members of the opposite sex.

You're allowed to like any person.

You're allowed to love any person.

You're allowed to change your mind about people as often as you choose.

If you like someone who doesn't like you in return, it's okay to try to do every reasonable thing to attract that person's affection. If he or she doesn't respond after a matter of time, then admit that this time you'd better look elsewhere.

If you feel that no one will ever be attracted to you, you're wrong. Someone will love you sooner or later, as long as you don't close yourself off to the idea of being loved. Expect to be loved.

An absolute truth: You are going to change. Over a matter of months or weeks you'll be able to notice some differences. All your friends will be changing, too. New things will happen.

Where to Get Help: If a love problem

Loving someone who doesn't love you in return can be painful.

has you down, you may feel it's the end of the world. Don't despair. You will feel better. If you think you need special help, go to a counselor. (*See* "Counselors," pages 66–67.)

Muscular Dystrophy. *See* "Handicaps," pages 83–84.

Parents and Brothers and Sisters.

Facts: It's common for kids to have mixed feelings about parents. Parents make mistakes, just as kids do. It's common for brothers and sisters to fight with each other. Or older kids in a family may not want to have the younger kids tag along when they go somewhere. Having such problems is part of being a family.

It's common to have both sad and happy times like this in a family.

What You Can Do: Learn to listen. You don't have to agree with what people say in order to listen to them. Let family members know you hear them. Ask questions. If someone else is right and you are wrong, admit it. If you don't feel like talking about something, say, "I don't feel like talking about that." Don't just stare; that can be very annoying. It can make you look as if you don't care. Accept the fact that people in a family sometimes don't agree.

Put yourself in the other person's place. If your little sister gets into your things, be aware that her desire to be like you may be behind her actions. If your big brother doesn't want you to come along,

realize that he needs to spend some time by himself. If your parents won't let you stay out until 2 A.M., ask yourself what you would do if it were your kid. Why might you say no?

If you feel your parents are being unfair about something, present your case. Be calm. List all the reasons you feel as you do.

Where to Get Help: Sometimes parents have deep problems that affect their kids. Some parents are alcoholics, for example, or child abusers. If your parents have problems like this, talk to a counselor. (*See* "Counselors," pages 66–67.)

Pimples. *See* "Acne," page 69.

Pregnancy. *See* "Sex," pages 89–90.

Running Away.
Facts: Kids often run away from home for very good reasons. One kid in 4 runs away because his parents beat him. Others have alcoholic parents, or have been kicked out of the house. In some cases, children run away because of a problem they consider terrible. It may be a failure in school or a "broken heart."

Whatever the reason, it is better to stay home and get help there. Runaway children are preyed upon by people who use them. Life on the street is not easy. Jobs for kids don't exist, so runaways often end up in trouble.

Where to Get Help: If you have run away and want to go home, go to a phone and call your parents collect. All you need is a dime. Ask the operator to help you.

If you don't want to call your parents, try a "runaway hotline." There are 4, and all are toll-free:

National Runaway Switchboard: 1 (800) 621–4000

    (In Illinois: 1 (800) 972–6004)

    Runaways: 1 (800) 231–6946

    (In Texas: 1 (800) 392–3352)

If you want to get in touch with your parents, the hotline staff will send messages for you. You do not have to tell your parents where you are, just that you're okay. The staff will also help you find a place to stay where you will be safe. Runaway shelters, mostly free, offer kids a place to sleep, food, and advice if they want it. They do not report you to the police or call your parents.

Other groups that help runaways are:
Salvation Army
Boys' Club
Girls' Club
Catholic Family Service
Family Service Association
Girl Scouts
YMCA
YWCA
Legal Aid Society

If you have not yet run away, the National Runaway Switchboard can find help for the problems that are making you think about escaping.

School. *See* "Homework," page 85, Feelings," pages 82–83, and "Learning Disabilities," pages 85–86.

Sex.

Facts: Sex isn't a problem by itself, but it can cause problems—like getting pregnant, catching venereal diseases (diseases you can get by having sex with someone who has them), and not knowing what it is about or what to do. Lots of adults want to avoid talking to kids about sex because they are afraid that by giving young people the facts they will be telling the kids to go out and *have* sex.

It's difficult to separate sex from related subjects, such as love and babies and religion. It's a big topic. One magazine said that kids under 16 are likely to have problems with their feel-

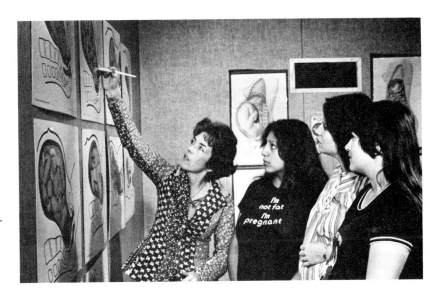

It's hard to separate sex from love, family, and religion. Here teenage mothers learn about the wonders of pregnancy.
(National Federation/ March of Dimes)

ings if they have sex. Some psychologists might not agree.

Where to Get Help and More Information: If you suspect you have venereal disease, call a V.D. hotline for help. The toll-free numbers are: 1 (800) 523–1885 or 1 (800) 227–8922. (In California, 1 (800) 982–5883.)

You can be cured if you are treated right away. By law, your parents don't have to know about your treatment. Don't fool around with V.D.; it can be dangerous. Clinics give free medical care.

If you can't get information and help about sex from your school, parents, or religious counselor, try:

Planned Parenthood Federation of America, Inc.
810 7th Avenue
New York, NY 10019

Local branches are listed in your phone book, but if you can't find one, write to the national office. Planned Parenthood offers:

• written information for small sums of money: *Sex Alphabet* (50¢), *Teensex: It's Okay to Say No Way* (25¢), and more:
• teen classes where you can get some answers about sex
• information about pregnancy and birth control
• help with pregnancy and birth control

Also consult:

March of Dimes
1275 Mamaroneck Avenue
White Plains, NY 10605

The March of Dimes is concerned with birth defects. One million teenagers become pregnant each year in the United States, and babies born to teenagers under 18 are nearly twice as likely to die at birth as those born to mothers 20 to 29 years old. The babies are also more likely to have birth defects. The March of Dimes has several programs that provide teenagers with information about and help with pregnancy.

Shyness.

Facts: Eight out of 10 people answering a poll said they had had problems with shyness, so if you are shy, you are

Saying hello to someone can be the first step in overcoming shyness.

not alone. Shyness has to do with *what you do* and *how you do it*, not with *who you are*. You aren't stuck with shyness the rest of your life.

What You Can Do: Make up a plan to take risks by reaching out to people. Start with something easy. For example, try saying hello to 2 or 3 kids at school. Do it for several days in a row. Then try something harder. You might say something else to one of the people you're saying hello to. Another thing you can do is listen to people. Really pay attention to what they say. Good listeners are hard to find. You don't have to be on stage to be a fun person.

Where to Get Help: If the problem of shyness is more than you can handle, talk to a counselor. (*See* "Counselors," pages 66–67, and "Feelings," pages 82–83.)

Sisters. *See* "Parents and Brothers and Sisters," pages 87–88.

Skin. *See* "Acne," page 69.

Smoking.

Facts: Smoking is bad for your health. People who smoke tend to die younger than those who don't. They are far more

This is a good sign to post where you live or study. Smoking will make it hard for your lungs to work— don't do it. *(American Lung Association)*

likely to get diseases like lung cancer, and their skin wrinkles sooner.

The nicotine in tobacco is a drug, and it is addictive. That means that when you start using it, you tend to become "hooked." Your body will find it difficult to give it up.

For these reasons, it is best not to start smoking. If you have begun smoking, stop.

If you think it is grown-up to smoke, ask yourself this: When I see kids smoking, do I think they're grown-up? Or are they just kids smoking?

Where to Get Help: 1. Smoking clinics. These often cost money. Some that don't cost money are offered by:

American Cancer Society
American Heart Association
American Lung Association
Seventh-Day Adventist Church

Look for the phone numbers of these groups and call for more information.

2. For the booklet "Clearing the Air: A Guide to Quitting Smoking," write to:

Office of Cancer Communications
National Cancer Institute
Bethesda, MD 20014

More Information: Write to:

1. American Lung Association
   1740 Broadway
   New York, NY 10019

2. Office on Smoking and Health
   5600 Fishers Lane
   Rockville, MD 20857

NOTE: Many kids are very worried about their parents' smoking. If you are, all you can do is to give them the facts. Let them know you care. It is very hard to give up smoking, so encourage them all you can

to try to quit. A good motto is: "If at first you don't succeed, quit and quit again!" Many parents *have* quit smoking because their children were so worried about it, so don't give up.

Stuttering.

Facts: Stuttering usually starts when children are 3 to 5 years old and often goes away when they become teenagers. The cause of stuttering has not been found. Boys are 4 times as likely as girls to stutter.

Winston Churchill, prime minister of England during World War Two, was a stutterer. Churchill was famous for his speeches. He controlled his stuttering by making a noise before speaking each sentence.

Everybody stutters at one time or other.

What You Can Do: If your friend stutters, don't say things like "Slow down." The less you say about it, the better.

If you yourself have this problem, get help. And remember what 13-year-old David Maschkowski, a stutterer, has said: "I know now that if a friend doesn't accept you because you stutter, he's not really a friend."

Where to Get Help: Speech therapists help kids who stutter. Someone in your school may be able to suggest one. Otherwise, call the National Easter Seal Society. Someone from the Society may be able to get help for you.

Some self-help groups have been started by:

National Stuttering Project
1269 7th Avenue
San Francisco, CA 94122

Suicide.

Facts: Every day 13 teenagers in the United States kill themselves. Many more try to end their lives and are saved. No one knows how many younger children try to commit suicide. If they succeed, it is often called an "accident."

Why do they do it? Some have trouble in school and fear failure. Others do it because someone they love has been lost to them through death, divorce, or the breakup of a romance. And there are other reasons. A lot of it comes down to, "So-and-so will be sorry when I'm dead." People who think this forget that if they are dead they won't *know* that people are sorry.

Some myths about suicide:

Myth: Once a person decides to take his or her own life, no one can prevent it.

The Truth: People who think about suicide have mixed feelings. They want to live as much as they want to die.

Myth: People who talk about suicide are just looking for attention. It's best not to *pay* attention.

The Truth: Yes, they do want attention, but they need it.

Myth: If a person talks of committing suicide, it's not a good idea to discuss it.

The Truth: Wrong. It's dangerous *not* to talk about it. Talking about suicide won't make the person do it, and might help him or her work through the problem and avoid death.

What You Can Do It It's You: Get help. Read "Where to Get Help" below. Don't be ashamed. Things may seem awful, but hard times don't last forever.

What to Do If It's Your Friend: Following are some signs that can warn you that your friend is thinking about suicide. Usually a friend is the one who learns first of a suicidal person's plans. Take your friend seriously.

1. Your friend says things like "I wish I were dead," "I'm empty," "Nobody cares," and "I'm no good." Everyone talks this way once in a while, but if your friend talks this way a lot, pay attention.

2. Your friend behaves differently than usual. Although usually outgoing, now he or she wants to hide in a closet. Or the friend that does very well in school starts getting low grades.

3. Your friend talks about dying a lot.

4. Your friend has problems with eating and/or sleeping.

5. Your friend begins to give things away. He or she might give you a favorite record album, for example. (That doesn't mean a gift has to be a sign of suicide.)

If you believe that someone you know is thinking about suicide, don't keep quiet about it. Talking to your friend won't make him or her go through with it. Ask questions. Don't say anything to make the person feel guiltier or more worthless than he or she already does. Don't say, "You're better off than most people."

Get help! Stay close!

Where to Get Help: 1. Tell your friend's parents or teacher or minister or priest or rabbi. Don't think you are betraying your friend by doing so, because he or she is probably not thinking straight. You are doing your friend a favor and very likely saving a life. Your friend is probably begging to be saved.

2. Call a Suicide Prevention Center. (See your phone book.)

3. Call a hospital. Call a doctor.

4. Talk to your school's counseling department.

Your rabbi, priest, or minister is a good person to discuss a problem with.

5. Find a counselor. (*See* "Counselors," pages 66–67.)

6. Call the American Association of Suicidology at 1 (303) 692–0985. Someone will tell you where to get help in your area. Write to this organization at the following address for booklets:

American Association of Suicidology
2459 South Ash Street
Denver, CO 80222

See "Feelings," pages 82–83.

Teeth. *See* "Braces," page 72.

Veneral Disease. *See* "Sex," pages 89–91.

Warts.

Facts: You don't get warts from picking up toads, but from a virus. Kids usually have cures they tell each other about, like putting milkweed juice on the wart. Ac-

tually, sometimes warts just go away by themselves.

Where to Get Help: If your warts trouble you, see your doctor.

More Information: Write to:

National Institute of Allergy and Infectious Diseases
9000 Rockville Pike
Bethesda, MD 20205

Ask for the free fact sheet on warts.

Weight (Fatness).

Facts: A kid with a fat parent (or parents) is more likely to be fat than a kid with thin parents. It's possible that a *tendency* to become fat is passed on from parent to child, but that doesn't mean the child *has* to be fat. Fat babies tend to have a weight problem later in life.

No child should go on a diet without seeing a doctor about it. Slow weight loss is best for your health; if you lose weight too fast, you tend not to keep it off.

Where to Get Help: See your doctor. Also, consider joining a group. Here are 3:

1. Weight Watchers International, Inc.
   800 Community Drive
   Manhasset, NY 11030
   Attn: Teen Department

Ask for information. To join a local group, call the number listed for Weight Watchers in your phone book. It is best to wait until you are 12 or 13, though. Children under 12 need a note from their doctor to join. Groups meet once a week for an hour to discuss their problems and learn about ways of losing weight. It costs money to join and there's a fee for each meeting.

Weight Watchers has camps for children. To find out about them, call 1 (800) 223–5600, or write to:

Weight Watcher Camps
183 Madison Avenue
New York, NY 10016

2. Overeaters Anonymous
   World Service Office
   2190 190th Street
   Torrance, CA 90504

Write and ask for information. To join a local group, call the number listed in your phone book for Overeaters Anonymous. Kids as young as 7 have joined. All you need to do is go to a meeting, which doesn't cost anything. Members of Overeaters Anonymous meet to share what they know, their strengths, and their hopes. They try to get over wanting to overeat. They want to learn to "eat to live," not "live to eat." There is no diet plan.

3. National Association to Aid Fat Americans, Inc.
   P.O. Box 43
   Bellerose, NY 11426

This is not a diet club, but a group of fat people who want to help themselves and each other. If you are over 11, you may want to join the NAAFA pen pal program. Write for an application.

See the section on "Weight," pages 94–95.

Zits. *See* "Acne," page 69.

Part 3: You Can Help Others, Too

by Lisa Ann Powell

Have you ever helped an old person carry packages or helped a lost child in a supermarket? How about locating the owner of a lost animal, or working as a volunteer in a hospital? There are lots of ways that kids can volunteer their time and services. How do you go about it?

Clubs. Most clubs have volunteer projects. Members raise money for causes and help in counseling other kids. Kids counseling kids sometimes works better than having adults advise young people.

Recreation Centers. Look in the phone book under your city or county for these. General training is given by many recreation centers to kids, who then help camp counselors, work in the office, or act as safety aides.

Petfinders. Some animal shelters have programs in which kids as young as 12 help find the owners of lost pets. They also find homes for stray and abandoned animals. Look in the Yellow Pages of your phone book under "Animal Shelters."

Health Centers. Kids help patients by visiting them, writing letters for them or reading to them, taking them for walks, and so on. Sometimes kids even work with physical therapy programs. Find out if your local health center has volunteer programs for young people.

Nursery and Day Care Centers. You can work with small children, showing them how to play games and make things. Sometimes volunteers help to keep kids safe on the playground.

Schools. Schools have service groups that visit hospitals and nursing homes, read to the blind, and so on.

In General. Volunteer programs for kids are usually listed in the Yellow Pages under headings like "Voluntary Action Programs" and "Youth Volunteer Programs."

Helping to clean up a beach after a disaster is one way to help others, too.

Kids put together toys and health care items for needy children in foreign lands. *(Dan Riordan, American Red Cross)*

Special Programs

Some charities have programs for kids, who help by collecting money and in other ways. Here are a few such charities:

American National Red Cross
17th and D Streets, N.W.
Washington, DC 20006

Local Red Cross chapters have various minimum ages. A phone call will answer any questions. Nearly 6 million young people are enrolled in Red Cross programs. Kids can:

• adopt a grandparent—visit, help with shopping, and provide friendship

Cleaning up a neighborhood helps everyone. *(Danilo Nardi, Freelance Photographer's Guild).*

• help with the bloodmobile—find donors, help with paperwork

• work with Special Olympics (*see* Chapter 8)

• visit sick people in the hospital

• aid the handicapped

The Red Cross also has a Youth Exchange program with foreign countries.

See "Accidents and Other Emergencies," pages 67–69, for Red Cross programs in health and safety.

Concerned Youth for Cerebral Palsy
United Cerebral Palsy Associations, Inc.
66 East 34th Street
New York, NY 10016

In California, children raised money for this organization with a "Rock-a-thon." Boston kids held a Monopoly marathon, with players using a giant board. Other groups have sponsored "walk-a-thons," "bowl-a-thons," and other activities to raise money.

March of Dimes
1275 Mamaroneck Avenue
White Plains, NY 10605

In 1938 the March of Dimes was established to fight infantile paralysis (polio), a frightening disease that had killed and crippled thousands of children. In 1955 Dr. Jonas Salk discovered a vaccine that prevented the disease and the Sabin vaccine followed a few years later. The fight was won. Today, kids who are vaccinated don't get infantile paralysis.

Now the March of Dimes fights birth defects, many of which can be prevented. Kids can help the March of Dimes in 2 ways:

1. By raising money for this charity. Groups can plan a "MOD-Mini-Walk," for

These kids are raising money in a Walk-a-thon.
(National Foundation, March of Dimes)

example, in which little kids and their pets walk around a block or playground as many times as they can and sponsors pay a certain amount for each round trip. This is only one money-raising idea. Write to the March of Dimes for more.

2. By educating other kids. Babies born to teenaged mothers are more likely to have birth defects than others. The March of Dimes has several programs that provide kids with materials to use in educating other children about this. Among the groups involved are student councils and Future Homemakers of America.

Clearinghouse on the Handicapped
Department of Education
3119 Switzer Building
Washington, DC 20202

Write for information about how young people can work with the handicapped.

Save the Children
54 Wilton Road, Dept. PCA
Westport, CN 06880

This group works to improve the lives of children. It gives money and other help to 400 communities everywhere in the world. People in these communities learn to help themselves and their children by using better farming methods, digging wells, and building health-care clinics and schools.

Every year Save the Children conducts a children's letter campaign, and kids also work to raise money for this group. (*See* pages 12–16.)

U.S. Committee for UNICEF
331 East 38th Street
New York, NY 10016

UNICEF works in more than 100 countries to help the children of the world. It improves their health, education, and general welfare with medicine, toys, school supplies, water pumps, and many other things. UNICEF will supply your group with ideas and materials for raising money.

Since 1950 kids have been collecting money on Halloween for UNICEF in an activity called UNICEF Day Trick-or-Treating. Adult leaders are in charge.

In Thanksgiving "family sharing" programs, a UNICEF container is put on the dinner table and family members put in money during the month before Thanksgiving.

Another money-raising activity is the Read-a-Thon. For each book a kid reads about another country, adults promise to give a certain amount of money to UNICEF.

Then there is the UNICEF-sponsored "Mini-Olympics," in which teams compete against one another in games. It can be teachers against students, girls against boys, one class against another class. Ticket money goes to UNICEF.

Finally, there are the UNICEF Greeting Cards. The more cards people buy, the more money UNICEF receives, so buy them for yourself or sell them to others through your club.

The National Commission on Resources for Youth, Inc.
36 West 44th Street
New York, NY 10036

This group is a national clearinghouse for programs in which kids help out in their communities. Its newsletter, which may give you ideas for your own club projects, is free. Just write for *Resources for Youth*. Many of the projects described are for high school kids, but there are some that involve children as young as 10.

Two major programs conducted by the Commission were Youth Tutoring Youth (YTY), in which kids helped other kids with their schoolwork; and Day Care Youth Helper, in which junior and high school students worked in day care centers.

Here are some projects reported to the Commission. They might give you an idea or two.

Teenagers in Vermont built toys for kids using lumber donated by local people.

Seventh graders in Colorado taught pet health and ran a pet clinic on school grounds.

Some British kids developed special

tools for disabled people, like alarm clocks for the deaf and page-turners for people without arms.

Junior and senior high school students in Minnesota staffed Consumer Complaint Bureaus. They followed up on calls until the problem was solved.

California kids surveyed the ways people used energy in their neighborhoods, then recommended ways to conserve to the city council.

Kids who studied dance and gymnastics performed for hospital patients.

Good swimmers in Scotland taught swimming to children with cerebral palsy.

Kids used art, TV, and radio to educate the public about problems in the community—rat control, fire hazards, and so on.

Children painted murals on the walls of buildings.

In Georgia, young people worked at a site where an ancient village once stood helping experts dig out and classify objects.

Native American children in South Dakota started a magazine to keep their culture alive.

Junior high school students staffed a rumor-control center at their school.

Kids developed programs to stop theft and vandalism in their schools.

Members of a 4-H Club in Missouri taught handicapped children how to ride horses and manage a stable.

Kids developed plans for fighting drug abuse, V.D., and other problems.

Children tracked down old citizens and taped their stories, building up oral history libraries in their communities.

Children analyzed pollution problems and brought them to the attention of authorities

Chapter *4*
ODD FACTS

Funny and Far-out Facts

A boy's first haircut is a big event on small island of Niue. Many people are invited to a big party. Each guest cuts a little piece of hair off the boy and then gives him money. One 7-year-old got $5,000 at his party. The money was put in the bank for the boy's future.

• The world's largest pizza was made by Lorenzo Amato in Wilton, New York, on October 8, 1978. It weighed 18,664 pounds and was cut into 60,318 pieces. It had 10,000 pounds of flour, 664 gallons of water, 316 gallons of sauce, 1,320 pounds of cheese, and 1,200 pounds of pepperoni. The money raised by Amato was given to Jerry Lewis's Kids—the Muscular Dystrophy Association Drive.

• There is a place in Norway called Hell. People love to go there on vacation and send back postcards that say: "Having a wonderful time in Hell."

• The Maya Indians loved to decorate their teeth. They filed their front teeth to sharp points and drilled holes in them, then filled the holes with beautiful jewels.

• A palindrome is a word or sentence that reads the same backward as forward. For example: Madam, I'm Adam. Another one: Step on no pets.

• *The Guinness Book of World Records* says that this is the hardest tongue twister: "The sixth sick sheik's sixth sheep's sick."

• About 10 million people in the world have the same birthday as you.

• In the summertime there is a very unusual way you can figure out the temperature. First, count the number of cricket chirps for 15 seconds. Then add the number 40. You will be very close to the real temperature.

This house in Rockport, Massachusetts, is made entirely out of newspapers. *(Selma M. Curtis)*

- On a golf ball there are 336 dimples.
- At Pigeon Cove in Rockport, Massachusetts, there is a house made of newspapers. The walls have 215 layers of paper. Even the furniture inside is made of newspaper. Over 100,000 copies of newspapers were used to build the house, and the work took 20 years.
- There are many pictures of Abraham Lincoln, but he is never smiling.
- Blood has lots of vitamins and minerals. In China people buy dried blood in the markets and use it as food.
- In the famous painting *Mona Lisa*, the woman has no eyebrows. At that time in Italy, women shaved them off.
- Licking stamps will never make you fat. The glue on each stamp has only one-tenth of a calorie.
- In 1859 a Frenchman named Charles Blondin went across Niagara Falls—on a tightrope. He was 160 feet above the

Mona Lisa shaved off her eyebrows to be fashionable. *(Ken Lambert, Photoworld/FPG)*

We usually smile when photographed, but President Abraham Lincoln never did in any photograph taken of him. *(Photoworld/FPG)*

water. Later he did it blindfolded. Then he did it on stilts. Finally, he surprised everyone when he went halfway across and stopped to have breakfast. He cooked some eggs, ate them, and crossed to the other side.

• Eskimos buy refrigerators so that their food will *not* freeze!

• Days and nights are very strange in a town called Hammerfest in Norway. Hammerfest has nothing but sunshine—around the clock—from May 14 to July 30. Then there is nothing but darkness from November 18 to January 30.

• The longest hair to be grown on a human head was 26 feet long. It belonged to a man in India and was measured in 1949.

• Honey never spoils. Honey found in the old tombs of Egyptian rulers still tastes good.

• There is a tiny bit of water in the middle of a kernel of popcorn. When the water gets hot, it becomes steam. Then it expands and the popcorn pops.

• Pirates put holes in their ears and wore earrings because they thought it helped them to see better.

• When the Beatles wrote the song "Yesterday," they at first called it "Scrambled Eggs."

• The fattest President of the United States was William Howard Taft, who weighed 332 pounds. Once he got stuck in a bathtub in the White House and had to be rescued by the servants.

• When Columbus sailed to America, every man on his 3 ships got two-thirds of a gallon of wine per day.

William Howard Taft was the fattest president. *(Paul Thompson, Freelance Photographer's Guild)*

• The people of Buenos Aires, Argentina, are very serious about their soccer games. Any fan who yells "Kill the umpire" will go to jail.

• Drop a raisin into a fresh glass of champagne. It will rise and fall in the glass.

• You can put only three-fourths of a gallon into a 10-gallon hat.

• The highest temperature ever recorded was 136.4 degrees in the shade. It happened in Al 'Aziziyah, Libya, on September 13, 1922.

• The shortest war in history was between England and Zanzibar in 1896. It lasted only 38 minutes. England won.

• The longest place name belongs to a hill in New Zealand. The name has 57 letters and means "the place where Tamatea, the man with the big knee who slid, climbed, and swallowed mountains, known as land-eater, played on his flute to his loved one." Here is how the name of the hill is spelled: Taumatawhakatangihangakoauauatamateapokaiwhenuakitanatahu.

• Before he became president of the United States, Grover Cleveland refused to fight in the Civil War. At that time, you could hire someone else to fight in your place. Cleveland did so because he had to stay at home and support his mother.

• A woodpecker has a pretty tough head. It can pound its head against wood at the rate of 20 times a second.

• The Queen of England's home, Buckingham Palace in London, England, has 602 rooms.

• Want to put 2 bowling lanes in your house? It will only cost you about $65,000!

• There are only 2 words in the English language that contain all the vowels—*a, e, i, o, u*—in the proper order. They are *facetious* and *abstemious.*

• Cinderella's slippers were made of fur, not glass. The story came from France, and a mistake was made when it was translated from French into English.

• It is very confusing for Americans to read a telephone book in Iceland. Names are listed by *first* names instead of last names.

• A flea can jump 200 times the length of its own body.

• The man who wrote all the Sherlock Holmes stories was an eye doctor. His name was Arthur Conan Doyle.

• Joan of Arc was found guilty of being a witch and was burned at the stake. Another charge against her was that she disobeyed her parents.

• One of the world's largest ice cream sundaes was made by Sealtest Foods in New York City. It was 12 feet tall, used

1,500 gallons of ice cream, and contained 50 pounds of chocolate chips. On top of it was 8 gallons of whipped cream.

• On the day Mark Twain was born, Halley's Comet was in the sky. He died 75 years later, the next time Halley's Comet appeared over the earth.

Halley's Comet was in the sky at Mark Twain's birth and death. *(Photoworld/FPG)*

• A house fly lives for only 2 weeks.

• Want to know how long it would take to toss a coin and have it land "heads up" 50 times in a row? A million people would each have to toss the coin 10 times a minute for 40 hours a week. And they would have to do that for 900 years!

• A regular lead pencil can write about 50,000 words.

• One of the oldest people in Russia, Medzhid Agayev, lived to be 143 years old. He guarded sheep for most of his life, and every day walked 6 miles to work.

• A frog must close its eyes to swallow.

Earth's largest living thing is the General Sherman Sequoia tree. *(Sequoia National Park)*

• The largest tree is the General Sherman Tree in Sequoia National Park, California. It is 272 feet, 4 inches tall—about as high as a 20-story building—and weighs more than 2,000 tons.

• An American typewriter has 43 keys and 84 symbols. A Chinese typewriter has one key and 2,500 symbols.

• A "phobia" is a fear, and some people have very strange ones. Here are just a few: Chromophobia is a fear of colors. Sitophobia is a fear of food. Verbophobia is a fear of words. Pedophobia means being afraid of children and dolls. Arachibutyrophobia is the fear of peanut butter sticking to the roof of the mouth.

• Every person in the United States eats about 8 pounds of pickles a year.

• Coca-Cola was invented in 1886. How to make it is still a secret that only 2 men know today. Even when these men travel to the same place, they fly on different airplanes so that in case one of them should die in an accident, the other would still be alive with the secret.

• To fill a teaspoon full of water would take 120 drops.

• Tycho Brahe was an astronomer from Denmark who had a very funny nose. The tip of it was gold. He had lost part of his nose when fighting a duel.

• In the first King Kong movie, made in 1933, the monster was really a hand puppet only 18 inches high.

• In San Luis Obispo, California, there is a special place to throw away your used chewing gum called "Gum Alley." On one side of the alley is a red brick wall. Thousands of people have stuck big wads of gum on that wall. They have written many words—and made many designs—all in different-colored, sticky chewing gum.

• An artist named Chanan Singh, from India, paints pictures on grains of rice. They are probably the world's smallest

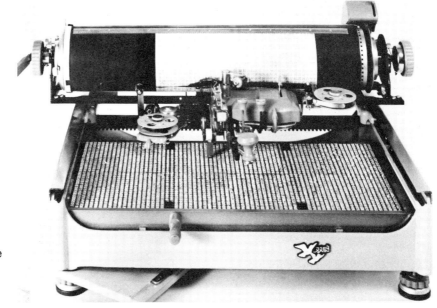

This Chinese typewriter has only one key to type 2,500 interchangeable symbols. *(Media Factory, Inc.)*

pictures, and so far he has painted more than 400 of them. He has a very steady hand and uses a paintbrush with only 1 or 2 hairs. Chanan Singh is always afraid that someone will accidentally eat one of his paintings!

• Every healthy person who lives for 70 years walks about 70,000 miles in a lifetime. That is about 18,000 steps a day.

• Child marriages and divorces are very common in Indonesia. In one part of that country, called Indramaju, many kids get married when they are 10 years old. Parents match up the children, and many couples are unhappy and end up getting a divorce. One 55-year-old lady who lives there has been married 50 times. Her shortest marriage lasted only 11 days.

• There are lots of crazy contests in the United States. One of the wackiest is the "National Rotten Sneaker Championship" in Montpelier, Vermont. Every year people show up in sneakers that are dirty, torn up, discolored—and very smelly. Winners get a new pair of sneakers and a can of Dr. Scholl's foot powder.

• Here is a great story for chocolate lovers. On January 2, 1980 the Blommer Chocolate Company in Chicago caught fire. In the building many 100-pound bags of chocolate began to melt, and soon there were big "lakes" of chocolate all over the place, some of them 30 feet wide and 3 feet deep. Firemen had a hard time putting out the fire. They had to keep licking the chocolate from their hands and wiping it from their eyes!

• The average teenage boy in the United States eats 1,917 pounds of food a year. The average teenage girl eats less—about 1,717 pounds a year.

Special Days, Weeks, and Months

JANUARY 1   **NEW YEAR'S DAY**

At the stroke of midnight on New Year's Eve, we welcome in the "new year." There is much noisemaking. Everywhere are the sounds of bells, car horns, sirens, firecrackers, whistles, and party horns. According to an old superstition, the noise drives away evil spirits that could bring harm in the new year.

FEBRUARY 2   **GROUNDHOG DAY**

According to a superstition, on this day the groundhog, which sleeps underground during the winter, leaves its burrow. If the animal sees its shadow, it ducks back into its burrow to sleep for 6 more weeks. This means there will be 6 more weeks of winter. If it does not see its shadow, the groundhog stays out of the burrow and this means spring is just around the corner. However, the National Geographic Service says that the groundhog's predictions have not been very good. He has been right only 28 percent of the time. There are many groundhog clubs, most of them in Pennsylvania. One in Wisconsin, the Sun Prairie Club, will send you a "groundhog birth certificate" if you were born on February 2. Just mail $1 to Chamber of Commerce, 243 East Main Street, Sun Prairie, Wisconsin 53590.

FEBRUARY 12   **ABRAHAM LINCOLN'S BIRTHDAY**

The sixteenth president of the United States liked to read aloud. "When I read aloud," he wrote, "two senses catch the idea; first, I see what I read; second, I hear it, and therefore, I can remember better."

FEBRUARY 14   **ST. VALENTINE'S DAY**

There is a town in Colorado called Loveland. The post office there is very busy early in February, because this is where people from across the country send their valentines. They want their valentines to be stamped with a special red seal, which usually has a cowboy cupid and a short poem on it. And, of course, it has the words "Loveland, Colorado." The valentines are then remailed and are on their way to the right people. Every year the post office handles about 200,000 valentines. Want to get that "romantic extra touch" for your valentines? Be sure they have the right address and postage on them. Send them to Postmaster, Loveland, Colorado 80537. They have to get to Loveland before February 6.

THIRD MONDAY IN FEBRUARY   **GEORGE WASHINGTON'S BIRTHDAY**

Almost everyone knows the story of George Washington and the cherry tree. At the age of 6, George chopped down his father's favorite cherry tree. His father was angry and asked him if he had done it. George said, "I cannot tell a lie. I did cut it with my little hatchet." Nice story, but it is not true. The tale was made up by a "Parson" Weems who wrote a book about Washington. More than 50,000 copies of the book were sold.

ALL OF MARCH   **PEANUT MONTH**

Africans used to worship peanuts which they called "goobers." The average person in the United States eats 8.4 pounds of peanuts a year. Of that amount, 3.8 pounds is in the form of peanut butter.

MARCH 1   **NATIONAL PIG DAY**

Pigs are not dirty, smelly animals. Sometimes they do roll in the mud, but that is because they have no sweat glands and are just cooling off the only way they can. Pigs are pretty smart and can learn tricks, like fetching a stick. Today many pigs are raised in "pig parlors."

MARCH 17   **ST. PATRICK'S DAY**

This day is in honor of an Irish saint—St. Patrick. The color of the day is green, and everyone loves to wear a shamrock. The biggest shamrock in the world is in O'Neill, Nebraska, where every year the citizens paint a huge shamrock 80 feet in diameter on the main highway.

A SUNDAY BETWEEN MARCH 22
AND APRIL 25   **EASTER**

Easter is a "movable" holiday. It falls on the Sunday following the first full moon after March 21, but before April 26. Astronomers have been figuring out the correct date for

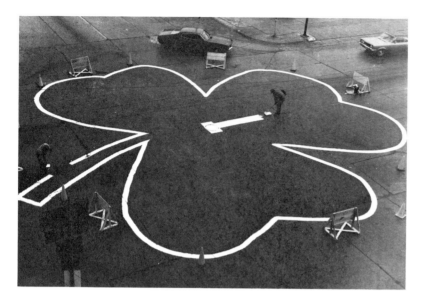

The world's largest shamrock is painted each year in O'Neill, Nebraska. *(Holt County Independent, O'Neill, NE)*

over 1,600 years. Finding two yolks in an Easter egg is said to be good luck, a sign that you will soon get a large sum of money. The most beautiful Easter eggs in the world are made by the Ukrainians. Their Easter eggs are called *pysanky*, and each egg has many different colors and designs. It takes many hours to make each egg. Melted beeswax, a needle, and many different dyes are used.

Ukrainian Easter eggs, called *pysanky*, are intricately designed and colored. *(Ukrainian Art Center, Los Angeles, CA)*

APRIL 1   **APRIL FOOL'S DAY**

Some zoos and aquariums have their telephones disconnected on this day. Why? Because of lots of silly phone calls. People ask for Mr. Fish, Mr. Camel, Mr. Wolf, Mr. Fox, or Mr. Shepherd.

FIRST WEEK IN APRIL   **NATIONAL MIME WEEK**

Put together your own mime show. (*See* Chapter 12.)

APRIL 22   **EARTH DAY**

Today is a day to honor the earth. Collect old newspapers and cans, and take them to recycling centers. Help clean up your neighborhood park. Get a group of kids together and talk about solving pollution problems. Every year more than 20 million people do something special today to help the earth.

MAY 1   **MAY DAY**

This is a day for making flower baskets and dancing around a Maypole. Hundreds of years ago women would get up very early on May Day and go to the countryside to wash their faces in the morning dew. This was supposed to improve their skin.

SECOND SUNDAY IN MAY   **MOTHER'S DAY**

Miss Anna Jarvis of Philadelphia made Mother's Day a national holiday. For most of her life, Anna took care of her mother and then her blind sister. Anna never married and never became a mother.

THIRD WEEK IN MAY   **PICKLE WEEK**

People were eating pickles more than 4,000 years ago. Today there are 36 different kinds of pickles. They are made from cucumbers, but no one is sure whether they are a fruit or a vegetable. The average person in the United States eats about 8 pounds of pickles a year. The Egyptian queen Cleopatra loved pickles; she thought they made her more beautiful. Why not try some "picklesickles"? Insert ice cream sticks into some large dill pickles and put them into a bucket of ice until they are very cold. Then munch away!

LAST MONDAY IN MAY   **MEMORIAL DAY**

This is a day to honor American soldiers who have died in war.

JUNE 14   **FLAG DAY**

The American national flag was adopted in 1777. No one knows who made the first United States flag. Many people think it was Betsy Ross, who lived in Philadelphia, but there are no records to prove that she did.

THIRD SUNDAY IN JUNE   **FATHER'S DAY**

Mark Twain, the famous writer who wrote *The Adventures of Tom Sawyer*, was always making jokes about everything. Here is what he wrote about his father: "When I was a boy of 14, my father was so ignorant I could hardly stand to have the old man around. But when I got to be 21, I was astonished at how much the old man had learned in seven years!"

FOURTH FRIDAY IN JUNE   **NATIONAL FINK DAY**

This is a special day for everyone with the last name of Fink. Finks from all over the country travel to Fink, Texas, a town that isn't on most maps—only on some maps of Texas. All of the Finks celebrate by playing many games and sports. They also pick a "Fink of the Year."

JULY 4   **INDEPENDENCE DAY**

Fireworks are always a big part of the Fourth of July. In 1976, called the "bicentennial" year, the United States was 200 years old. On July 4 of that year there was a very special fireworks program in Washington, D.C. More than 33 tons of fireworks were set off at a cost of more than $200,000.

JULY 11   **CHEER-UP-THE-SAD-AND-LONELY DAY**

Do something nice for a lonely person. You might pick some flowers or bake some cookies. Most important of all are friendly smiles and cheerful words.

AUGUST 1–7   **NATIONAL CLOWN WEEK**

Want to be a clown when you get older? In Venice, Florida, there is a college, called Ringling Bros. and Barnum & Bailey Clown College, that does nothing but train clowns.

These two celebrate National Clown Week.
(Ringling Bros. and Barnum & Bailey Combined Shows, Inc.)

You have to be 17 years old to apply to the school, and it takes only 9 weeks to graduate. Some of the subjects you would study are Elephant Riding, Juggling, Slaps and Falls, and Explosive Surprises!

SECOND SUNDAY IN AUGUST   **FAMILY DAY**

This is a good day for a family picnic. You might want to start tracing your family history. (*See* Chapter 2.)

FIRST MONDAY IN SEPTEMBER   **LABOR DAY**

This day honors all men, women, and children who work. About 140 years ago many children worked in mills that made cloth. They were not treated fairly. Most of these kids worked for 70 hours a week—that is, about 12 hours a day, 6 days a week. The pay was $2 or $3 a week. Some working kids were only 6 years old.

FIRST SUNDAY AFTER LABOR DAY   **GRANDPARENTS' DAY**

Spend the day with your grandparents. Consider making them a gift, such as a "family tree" that shows the names and relationships of all your relatives, a scrapbook of all the kids in the family, a very special greeting card.

A scrapbook of family memories makes a fine Grandparents' Day present. *(Big Brothers/Big Sisters of America)*

FOURTH SUNDAY IN SEPTEMBER   **GOOD NEIGHBOR DAY**

This is a day for helping others. Plan a picnic for handicapped people, or invite elderly people from your town to visit your school. They can tell you what it was like when they were kids. Awards are given to schools that do worthwhile projects. For information, write to Good Neighbor Foundation, Drawer R, Lakeside, Montana 59922.

FOURTH WEEK IN SEPTEMBER   **RESPONSIBLE PET CARE WEEK**

All pets need proper care. For free pamphlets on pet care, write to The American Humane Association, P.O. Box 1266, Denver, Colorado 80201. Remember to tell them what kind of pet you have.

SECOND WEEK IN OCTOBER   **INTERNATIONAL LETTER-WRITING WEEK**

Write to a friend in another country. Remember to use lightweight stationery and to send the letter "airmail."

SECOND SATURDAY IN OCTOBER   **NATIONAL JOGGING DAY**

Over 11 million Americans now jog, and many of them are children. One champion marathon runner, Maryetto Boitano, started running when she was 6. She's now 38.

SECOND MONDAY IN OCTOBER   **COLUMBUS DAY**

Christopher Columbus came to America in 1492, but he thought he had found a new route to Asia and never knew that he had discovered a new continent.

OCTOBER 15–21   **NATIONAL JOKE-TELLING WEEK**

Can you tell a good joke? If not, here are some good hints. Stick to familiar subjects. Practice your jokes before you tell them to friends. Never stop in the middle of a joke and say, "Sure you haven't heard this one?"

THIRD WEEK IN OCTOBER   **NATIONAL POPCORN WEEK**

The average kid in the United States eats about 33 quarts of popcorn a year. Almost all the popcorn in the world is grown in the United States. When Columbus discovered the West Indies, the natives were wearing popcorn corsages. Here is how to make perfect popcorn:

1. Warm a heavy pan.
2. Pour in ¼ cup cooking oil. Never use butter.
3. Let oil get hot. Then drop in several kernels of corn.
4. When kernels start to spin, pour in more kernels. Use just enough popcorn to cover the bottom of the pan.
5. Cover pan with lid. Shake gently.
6. When you hear the last few pops, take pan away from heat.

LAST WEEK IN OCTOBER   **NATIONAL PRETZEL WEEK**

Ever wonder how the twisted pretzel got its shape? It happened over 1,300 years ago either in France or Italy. A monk (a religious man) was baking bread and had some strips of dough left over. In those days children did not pray with their hands held together, but folded their arms across their chests instead. The monk twisted his extra dough strips to make them look like the children's arms. Today the United States makes 400 million pounds of pretzels a year. There are 28 different kinds.

OCTOBER 31   **HALLOWEEN**

The first jack-o'-lanterns were made by Irish and Scottish children from large, hollowed-out turnips or beets, not pumpkins. The children carved faces on them and put candles inside of them. Called "bogies" and "punkies," the jack-o'-lanterns were used to scare evil spirits away.

NOVEMBER 11   **VETERAN'S DAY**

All American soldiers are honored on this day. There are special ceremonies at the Tomb of the Unknown Soldier in Arlington National Cemetery in Washington, D.C. There are really 3 soldiers buried in the tomb—one from World War One, one from World War Two, and the third from the Korean War.

FOURTH THURSDAY IN NOVEMBER   **THANKSGIVING DAY**

The first Thanksgiving took place in Plymouth, Massachusetts, in 1621. About 140 persons, including 90 Indians, gathered for the event, which lasted three full days. The meal included turkey, deer, pigeons, partridges, geese, duck, clams, eels, oysters, corn, squash, and pumpkin.

DECEMBER 25   **CHRISTMAS**

Ever wonder how fast Santa Claus has to move on Christmas in order to deliver all the presents? He has to visit 2 billion families in 24 hours. He and his reindeer travel at about 70,000 miles an hour, and he can stay at each house for only one-half of one ten-thousandth of a second!

Animal Facts and Feats

The mouse deer is a real deer so small you could hold it in your hand.

If you make a gorilla mad, it might stick out its tongue at you.

Penguins can't fly, but they can dive. One kind of penguin can stay deep under the water for 18 minutes.

Scientists have invented a new kind of bacterium that eats oil. If a boat spills oil, which can kill sea animals, the bacterium eats it.

One type of spider spins a whole web in 20 minutes. It weaves at the rate of 1,000 operations a minute.

A whale's mouth is so big a man could stand up in it, but the whale couldn't swallow him because its throat is too small.

The biggest frog in the world lives in Africa. It is so big it can knock a person down.

The giant clam weighs 500 to 1,000 pounds. It's as broad as a table, and the pearl it grows is the size of a golfball. It is probably not true that giant clams clamp down on divers' legs to hold them under the water.

When half-grown rats sit too close to one another, their tails sometimes get knotted together.

Some swans and other water birds carry their young ones across the water on their backs.

An albatross, a big seabird, can fly for 6 days without moving its wings. The rea-

An albatross can glide on air currents for 6 days.
(American Museum of Natural History)

sons? The albatross glides on air currents, has more wing feathers than most birds, and is shaped for flying. Albatrosses can even sleep while in the air.

A family of shrews makes a chain when danger threatens. One baby grabs another's tail in its mouth, its tail is held in the mouth of the next baby, and so on down the line. In this way nobody gets lost.

The whirligig beetle has a set of eyes for seeing above water and another set of eyes for seeing underwater.

An ant's sense of smell is as good as a dog's.

Some fish can live while frozen in ice because the freezing temperature of their blood is lower than that of water.

Porcupine fish blow themselves up to twice their usual size with air or water. Their name comes from their sharp spines.

The giant squid has arms as long as 50 feet and an eye as big as a paperback book. A tough animal, the giant squid has been known to fight whales.

The tree snake can "fly" from a tree by flattening its body and riding the air.

A beaver can cut down a fairly large tree, cut it into logs, and drag it to the water's edge in one night. It's teeth grow throughout its life. If it didn't chew, they'd get too long.

Fleas, which have no wings, can jump 100 times their height. If humans could jump as high as a flea, they could leap to the top of a 40-story building.

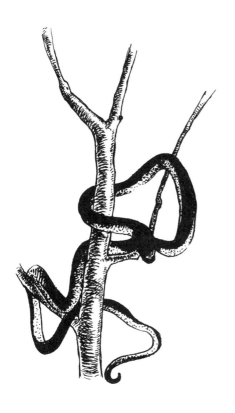

This tree snake is able to flatten its body and "fly" by gliding in air.

The python is one of the big eaters of the world. It can eat a grown leopard.

Eagles keep the same nest throughout their lives. Some eagle nests weigh as much as a ton.

The python, a kind of snake, can eat a grown leopard. It takes 12 men to hold a python down.

Hummingbirds can fly straight up like little helicopters. They can also fly backwards.

If a glass snake (a kind of lizard) is grabbed by its tail, the tail snaps off. The tail pieces wiggle. The glass snake then grows a new tail.

If a live sponge is broken into pieces, each piece will turn into a new sponge like the one it came from.

Offbeat Facts About Kids in History

The ancient Egyptians thought children could see into the future.

Aristotle, a thinker of ancient Greece, said children had bad memories because their heads were heavy compared to the rest of their bodies.

In ancient Greece children read books that were sometimes 12 feet long! The books were scrolls, long pieces of paperlike stuff wound around a couple of sticks.

In the year 1212, 30,000 children marched away on a Children's Crusade. Their leader was a 12-year-old shepherd boy named Stephen, who led them to a French port, Marseilles. There 2 men, Hugh the Iron and William the Pig, offered them free passage on ships to the Middle East, where they wanted to go. There they planned to help take back the Holy Land from the Saracens. Instead, the children were taken to Algeria and sold as slaves. Some worked for the gov-

Thousands went on the Children's Crusade in 1212, but only one returned to tell the story.

In ancient Greece kids studied from scrolls that were sometimes 12 feet long.

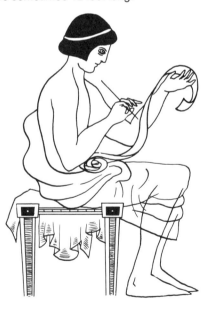

ernor of Egypt as translators and secretaries. Only one person, a young priest, was able to get back to France to tell their story.

Fra Filippo Lippi, a painter in the fifteenth century, was the first to draw babies as they really are. Before he came along, a baby's head was shown as one-sixth as long as its body, as is true of an adult. Fra Filippo Lippi saw the head as it really was—one-fourth the length of a baby's body.

In the 1500s and 1600s, whooping cough was treated by putting a live frog in the sick child's mouth. Another "cure" was to hold an old spider over his head. As it was hanging there, someone would say:

Thank goodness this cure for whooping cough isn't in use today—it didn't even work!

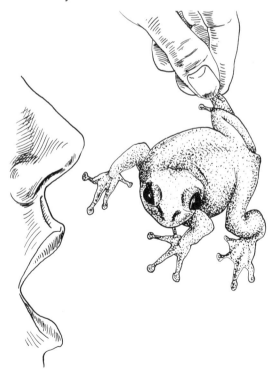

Spider, as you waste away,
Whooping cough no longer stay.

Beginning in the 1600s, boys wore skirts until they were 6 or 7. They were then "breeched"—taken for a suit of clothes that included pants. Little girls wore corsets with whalebone or steel bands sewn into them. The corsets were so tight, the girls couldn't bend over.

In the 1700s at least one writer objected that children were eating junk food. He wrote about a child who "ate trash until he could eat nothing else."

The Society for the Prevention of Cruelty to Animals was the first group to help abused children.

The first mill in America opened in 1791. In this mill 9 children ran spinning machines for 14 hours a day, 6 days a week. By 1796, 100 children, aged 4 to 10, were working in another spinning mill.

In 1822 Clement Moore wrote "Visit from St. Nicholas," the poem that begins, " 'Twas the night before Christmas. . . ." He created the poem for his own children.

Homeless children from city slums in the eastern part of the United States were sent west to get a better chance in life. They traveled on "orphan trains" that stopped at towns along the way. When they arrived in each town the kids put on tags that showed their names and birth dates, then got off the train. Townspeople looked them over. If a couple liked a child, they might adopt him or her. The

In the 1800s children worked for 14 hours a day, 6 days a week, in textile mills and factories. They had no time for school or play.

kids who weren't chosen traveled on to the next stop. Between 1854 and 1904 more than 100,000 orphans found a home this way.

In 1885 heaps of sand were dumped in 2 places in Boston. They were the start of the first public playgrounds.

The baby doll was invented in the 1800s. Late in the century most rich children had fancy doll houses, tiny doll carriages drawn by toy horses, and little doll wristwatches.

"Penny dreadfuls," books for children in the late 1800s, were full of action and violence. They had titles like *Castle Fiend, Varney the Vampire,* and *Feast of Blood.* Many grown-ups hated them, but most children loved them. Other books were different: *Little Women, Treasure Island, Rebecca of Sunnybrook Farm.* And there were those starring boy heroes like Frank Fearless and Dick Dare.

Elsie Leslie was an early child star on the stage. In one play, *The Prince and the Pauper,* based on the book by Mark Twain, she played 2 parts. Both were roles for boys—one was a prince, one was poor—and they looked exactly alike.

Twain made her a pair of cross-stitched slippers as a present. They were red, blue, gold, and green.

A rich child from the 1800s with her doll, book, toy horse, jewelry, and cats. In those days the gap between the rich and other people was very wide.

Chapter 5
YOUR RIGHTS AND THE LAW

THE DECLARATION OF
THE RIGHTS OF THE CHILD

In 1959 the United Nations declared that children have special rights, and these were listed in "The Declaration of the Rights of the Child." According to the United Nations, children everywhere in the world have the right to:

1. *Enjoy the rights listed.* The rights are for all children. Children should not be kept from having their rights because of race, color, sex, religion, or nationality.

2. *Be able to grow in a healthy and normal way, free and dignified.* Children should be specially protected, and should be given special opportunities to grow.

3. *A name and nationality.*

4. *Social security.* This includes a decent place to live, good food, health care, and opportunities to play.

The law deals with kids too, and lawyers spend many years studying our laws so they can help us if we commit a crime or need legal assistance. *(Dave Grube, Freelance Photographer's Guild)*

5. *Special treatment, schooling, and care if handicapped.*

6. *Love and understanding.* Children should be raised so that they feel secure and loved, with their parents, if possible.

7. *Free schooling and opportunity to play. Equal opportunity to become everything they can be.*

8. *Prompt protection and relief in times of disaster.* If there is an earthquake or war or other disaster, children should be taken care of right away.

9. *Protection against all kinds of neglect, cruelty, and being used by others.*

10. *Protection from any kind of unfair treatment because of race or religion.*

"It's the Law!"

What law? State? Federal? Knowing what the law says is not always easy. Laws change. Yet, confusing as they sometimes seem, they are based on a core of thought that makes sense. You can be *pretty* sure you will not violate the law and will stay out of trouble if you never do anything that takes away the rights of someone else. Other laws, though, are meant to protect *you*. You hurt yourself, mostly, if you don't go to school, and so the law says you must go to school until you are a certain age. One reason for this is that children once were made to work when they were very young. Their parents didn't allow them to go to school. So if a law seems unfair to you, look at it. Maybe it is fairer than you think.

There is a layered system of laws in the United States. On the top is federal law; Congress makes laws for all people in the United States. They are like a big umbrella over everyone. For instance, there are federal laws about child labor. For one thing, children under 16 cannot work full time for people who do business with people in more than one state.

Each state makes laws about matters

These students learn how the law works by conducting a mock trial.
(Michael D. Sullivan)

within the state, and the laws they make must not conflict with federal laws. For instance, state laws about child labor may say that younger children can work for some employers who do business only within the state.

Counties and towns also make rules. A town may require that you need a license for your bicycle, for example.

Laws can be tested in the courts. Sometimes a law is declared unconstitutional by the U.S. Supreme Court. That means the law conflicts with what the Constitution says and so is no longer legal.

Laws About Family Matters

Under the law, your parents have the right to tell you what to do. They can punish you, tell you what friends you can play with, set a bedtime hour, and more.

To make you obey, your parents have the right to hit you, but they are not supposed to hit you so hard that they injure you. If they do, they can get in trouble with the law.

Some laws in other countries are different from those in the United States. In Sweden, for example, it's against the law for parents to hit their children. Furthermore, Swedish parents aren't allowed to shame their children, insult them, or lock them up in a closet. How can parents make their children obey? By helping them "develop an inner voice," experts say. The idea behind the law in Sweden is that you can't do things to a child that you can't do to an adult.

Your parents have to take care of you—give you proper food, clothes, and a place to sleep.

You have a right to go to school, and your parents must not make it hard for you to go. However, your parents do not have to send you to college.

Your parents may not take away any rights you have under the law.

You must live where your parents want you to live. If they move, they can make you go with them.

No one, not even a parent, is allowed to take away money someone else gives you as a gift. For example, if your grandmother dies and leaves you $1,000, that money belongs to you. Because you are a child, though, sometimes a bank officer may take care of it until you are older,

If your parents move, they can make you move with them, according to the law.

perhaps 21. Your parents can't spend this money, even on you, without asking the bank officer.

Your parents do not have to pay you for work you do for them, and they have a right to the money you earn. Of course, most parents wouldn't want to take money earned by their kids away from them. In some places children can, under the law, go to court to try to force their parents to give back to them money they have earned.

In some places, parents must pay for all or part of any damage you cause. If, for example, you run through a neighbor's garden and wreck some prize flowers, your parents may be made to pay for what you did. Some states where this is true are Alaska, Arkansas, Colorado, Georgia, Idaho, Indiana, Kentucky, Massachusetts, New Mexico, Oklahoma, South Dakota, Tennessee, Texas and West Virginia.

Child Abuse

Some parents treat their children very badly. (*See* "Child Abuse," page 74.) Soon after a case of child abuse is reported, it becomes a legal matter. It is the law that the child be given a lawyer to present the case at a court hearing. Usually, the child is not allowed to appear in court, but is permitted to stay with the parents during the hearing if there is no danger from them. If there is an emergency—for instance, if the parent threatens the child's life—the child will be taken away from home and placed in a foster home or other safe place.

Divorce

If your parents divorce, which one will you live with? This question is often de-

Twelve-year-old Walter Polovchak went to court to receive political asylum in the U.S. when his folks returned to Russia. *(Wide World Photos)*

cided by parents and children together. When parents don't agree, it is decided in court. One parent may be given custody. That parent is then in charge of you and provides you with your main home. The other parent has "visitation rights," which means he or she can see you at certain times. You might spend weekends with that parent or live with him or her during summer vacations. In some states, "joint custody" is allowed. Then both parents have custody of you and you divide your time between them.

Children don't have much say in child custody cases. In some states, like California and Colorado, children's wishes are taken into account. Age has something to do with it. When the involved children are 12 years old or more, the courts are likely to pay more attention to their wishes. But usually the court judge decides "in the best interests of the child." The child might not agree with the judge's opinion.

More and more, children in divorce cases are allowed to have lawyers, who present their side of things.

After the divorce, you have the right to see both parents, and your parents must keep on supporting you.

The parent who does not have custody may not kidnap you. If such a thing happens, call home collect.

Adoption

In almost every state, adopted children are not allowed to find out who their natural parents are. In the states where they can, they must be 18 or more. After a child is adopted, the birth certificate is "sealed" and no one is allowed to see it.

Laws About School

Generally, teachers and principals are considered by law to be acting in the place of parents. They have many of the same rights to control you that parents do.

If you skip school, the truant officer may come ask where you have been.

School Attendance

In every state except Mississippi, it is the law that you must go to school for a certain time in your life. If you don't, you and your parents can be arrested. Your parents or the person you work for cannot stop you from going to school, or make it hard for you to attend school. However, sometimes it is okay for your parents to teach you at home or for you to go to a private school.

Children who skip school without a good reason (like being sick) are called truants. If you skip school more than a certain number of days, you might end up in court.

Your Years in School, State by State Chart

To read the chart: Find the state in which you live, then read across. If the first age is 7 and the second is 16, that means you must go to school from the time you are 7 until you are 16 or graduate from high school.

STATE	SCHOOL AGE			SCHOOL AGE	
	From	To		From	To
Alabama	7	16	Nebraska	7	16
Alaska	7	16	Nevada	7	17
Arizona	8	16	New Hampshire	6	16
Arkansas	7	16	New Jersey	6	16
California	8	16	New Mexico	6	17
Colorado	7	16	New York	7	16
Connecticut	7	16	North Carolina	7	16
Delaware	7	16	North Dakota	7	16
District of Columbia	7	16	Ohio	6	18
Florida	7	16	Oklahoma	7	18
Georgia	7	16	Oregon	7	18
Hawaii	6	16	Pennsylvania	8	17
Idaho	7	16	Rhode Island	7	16
Illinois	7	16	South Carolina	—	16
Indiana	7	16	South Dakota	7	16
Iowa	7	16	Tennessee	7	16
Kansas	7	16	Texas	7	17
Kentucky	7	16	Utah	6	18
Louisiana	7	16	Vermont	7	16
Maine	7	17	Virginia	7	16*
Maryland	7	16	Washington	8	18
Massachusetts	7	16	West Virginia	7	16
Michigan	6	16	Wisconsin	7	16
Minnesota	7	16	Wyoming	7	16
Mississippi	—	—	Commonwealth of		
Missouri	7	16	Puerto Rico	8	16
Montana	7	16			

NOTE: In some states you may be able to quit school or go part-time after you finish a certain grade (usually the eighth grade) *if* you have a job.

*In Virginia, the age for leaving school depends on local laws.

Your Rights in School

You have the right to say what you think in school *if* you do not stop others from working or make them break rules, and if you do not interfere with what's going on in the classroom. Be careful, though. It is always best to be polite. Make sure you are just saying what you think, not disobeying a rule. There is a fine line there.

Examples of saying what you think:
Your school does not have a free lunch program.
You think it should, and say so.

Your teacher says something which you think is wrong.
You say so.

Examples of disobeying the rules:
Your teacher tells you to stop passing

It's usually against the rules to pass notes to your classmates during classroom time.

notes and pay attention. You don't obey. Then you are breaking a rule.

You swear at someone. You are probably breaking a school rule. You may not swear or use obscene language anywhere without risking getting in trouble.

You have the right to say what you wish in writing. If you write for the school newspaper, you may write whatever you want to *if* what you say is really true. In any case, it is not a good idea to ridicule people. Be very careful that your facts are right and that you are being fair.

No one, not even the principal, may make you talk to the police.

You may not be stopped from taking a class or playing on a school team just because you are a girl or boy.

You and your parents have the right to see your school record.

The school may not make you buy gym clothes, but you must wear the kind of clothes to gym that will allow you to participate in the activities.

Other School Laws

It is against the law to hold religious services in public schools.

Your locker may be searched; it is within the law for a teacher or principal

You cannot be kept off a school team just because you are a girl (or boy).

A teacher or principal can, under the law, search your locker.

to do so. Put nothing in your locker that could get you in trouble.

In some places you have to wear certain kinds of clothes to school and to look a certain way. However, the courts are giving students more rights in this matter. Rules about the way you look in school have to be fair.

It is against the law for children to be made to go to a certain school because of their color or sex or beliefs. However, parents have the right to send their child to a parochial or private school.

Avoiding Trouble in School

If you follow your school's rules of being polite and not hurting people or things, you're pretty safe. In most schools it is against the rules to:

1. Talk back to or disobey a teacher
2. Swear or use obscene language
3. Smoke
4. Use alcohol or other drugs

5. Start or join a secret club (If you want to start a club, ask your teacher how to do it.)
6. Disobey any school rule when in school or on your way to and from school
7. Damage school property on purpose
8. Hit someone
9. Throw things in the classroom or lunchroom
10. Damage library books or take them without signing them out
11. Cheat on tests

And more . . .

Laws and Rules About Punishment in School

Hitting:

In most states a teacher or principal may hit you if you do something wrong. In the following places it is against the law to hit a student: Maine, Massachusetts, New Jersey, District of Columbia, Baltimore (Maryland), and Chicago (Illinois), Kalamazoo and Grosse Point (Michigan), New York City, Pittsburgh (Pennsylvania), Portland (Oregon), Groton (Connecticut).

Even where hitting a student is within the law, there are rules about it. In some places only a principal or superintendent may hit you. And the person who hits you may not hit you hard enough to really hurt you.

Suspension:

To suspend a student means to kick the student out of school for a few days. In most states only a principal, superintendent, or school board may suspend you; in others it is not allowed at all. It is against the law for the school to suspend you for something your parents have done. For example, if your parents don't come to school when asked to, the school may not suspend you. You have a right to a hearing (a meeting of everyone who has anything to do with it).

Silas Brisco was suspended from a Chicago school for wearing an earring. People at the school thought he was wearing it to show he belonged to a local gang, since members of the gang all wore one earring. Brisco, a black student, said it was a symbol of racial pride. He fought the suspension, but was suspended for 17 days.

Being Expelled:

To expel a student means to kick the student out of school forever or for a very long time. This is very serious. In many places it is against the law; in others only the school board can do it. Remember, you have a right to go to school.

Being Transferred:

To transfer a student means to send the student to another school. In most places it is against the law for the school to do this to punish you.

Laws About Working

It is usually against the law for children under 18 to:

1. Work in factories, on railroads, or on boats
2. Work in bars, liquor stores, bowling alleys, or pool halls
3. Work in places that sell or buy things from other states
4. Sell tobacco
5. Ride or work on dangerous machines

In many places it is against the law for children to:

1. Sell door to door (In some places all people who sell door to door must sign up with the police. Before you sell anything, even Girl Scout cookies, check the law first.)
2. Deliver anything, even newspapers, from a car or truck
3. Shine shoes, sell newspapers, or sell anything on the street

Children may not work before 6:00 A.M. or after 7:00 P.M.

Children must not spend more than 8 hours a day in school and at work. That means if you go to school for 5 hours a day, you may only work 3 hours a day.

Usually, rules about working hours do not count when it comes to babysitting, delivering newspapers, mowing lawns, shoveling snow, and doing odd jobs for people.

For any other work kids need a work permit. If you want to pick strawberries for pay on a large farm or you want to bag groceries at a supermarket, you will need a work permit. (*See* "Getting a Work Permit," page 286, and "Legal Stuff," pages 287–289.)

Other Laws

As a child, you really have fewer rights under the law than grown-ups have, but the law is easier on you sometimes. It is supposed to help you, so although you are not as free, you are more protected. Following are some additional rights (and limitations) that apply to kids.

In some states you can own land. In others you can't.

You can go to court to get back something that belongs to you or to get money if you have been hurt in some way. Usually you need a parent and a lawyer with you.

As is true during school hours, you have a right to say and write what you wish if you do not swear or use obscene language or write something untrue about another person (libel).

You have the right to worship as you want to.

You may stop a big kid from beating up a smaller one.

You may not drink liquor until you are a certain age, usually 18 or 21.

You may not vote or run for public office until you are at least 18.

You usually may not make a contract (legal agreement). If you do, it will not hold up under the law.

If you write a will, it will not be any good under the law because you are a child.

You do not have the right to a jury trial (though this is changing).

Miscellaneous, But Important: It Is Against the Law to . . .

Usually, if you do nothing to hurt anyone or anything, you will not get in trouble with the law.

It may seem that there are lots of laws to hedge you in, but remember that they protect you, too.

Almost everywhere in the United States it is against the law for kids to:

1. Throw things on the road that might damage a car or hurt a person; or throw things anywhere when the result is to make a place look ugly. (Don't throw candy wrappers, empty bottles, and other trash in the street.)

2. Throw things at cars, buses, or trains.

3. Write on, steal, or damage highway signs.

4. Use fake money (slugs) in telephones and machines that sell things.

5. Refuse to give up the telephone when someone breaks in with an emergency call.

6. Use drugs, sniff glue, smoke, or drink alcohol.

7. Play games to win money (gamble). It is okay to play games with play money.

8. Blackmail people—say you will tell on them unless they pay you something.

9. Extort money from people—make them pay you because they are afraid you will hurt them if they don't. (For exam-

ple, it is against the law to frighten another child into giving you his or her lunch money.)

10. Use bad language.

11. Steal from a store (shoplift).

12. Make someone else break the law. (For example, it is against the law for you to get someone else to steal something for you.)

13. Keep something you find without trying to learn who the owner is.

14. Buy or take something that someone else has stolen.

15. Make a lot of loud noise.

16. Shoot a gun.

17. Refuse to "break it up" when the police tell you to.

You must "break it up" when the police tell you to. "Hanging out" is sometimes against the law.

18. Set fire to something.

19. Abandon or not take care of an animal you own.

20. Be mean to any animal.

21. Go on someone's property without asking permission.

22. Sell or give tobacco to another child.

23. Write on the walls of buildings, rest rooms, and other public places.

24. Break things that don't belong to you.

25. Fool around on railroad tracks.

26. Hang around a school where you don't belong.

27. "Borrow" or take a car, bicycle, or anything else without asking the person who owns it.

28. Make fun of, scare, or hurt in other ways children who are new in school. (This is called "hazing.")

29. Go to places where it is against the law for children to be.

30. Hang out with criminals.

31. Run away. (*See* "What Happens If You Run Away," page 130.)

32. Work at a job that is against the law.

33. Beg.

34. Skip school (truancy).

And more. . .

In some places there are special laws. Find out if it is okay where you live to:

1. Be out after a certain time of night (curfew).

2. Pick wildflowers.

3. Start a fire on a beach or in a park.

4. Light a firecracker.

5. Camp overnight.

6. Ride a skateboard on the street or in a parking lot.

7. Hunt animals. (Ask in your sporting goods store for the rules.)

8. Fish. (In some places children don't need a license to fish. Ask in your sporting goods store.)

9. Own a dog. (Usually you need to get a license for a dog. In most places dogs must be kept in a yard and walked on a leash.)

10. Own a cat. (In some places you need a license to keep a cat.)

11. Hitchhike. (If it is allowed, usually you may not do it on a freeway or ramp. You must stand off the road's shoulder or on the curb, and you must have asked your parents if it's okay. It is not a good idea to hitchhike—you can get into serious trouble if you are picked up by the wrong person.)

Status Offenders

A "status offender" is a kid who has done something illegal which really hurts no one but him- or herself—like skip school or run away or break curfew. Some kids who are status offenders end up in jail. The federal government and state governments are trying to change this.

What Happens If You Run Away

Every year about half a million kids run away from home. Most are sent back to their families. Because of your age, you don't have the right under the law to run away or be on your own. The police have to pick you up.

When the police find you, what happens to you depends on where you are. Usually, the police make sure you live where you say you do, then send you home. Your parents may come and get you, or the police will find another way (for example, a bus) to send you back. If there is no way to send you home right away, you may spend a few days in a place for children without a home, a house with a family, or a kids' jail for children who have broken laws.

See "Running Away," pages 88–89.

Arrest and the Courts

The Juvenile Justice and Delinquency Prevention Act of 1974 says that states must change the way they treat kids who break the law. They must find other ways to handle them besides locking them up. (At present about a million kids are locked up, either in adult jails or detention homes.)

One way is to make child lawbreakers pay money for damage they have caused.

Instead of going to jail they are sometimes made to work. Kids have worked in state parks and in neighborhood clean-up programs to earn the money they need to pay for the wrongs they have done. Sometimes kids who have done nothing worse than run away or commit one small crime are thrown in jail with hardened criminals who have committed armed robbery or murder. Of course this is not fair, and besides, being in such places can lead kids into a life of crime rather than away from it. To keep this from happening, many communities and states have worked out other ways of dealing with kids in trouble than sending them to jail.

In Denver, juries of junior and senior high school kids decide sentences for young lawbreakers. The kids on trial have not been in trouble before, have agreed that they are guilty, and have promised to do what the jury says. The juries have handed down some interesting sentences:

- Get a job.
- Pay money for the damage done.
- Write a letter of apology to a police officer.

One jury of young people told a father he should not belittle his son anymore. The father was "part of the problem," they said.

Only a very few kids who get in trouble with the law are sent to jail—rarely to jail with adults.

If You Are Arrested

Remember this: If a police officer arrests you, you do not have to tell him or her anything. The officer should tell you that you have the right to be silent. This is true whether or not you have done something wrong.

Do not try to stop a police officer from arresting you. If you do, you may get in more trouble or be hurt. Stand still. Don't reach for something in your pocket or make any quick moves. Police officers are sometimes nervous, because people they arrest might attack them.

It is against the law to go limp to make it hard for the officer to arrest you.

Unless you are caught in the act of doing something wrong, the officer must have a warrant for your arrest. A warrant is a piece of paper issued by a judge on which is written your name and what you are supposed to have done wrong. The officer must show it to you if you ask to see it.

If an officer catches you doing something wrong, he may search you for things that have something to do with what you did wrong. For example, if you are caught stealing, he or she may search you for the thing you stole. Don't try to stop the search. However, it is a good idea to say you do not want to be searched. If you do, it is less likely that anything the

The police can search you, if you've been caught doing something wrong.

If you are arrested you can make 2 phone calls in most states—to call someone who can help you.

officer finds on you may be used against you later in court.

Being Booked

The officer will take you to the police station where you will be "booked." You may have your fingerprints and picture taken. A record of your arrest will be written down. You still do not have to say anything.

Remember this: You have the right to call someone to help you. In most states you are allowed 2 phone calls. Call some-

Of the cases that end up in court, 3 out of 10 end in probation. *(J. Berndt; Stock, Boston)*

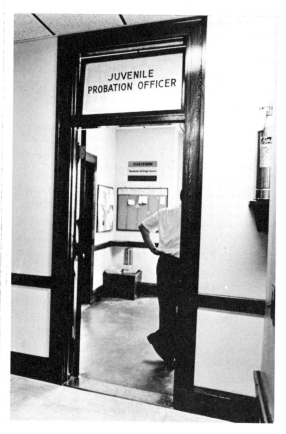

one who can really do something—a parent or other adult you trust. Don't call your best kid friend.

What Happens Next

What happens next depends on how bad the thing you did was, on the quality of your home, and on whether or not you have done anything wrong before. The next step will be *one* of the following:

You will be sent home.

You will be sent home but will be told to go to court at some other time.

You will be put in a home or other place that cares for children if you have no home or if your home is not a good place for you to be.

You will be put in a hospital if you are sick.

You will be put in a kids' jail (detention home) until your trial comes up. This will not happen unless you have done something really bad—for example, shot a person with a gun. Children under 12 are almost never put in detention homes unless they might hurt themselves or other people.

While You Are Waiting to Go to Court

You may not have to go to court. If you do, a probation officer will look into your home life, your history, your school record. A report will be written telling what your problem is and what should be done about it.

You have the right to appear in court with your parents.

If You Go to Court

Almost all states have juvenile courts that handle cases for or about children. In juvenile court there is no jury, only a judge. The judge is usually used to dealing with kids.

Remember these rights:

• You have the right to stay silent.

• You have the right to a lawyer. If your parents can't pay for one, the court must get one for you at no cost.

• You have the right to have enough time to get your parents in court with you.

• You have the right to ask questions of anyone who speaks against you in court.

In court, the judge will first decide if your case can be dismissed. If it is, you can go home and it is all over. If it is not, he will hear your case. Everyone who has anything to do with it will be there to tell about it. Your lawyer may say a few things, too.

Then the judge will decide what will happen to you. What are your chances? Of all the children who end up in court:

• Three out of 10 have their cases dismissed.

• Three out of 10 are put on probation. That means they go home, live their lives, and follow rules the court sets up. A child on probation may not be allowed to go out at night, for example. A probation officer has some say about what the child is allowed to do.

• Only 1 out of 10 goes to a kids' jail. Only children who have done something very bad or have been in court many times before are sent to jail. Most of the "children" who go to jail are over 12 years old. The court would rather have you at home.

• The rest go to a foster home or some other place.

Laws About Walking

Don't sit or stand on the street or sidewalk so that you get in the way of traffic.

Don't jaywalk. Cross the road at a light or marked crosswalk. If it is a long street with no lights or crosswalks, cross anywhere, but be careful.

Walk on the sidewalk. If there is none, walk on the left side of the road facing traffic, as far off the road as you can get.

Laws About Bicycles

Licenses

In most places, you need a license for your bicycle. It doesn't cost much—usually about a dollar. Having a license protects you. If your bike is stolen, it can be found through your license number. You can get a license from the police or from a bike store.

Equipment

Your bike should have:

1. A brake that will make one wheel skid on a dry road
2. Handlebars lower than your shoulders
3. A seat
4. Pedals not more than 12 inches above the ground when they are as low as they can go

Riding

Do not ride after dark if you can help it. If you do, you should have a white light on the front and a red reflector on the back.

Ride as close to the right-hand side of the road as you can.

Keep at least one hand on the handlebars.

Do not ride on a bike with another person.

Do not hitch a ride on a car or bus by hanging on to it while it is movng.

Use hand signals when turning.

Stop at stop signs and red lights. Count to 10 before going again and check twice to make sure nothing is coming.

Stay off freeways and ramps.

Laws About Minibikes and Go-carts

It is against the law to ride a minibike or go-cart in an alley or street without a license. To get a license, usually you must have brakes, lights, fenders, a windshield, windshield wipers, and a muffler. You must also have a driver's license.

To be safe, ride your minibike or go-cart off the street. If you want to go on someone else's property, be sure to first ask if it's okay. If the person doesn't want you there, do as he or she says.

Plainclothes policemen check a young motorcyclist's license. Make sure to have a license when *you* drive. *(Anestic Diakopoulou; Stock, Boston)*

For safety, you should always give the proper hand signal when turning or stopping.

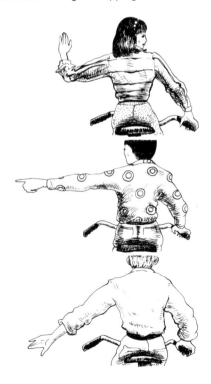

Laws About Drivers' Licenses

This chart tells you when you are allowed to have a driver's license. Look up your state, then read across.

	AGE		
	Regular License		**Juvenile License**
STATE	**After Driver Education**	**Without Driver Education**	
Alabama	16	16	
Alaska	16	16	
Arizona	16	16	
Arkansas	16	16	
California	16	18	14—only between home and school
Colorado	21	21	16
Connecticut	16	18	
Delaware	16	18	
District of Columbia	18	18	16
Florida	16	18	
Georgia	16	16	
Hawaii	15	15	
Idaho	16	16	14—only for certain hours
Illinois	18	18	16—only for certain hours
Indiana	16	21	
Iowa	16	18	14—only between home and school
Kansas	16	16	14—only between home and school
Kentucky	16	16	
Louisiana	17	17	15—only for certain hours
Maine	15	17	15—only between home and school
Maryland	16	18	
Massachusetts	18	18	16½—only for certain hours
Michigan	16	18	14—only between home and school
Minnesota	16	18	15—only for certain hours
Mississippi	15	15	
Missouri	16	16	
Montana	15	16	

	AGE		
	Regular License		Juvenile License
STATE	After Driver Education	Without Driver Education	
Nebraska	16	16	14—only between home and school
Nevada	16	16	14—only between home and school
New Hampshire	16	18	16—only between home and school
New Jersey	17	17	16—only for farming use
New Mexico	15	16	
New York	17	18	16—only for certain hours
North Carolina	16	18	
North Dakota	16	16	14—only between home and school
Ohio	16	18	14—only in special cases
Oklahoma	16	16	
Oregon	16	16	14—only between home and school
Pennsylvania	17	18	16—only for certain hours
Rhode Island	16	18	
South Carolina	16	16	15—only for certain hours
South Dakota	16	16	14—only for certain hours
Tennessee	16	16	14—only for certain hours
Texas	16	18	15—only in special cases
Utah	16	17	
Vermont	18	18	16
Virginia	16	18	
Washington	16	18	
West Virginia	16	18	
Wisconsin	16	18	14—only for certain hours
Wyoming	16	16	14

If You Get a Traffic Ticket

When you get a ticket for breaking a law about bikes, minibikes, go-carts, or walking, the officer makes you sign it. When you do, that is your promise to come to court. The ticket tells you where and when. Signing the ticket does not mean you are guilty.

WARNING: Always go to court if the ticket tells you to do so. If for some reason you can't get to court at the time the ticket specifies, call the court to change the date or time. This is very important. You can get in more trouble for not showing up in court than for breaking the traffic law in the first place.

When you do go to court, a traffic officer or someone else will meet with you and your parents, and you will get a chance to tell your story. If you say you are not guilty, you can ask for a hearing. If you say you are guilty, the traffic officer will sentence you right there. Usually your sentence will be one or more of the following:

- A warning not to do it again

For some traffic tickets you can pay the fine by mail. Otherwise you have to appear in court at the time set on the ticket.

- A fine
- Writing something about the law you broke

To Get Legal Help

Call the local branch of the Legal Aid Society if you need a lawyer. National organizations that may give you information are:

1. Youth Law Center
   1663 Mission Street
   San Francisco, CA 94105

2. National Juvenile Law Center
   3701 Lindell Boulevard
   P.O. Box 14200
   St. Louis, MO 63178

3. American Civil Liberties Union
   Juvenile Rights Project
   132 W. 43rd Street
   New York, NY 10016

4. NAACP Legal Defense Fund
   1790 Broadway
   New York, NY 10019

Be sure to mention your age and problem in your letter.

Chapter *6*
REAL PEOPLE AND UNREAL SUPERPEOPLE

Famous Children

A Five-year-old King

Louis the Fourteenth of France
Born: 1638
Died: 1715

When Louis was born, a 6-day holiday was declared in France. People marched in parades and rang bells. Guns boomed. Bonfires burned. It was all for the baby Louis, the Dauphin, which means both "prince" and "dolphin" in French.

Five years later, his father, King Louis the Thirteenth, died. As his oldest son, Louis was next in line to become king. Dressed in purple, he sat on a throne in the French *Parlement*, which was something like our Congress. To the men below, he made a short speech. It went: "Gentlemen, I have come to see you to give proof to my *Parlement* of my affec-tion and good will. My chancellor will speak further to you." Obviously, Louis didn't write that short speech himself.

Though he was king, he didn't really rule. His mother, the Queen, and other adults made the decisions. He didn't get away with much. True, he ate junk food once in a while, and he had a pony. But when he didn't behave, he was punished. For example, his mother made him stay in his room for 2 days for saying a swear word when he was 6.

And he wasn't a snob, despite being king. As a little child, he played at being grown-up with his friend Marie, who was the daughter of a servant. In their games *she* was queen and *he* was the servant. However, his teachers taught him that he was important. Once he was made to write, "Honor is due to kings; they do just what pleases them." He must have wondered about that, since he couldn't do everything he pleased.

Louis's seventh birthday party was wonderful. It included an animal ballet starring monkeys, bears, ostriches, and a parrot. At this time he learned to use a sword, to march, and to ride horses. As a child, he loved playing with silver toy soldiers, and he liked war all his life. A little fort, built in the palace garden, had little guns that could really shoot (though the "bullets" were blanks).

During much of Louis's childhood, his life was in danger because a group of people was trying to take over the government. Once the royal family was trapped in the palace. Outside mobs of people yelled, threatening to come in and kill them. Louis's little brother was scared. Louis drew his sword to show he had some power, then put his arm around his brother to comfort him.

At 16, Louis was finally crowned king. He was called the Sun King, and his court was very fancy. During his reign he took a lot of land for France. And he finally learned how important he was. One of his famous remarks was, *L'Etat, c'est moi,* which means, "I am the State." And *that* means he had all the power and knew it.

The Eight-year-old Diarist

Marjory Fleming
Born: 1803
Died: 1811

Do the arithmetic: Subtract Marjory's birth year from the year she died. She was only eight years old when her life ended. Yet the story of her life is given in books that contain biographies. Her writings appear in books of literature. Why? She was a writer who charmed the world.

Marjory was very brainy. At age 3 she could read. Until she was 5, she lived with her parents in a small town in Scotland. The family had pets—10 birds, including a hawk, and a dog named Help.

When Marjory was 5, her 17-year-old cousin Isabella came to visit, and the 2 girls liked each other right away. The age difference didn't seem to matter. Isabella asked if Marjory could come to live with her in the city of Edinburgh. The Flemings agreed.

Isabella was her teacher as well as her friend. For 2 hours each day the 2 girls worked on Marjory's lessons. Marjory liked history, and wrote a long poem to Mary, Queen of Scots, after reading about her. She also wrote in her journal. Here's what she had to say about arithmetic: "I am not going to tell you the horrible and wretched pleage [plague] that my multiplication table gives me. . . . The most Devilish thing is 8 times 8 and 7 times 7. . . ." Marjory loved 9 times 9, though.

Here is part of one of her letters:

"I sit down on my botom to answer all your kind and beloved letters which you was so good as to write to me. This is the first time I ever wrote a letter in my Life.

"There are a great many Girls in the Square and they cry just like a pig when we are under the painfull necessity of putting it to Death."

Marjory loved animals. She wrote in her journal, "There is a dog that yels continualy & I pity him to the bottom of my heart indeed I do." (You may notice her spelling and punctuation needed some work.) And: "The Casawary is a curious bird & so is the Gigantick Crane & the Pelican of the Wilderness whose mouth holds a bucket of fish & water."

She was not always good. On July 12,

1810, she described a temper tantrum: "I confess that I have been more like a little young Devil . . . for when Isabella went up the stairs to teach me religion and my multiplication and to be good and all my other lessons I stamped with my feet and threw my new hat which she made on the ground and was sulky. . . ."

In 1811 Marjory returned to her parents' house. That fall she got the measles. She seemed to get better, but then was sent to bed again with "water on the brain." Her mother had given her sixpence for being "patient in the measles," and Marjory wanted to get well so she could use the money to buy Isabella a New Year's present. But it was not to be. Her headaches grew worse. On December 19, she whispered, "Oh, mother, mother." Then she died. Her father felt so bad about it that he didn't allow anyone to say her name ever again.

Fifty years later her writings were found and published.

The Calculating Boy

George Parker Bidder
Born: 1805
Died: 1878

The problem was: The moon is 123,256 miles from the earth. Sound travels at the rate of 4 miles per minute. How long would it take for battle sounds from the earth to reach the moon?

The 9-year-old boy gave the answer* in less than a minute. He had figured it out in his head. The people in the audience were amazed, and some thought there was a trick. There wasn't.

The boy was George Bidder, and his

See next page for the answer.

talent with numbers was very unusual. No one taught him what he knew, though his brother had shown him how to count. George said that the numbers were his friends. He knew how they related to one another. On his own, he figured out how multiplication worked by arranging shot (small round pieces of lead) in rows like this:

By counting the shot, he proved to himself that 8 times 8 is 64.

George's father didn't make much money, and when he saw how smart his son was he took him on tour. People paid to see George do arithmetic in his head, and called him "the Calculating Boy." George later said he saw the answer to problems in his mind's eye.

When George was 11, this number was read to him backwards: 2,563,721,987,-653,461,598,746,231,905,607,541,128,-975,231. He was able to recite it forward, without seeing it. An hour later he still remembered the number and repeated it exactly.

When George was 12, Sir William Herschel, a famous astronomer, gave him the following problem to do in his head:

Light travels from the sun to the earth in 8 minutes. The sun is 98,000,000 miles from the earth. It would take light 6 years and 4 months traveling at the same rate to reach the nearest fixed star. Each year is 365 days and 6 hours. Each month is 28 days. How far is the star from the earth?

George's answer was correct.†

At one of his shows about this time, a smart aleck asked, "How many bulls' tails would it take to reach the moon?"

George's answer was fast: "One, if it's long enough."

Because he was on the road so much, George got very little schooling until he was older. But he made up for it. At college he won the mathematics prize and when he grew up he became an engineer and was very well thought of. He never lost his ability to do arithmetic in his head.

Answers to George Bidder's problems:
*21 days, 4 hours, 34 minutes.
†40,633,740,000,000 miles.

A Small Person with a Big Personality

Charles Sherwood Stratton (General Tom Thumb)
Born: 1838
Died: 1883

When Charles Stratton was 5, he was an inch over 2 feet tall and weighed 15 pounds. For some reason he had stopped growing. With his rosy cheeks and light hair, he was very appealing. He also was smart and full of energy.

Charles's mother took him to see the showman, P. T. Barnum. Barnum said later that Charles was "the smallest child I ever saw that could walk alone." A good addition to his show, Barnum thought. At

Tom Thumb was only 40 inches tall, but had a large personality. In 1863 he married his sweetheart, Lavinia Warren, in a grand wedding.

his American Museum, he already had jugglers, magicians, trained fleas, and glassblowers. A small person would round things out. He hired Charles with his mother and father. The family was paid $7 a week and had all expenses paid.

One of the first things Barnum did was give Charles a new name—General Tom Thumb. The name Tom Thumb came from an old legend about a tiny knight, named Sir Tom Thumb, who lived in a gold palace and rode in a coach drawn by 6 white mice. In the story, Sir Tom Thumb was killed while fighting a spider. The "General" part of the new name was a joke.

Barnum taught Tom, as Charles was now called, to sing, dance, act, and tell jokes. When Tom became very good at it, Barnum said he was ready to go on stage. Barnum was not a trustworthy person. In his ads, which were lies, he said Tom was 11 years old and came from England. People flocked to see Tom. He usually began his act by saying, "Good evening, ladies and gentlemen. I am only a Thumb, but a good hand in a general way in amusing you."

In his act, Tom fought mock battles with very tall people. He danced a jig on a wooden plate held by 8-foot Angus Mc-Askill. Children came up on stage to play with this person who was so small.

When Tom was 6, Barnum took him to Europe on a ship. When they left, at the docks were 80,000 people who had come to see Tom off. When the ship landed in England, crowds were waiting, so Tom's mother wrapped him up like a baby and sneaked him off the ship.

In England Tom met the Queen and the rest of the royal family. In his show for them, he danced the horn pipe and imitated Napoleon, a ruler of France. On the way out, he tried to walk backwards—a rule people who meet the Queen are supposed to follow—but because he was so small, he couldn't walk fast enough to keep up with the others. He had to walk backwards a few steps, then turn and run forward, then go backward again. To make things worse, the Queen's pet dog attacked him and Tom had to beat the dog off with a cane.

At another meeting with the Queen, he sang "Yankee Doodle" because it mentioned a pony. When he sang the word "pony" he pointed to the Queen, because he had seen a pony outside the palace and wanted it as a present. He didn't dare ask for it right out. But the Queen didn't get the message, and gave Tom a gold pencil instead.

Tom's act was bringing in so much money that Barnum gave him part of the profits. By the time Tom was an adult, he had grown 15 inches and was very rich. Barnum had added more little people to his show. One was Commodore McNutt. Another was Lavinia Warren, who had taught third grade. Both McNutt and Tom fell in love with Lavinia. Once McNutt became so jealous that he punched Tom. But Tom won Lavinia. They were married in 1863, and 2,000 people came to the wedding.

On their wedding trip, the two met President Abraham Lincoln before going on to live in Tom's house in Connecticut. The house had furniture just the right size for them. Tom owned horses, big sailboats, and other houses.

For the rest of his life, Tom sometimes traveled with Lavinia in the circus or on world tours. During his lifetime, 20 million tickets to his show were sold. Tom once said, "I feel I am as big as anybody." He was.

The Real *Alice*

Alice Liddell
Born: 1852
Died: 1934

Five friends in a boat. The three Liddell sisters: Lorina (13), Alice (10), and Edith (8). Charles Dodgson who taught mathematics. Robinson Duckworth, who could sing. They rowed up the Isis River that runs by Oxford University in England. The day was July 4, 1862. During the afternoon they beached the boat at Godstowe and had tea on the grass near some haystacks. An ordinary day.

But sometime during the afternoon, Dodgson began to tell a story about a little girl named Alice who fell asleep and dreamed she went down a rabbit hole. While underground, she had some curious adventures. . . .

As they were rowing, Dodgson kept spinning his tale. "Are you making it up?" asked Robinson.

"Yes," replied his friend. "I'm inventing it as I go along."

This was not the first story tale Dodgson had told. It was his habit to tell a story when he took pictures of children, one of his hobbies. The better the story, the more likely the children would be still and the pictures wouldn't turn out blurry. Most of his stories, though, were forgotten after they were told.

Not this one. At the end of the day, Alice said, "Oh, Mr. Dodgson, I wish you would write out Alice's adventures for me."

Dodgson said he would try.

The story was published under the title *Alice's Adventures in Wonderland.* As the author, Dodgson used the pen-name Lewis Carroll. The book, of course, became famous.

Who was Alice? She was the daughter of the Dean of Christ Church at Oxford. Very pretty, she had dark hair and eyes like a deer. She was polite, curious, and trusting. As one of Dodgson's friends said, Alice was "an ideal child-friend." And perhaps important for a storyteller, she was a perfect listener.

Many of the characters in *Alice's Adventures in Wonderland* were taken from real life. Dodgson himself was the model for the Dodo. Thin, with one eye higher

Alice's Adventures in Wonderland was written by Charles Dodgson for a real Alice Liddell.

than the other, he also looked like the Gryphon, and like the Cheshire Cat, he smiled a lot. Duckworth was the Duck. Lorina was the Lory. Edith was the Eaglet. And Alice, of course, was Alice.

One evening, during the time Dodgson was writing the story, the Liddell girls sang him a serious song. The first line went: "Star of the evening, beautiful star." That song was the model for the poem "Turtle Soup" in *Alice*. Its first line was, "Soup of the evening, beautiful soup."

Dodgson kept up his friendship with the Liddell children. They went to see a magic show, watched fireworks, and played croquet together. And there were more picnics on the river.

Alice grew up to be beautiful, smart, and witty. She married and had 3 children—all boys. But her claim to fame was as the model for the heroine of a famous children's story.

"The Chess Machine"

José Capablanca
Born: 1888
Died: 1942

For three days, 4-year-old José watched his father play chess with a friend. On the third day, he noticed something.

The piece called the knight could be moved 2 ways:

 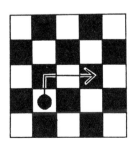

In any case, it always moved from a black square to a white one, or from a white square to a black. José's father moved a knight from a white square to a white, and after the game was over, José pointed this out. He laughed and said his father had cheated. Angry, his father said José didn't know anything about chess, and in response, José challenged his father to a game. Knowing the child had never played before, his father humored him. José won. They played another game. José won that one, too.

Until he was 8, José didn't play chess very much. Doctors thought it would be bad for him—it might strain his brain— but on his eighth birthday he was taken to the Havana Chess Club. Havana, Cuba, was then famous for chess; many great chess players came there. José started playing the game. He was serious about it, though he didn't read chess books, which showed standard plays that had worked in the past. Since José hadn't studied these, he played by instinct. His instinct was very good.

When José was 12, he played a match against the Cuban champion. He won, and became the chess champion of Cuba.

When José was 20, he traveled throughout the United States playing chess. Of the 734 games he played, he won 703.

Two years later he tried to enter the San Sebastián Tournament, but some of the important players didn't want to let him in, thinking he wasn't a good enough player. Finally they gave in. José Capablanca won the tournament.

In 1921 Capablanca became chess champion of the world. He still played by instinct. He once said, "To play chess requires no intelligence at all." His end game was very good, said the critics, who called him "The Chess Machine."

Capablanca made a number of statements about chess that reporters quoted. One famous one was, "In this world the winning player is always lucky."

Brain in a Hothouse

William James Sidis
Born: 1898
Died: 1944

The father of William Sidis had an idea to prove. His idea was that if children were pushed, they could learn "faster than a jack rabbit runs." When William was born, his father got his chance to find out if he was right. At 9 months, William was given alphabet blocks. At the age of 4, he could type in English and French. The pressure on William's brain to learn fast seemed to be working.

In first grade, William knew more about fractions than his teacher. In 6 months he went through 7 years of schoolwork. At the age of 8, he knew 6 languages, and at 9 he was ready for college. Harvard College wouldn't let him in until he was 11.

William was the youngest person ever to enter Harvard. In his first year there, he gave a lecture on the fourth dimension. The 100 professors and students in the audience were amazed; in fact, many weren't smart enough to know what he was talking about. One of the professors said William was slated to be a great mathematician, and the story of his lecture was published in the newspapers. William—blue-eyed, sandy-haired, 11 years old—was famous.

A year later, he broke down. His overloaded brain started complaining, and

William James Sidis, child genius, went to Harvard at the age of 11. *(Harvard Univ. Archives)*

William had to take a rest cure. When he was in good health again, he went back to college. He was a loner. His parents made matters worse by dressing him like a little kid. When he was 16, the year he graduated from Harvard, he was still in short pants. He told reporters, "I want to live the perfect life," and that, to him, meant being alone. He said he would never marry.

After going to law school, he taught for

a while, then dropped from sight. He was a strange man. Because William didn't bathe enough, he looked and smelled dirty. He hated his father. When someone told him his father had died, he said he didn't want to hear about it.

All his life William was interested in an odd thing—transportation lines. He enjoyed knowing how they connected with one another. At 14 he had written a poem about how to transfer from one line to another in the Boston subway system. He collected 1,600 transfers, pieces of paper used to transfer from one bus or subway to another. Each was different. In 1926 he published a book called *Notes on the Collection of Transfers,* a collection of jokes, weird facts, and poems about transportation lines and how they connected. He called himself a peridromophile—a lover of roundabout ways.

As an adult, William just wanted to be alone. He worked as a clerk, and played dumb. When a reporter found him and wrote about him, he sued the magazine the reporter worked for. "All I want to do is run an adding machine, but they won't let me alone," he said.

He died at the age of 46—alone.

The Real Christopher Robin

Christopher Robin Milne
Born: 1920

As a little boy, Christopher saw his father for only a short time each day. This is not unusual in rich English families. As was the custom, Christopher was taught and taken care of by his nanny, a woman hired for the job.

His father thought little children had lots of ego and were somewhat heartless. However, he liked to write about them. To get material for his poems and stories,

he paid a lot of attention to what Christopher did, and his son became the main character in his writings. When Christopher was 4, his father's first book of poems for children—called *When We Were Very Young*—was published. And in the next 4 years there were *Winnie-the-Pooh, Now We Are Six,* and *The House at Pooh Corner.*

The books were very popular. Children loved hearing about the characters Christopher Robin (the author used his son's real name), Pooh the bear, Piglet, Eyore, Kanga, Roo, and Tigger—characters modeled after the real Christopher Robin's toys. In the stories, Christopher Robin did cute and funny things, like build a "heffalump trap," as he did in real life. Many other things in the poems and stories were true. There were a real 100-Acre Wood (only it was larger) and a real Poohsticks Bridge.

Reporters came to visit the real Christopher Robin. They wanted him to be cute like the character in the book, and when he wasn't, they put words in his mouth. A reporter Christopher liked found him in

The stories of Winnie-the-Pooh and Christopher Robin are based on a real boy, who hated being teased about the stories his father wrote.

the gym, where he was exercising to build himself up because his parents thought he was too thin. This reporter wrote a story about how good Christopher was at climbing a rope. Christopher liked that story.

At age 10, Christopher was sent away to a boarding school, and he saw his parents only on vacations and holidays or when they came to visit. As a small child, he had liked the fame of being the model for a book character, but in school he came to hate the fame, at least part of the time. The other boys teased him, especially about the poem called "Vespers," which tells about little Christopher Robin saying his prayers. He did say prayers when he was 3, and he still said them, but he didn't like to be teased about it. Some of the boys played a phonograph record of the poem over and over. Finally the joke wore thin. When the boys gave the record to Christopher, he smashed it.

Luckily, it was about the time he went away to school that Christopher and his father became close. And strangely, it was then that his father stopped writing about Christopher Robin.

Today, Christopher Robin Milne runs a bookstore with his wife. He is still thin. His toys—Pooh, Piglet, and the rest—are in a glass cabinet in a publisher's office. In 1975 he wrote a book about what it was like to be a character in his father's stories. He says about his toys, "My toys were and are to me no more than yours were and are to you. . . . Fame has nothing to do with love."

Little Miss Miracle

Shirley Temple
Born: 1928

Mothers curled their daughters' hair in Shirley Temple curls. The daughters played with Shirley Temple dolls. They entered Shirley Temple contests. They cut out Shirley Temple paper doll clothes.

Who was this famous Shirley Temple? A little girl, a child movie star.

When Shirley was 8 she made $500,000 a year—before taxes. In those days, the 1930s, times were hard in the United States. Millions of people were out of work, and heads of families stood in line for free soup. But thousands of those poor people paid money to go to the movies to see Shirley Temple. Watching the bright

Shirley Temple danced with Bill (Bojangles) Robinson in *The Little Colonel.* (*Wide World Photos*)

little child sing and dance cheered them up.

Her career began when she was 3. At her dancing school, a talent scout from the movies coaxed her out from behind the piano where she was hiding. After seeing what she could do, he chose her for the movies. Her salary then was $10 a day.

Her first movies, short features, were called *Baby Burlesks*. Like other kids in the cast, Shirley wore diapers as a part of the joke. Being an actress wasn't always fun. Once Shirley was put in a cart hitched to a blindfolded ostrich, and when the blindfold was yanked off, the scared ostrich started running wildly. Shirley, bouncing in the cart, was terrified.

By the time Shirley was 6, she was starring in long movies. Her mother was her coach. While Shirley was acting, she called out, "Sparkle, Shirley, sparkle." The girl was a good actress, singer, and dancer, and besides, with her dimples and blond curls, she was very cute. Her first big movie was *Stand Up and Cheer* in 1934. Movie people called her "Little Miss Miracle" because she was so popular.

When Shirley was 7, she got 5,000 letters a week from fans. One woman cut off one of Shirley's curls as a keepsake. People sent presents to the little actress. The kangaroo she got had to be given away because it jumped the fence. On her eighth birthday she received 1,000 cakes.

Shirley's mother made sure she wasn't spoiled by all the attention. She gave her daughter only $4.25 a week as an allowance; the rest of her money was put in the bank for later. Shirley had to eat spinach 4 days a week. Once she talked the people from the studio restaurant into

teaching her mother a lesson. They sent in a whole plate of spinach for her mother's lunch. The lesson didn't work. Shirley still had to eat her spinach.

Shirley *did* know how important she was. When a reporter tried to interview her mother, Shirley said, "Why don't you interview me? I'm the star." At age 11, she achieved one of her dreams—to play the lead in *The Little Princess*.

When Shirley grew up, she didn't make many more movies, but she did star in a couple of television shows. With her husband, Charles Black, she had 2 children. In the late 1960s, Shirley Temple Black went into politics, and in 1974 she was appointed U.S. ambassador to Ghana, a country in Africa. She has worked in a number of ways to help people. After her operation for cancer, she broadcast a message to get other people to watch for signs of the disease. She is still a miracle.

The Girl Whose Secret Writings Became Famous

Anne Frank
Born: 1929
Died: 1945

Anne Frank's best friend, "Kitty," was a book with a red-checked cover that she had been given on her thirteenth birthday. In its pages she wrote her secret thoughts. At first, she told about what happened to her in school. Her math teacher made her write a theme called "A Chatterbox" because she talked too much in class. Boys were beginning to be interested in her. She wasn't sure about how to handle them.

At that time Europe had been at war for 3 years, and Holland, where the Franks lived, had been captured by the German Nazis. The Nazis hated Jews. Under the

Anne Frank and the entrance to the Annex, her family's hiding place from the Nazis in Amsterdam during World War II. *(Anne Frank House)*

Nazis, Jews were forced to wear yellow stars, to stay in at night, and to obey other rules. Millions were sent to concentration camps, where many were worked to death or killed. The Franks, who were Jewish, had been able to live for a time in the open. Then they learned that Margot, Anne's sister, had been chosen to go to a camp, and it was time to go into hiding. Anne's diary was a month old.

Eight people lived in the Franks' hiding place, called the "Secret Annex." There were the four people in the Frank family;

Mr. and Mrs. van Daan and their son, Peter; and Mr. Dussell, a dentist. The Annex was in the building where Mr. Frank had had his office. During the day they couldn't flush the toilet, for if they did, people working nearby might hear. They could look outside only through a slit in the curtain, and the opening to the Annex was hidden by a bookcase. Anne wrote, "It is like a very peculiar boarding house." At first she liked it. Friends brought them food, books, and news of what was happening.

Then the Annex started to feel crowded. The van Daans fought with one another, and Anne had problems with her mother. She told Kitty, "Mummy sometimes treats me just like a baby, which I can't bear," and "I feel lonely as if there were a great vacuum around me."

Anne told her diary nearly everything. She was jealous of Margot, and her own appearance and personality bothered her. She wanted to have blue eyes (hers were brown) and straighter teeth. Her temper tantrums made her feel guilty. She wrote, "Then suddenly the ordinary Anne slipped away, and a second Anne took her place, a second Anne who is not reckless and jocular, but one who just wants to love and be gentle."

During the time the Franks were in the Annex, Anne grew up. Pencil marks on the wall showed that she was growing taller. She fell in love—and out of love—with Peter van Daan. And she became more thoughtful. Toward the end, she wrote, "I can feel the suffering of millions. . . ." And, "I must uphold my ideals, for perhaps the time will come when I shall be able to carry them on."

In August 1944 the Nazis found the Annex, and all 8 of the people who lived there were arrested. One of the Nazis dumped out the contents of the briefcase in which Anne kept her writings. A few days later, Dutch friends found Anne's papers and put them in a safe place.

Anne and the others were sent to a concentration camp. She died in March 1945 at the age of 16.

Anne's father survived, and after the war he found Anne's diary and it was published. Millions of people have been moved by *The Diary of Anne Frank*. The writing is vivid and true to life. Anyone who reads the diary knows Anne—her faults, her loving personality, her feeling for living.

The Secret Annex has been kept as it was when the Nazis came. The marks on the wall that show Anne's height at different ages are still there, and her pictures are still tacked on the wall. There are movie stars, a photograph of Princess Elizabeth of England, a sketch of a chimpanzee's birthday party.

Anne wrote in her diary, "I want to go on living even after my death." She did.

"A Very Old Soul . . ."

Gary Coleman
Born: 1967

By the time he was 5 years old, Gary Coleman had had 3 kidney operations. The last one—when a kidney taken from

Gary Coleman hugs his People's Choice award for favorite young performer. *(Wide World Photos)*

someone else was put into his body—may have saved his life. When he was 11, he said, "the reason I survived is that I had a kidney that wouldn't give up. Now I got a Greek kidney donated from a kid who was hit by a car."

Perhaps because of his kidney disease, Gary is very short. Medicine he has to take has puffed out his cheeks. He's a delightful kid. In his wise-guy way, he has said, "I'm huggable, cute, sweet, adorable, et cetery." He is also smart. He could read at age 3½, and memorizing lines is easy for him.

In the television series "Diff'rent Strokes," he steals the show, playing one of 2 black children adopted by a rich white man. When he works away from his home in Zion, Illinois, his mother goes with him. His father works for a drug company in Zion. The family doesn't like to be separated, but it's necessary.

Gary is an only child who likes trains, planes, and model cars. In spite of his fame, he has his feet on the ground. He's a good actor who understands timing and body language, and grown-up actors respect his work. One calls him "a very old soul."

His career as a model began when, at the age of 5, he wrote to Montgomery Ward to tell the company what a good model he would make. Montgomery Ward hired him. So did McDonald's and other companies.

Will he stay in the television business? "Television is fun, but it's hard, and if it gets too crazy I may just do it as a part-time thing," he has said. His mother agreed. "If this is what Gary wants to do, he should have the chance. But if he wants to quit next year, that's also fine with me."

Childhoods of Famous People

Fairy Tale Author

Hans Christian Andersen
Born: April 2, 1805
Died: August 4, 1875

He was an ugly duckling.

Altogether he wrote 156 fairy tales. Among his most famous stories are "The Ugly Duckling," "The Princess and the Pea," "The Emperor's New Clothes," and "The Red Shoes." His name was Hans Christian Andersen.

Born in a slum in Odense, Denmark, Hans had a difficult life. He grew up in a tiny one-room house. His father was a shoemaker but could not afford to give leather shoes to Hans, and so the boy had to wear wooden ones. His mother could not read or write and was superstitious. His grandmother lied all the time, and his grandfather was insane.

To make matters worse, everyone made fun of the way Hans looked. He was tall and lanky, his hands and feet were large, and his eyes were small and very close together. But the worst feature was his nose. It was much too big for his face.

To cheer himself up, Hans created a make-believe world. For hours and hours he played with his toy theater. It had tiny wooden actors that he himself had carved; he even sewed costumes for the small figures. He also made up short plays and acted out all of the parts. When

Hans Christian Andersen was considered an ugly duckling whose dreams came true. *(Wide World Photos)*

he was 7, his parents took him to see his first play, and from then on Hans dreamed of being a famous actor. He would often sit in front of a mirror with his mother's apron over his shoulders, pretending that the apron was a knight's cloak.

When Hans was 14, he went alone to the big city of Copenhagen to become an actor. His mother cried. In his pocket was $14. First, he went to the Royal Theater, the most important theater in the city, where he acted for the manager and asked for a job. He was turned down.

For 3 years he tried hard to become famous, but the people at the Royal Theater still rejected him. They said he was not a good actor and not a good writer. "We only hire people with an education," they said.

Hans returned to school when he was 17, and was placed in the beginner's class. The lessons were difficult and the teacher was mean, but he worked hard and got good grades. He decided to become a writer instead of an actor. However, he was lonely and unhappy. Every night he wrote down his feelings in his diary, and later used some of those thoughts in writing "The Ugly Duckling," a fairy tale about an ugly baby duck that nobody wanted. In real life Hans thought *he* was the ugly duckling.

He wrote his first fairy tales when he was 30. He needed money, but did not think the stories would have much success. How wrong he was. People all over the world loved the stories. Even today, more than 100 years later, his fairy tales are enjoyed by both children and adults. His dream of becoming famous had come true.

Poet

Elizabeth Barrett Browning
Born: March 6, 1806
Died: June 29, 1861

She was a child prodigy.

Elizabeth Barrett was a very smart little girl who was reading adult books when she was 4. By the age of 6 she was writing poems and had even started to write a book. Sometimes Elizabeth wrote in the English language and sometimes in French. Everyone called her a "prodigy"—a child with very special talents.

Elizabeth had 11 brothers and sisters and grew up in a beautiful country house

Elizabeth Barrett Browning, a child prodigy who later got sick, became a famous poet. *(Wide World Photos)*

in a place called Hope End in England. She was a very happy girl and loved to climb trees and ride her pony. Elizabeth's grandmother was often upset because the little girl was a tomboy and would rather go fishing than sew. Even though she was small in size, Elizabeth had lots of energy and was usually the leader when the children played games.

Reading and writing were her favorite hobbies. She always wrote special poems for family birthday parties and for holidays, and all of her writing was filled with imagination and deep feelings. Elizabeth was so confident that one day she would be a well-known writer that she wrote the story of her life when she was 14!

A terrible accident happened to Elizabeth when she was 15. As she was mounting her pony, the heavy saddle slipped and fell on top of her. Elizabeth's spine was badly hurt and she had to stay in bed for a few months. It was the first of many times that she would have to rest in bed to get well.

After the accident she was not a very strong girl and often caught bad colds. At times she coughed so hard that she spit blood, and some doctors guessed she had tuberculosis, a disease of the lungs, but none of them were sure of that diagnosis. Elizabeth spent many long months— even years—in bed. But she tried not to be sad and depressed and spent all of her time writing poetry. Elizabeth's father always worried about her health and protected her too much. When she was sick, Elizabeth hardly ever left her bed and was allowed very few visitors. She was quite famous but very lonely at the age of 39 when she met Robert Browning.

Robert Browning was a handsome and very popular man. He was also a well-known poet and a big fan of Elizabeth's. His first letter to her began, "I love your verses with all my heart, Miss Barrett." He went on to say, "I do, as I say, love these books with all my heart—and I love you too." For many weeks they wrote letters to each other. Finally they met. Robert knew immediately that he wanted to spend the rest of his life with Elizabeth, and she was so excited that she could not sleep well for many nights. After little more than a year, they decided to get married. Because Elizabeth was afraid to tell her father, they ran away and were wed in secret.

Elizabeth and Robert spent 15 happy years together, and for a while her health even improved. Many books have been written about the great love they had for each other. Elizabeth died—smiling—in Robert's arms when she was 55.

Helper of the Blind

Louis Braille
Born: January 4, 1809
Died: January 16, 1852

He became blind when he was 3.

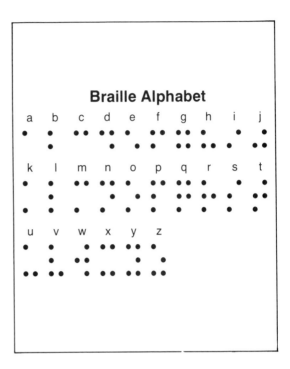

Braille Alphabet

The Braille family lived in a village near Paris, France. There were 4 children, and Louis—a handsome child with big blue eyes and curly blond hair—was the youngest. The boy was very smart, and his father hoped he would grow up to be a teacher. But then a terrible accident happened.

Louis's father was a saddle and harness maker, and his children often played in his shop. When Louis was 3, he disobeyed his father and picked up an awl (a pointed tool used to make holes in leather) to use on a scrap piece of leather. The leather was tough, and Louis pounded harder and harder to make the holes. All at once, the awl accidentally went into his left eye. The little boy screamed with pain as he was rushed to the doctor. Soon an infection started in his injured eye, then spread to the other eye. For 2 weeks Louis stayed in a very dark room with bandages wrapped around his eyes. Finally the bandages were removed and the doctor asked Louis what he could see. In a frightened voice, Louis answered, "Nothing." He was totally blind.

Louis's father made him a cane, and the little boy explored his home. He learned where everything was and how it felt. When he was old enough, Louis went to school and tried to memorize everything the teacher said. The future did not

look good for him. In those days blind people either became beggars in the city streets or ended up in homes for the poor. Luckily, however, the village priest heard of a school where blind children could learn skills. Even more surprising, they could learn to read!

When Louis was 10, he entered the National Institute for Blind Youth in Paris, where the children learned to read by a system called "embossing." Letters of the alphabet were pressed into thick, heavy paper, and this left raised outlines on the other side of the paper. Students would then feel the outlines with their fingers and could read—letter by letter. But the letters had to be big and sometimes a book page had only 2 sentences on it. Each book had to be divided into as many as 20 parts, and each part weighed 20 pounds.

One day a retired army captain named Charles Barbier came to the school. Barbier had invented a secret code—dots and dashes embossed into paper—that was used in time of war. He hoped that it would help blind people to read, but it turned out to be too confusing. When Louis was 12, he started to improve upon Barbier's system. He used only dots, pressed into paper, that represented the letters of the alphabet. By the time he was 15, Louis's new system of raised dots was finished. It was simple—and it worked.

It took many years for the French government to accept the Braille system. When Louis Braille died, he had no idea how many people he would help. On the door of the house where he was born are these words: "He opened the doors of knowledge to all those who cannot see."

Founder of the American Red Cross

Clara Barton
Born: December 25, 1821
Died: April 12, 1912

She wanted to be a soldier.

Clara Barton never had any dolls or toys when she was a child. Her mother was very strict and thought that toys were a waste of time. Luckily, Clara lived on a farm near North Oxford, Massachusetts, and had a lot of pet animals. Her favorite was a dog named Button. At age 5 she learned to ride a horse—without a saddle. She had 4 older brothers and sisters.

Clara loved to play military games with her father, who was once an army officer under "Mad Anthony" Wayne, a general

in the Revolutionary War. Their most exciting game was called "Battle." One army was represented by yellow grains of corn, the other army by red grains of corn. Little Clara became expert at the game and often told her mother that she wanted to be a soldier and go to war when she grew up.

When Clara was 11, her brother David fell from the barn roof and was seriously injured. For the next 2 years Clara took care of her brother, day and night. Sometimes the task was unpleasant. In those days people wrongly believed that blood-sucking worms, called leeches, could cure sick people. The worms were put over big blood vessels to drink the patient's blood. Clara was sick at the sight of blood, but every day she put the leeches on David.

She was average-looking and had thick brown hair and brown eyes. In school Clara was very bashful, but she did get good grades. When she was 15, Clara met

Clara Barton, bashful as a child, became a nurse during the Civil War and later founded the American Red Cross.

an Englishman named Mr. Fowler. Mr. Fowler told people what they were really like by looking at the bumps on their heads, a practice called phrenology. He told Clara that she would make a good schoolteacher. Shortly afterward, Clara began to teach school, and remained a teacher for the next 18 years. After that, she worked for the government in Washington, D.C. The job was a good one and it paid a decent wage. Not many women had good jobs at this time, and some of the men at Clara's job resented her. Behind her back, they called her a "pest in petticoats."

She did not become a nurse until she was almost 40 years old. During the Civil War, Clara became a heroine as she cared for the sick and wounded from the North and the South. The soldiers called her the "Angel of the Battlefield." She was slim and only 5 feet tall, but she was not afraid to drive a supply wagon through gunfire to the front lines.

After the war, Clara went to Europe to take a rest, and while she was there she learned of a group called the Red Cross. Many different countries belonged to this group, and each pledged to care for wounded soldiers in time of war. Clara wanted her own country to join, so she went home and organized the Red Cross in the United States. It not only provided service in time of war but also gave help to Americans during floods, fires, and other national disasters.

Clara Barton lived to be 91 years old. We know much about her life because she kept diaries for over 60 years.

U.S. President

Theodore Roosevelt
Born: October 27, 1858
Died: January 6, 1919

He rebuilt his body.

Theodore Roosevelt was the twenty-sixth president of the United States. In addition, he was a naturalist, explorer, rancher, soldier, and boxer. Everything he did required courage and physical strength.

As a boy, however, Theodore was a weakling. He suffered from severe attacks of asthma, a sickness that makes breathing difficult. Often he could not fall asleep because he was gasping for breath, and on many nights he went to sleep sitting up in order to breathe better. The illness caused him to become very thin and frail.

One day, while riding on a stagecoach, Theodore realized how helpless he was. The only other passengers on the stagecoach were 2 boys, both about 14 years old, the same age as he was. The boys pushed him around and made fun of him. Although he did not get hurt, Theodore was embarrassed, and told his father what had happened. Together they planned to change his weak body into a strong, healthy one.

To begin with, Theodore learned to box. His parents set up a gym for him in their house and hired an ex-prizefighter to train their son. At first, Theodore was slow and awkward, but he worked hard and improved quickly, and his body became sturdy and muscular. Other sports began to interest him, and soon Theodore was spending a lot of time outdoors. He went hiking, hunting, and horseback riding. At about the same time, he got his first pair of glasses. Until then, he had often stumbled over objects but had not known that his eyesight was bad. He later recalled, "I had no idea how beautiful the world was until I got those spectacles."

Theodore entered Harvard University

Theodore Roosevelt, sick as a child, decided at 14 to conquer his ills. *(National Park Service)*

As a "Rough Rider" Roosevelt became a national hero. *(National Park Service)*

and graduated twenty-first in a class of 158. He went on to hold many different jobs, but people really began to notice him during the Spanish-American War. In that conflict he was a colonel in charge of the "Rough Riders." His victorious

charge up San Juan Hill in Cuba made him a national hero.

Even after he was elected president of the United States, Roosevelt kept his body in shape. He even boxed in the White House. Once, his opponent landed a hard blow to his left eye, and Roosevelt became blind in that eye because of the accident.

Roosevelt loved to go hunting. He once cornered a bear but would not shoot it because it was so small. Instead, he ordered that the bear be set free. Newspaper reporters covered the story and named the cub "teddy bear," after the president. It was the first time the term was used, and after that, teddy bears became a national fad.

Even as he grew older, Roosevelt remained active. When he left office, he went big-game hunting in Africa. Another trip took him to South America, where he explored areas that no one else had ever seen. Everyone admired his stamina. When Roosevelt died in his sleep at the age of 60, his son sent a telegram to the other relatives. The message said, "The Lion is dead."

Magician

Harry Houdini
Born: April 6, 1874
Died: October 31, 1926

He could pick locks when he was 12.

His real name was Ehrich Weiss and his parents came to Appleton, Wisconsin, from Budapest, Hungary. When he was 6, Ehrich performed his first trick by making a dried pea suddenly appear in a cup. Then he learned how to make a quarter disappear from his hand—and then reappear.

Ehrich got his first job, with a local circus, when he was 9. He did a simple trapeze act and called himself "Ehrich, the Prince of the Air." Soon he was doing rope escape tricks. Members of the audience were invited to tie him up, making as many knots as they wanted. Then Ehrich would quickly work his way free from the large tangle of ropes. The crowd was amazed at how easily he escaped.

Ehrich's family was poor and he had to earn money to help support them. When he was 12, he got a job with a locksmith, and within a short time he could pick any lock given to him. He would secretly break into his mother's cupboard where the cakes and cookies were locked, and relock it after eating some of the delicious pastries. Mrs. Weiss was completely puzzled, since she was the only one with a key to the cupboard.

Harry Houdini loved magic tricks as a kid, and he became the greatest escape artist of all time. *(Wide World Photos)*

When his family moved to New York City, Ehrich became a tie cutter. He was 14 years old and spent all of his spare time reading magic books and practicing new tricks. One day he read a book about a fabulous French magician named Robert Houdin and was impressed by Houdin's exciting life. It was then that

Ehrich added an *i* to the name Houdin and began to call himself "Houdini."

He was the "Escape King." In his lifetime Houdini escaped from many places, including bank safes, iron boxes, and straitjackets. He even escaped from a coffin that was buried 6 feet under the ground. With his hands tied or handcuffed, he sometimes jumped from a bridge into the ocean. But the "Chinese Water Torture" was probably his most famous escape act. He was locked—upside down—in a tank, which was then filled with water. He always got out—wet and gasping for air, but safe.

Much of Houdini's success was due to his incredible physical strength. He once said that every one of his muscles was "a worker," and he used his toes as if they were his fingers. He never smoked or drank alcohol.

When Houdini was 52, a college student asked him if he could punch him to see how strong the magician really was. Houdini agreed and the student hit him three times in the stomach. Days later Houdini died—on Halloween night—of a ruptured appendix.

Painter

Pablo Picasso
Born: October 25, 1881
Died: April 8, 1973

He could draw before he could talk.

His full name was Pablo Diego José Francisco de Paula Juan Nepomuceno Cipriano de la Santissima Trinidad. He

Picasso disliked school and spent most of his time drawing. He became a world-famous artist. *(Wide World Photos)*

painted under his mother's name, Picasso. Born in Malaga, Spain, Picasso became one of the greatest artists of the twentieth century.

Picasso's mother claimed that his first words were "piz, piz"—short for *lapiz*, the Spanish word for pencil. Relatives said that Picasso was able to draw pictures long before he could talk. As a child, he was happy to work alone, for hours at a time, with his paper and pencils. Picasso's father, Don José, a painter, was delighted that his little boy was so talented.

Getting young Pablo to go to school was a real problem. He thought school was a waste of time and hated it. He would often refuse to go to school unless he could take along one of his father's pigeons. (His father painted many pictures with pigeons and owned some that he used as models.) In class, Picasso was allowed to pick up the lid of his desk and put the pigeon behind it.

The boy spent most of his time drawing instead of studying. When he was only 8 years old, Picasso completed his first oil painting, a picture portraying a bullfight. It was beautiful and full of many colors. Even after he became famous, Picasso never sold that first painting.

Picasso sometimes did a little work on his father's paintings. Don José would paint pictures of pigeons and leave out the feet, then ask his son to paint them in. To make sure Pablo did the job just right, his father would cut off the feet of a dead pigeon and pin them to a board in the proper position. Picasso would then copy every detail of the feet until his father approved of the work.

When Picasso was 14, his family moved to the big city of Barcelona, where the boy hoped to attend the School of Fine Arts. To get into the school each student had to do a very special painting as a test, to be completed in one month. Picasso finished the picture and passed the exam in *one day*. He later said, "I looked at it for a long time and thought whether there was anything I could add to it. But I could see nothing, absolutely nothing."

Picasso lived a long and full life. Museums around the world display his works. In addition to paintings, Picasso created many drawings, sculptures (figures usually made from stone, clay, or metal) and other kinds of art. Some of his works sold for as much as a million dollars. When he died at 92, Picasso was very rich, with more than $240 million.

U.S. Army Officer

George Smith Patton, Jr.
Born: November 11, 1885
Died: December 21, 1945

As a kid, he was a "private."

George Patton's fellow soldiers called him "Iron Pants," "Gorgeous Georgie," and "Old Blood and Guts." Those who served under him both feared and respected the man who never wanted to be anything but a soldier.

George grew up on a big ranch near Pasadena, California. As a young boy, he had 2 horses that he loved to ride fast across the open land. Fishing was also a favorite sport and George's father often took him fishing in the Pacific Ocean. George even had his own sailboat, called "The Elaine."

He was born into a family of military men. One of his grandfathers was a colonel in the Civil War and died in battle. The other grandfather was a captain in the Army, and George's father studied at the Virginia Military Institute. Dressed up in blue coats with brass buttons,

In a childhood game of soldiers, Patton was outranked by his sister. *(Wide World Photos)*

George and his sister Nita often played "soldier." As their father left for work in the morning, the children would stand together and give him a big salute. George always wanted to be a private, and his sister was the major. He was too young to know that major was a much more important rank! When he got his first sword, George ran outside and attacked a cactus, but he was careless and got stuck all over with the sharp prickles of the plant.

In school, George was a pretty good student. History was his best subject; he was always amazed by the clever battle plans of great warriors like Alexander the Great. But George did have one big problem in school: He could not spell. Some of the words he misspelled were: climbing (he spelled it "climeing"), always ("alwaies"), and war ("ware").

Like his father, George went to the Virginia Military Institute. Then he went to West Point. When he wanted to marry his teenage love, Beatrice Banning Ayer, he had to explain to her father why he wanted to be a soldier. George sat down and wrote Mr. Ayer a letter. In it he said: "Why I want to be a soldier? I only feel it inside. It is as natural for me to be a soldier as it is to breathe and would be as hard to give up all thought of it as it would be to stop breathing."

From that time until he died, Patton was never anything but a soldier. But he did do a few things that surprised many people. In 1912, when he was 27, he competed in the Olympic Games in Sweden. Entered in the pentathlon (a contest with 5 different events), he came in fifth. Also, Patton wrote poetry all of his life. Some of his poems were "Fear," "A Soldier's Burial," and "Marching in Mexico."

George Patton became a hero in World War Two. When fighting the enemy, his motto was "Grab 'em by the nose and kick 'em in the tail." Many people did not like him because he bragged a lot and had a terrible temper, but everyone admired his courage. He received many medals for bravery, and at the end of the war he was a 4-star general.

Actor Comedian

Charlie Chaplin
Born: April 16, 1889
Died: December 25, 1977

"The little tramp" became a knight.

Charlie Chaplin was born in a slum in London, England. His mother was a

Charlie Chaplin, who started acting when he was 5, starred with Paulette Goddard in *Modern Times*. *(Wide World Photos)*

singer and dancer, and his father was a singer and comedian. However, the Chaplins separated when Charlie was only 2 years old because Charlie's father was an alcoholic and was often violent.

Charlie first appeared on stage at the age of 5. His mother was singing at a theater when, all of a sudden, she lost her voice. The audience began to laugh at her, and then they got angry. The manager of the theater quickly pushed little Charlie, who was standing nearby, onto the stage, and the boy began to sing in a loud, clear voice. The audience liked him so much that they threw money at him. In the middle of the song, Charlie stopped to pick up the coins and shouted, "Wait 'til I get it all and I'll sing a lot." The crowd laughed and applauded and begged for more.

Mrs. Chaplin sold the family's belongings in order to get money. When there was nothing left to sell, she and her 2 sons had to go to the poorhouse. Charlie was only 7 and his older brother, Sydney, was 11. Shortly afterwards, the boys were taken away to an orphanage.

Life became very difficult for the Chaplin family. The boys were in and out of orphanages, they usually had little to eat, and their clothes were faded and torn. At one point they moved in with their father, who was living with a woman who was an alcoholic. Sometimes the boys were locked out of the house and had to sleep in the streets. Their father finally drank himself to death, and their mother went insane.

Together, Charlie and Sydney set out to become actors. They worked hard at many small acting jobs, and Charlie became a top comedian with a pantomime group that came to the United States to perform. Then he began to act in American movies. After only a year he was a big success as a comedian, making $10,000 a week. His trademark was his funny costume—baggy pants, big shoes, a derby, and a coat that was too tight. Charlie also had a fake mustache and carried a cane. People everywhere called him "the little tramp."

For many years Charlie wrote his own movies in addition to acting in them. Some Americans did not like Chaplin's later movies because they told his opinions on what was good and bad about government. They called him a "traitor." When Chaplin was 63, he took his family out of the country for a vacation. When he wanted to come back, the United States government said no.

Chaplin did not return to the United States for 20 years. He came back to accept an Academy Award—the highest honor in the movie business. When he walked onto the stage in Los Angeles, the audience jumped to its feet and clapped for many long minutes. Chaplin almost cried as he was handed the award. Three years later the Queen of England knighted him and he became "Sir" Charles

Chaplin. It was quite a moment for a man who once wore rags and lived in a slum.

Baseball Player

George Herman ("Babe") Ruth
Born: February 6, 1895
Died: August 17, 1948

He grew up in a reform school.

As a boy, Babe Ruth was always in trouble, and his neighbors thought he was headed for a life of crime. Even Babe Ruth agreed. When he grew up, someone asked him about his childhood. Babe said, "I was a bum when I was a kid."

He was born in a small house in Baltimore, Maryland. Both of his parents were German. His father was a bartender in a saloon and was always busy. His mother also worked in the saloon. He had one younger sister. Nobody paid much attention to him.

Babe chewed tobacco and drank whiskey. He roamed the streets late at night and hung around pool halls. He was even caught stealing. Before Babe turned 8, his parents put him in St. Mary's Industrial School for Boys. It was partly a reform school and partly an orphanage, and Babe stayed there until he was 20.

St. Mary's had 800 boys 7 to 21 years of age. The boys got up at 6:00 in the morning and went to bed at 8:00 at night. All of the boys learned special skills, and Babe spent most of each day in the classroom. He was taught to make cabinets and learned how to roll cigars. He also worked in the tailor shop, where he put collars on shirts and was paid 6¢ a shirt.

Baseball was the favorite sport at St. Mary's, and Babe was usually the catcher. Brother Matthias, a religious teacher at the school, was one of the men

Babe Ruth, a troubled boy, became baseball's home-run king. *(Wide World Photos)*

walked out on the field. People cheered the teenager with the pushed-in nose, wide mouth, and crewcut.

When Babe left the school to try to make a living as a baseball player, he first played for a team in Baltimore. The other players called him Babe because he looked so young, and the nickname remained with him for the rest of his life. The second team he played for—this time both as a pitcher and an outfielder—was the Boston Red Sox. Then came the New York Yankees. With the Yankees, Babe became famous around the world.

Babe Ruth was the home-run king; no other baseball player had ever hit so many homers. Sports fans jammed into baseball stadiums to see Babe play and screamed with joy when he took a big, powerful swing at the baseball. He hit the ball very hard and very far. The game became much more exciting. When he retired, he had been at bat 8,399 times and had hit 714 home runs. He was the greatest baseball player who ever lived. People often asked Babe how he hit so many home runs. He simply said, "I just keep swinging."

Prime Minister of Israel

Golda Meir
Born: May 3, 1898
Died: December 8, 1978

> *Next to her picture in*
> *her high school yearbook:*

> *Those about her*
> *From her shall read the perfect*
> *Ways of honor.*

In a book about her life, Golda Meir wrote that what she remembered most about her childhood was "poverty, cold, hunger, and fear." Her parents were

in charge of baseball. He was the first to notice Babe's talent, and suggested that the boy become a pitcher. By the time he was 16, Babe was the school's star baseball player. There was much excitement when the long-legged Babe Ruth

Golda Meir worked on a kibbutz (a cooperative farm) in pre-state Israel. *(Consulate General of Israel, New York)*

Jewish and lived in Kiev, Russia, where Jews were second-class citizens. Her father, a carpenter, had a hard time finding work.

Sometimes the Cossacks—government soldiers on horses—would come thundering through the streets of Russian towns, burning Jewish homes and killing Jewish people. Golda was only 4 when her father tried to explain why this happened. He said that most people in Russia were poor, had miserable lives, and needed someone to blame for their unhappiness. The Jewish people were blamed, mostly because they were different. They had a different religion, different customs, even a different language.

Golda's father wanted a better life for his wife and 3 daughters, so he left Rus-

sia for America and settled in Milwaukee, Wisconsin, leaving his family behind until he could afford to send for them. They moved to another town, called Pinsk, where Golda became even more aware of how badly the Jewish people were treated. One day she and a girl friend were playing in the yard when a man walked up to them and hit their heads together. He said, "That's what we'll do with all the Jews. And then we'll be through with them." Golda never forgot that day.

Finally, after 3 years, Golda's father sent for his family. In Milwaukee, Golda learned English quickly and got good grades in school. When she was in the fourth grade, she raised money to buy textbooks for poor children. It was her own idea, and everyone was impressed by her leadership and confidence. Later in her life she would raise a great deal of money for a very important reason—to help the Jews make a new home for themselves in a new land.

Golda was very pretty and received much attention from many young men. Her mother was very upset when she announced that she wanted to become a schoolteacher, for at that time the law in Wisconsin did not allow schoolteachers to get married. There was a big argument and Golda ran away from home to live with one of her sisters, who had moved to Denver, Colorado. After a year, Golda returned to Milwaukee, where she did become a schoolteacher.

As she grew older, Golda became active in groups that wanted to form a new country where Jewish people could live in peace, without fear. For many years she worked hard to get money for that country, to be called Israel. After Golda got married, she and her husband moved to the land that years later did become the state of Israel. When she was 70, Golda was chosen to lead the country as prime minister—the highest job in the government.

"Public Enemy Number One"

John Dillinger
Born: June 28, 1903
Died: July 22, 1934

As a kid, he led "The Dirty Dozen."

John Dillinger grew up to be one of the most famous bank robbers of all time. He was so hard to catch that the FBI called him "Public Enemy Number One." There was a $25,000 reward for anyone who helped to capture him.

He was born in Indianapolis, Indiana, where his father owned a grocery store. Mr. Dillinger was very strict and punished John when he did anything wrong. John's mother died when he was only 3 years old. He was brought up by his father and older sister, Audrey. Cuter than most of the kids in his neighborhood, he had big blue eyes and light brown hair.

In school John was pretty quiet. If his report card was bad, he didn't give it to his father. Instead, he signed it himself and told Mr. Dillinger that he had lost it. Most of his teachers said that John didn't cause much trouble. He was very good in sports, especially baseball. His Sunday school teacher spoke well of him. "He always tipped his hat to me," she said.

When he was in the sixth grade, John was the leader of a neighborhood gang called "The Dirty Dozen." Sometimes the gang would steal coal from the Pennsyl-

John Dillinger was shot by FBI agents a few months after this picture was taken. *(Wide World Photos)*

vania Railroad yards, then sell it and split the money. But one night they got caught. All the boys were scared to death when they had to go to court—except John. He stood before the judge with his hat on, and he was chewing gum. The judge told him to get rid of the chewing gum and take off his hat. John looked right at the judge and took the gum from his mouth. Then he smiled and stuck it right on the tip of his hat. The judge said to him, "Your mind is crippled."

When John was 12, the Dillingers moved to a farm. John hated the farm and his life began to change for the worse. Sometimes he would stay out all night. He and his father had terrible fights. After a few years he dropped out of school. He still did a little reading, but only liked stories about the Wild West. The outlaw Jesse James was his hero.

When he was 20, John went to jail for robbery. When he got out, he formed a gang that robbed banks in 5 states. Once John got caught and was put in an "escape-proof" jail. He carved a gun out of wood and painted it with shoe polish. The sheriff was too scared to see that it was a fake gun, and John easily escaped. He loved to tell this story of how he fooled the law.

Newspapers everywhere published stories about John Dillinger. It seemed that no one would ever catch up with him. But the FBI did. One night, as John was coming out of a movie theater, FBI agents were waiting for him. He tried to escape. The agents shot him to death.

Civil Rights Leader

Martin Luther King, Jr.
Born: January 15, 1929
Died: April 4, 1968

At 6 he learned the meaning of segregation.

Martin Luther King spent his life trying to get equal rights for black people. When Martin was a child in Atlanta, Georgia, black people had to sit at the back of the bus. White people and black people went to different schools. They sat in different parts of movie theaters and used separate public rest rooms. A black person could not use a water fountain if it was in a "for whites only" park. This kind of separation of black and white people is called "segregation."

Martin first learned about segregation when he was 6. Two of his best friends were white boys, and Martin played with them every day. When the 3 friends became old enough to start school, the white boys went to a school for white children and Martin went to a school for blacks. At that time, the mother of the white boys told Martin that he should not come around anymore because he was a "Negro." Martin began to cry and ran home to ask his mother what that meant. She told him the history of the Negro—about slavery and the Civil War. Then she told him about the problems he would face. But she added, "You must not think that you are not as good as everyone else."

In spite of the problems of black people in America, Martin had a very happy childhood. His father was a Baptist minister and his mother was a schoolteacher. His parents were warm, loving people and spent much time with their 3 children. They lived in a 12-room house in a very nice neighborhood. They were not poor. As he got older, Martin learned that most black people were not as fortunate as he was.

In high school Martin did very well. He

The late Rev. Martin Luther King, Jr., makes a speech at a civil rights rally. He inspired many with his boyhood dream of an America free of racial prejudice. *(Doug Harris, Design Photographers International, Inc.)*

was active in sports and was so smart that he skipped 2 grades. Like his father, he was very good at expressing himself, and his friends would sometimes tease him because he used big words. Martin graduated from high school at the age of 15 and went on to college.

He then became a minister and began the long struggle to get laws passed to make life better for black people in America. He wanted his people to have the right to vote, the right to good jobs, and the right to a good education. And he fought to end segregation of public places like buses, libraries, and elevators.

King believed that changes should come about in a peaceful way, and organized many peaceful marches, demonstrations, and sit-ins. He also traveled around the country to speak out about black problems. He accomplished much before he was killed in 1968.

Many people will always remember his famous "I have a dream" speech. In it he said, "I have a dream that my four little children will one day live in a nation where they will not be judged by the color of their skin but by the content of their character."

Superpeople with their superpowers can seem, in our mind's eye, to leap from the comic pages. They are fun to read about, but are only fiction!

Comic Book Superpeople and Their Superpowers

Batman

Real name: Bruce Wayne.

Secret of superpowers: He trained himself to be superpowerful and supersmart. When his father and mother were killed by a crook, he made a vow to spend his life fighting crime.

Friends: Robin, the Boy Wonder (really Dick Grayson, circus high-flyer). Batwoman, who also is in the circus. Batgirl, Batwoman's niece. Bat-Hound, a dog. Bat-Mite, a creature from another dimension.

Some enemies: The Joker (has green hair). The fat Penguin, with his jet umbrella. Riddler, who leaves clues about his crimes in riddles. Bizarro. Swamp Thing. Felix Faust, sorcerer.

Some other facts: He lives in Wayne Mansion in Gotham City. In the cellar is a Batcave. He owns a Batmobile and a Batplane. He lassos criminals with his Batarang.

Captain Marvel

Real name: Billy Batson, orphan boy, or Captain Mar-vell from outer space.

Secret of superpowers: At the far end of a subway ride, he found the Wizard Shazam. The Wizard was 3,000 years old. By saying "Shazam," the Wizard said, Billy could become the "World's Mightiest Mortal." He would have:

    *S*olomon's wisdom
    *H*ercules' strength
    *A*tlas's stamina
    *Z*eus's power
    *A*chilles' courage
    *M*ercury's speed

Friends: Mary Marvel, Billy Batson's twin (real name Mary Bromfield). Cap-

tain Marvel Junior, really Freddy Freeman, crippled newsboy.
Enemies: Mr. Mind, evil genius worm. Dr. Sivana, mad scientist. Sivana Junior and Georgia Sivana, his children.

Flash

Real name: Barry Allen, scientist.
Secret of superpowers: When he was hit by a lightning bolt, he became the fastest man on earth. He named himself Flash after an old comic book hero, Flash Gordon. Over a short distance, he is faster than Superman.
Enemies: The Turtle Man.

Green Lantern

Real name: Hal Jordan, test pilot.
Secret of superpowers: A green lantern battery. The battery charges a power ring for 24 hours. The battery was given to Hal Jordan by a red-skinned creature from outer space. The Green Lantern now works for the Guardians of the Universe, who live in Oa, in outer space. They have blue skins and bald heads. Sector 2814 is his territory in space.
Friends: Other members of the Elite Green Lantern Corps. Pieface, his mechanic. Carol Ferris, his girl friend and boss.
Enemy: Sinestro.
Weak spot: His ring doesn't work against yellow.

Incredible Hulk

Real name: Dr. Robert Bruce Banner, scientist.
Secret of superpowers: He was caught in a nuclear explosion, and gamma radiation changed him. When things are calm, he is Bruce Banner. When he gets upset, he becomes the Hulk. The Hulk has green skin, weighs 1,000 pounds, is 7 feet tall. His strength is incredible.
Friends: Fred Sloan, writer. Betty Ross, girl friend. Trish Star, who works for Sloan and has one arm.
Enemies: Tyrannus, who turns into flame. Arizen Turk, who lives in Tunnelworld. Omegatron. Anything Man.

Popeye

Real name: Popeye, a sailor.
Secret of superpowers: When Popeye eats canned spinach, he becomes superpowerful. His muscles swell, and he can lick anyone.
Friends: Olive Oyl, his girl friend. J. Wellington Wimpy, who loves hamburgers.
Enemies: Bluto
Statue: A statue of Popeye stands in Crystal City, Texas. It was put there by spinach farmers. However, they would rather people ate fresh spinach, not spinach from a can.

Sabraman

Real name: Daniel Bar-On, Israeli. Works for superagency in Israel.
Secret of superpowers: He can shoot radioactive rays from his eyes. He is so fast he can cross oceans in a split second. His body cannot be attacked because he can surround himself with a magnetic field. Sabraman's parents were killed by the Nazis in World War Two. The Sabra part of his name comes from the Israeli word sabra, meaning a native Israeli. It also is the fruit of a cactus—prickly on the outside, sweet on the inside.
Writer: Sabraman was created by Uri Fink when he was 15. He lives in Tel Aviv, Israel.

Siopawman

Secret of superpowers: Bullets and blows don't hurt him. He was sent to Earth from the planet Siopaw. He was not liked there because of his looks. He has a big nose, fat body, and bald head. He wears an *S* on his chest, and his cape covers a patch on his shorts.

Enemies: Jello-man, who quivers and shakes. Vegetable creatures. Creatures from outer space. Ordinary crooks.

Where you can read about him: This comic character is from the Philippines. To get a copy of a Siopawman comic book, you'll probably have to go there.

Spiderman

Real name: Peter Parker, student at Empire State University and newspaper reporter.

Secret of superpowers: He was bitten by a radioactive spider, which gave him the power to climb walls and act as a human spider. His web-shooters spin rope lines. He can grow new arms.

Friends: Aunt May.

Enemies: Morbius, vampire-ghoul, really a scientist. Black Cat. Mysterio. Lizard. Swarm of killer bees.

Superman

Real name: Kal-el of planet Krypton. Clark Kent, on Earth.

Secret of superpowers: Kal-el was born on the planet Krypton, which was due to explode. His parents sent him into space to save his life. On earth he was adopted by Jonathan and Martha Kent, who called him Clark. When he grew up he became a reporter in the city of Metropolis. However, he also has another identity—Superman. After he changes into his costume in a phone booth, he can show his powers. He can fly faster than a speeding bullet or the speed of light. He can leap over tall buildings or to the edge of the universe. He has superhearing. His X-ray vision allows him to see through walls. His breath is supercold. He can lift a railroad train. These powers come from Earth's sun. As Superman, he fights for truth and justice. When people see him blasting through the sky, they say, "It's a bird. It's a plane. It's . . . Superman!"

Friends: Jimmy Olsen, newsboy. Lois Lane, his girl friend. Supergirl, his cousin from Krypton, also called Linda Danvers. Linda Danvers now works in the New Athens Experimental School in Florida.

Enemies: Mr. Mxyzlptlk, who can be sent to another dimension if you say his name backwards. Toyman. Lex Luthor, bald mad scientist. Green computer person Braniac.

Weak spot: Can be hurt by kryptonite, particularly if it's green.

NOTE: In the real city of Metropolis, Illinois, there is a Superman Square. On a water tower is a 19-foot picture of Superman.

Wonder Woman

Other name: Diana Prince, who works for the U.S. government.

Secret of superpowers: She came from Paradise Island, where only superwomen called Amazons live. The Queen, Hippolyte, gave Wonder Woman her powers. (One story has it that Wonder Woman was a statue brought to life by Hippolyte.) At the age of 3, Wonder Woman could pull up a tree by the roots. At age 5, she could run as fast as a deer. Her bracelets keep her safe; bullets bounce off them. When she ropes someone with her golden lasso, that person must do as she says. There is a radio in her headband. Her belt has taken from her all wishes to do evil. Her robot plane is invisible and goes 3,000 miles an hour, and she can make it come to her by sending out thought waves. When Steve Trevor, a pilot, crashed on Paradise Island, Wonder Woman fell in love with him and brought him to the United States. If she had stayed on Paradise Island, she would have lived forever; in the United States, she won't. Steve Trevor works with her to fight crime.

Friends: Nubia, her black sister. Steve Trevor.

Enemies: Spies. Mars, god of war.

Her creator: Dr. William Marston, who created Wonder Woman, was a psychologist. He used the pen name Charles Moulton. He believed that women are powerful, smart creatures. Why not have a superheroine? Why should all superpeople be male? So he invented Wonder Woman.

Weak spot: If her bracelets are chained by a male, Wonder Woman can lose her powers.

Childhood Around the World

Some Facts and Figures

Number of children in the world: about 1½ billion.

Number of children aged 5 to 13 in the United States: about 37 million.

Number of children in the world who are poor and hungry: 250 million.

Number of children in the United States who are poor: 1 out of 5.

Number of children in the world who don't finish elementary school: more than a billion.

In Asia, 14 out of 1,000 children under 13 work for a living.

In South America, 6 out of 1,000 children under 13 work for a living.

In Europe and the United States, one out of 1,000 children works for a living.

Some Customs and Facts

Alaska. The Inuits, sometimes called Eskimos, think children need years to learn to behave. Inuit children are almost

A 5-year-old farm worker brings in a basket of fruit in Florida. *(Anne Sager, Photo-Researchers, Inc.)*

A refugee from Kampuchea carries water to his family in a camp in Thailand. *(UPI, Inc.)*

never punished, and their parents never hit them. Sometimes, if driven far enough, parents *do* punish their children—by making fun of them.

Mexico. The Huichols, Mexican Indians, teach their children to use a bow and arrow. The children dress in garments with fancy stitching and big hats. Among their favorite games are soccer and volleyball.

New Guinea. Native boys 10 to 13 years old undergo a test to enter the adult male group. They are made to sit by a fire with nothing to drink or eat. For nights, they are kept sleepless. Men dressed in leaves

sneak up and scare them, and stone axes are put to their throats. After they have proved they are brave, they are painted with red oil and feathers are put on their heads. They are then adults.

A favorite game in New Guinea is a card game like hearts. People play it sitting on the ground.

Kampuchea. The government of Kampuchea (the country's name used to be Cambodia) has been changed by force several times in the last few years, and this has affected the people living there. In 1979 a story in the *Los Angeles Times* told what happened to one 12-year-old boy, Lim Hua. When he was little, his life was peaceful. He rode his bicycle, went to school, visited the temple. His father made a good living as a baker. Then soldiers came and his family was sent into the jungle to work. He worked 10 hours a day and there was no school to go to. His father was killed. For 4 years, he and his family lived under a tree. Once he was so hungry he ate marigolds, and they made him sick. He and the rest of his family walked out of Kampuchea and entered Thailand in 1979. As refugees, they lived under a temple porch. Lim Hua saved plastic bags to put on the ground so that the family would be more comfortable sleeping. "It had been very dark in Cambodia," he said.

China. Because most women in China work, their children are taken care of in day care centers. These are free. So are the schools.

Children in China play tug-of-war games. However, they are taught to cooperate when they play, not try to win.

Movies in China cost 5¢ for students.

Disco dancing in public places is against the law in China. Children dance

A kite festival takes place in Japan in early May.
(Japan National Tourist Organization)

at home with the music going full blast, and their parents are annoyed by the noise. For that reason, many are trying to get public disco made legal.

Japan. Education is so important in Japan that many children work too hard at their studies. Others give up. One study found that 7 out of 10 high school kids were unhappy about school.

In early May in Japan, men fly kites to celebrate the birth of their first-born sons. They try to knock each other's kites out of the sky. In March, girls have a day, too. Their day features dolls.

India. In Sumdah, in the high mountains, children wear pants without seats until they are toilet-trained. Puppet masters and dentists set up shop in the street.

Zimbabwe. In 1978 there was fighting in Zimbabwe, an African country that used to be called Rhodesia. An essay context

called Rhodesia Through a Child's Eyes was held that year. Children wrote about their lives.

Sibanda Bakesela, 12, wrote about sitting around the campfire in the evenings. He and other people in his village live in mud huts with straw roofs. "Before we go to sleep," he wrote, "my grandfather and some boys sit at a bonfire. Then all my family sit around it, listening to stories told by my grandparents. Sometimes early in the morning, grandfather wakes all the little boys and tells them his life history as a little boy, and teaches them how to do woodwork."

Wild animals—zebras, impalas, kudus, and others—are common. Much of the land is still wild. S. Landy, age 12, wrote, ". . . there is still much wild beauty which has not yet been destroyed by man."

Timothy Sikwiye, 12, was frightened by the fighting. "I do not sleep in the night," he wrote. "There are many soldiers moving in the night. Many people were killed in the night. . . . Help me, please. I am afraid; where can I go?"

Kenya. In the African country of Kenya, the family is important. New babies ride strapped to their mothers' backs. When they cry, they are fed and held. By the age of 5, children are working. They take care of the animals or smaller children. A good deal of freedom is given to them.

In the villages, children don't have toys bought in stores; they make their own. The leafy tops of banana trees are cut off to make rafts on which to float down the river. Soccer balls can be made of palm leaves. Most of the village children have never seen electric lights or flushed a toilet.

Kenyan children want to go to school.

Charity Tayani, a ninth grader, said, "My family works hard to give me a chance, so I owe them everything. When I marry, if my family comes to my house, or anyone from my tribe, I will find them jobs. I am the lucky one."

Israel. All children in Israel have to go to school. Some children in Israel live on kibbutzim. A kibbutz is a community where people own all the property and machinery in common and share the work and food. All basic decisions are made by the membership democratically. Children on kibbutzim often live in Children's Houses and are taken care of by people who enjoy children. The family gets together for dinner and for a few hours at other times during the day, but at night the children from the kibbutz usually sleep in the Children's House away from their parents.

The Union of Soviet Socialist Republics. In Moscow, a big city, most children 2 to 6 years old are in nurseries because their mothers work. Grandmothers (*babushkas*) often pick up children at the nursery or at school.

Children talented in sports can go to special sports schools in the U.S.S.R.

West Germany. In West Germany, children have a say about which parent they will live with in divorce cases. Those under 14 are asked what they want, and their wishes taken into account when the judge makes his decision. Those who are 14 and older can choose which parent they want to live with.

Austria. In Vienna, an old Austrian city, many kids are still taught old-fashioned dances, like the waltz, at dancing school. Boys learn to greet a woman by kissing her hand.

Great Britain. In 1975 a Children's Act was passed in Great Britain. Under this law, children with problems are given free help. Now there are centers where children can go to get free help from lawyers.

Sweden. It is against the law for anyone to hit a child in Sweden. Parents can't even spank their kids. Children have an ombudsman (a special government official) who stands up for their rights. Anyone who has a problem can call the ombudsman. Usually the child is given the name of someone who can help. One woman who was an ombudsman said, "In every country, the child is the blossom of life."

There has been a plan to pass a law that would give children the right to divorce their parents. It has not become a law—yet.

Norway. Norway also has an ombudsman (a kind of impartial referee) for children. In Lapland, the reindeer herds go on long fall and spring journeys to get to the grass. The owners of the herds go along, and Lap children have time off from school to go also. It is important for young people to learn the routes the reindeer follow, because when they grow up they may be in charge. Many Lap families use snowmobiles to herd the reindeer.

Children on an Israeli kibbutz enjoy a musical moment. Does the donkey enjoy the music too?
(Consulate General of Israel, New York)

Some want to be trampoline champs. *(David S. Strickler, Freelance Photographer's Guild)*

Others prefer reading. *(Joe Craig, Freelance Photographer's Guild)*

Chapter 7
BODY AND MIND

Questions and Answers About Your Body

How fast does the air travel when you sneeze?
A hundred miles an hour.

What makes your knuckles crack?
Bubbles popping! There is a fluid around the joints of your finger bones. When you stretch your fingers, the pressure on the fluid changes, little bubbles form in the fluid, and they pop. Want to crack the same knuckles again? You have to wait about 15 minutes.

What determines the color of your skin?
Special cells in the skin make a substance called melanin, which determines the color of your skin. People with just a little melanin have light-colored skin; those with lots of melanin have dark-colored skin. This substance is also the cause of freckles.

How do you get "goose bumps"?
Each hair on your body grows in its own shaft, called a follicle. If you get cold or scared, the smooth muscles around the follicles contract. This gives you goose bumps and makes the hairs stand upright.

How long does an eyelash live?
About 150 days.

How did the saying "Beauty is only skin deep" get started?
Human skin is not very deep. Nowhere on the body is the skin more than 3/16 of an inch thick.

Why do some people have dimples?
Dimples are caused by muscles in your face. These muscles are unusual because they are attached to the skin; most muscles in your body are attached to bones. When some people smile, certain muscles make dimples.

Types of Fingerprints

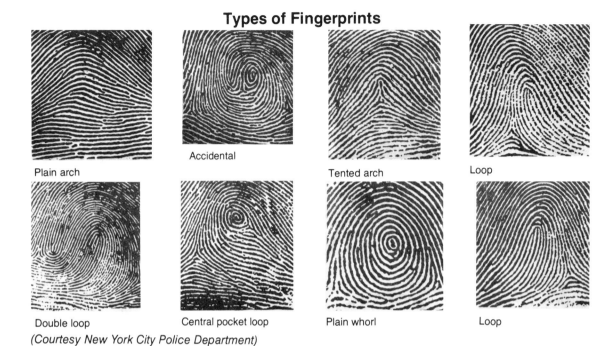

Plain arch

Accidental

Tented arch

Loop

Double loop

Central pocket loop

Plain whorl

Loop

(Courtesy New York City Police Department)

Why are fingerprints a good way to identify people?
The ridges of skin on the fingertips have lots of sweat pores, and that is why people easily leave fingerprints after they touch something. The FBI has over 169 million fingerprints on file. *None are exactly alike.* Here are the 8 basic kinds of fingerprints on file. *None are exactly alike.* There are 8 basic kinds of fingerprints. Use an ink pad to make your own fingerprint, and check the chart above to see what type you have.

like you?
It is almost impossible. The odds against this happening are one out of a number too big to write out. It is a 1 followed by 9,031 zeros! (This answer is not true of kids who are identical twins.)

How many bones do you have in your body?
A baby has 330 bones. An adult has only 206 bones. This is because many of the baby's bones have joined together by the time it grows up. Some people have an extra bone in the arch of their foot. Also, one out of every 20 people has an extra rib.

What is the largest bone in the body?
The largest bone in the body is the thigh bone. It measures about 20 inches in an adult who is 6 feet tall.

What is the "funny bone"?
This is a bone in your elbow. The term *funny bone* came from the real name of the bone, humerus. (Get the joke?) But nothing is funny when you hit the funny bone. A big nerve rests against this bone just beneath the skin, and you won't laugh if you hit that nerve against something hard. You might even cry.

How many cells do you have in your body?
Everything that is alive is made of cells.

They are so tiny that you need a microscope to see one. You started out as one cell. Today you are made up of 55 trillion cells!

When are people the healthiest?
People are healthiest between the ages of 5 and 15.

When do kids stop growing?
Boys achieve 98 percent of their height when they reach the age of 17¾. Girls reach 98 percent of their height by the time they are 16½.

Why is there wax in your ears?
In your ear are 4,000 special glands that make wax. The wax catches tiny insects and other things that don't belong in the ear.

What happens when you go "off balance"?
Deep inside the ear are 3 canals that are partly filled with liquid. These "semicircular canals" help you keep or lose your balance. When you move around, the liquid moves around and sends messages to the brain, telling it what you are doing. Then signals go from the brain to your muscles, telling your muscles to keep you steady. But if you spin around quickly, you might get dizzy and fall down be-

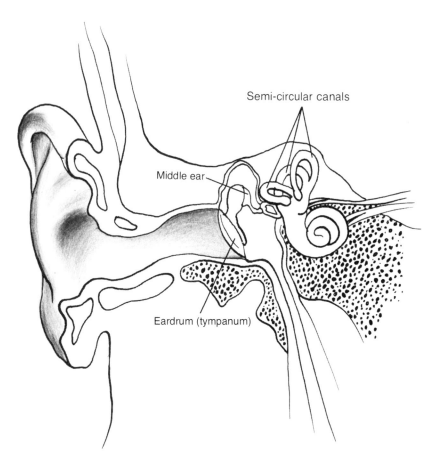

Semi-circular canals

Middle ear

Eardrum (tympanum)

In the inner ear are 3 canals filled with liquid that helps you keep your balance.

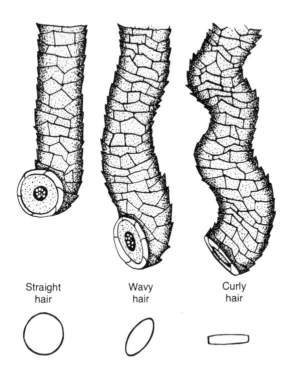

Straight   Wavy   Curly
hair   hair   hair

Whether your hair is straight, wavy, or curly depends on the shape of the shaft of the hair.

cause the fluids in the canals have been moving too fast. The brain gets more messages than it can handle, and you are thrown "off balance." But in a very short time you get back to normal.

Why can some people wiggle their ears?
Most people *cannot* wiggle their ears. Those who can are able to use muscles that are attached to their outer ears. Everybody has these muscles but not everyone is able to use them. Can you?

How long does it take to blink your eyes?
About ¾ of a second.

What causes color-blindness?
The inner lining of the eyeball, called the retina, contains many tiny rods and cones. The rods allow you to see black

and white; the cones let you see colors. In some people the cones don't work well, and these people are color-blind. A color-blind person usually has trouble with reds and greens.

When is your eye still?
Never. The eye is always moving, even when you are staring at something. The tiny muscles in the eye move about 100,000 times a day to let you see. For your leg muscles to get the same amount of exercise, you would have to walk 50 miles.

Are kids today taller or shorter than kids who lived 100 years ago?
They are taller by about 6 inches.

How many sounds can you hear?
You can hear between 350,000 and 400,000 different sounds.

How fast does your hair grow?
Hair on your head grows about one-hundredth of an inch a day. As you get older, it grows a little slower. You have about 100,000 hairs on your head, and each one lives from 2 to 4 years. During an average lifetime the hair grows 25 feet!

Why do some people have straight hair and others have wavy or curly hair?
It all depends on the shape of the hair follicle, the shaft in which each hair grows. People with round follicles have straight hair. Others have oval follicles; they have wavy hair. Slit-shaped follicles make curly hair.

What is the heaviest organ in the body?
The liver. It weighs 3½ pounds in an adult, or about 5 times more than the heart.

How much air do the lungs use in one day?
About 12,500 quarts.

Why do people yawn?
In the lungs are millions of tiny air sacs

called alveoli. Changes in the alveoli cause you to yawn. When you are sleepy, you are not breathing deeply enough to get enough oxygen. The alveoli are not filled with air. So your brain sends out a message, telling you to take a long breath. That long breath is a yawn.

What is the hardest substance in the body?
If you guessed that it is the bones, you are wrong. The hardest substance is the enamel that coats your teeth. However, unlike other parts of the body, enamel cannot fix itself if it is damaged.

How fast do your fingernails grow?
About 1/25 of an inch a week. They grow faster on the hand you use the most. If you are right-handed, your right fingernails grow faster. If you are left-handed, the left fingernails grow faster.

How important is your thumb?
The thumb does 45 percent of all the work done by your hand.

How much blood does your heart pump?
In an adult there are 5 to 6 quarts of blood, which are constantly pumped back and forth by the heart. In one day the heart recycles 5,000 to 6,000 quarts of blood through 60,000 miles of blood vessels. It is an amazing feat since the heart is only about the size of a fist and doesn't even weigh one pound.

Why does your nose run when you cry?
When you cry, many of the tears fall on your cheeks, but some stay in the eye and then go into a tiny tube, or duct, that leads to the nose. The result is a drippy nose.

How much spit (saliva) does your mouth make every day?
About half a quart.

How do humans taste foods?
Every person has 9,000 "taste buds" on the tongue. These special cells tell you 4 kinds of taste: sweet, salt, sour, and bitter. The sweet buds are on the front of the tongue, and the sour buds are behind them. The bitter buds are at the back. Taste buds are also found on the roof of the mouth and at the back of the throat.

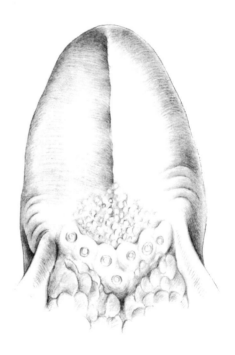

The tongue has over 9,000 taste buds on the top and bottom, along with glands to make saliva (spit).

Why does your stomach growl when you are hungry?
Your body changes the food you eat into substances it can use, and one of the most important of these is glucose, a kind of sugar that gives you energy. When your body doesn't get enough food, it cannot make all the glucose it needs. A large nerve, the vagus nerve, goes into action if

there is too little glucose. The nerve makes the stomach muscles pull in, and that makes you feel hungry. And what if there is air in your stomach when this happens? Then you hear a growl.

How big is the stomach?
The stomach grows to be 10 inches long. When empty, it looks like a flat balloon, but it can get pretty big when you eat. An adult stomach can hold 2 quarts of food.

How many different smells can humans smell?
The average person knows 4,000 different smells. Some people with a very special sense of smell know 10,000 different scents! People who test perfumes have this special talent.

How long can you live without water?
Only about 10 days, because 60 percent of your body is water.

How many muscles does it take to smile?
It takes 17 muscles to smile. Forty-three muscles are used when you frown.

How much work do your muscles do?
You have more than 600 muscles in your body, and they all do different amounts of work. But what if you could add up all the amounts? The work would equal picking up 24,000 pounds and putting it on a 4-foot-high shelf.

What's Puberty?

Going through "puberty" can be scary. Puberty is the time between childhood and adulthood, the time when the body changes and grows. Many kids don't know what to expect; they look around at other kids. But no 2 people are alike—body changes happen in different people at somewhat different times. Many kids ask the same questions. Here are just a few of them.

Special Questions and Answers for Girls

When do most girls get breasts? How do I know what size I will be?
There is no *normal* age at which the breasts begin to grow. Every girl's body has its own special way of growing. Some girls worry that they will always be "flat." All girls go through the same 5 stages as their breasts grow. Here are the 5 stages and the *average* ages for each. Remember: Don't panic if your growth is different.

Stage 1: Under the nipple is tissue, a group of alike cells. The tissue will grow and push outward on the nipple. The swelling is very small but you can tell the difference. Average age: 10. But: It can happen as early as 8 or as late as 13.

Stage 2: Breast buds begin. The area around the nipple starts to get bigger. It is called the "areola." Also, the breast itself starts to form a mound. Average age: 12. But: It can happen as early as 8 or as late as 15.

Stage 3: Both the breast and the areola grow larger. Average age: 13. But: It can happen as early as 9 or as late as 15.

Stage 4: The nipple and areola form a mound that seems almost separate from the mound of breast that is still growing. Average age 14. But: It can happen as early as 11 or as late as 16.

Stage 5: The areola again becomes part of the breast mound. It flattens into the center of the breast. Average age: 16. But: It can happen as early as 12 or as late as 19.

It's hard to tell just how large your breasts will become. Look at the female relatives in your family. Include both your mother's and your father's relatives. If most of the women are small-breasted, you will probably be the same way. If they have large breasts, then chances are you will be large-breasted. However, that method is only guesswork. You will probably just have to wait and see how you turn out!

What does pubic hair look like and how fast does it grow? Is it the same color as the hair on your head?
Pubic hair grows around your sex organs. It can grow before or after breasts start to grow. Again, everyone's body is different. There are 4 stages to watch for.

Stage 1: The first hair shows up. It is thin and straight. Average age: 13. But: It can happen as early as 9 or as late as 15.

Stage 2: The hair becomes coarse and starts to curl. It gets darker and spreads out. Average age: 13. But: It can happen as early as 10 or as late as 16.

Stage 3: Hair looks about the same as an adult's, but it still covers a small area. Average age: 14. But: It can happen as early as 11 or as late as 17.

As a girl grows up, her breasts go through several stages of development.

Stage 4: More and more hair grows. It fills out to look like an upside down triangle. Average age: 15. But: It can happen as early as 12 or as late as 19.

Pubic hair is somewhat the same color as the hair on your head, but it can be many shades darker.

When do "periods" start? How much do you bleed? Will I get cramps? When do periods stop?
The real name for "periods" is menstruation. It is the most important change that happens to a girl's body. It means you are growing into an adult and that you can someday have a baby. Girls usually get their first period between the ages of 10 and 16. Many start at 12 or 13. Some girls are afraid at first; the blood scares them. But there is really very little bleeding—only a few ounces. Some girls get cramps with their periods. Exercise helps if you do. get cramps. You should learn as much as you can about your periods. Most women have them until they are 50 or older.

Special Questions and Answers for Boys

Am I growing as fast as other boys? When will my penis get larger? When will I get more body hair? When will my voice get deeper?
The differences in how boys grow are even greater than the differences in how girls grow. Luckily, there are some guidelines. Here are the usual stages. Remember: The ages given are an *average.* You might not fit exactly into some of the stages.

Stage 1: The 2 testicles grow larger. They look like Ping-Pong balls and are located inside a bag called the scrotum. The scrotum hangs under the penis. Average age: 11. But: It can happen as early as 8 or as late as 15.

Stage 2: Hair appears around the penis. It is straight and thin. Average age: 12 or 13. But: It can happen as early as 10 or as late as 15.

Stage 3: Both the penis and the testicles show a noticeable growth. Average age: 13 or 14. But: It can happen as early as 11 or as late as 15.

Stage 4: The area around the nipples on the breasts gets bigger. The nipples may become slightly raised. Also, pubic hair spreads over a greater area. It is coarser and thicker. Average age: 14. But: It can happen as early as 11 or as late as 16.

Stage 5: Hair shows up in the armpits and above the upper lip. The voice becomes deeper. Average age: 14 or 15. But: It can happen as early as 12 or as late as 18.

Stage 6: Hair appears on the face. It also grows on the chest, arms and legs. Average age: 17. But: It can happen as early as 14 or as late as 19.

Is my penis a normal size?
There is no normal size for young men. There isn't even a normal size for adult men. A fully grown man has a penis that *averages* between 3 and 4 inches when not erect. Penis size is not based on how short or how tall you are. Also, penis size has nothing to do with how masculine you will become. Most of all, size will not make you a good or bad lover.

At what age can I get a girl pregnant?
As soon as a boy's body is making sperm, he can be a father. This can happen as early as 12 years old—sometimes even younger.

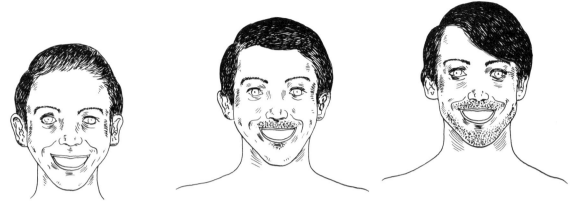

As a boy grows up hair begins to grow above his upper lip and on his face, chest, arms, and legs.

I am pretty short. Can I do anything to make myself taller?
No. How tall you will be has already been decided by the "genes" you got from your parents. These genes are special structures that determine the color of your eyes, your height, and lots of other things. Boys grow the most between the ages of 11 and 16. Some 14-year-old boys may be 4 feet 7 inches tall. Other 14-year-old boys may be 6 feet 2 inches tall. That is a difference of 19 inches! If your parents are tall, there is a good chance you still have some growing to do. Just give yourself some time.

There are many great books about your body. They will answer questions you are afraid to ask. Here are the names of 2 very good ones.

Kathy McCoy and Dr. Charles Wibbelsman, *The Teenage Body Book* (New York: Pocket Books, 1978).

Dr. Marvin J. Gersh and Dr. Iris R. Litt, *The Handbook of Adolescence* (New York: Dell Publishing Co., 1971).

The War Against Weight

Being fat is not healthy. It can lead to heart disease, high blood pressure, and other ailments. Being fat is sometimes a miserable experience. Nobody likes to be called Fatso, Porky, or Chubs. Blimp, Lardo, and Jellybelly are just as bad.

It's hard to say what is a "right" weight for anyone. It depends on your height and your build. However, there are 2 tests for finding out whether you have too much fat on your body.

Test 1: Pinch Test
Use your thumb and finger to pinch the flesh on one side of your waist. Or pinch the flesh on the back of your upper arm. Can you pinch an inch of flesh? If so, you are carrying around too much fat.

Test 2: Ruler Test
Take off your clothes and lie flat on the floor. Put a ruler—lengthwise—on your body. One end should be on your rib cage;

Too much junk food can make you fat. Cutting out snacks is a good way to lose weight.

the other end should point toward your hip bones. The ruler will be like a bridge from your shoulder to your knee. If the ruler rests on your bones, you are okay. If it rocks back and forth, you have too much fat.

Check with your doctor or school nurse to find out what you should weigh. Some kids really do have weight problems; others just think they do. Many girls want to be like fashion models and try to get too skinny. If you want to lose weight, you will have to eat less and exercise more.

The food you eat is measured in calories. Girls from ages 12 to 18 usually eat 2,000 to 2,400 calories a day. Boys from 12 to 18 eat 2,500 to 3,000 calories a day. If you want to lose weight, you will have to eat fewer calories. One pound of body weight equals 3,500 calories. Want to lose one pound of body fat a week? You

will have to get rid of 3,500 calories. That means 500 fewer calories a day for 7 days.

It is important to eat 3 meals a day. They must be nutritious—the body needs good food to stay healthy. Every day you should eat food from these 4 groups:

1. Meat, fish, and eggs
2. Fruits and vegetables
3. Bread and cereal
4. Milk and milk products

A doctor can tell you exactly what to eat to lose weight. There are many books that will tell you how many calories are in different foods. You can buy a calorie book in most supermarkets, or you can get one through the mail. Send $1 to Superintendent of Documents, U.S. Government Printing Office, Washington, D.C. 20402.

Eating less junk food is a good way to start losing weight. Junk foods are foods with lots of sugar and fat, and most of

JUNK-FOOD SCOREBOARD

It would take a whole book to list all the junk foods. Here are just some of the popular ones.

FOOD	AMOUNT	CALORIES
Candy		
Almond Joy (Peter Paul)	1 oz.	141
Baby Ruth	1 oz.	123
Chunky	1 oz.	131
Clark Bar	1 oz.	133
Cracker Jack	1 oz.	151
Fifth Avenue	1.2 oz.	160
Good N' Plenty	1 oz.	164
Hershey's Almond	1.05 oz.	164
Kit Kat	1.125 oz.	161
Mars Almond Bar	1 oz.	135
Milk Duds	12 pieces	165
Milky Way	1 oz.	120
Mister Goodbar	1.3 oz.	203
M&M's Plain	1 oz.	140
Mounds (Peter Paul)	1 oz.	142
Nestle's Crunch	1 oz.	150
Reese Peanut Butter Cups (2)	1.2 oz.	184
Snickers	1 oz.	130
Sugar Daddy	1.1 oz.	121
Three Musketeers	1 oz.	120
Cakes and Pies		
Hostess Ding Dongs	1 cake	170
Hostess Filled Cupcakes	1 cupcake	160
Hostess Fruit Pies	1 pie	435
Hostess Snoball Cakes	1 cake	135
Hostess Twinkies	1 cake	145
Morton Pastry Shop Mini-Pies	1 pie	240
Mrs. Smith's Apple Pie	1/6 pie	295
Sara Lee Brownies	1/8 cake	195
Sara Lee Original Cheese Cake	1/6 cake	240
Cookies and Chips		
Lay's Potato Chips	1 oz.	156
Frito-Lay Chee-tos	1 oz.	160
Frito-Lay Doritos Nacho Cheese Tortilla Chips	1 oz.	140
Frito-Lay Fritos	1 oz.	156
Granny Goose Thick Potato Chips	1 oz.	175
Nabisco Biscos Sugar Wafers	1 oz.	150
Nabisco Chips Ahoy	1 cookie	53
Nabisco Chocolate Pinwheels	1 cookie	140
Nabisco Fig Newtons	1 cookie	55
Nabisco Oreo Chocolate Sandwich Cookies	1 cookie	50
Pepperidge Farm Brownie	1 cookie	55
Pepperidge Farm Cinnamon Sugar	1 cookie	53
Pepperidge Farm Fudge Chip	1 cookie	53
Pepperidge Farm Irish Oatmeal	1 cookie	50
Pepperidge Farm Milano	1 cookie	63
Pringles New Fangled Potato Chips	1 chip	7.5
Wise Potato Chips	1 oz.	162

them have almost no nutritional value. Some have a little nutrition but not enough to make up for the loads of calories in them. For example, 6 Hershey Kisses have 150 calories (no nutrition). A raw carrot has 20 calories. A medium-size apple has 80 calories. A small baked potato has 90 calories.

Exercise uses up calories and thus helps you to lose weight. A good rule to remember: "Don't sit—stand. Don't stand—walk. Don't walk—run." The more you move around, the more calories you use up. Some activities are very good for using up lots of calories.

ACTIVITY	CALORIES LOST EVERY HALF-HOUR
Walking quickly (3 miles an hour)	120
Riding a bike (9 miles an hour)	150
Skiing	240
Ice skating	240
Swimming (doing the crawl or breaststroke)	350
Running (6 miles an hour)	400

Sugar

Every year you eat about 128 pounds of sugar. Much of that sugar is in junk food. On the average, each person eats about 33 pounds of candy, 50 pounds of cakes and cookies, 63 dozen doughnuts, and 363 bottles of soda pop every year. Most of the time you know when you are eating something with lots of sugar. It tastes very sweet. But many of today's foods have "hidden" sugar in them. Here are just some of them: bread, soup, canned vegetables, lunch meats, salad dressing, potato chips, baked beans, bacon, ketchup, mayonnaise, and pickles.

Doctors have known for a long time that "refined" sugar does nothing good for your body. Refined sugar is the kind you put on cereal or in a glass of iced tea. It started out as sugar cane or sugar beets, but then it went to a factory where it was made into crystals. This refined sugar is the kind used in most of our food. It has no vitamins and no minerals. Sugar is nothing but "empty calories," which

means it won't give your body any nourishment. But it will help you to gain weight!

Dentists have a lot to say about sugar and tooth decay. About 90 percent of all children have tooth decay. At this very minute, the average American has 5 unfilled cavities. By the time they get to age 60, one-third of all Americans have no teeth at all. It costs us about $3 billion a year to fix our teeth.

New studies on sugar have produced even more bad news. They show that too much sugar can hurt almost every organ in the body. It can play a part in heart disease. Doctors are now thinking that it might be causing personality and behavior problems in kids.

If you want to eat less sugar, here are some tips to follow:

1. Eat less junk food. If you crave sugar, eat more foods with "natural" sugar in them. Apples, oranges, and other fruits are good substitutes.

ADDED SUGAR IN CEREALS

	SERVING SIZE	TSP SUGAR IN SERV.	SUGAR % WEIGHT
General Mills Cheerios	1¼ cup	.2	3.6
GM Wheaties	1 cup	.7	11
GM Total	1 cup	.7	11
GM Kix	1½ cup	.5	7.1
GM Lucky Charms	1 cup	2.7	39.3
GM Nature Valley Granola Cin & Raisin	⅓ cup	1.7	25
Post Alphabits	1 cup	2.7	39
Post Raisin Bran	½ cup	2.2	32
Ralston Purina Cookie Crisp (choc chip)	1 cup	3	46
Kellogg's Fruit Loops	1 cup	3.5	50
Kellogg's Sugar Pops	1 cup	3.2	46
Kellogg's Special K	1¼ cup	.5	7.1
Kellogg's Corn Flakes	1 cup	.5	7
Kellogg's Raisin Bran	¾ cup	.7	10.7
Kellogg's All Bran	⅓ cup	1	14.3
Kellogg's Apple Jacks	1 cup	4	57
Kellogg's Sugar Frosted Flakes	⅔ cup	2.7	39
Kellogg's Country Morning	⅓ cup	1.5	21
Kellogg's Rice Krispies	1 cup	.7	11
Kellogg's Sugar Smacks	¾ cup	4.0	57
GM Boo-Berry	1 cup	3.2	46
GM Cocoa Puffs	1 cup	2.7	39
GM Count Chocula	1 cup	3.2	46
GM Golden Grahams	1 cup	2.7	39
GM Crazy Cow	1 cup	3.0	43
Nabisco 100% bran	½ cup	1.5	21.4
Instant Quaker Oatmeal with cin & spice	1⅝ oz.	4	35.2
Quaker Captain Crunch	¾ cup	3	43
Quaker Life	⅔ cup	1.2	18
Quaker 100% Natural Cereal	¼ cup	1.5	21
Shredded Wheat	1 biscuit	—	—

Source: August 1979, Nutrition Action, Center for Science in the Public Interest. Membership is available for $15.00 per year. CSPI, 1755 S Street N.W., Washington, D.C. 20009.

2. Stay away from candies that stick to your teeth. Chewy, sticky caramels stay on your teeth longer than other candies. So does chocolate. The longer a sweet candy stays in your mouth—and on your teeth—the better chance for tooth decay. Candy that you suck on, like lollipops, stays in your mouth for a long time. Cough drops are also bad; try not to eat them. And then there is chewing gum . . .

3. Read food labels. Start by checking out the food in your cupboards and refrigerator. You will be surprised at how many "regular" foods contain sugar. Even some foods called "health foods" have sugar. Look at the order in which the ingredients appear. They are listed in order of largest amounts to smallest amounts. See how far up sugar is on the list. Don't be fooled by other names used

for sugar. Sucrose, glucose, dextrose, fructose, maltose, and corn syrup are all sugars.

Many kids eat cereal for breakfast. All the ads on television talk about vitamins and minerals. They use words like "healthy," "strong," and "fortified." However, they don't talk about sugar. Some cereals have sugar as the first ingredient on the label. Want to see how much sugar is in the cereal you eat? Look at the chart on page 191. The first column tells you the serving size. The second column tells you how many teaspoons of sugar are in that serving. The most important column is the last column. It tells you the *percent* of sugar in the serving of cereal. For example, one cup of Apple Jacks is 51 percent. More than half of the serving is sugar!

Snack Foods

There are good snacks and there are bad snacks. Everyone knows that candy, cookies, and potato chips are bad snacks. Good snacks are foods that are nutritious and tasty. Fruits and vegetables are high on the list of good snacks. So are whole wheat crackers and sunflower seeds. Yogurt is great, but check out the label. It should be low-fat and it should not have sugar.

Popcorn is a pretty good snack food. It is a whole grain and has between 25 and 55 calories per cup when popped. If you are not on a diet, you can add a few drizzles of butter. That's only 15 extra calories. Go light on the salt. If you get

THE BEST	STILL OKAY
Carrot sticks	**Popcorn**
Celery sticks	**Peanuts**
Low-fat yogurt	**Peanut butter**
Fresh fruit	
Fruit juices	
Sunflower seeds	
Whole wheat crackers	
Vegetable juices	

bored with plain popcorn, add some spices and herbs for flavor. Try adding grated lemon or orange rind. You might try this recipe:

SLIMMER'S POPCORN TREAT

5 quarts popped corn
¼ cup soft low-cal margarine
¼ cup grated Parmesan cheese
1 teaspoon dried thyme, crushed
¼ teaspoon onion salt
¼ teaspoon garlic powder

Keep popped corn warm. Cream together margarine, cheese, and seasoning. Pour off any water that has worked out of the margarine. Toss cheese mixture with popped corn. About 75 calories per cup.

Peanuts and peanut butter are good snacks because they are high in protein, but they are also high in fats. You have to be careful not to eat too much if you are watching your weight. Also, it is better to eat nuts with no salt or very little salt. Two tablespoons of peanuts have 105 calories. One tablespoon of peanut butter has 95 calories. Buy peanut butter without sugar. Here is a good treat:

BANANA AND PEANUT BUTTER DELIGHT

½ banana
½ teaspoon lemon juice
1½ teaspoons peanut butter

Slice banana in half lengthwise. Place slices in small baking dish. Sprinkle with lemon juice. Spread peanut butter on each banana slice. Bake at 350° for 20 minutes or until banana is soft. One serving is 90 calories.

Some Weird Foods

The winning entry in the 1976 *Ver de Terre* Recipe Contest was Applesauce Surprise Cake. The "surprise" was dried, chopped earthworms. It's not such a surprise if you know French. *Ver de terre* means "earthworm" in that language. Other prize-winners were earthworm omelet and earthworm stuffed peppers. The worms used in the recipes were first washed in cold water, then boiled.

People throughout history have eaten worms. American Indians did. The Tainos left the pulp of zamia plants in the sun until it was full of maggots, then made wormburgers out of it. It was a good thing they waited for the maggots—zamia has poison in it, and the maggots drew it out. Mexican Indians served agave worms with guacamole. Back in the Middle Ages in Europe, worm powder was used as medicine.

"Nobody loves me. I'm going into the garden and eat some worms" may be a true saying for some people. Actually, worms are good food, full of protein. So it's not such a joke after all. If you can eat shrimp and oysters, why not earthworms?

The weight of earth's insects and their larvae is greater than the weight of all the earth's other animals. They're full of protein, too. Chicken has about one-fifth protein by weight. Termites have twice as much. Grasshoppers 3 times as much. Carol and Dennis Miller, experts on insect eating, made up some recipes. Jiminy

Bread, named after Jiminy Cricket, is made of roasted grasshoppers. First you fatten your grasshoppers on corn meal, then you fry them and use them in making bread. Termites can be cooked with rice, sesame seeds, and onions. You can't tell the termites from the rice. Bees taste like straw. The Millers like Bee Croutons in their salads.

Some 2,000 years ago, Chinese travelers carried dried snakes as their trail food. Chinese also eat bird's-nest soup. It is made from seaweed that birds have eaten, then thrown up to "glue" their nests with.

Anyone for earthworm pizza? Termite cookies? And why not, except that you're probably not used to them? Perhaps dipped in chocolate?

The Incredible Human Brain: It's All in Your Head

Your brain is what tells you to be scared of a tiger—or not to be!

Without a brain, a kid would not run from a tiger. He wouldn't know a tiger is dangerous. Nothing would tell his feet to start moving. He wouldn't yell. The brain is a fantastic thing.

The human brain is about 3½ pounds of gray and white gelatin-like stuff plus some brain stem. It weighs only one-fiftieth as much as the body, yet it uses one-fourth of the blood's oxygen.

The brain is protected in the fortress of the skull. The bony skull is curved and a curved surface gives greater protection than a flat one. Blows are likely to slide off it.

It's a good thing. The brain is a miracle that needs protecting. It's an information storage place. In your lifetime 100 trillion bits of memory are stored there.

facts/facts/facts ....
ideas/ideas/ideas ....
faces/pictures ....

a how-to library: how to put facts and ideas together, how to figure out problems. . .

The brain knows:

the amount of finger pressure needed to hold an egg, a pencil, or a bowling ball
what love, pleasure, anger, and fear are
that a rose is a rose is a rose

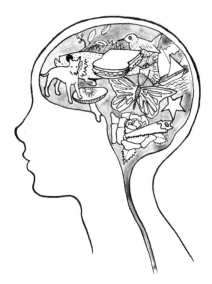

In a lifetime the brain will store 100 trillion (100,000,000,000,000) bits of information.

That's not all. The brain keeps you breathing and your heart pumping. Without your brain, you wouldn't be able to see, hear, talk, write, feel, think, live.

Every part of the brain has a job or jobs to do and more than one part of the brain may do the same job. The brain has wonderful back-up systems. If one part of it gets knocked out, another part can take over. The brain has 3 main parts.

The brain stem is a switchboard that sends messages from your body to the proper part of the brain. It contains structures that control the heat of your body (like a thermostat), your blood pressure, waking, sleeping, and other functions. In the brain stem is the pituitary gland, the main chemical plant. It triggers hormones that control aggressiveness, sex drive, hunger, and other feelings.

The brain is a drugstore, and it fills its prescriptions in split seconds. Just before an accident, for instance, your brain sends a chemical called norepinephrine through your body. It comes from a group of cells this size: ●. The chemical is a messenger. Alert! Alert! It starts another chemical—adrenalin—flowing.

When you are hurt, the brain sends out another chemical—enkaphalin. Enkaphalin is a terrific pain-killer. It's better than anything that comes out of a bottle. Ever notice that when you're hurt you don't feel the pain right away? That's enkaphalin at work.

The brain is a message center. It's like a big telephone exchange with messages coming in and out all the time. Each second the brain receives more than 100 million nerve messages from your body, and it knows what to do with them.

The stem acts like a switchboard for messages between the two other main parts of the brain—the cerebrum and the cerebellum—and the body.

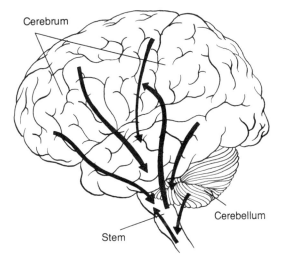

Cerebrum

Cerebellum

Stem

Shaped like a butterfly, the cerebellum is the part of the brain that controls balance and coordination. It's a feedback center for your movements. Without it, you wouldn't be able to stand up or walk.

The cerebrum sits on top of the brain stem and resembles a mushroom or a walnut kernel, with its 2 sections and wrinkles. The gray matter on the outside is the cerebral cortex. The white matter, inside, consists of cable-like connections with the rest of the brain and nervous system.

The cerebral cortex is wrinkled for a reason: Its wrinkles allow more surface to be stuffed into the skull. Spread out, it would cover 1½ square feet.

The cerebral cortex is where most thinking happens. It also handles such functions as seeing, hearing, feeling, tasting, remembering, speaking, and writing.

The right side of the brain controls the

Each side of the brain controls the opposite side of the body.

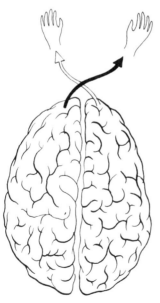

left side of the body; the left side of the brain controls the right side of the body. The 2 sides are not the same, although if one side is knocked out, the other can take over. In most right-handed people, the left side of the brain is the strongest, and the opposite is usually true of those who are left-handed. The left side of most right-handed people's brains is the seat of language and analysis, while the right side governs understanding of space and artistic matters such as music. It is the right side of the brain that recognizes faces.

The cortex is like a big map of the body. In it, are centers for hearing, seeing, feeling, and so on. In fact, if a brain surgeon were to probe a part of it you would "see" or "hear" things.

Each part of the brain controls a separate part of the body, as this diagram shows.

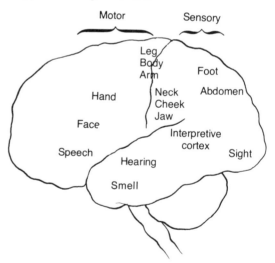

How does it all happen? Because of the workings of very small units—the cells. Inside the brain are a trillion of these tiny structures. Scientists know about brain cells, called neurons, from looking at

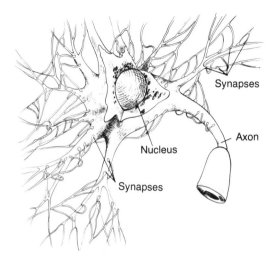

Brain cells are called neurons. All the working of the brain takes place within the cell network.

them through very powerful microscopes. If you could look, you'd see something like the drawing just above.

The axon sends messages out from the cell body. It can be fairly short or quite long. The longest axon reaches from your brain to your big toe.

The cells are connected to one another

in what scientists call a feltwork, which resembles the pattern of the material in a felt hat.

By means of these many connections, one neuron can feed into hundreds or thousands of others.

Through the connections the cells send messages, which zip along like electric impulses. They travel between the brain and the body parts at speeds from one mile an hour to 345 miles an hour. Each cell transmits its message to the next one at a synapse.

Some signals excite the cell to move the message through; others stop the message. This is done by chemicals at the synapse.

The cell body makes sense out of the message, then sends it on to another cell or cells.

Here are the connections for seeing. The retina of your eye is lined with cells that respond to what you look at. Messages are sent along the optic nerve to the visual center of the brain, which is

Each neuron is connected to another at a synapse, shown here, where messages can cross.

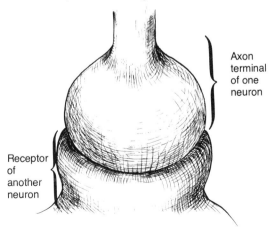

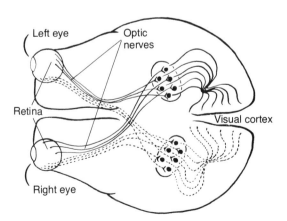

Your brain "tells" your eyes what they are "seeing" through a network like this.

1

2

3

something like a screen on which your brain sees what your eyes have just seen.

Let's return to the kid and the tiger. Before the kid sees the tiger, his cerebellum and the other parts of the brain keep him standing upright. His brain stem keeps him awake and breathing with his blood at the right pressure and temperature at 98.6° Fahrenheit.

Along comes the tiger. The kid's retina flashes the image of the tiger to the visual center. It goes from there to a center where memory is stored. The memory center says "loose tiger equals danger." Message to chemical factory: norepinephrine, GO! Alert! Alert! Adrenalin floods the kid's body. His blood pressure goes up and his heart beats faster. His energy level is up. The kid is aware of fear. Messages speed to his muscles—run!

He runs. The speech centers in the brain send the messages that start him shouting for help.

Of course, this is only a rough sketch of the millions of complex message connections that take place. Luckily, the kid doesn't have to think about *that!*

Facts About the Brain

The brain can "look at" itself.

The brain can't feel pain. Brain surgeons can operate on the brain while the patient is awake. Yet it is the brain that "feels" pain in other parts of the body.

During the first 6 months of a baby's

When the kid first spots the tiger (1) a message flashes from his brain, telling him danger (2)—run (3)!

life, its brain doubles in size. At age 3, the brain is two-thirds the size it will finnally be.

There's a lot of unknown territory in the brain. Scientists have much to discover about it.

Girls tend to be better at talking and writing than boys. Boys tend to be better at understanding space relationships and mechanical things (like how blocks fit together) than girls. However, some girls are better with blocks than talking, and some boys are better at talking than blocks.

Is a Computer Better Than a Brain? Answer: Yes and No

Like a brain, a computer can:

- store information
- give information back when asked
- solve problems
- make decisions

A computer can be better at "number-crunching" than a human brain. It works faster in doing arithmetic.

Computers now can:

- compose music and draw pictures
- play chess and checkers better than many human players
- drill you in your school subjects, telling you if you're right or wrong
- start the sound of a dog barking if someone breaks into your house

A computer can do many things, but only what a person tells it to. *(Tad Goodale, Boston Children's Museum)*

• water the lawn when the ground gets dry

• open the door when you say "Open up!"

• match partners for a dance

• predict the weather

• translate one language into another, even out loud

• and more, more, more. . . .

They can't do most of these things as well as people can. For instance, computers are not yet very good at translating.

A human brain, too, is a better memory bank. It is better at putting ideas into action. It puts computers in the dark when it comes to creating art and ideas. And it is still true that most computers can only do what a human tells them to do.

How to Take a Test—Some Tricks

Before the Test

Remember that somebody made up the test. That somebody is just another human being. It could be a teacher or a person who works at a testmaking company.

The world won't end if you don't pass the test. You may even look upon a test as a means of helping you to find ways to improve. Most of us don't see tests that way, though. We're not that high-minded.

We live in a world of tests. If you get stuck while taking a test, relax your brain for a while. *(Ulf Sjöstedt, Freelance Photographer's Guild)*

Many people are nervous about taking tests. If you're one of those people, try to think of a test as a big game or problem to solve.

In the Room Before You Start

Listen carefully to the instructions. Be sure you know how much time you have to take the test.

Skim the test fast before you begin. Plan your strategy. Maybe you'll want to do the easy questions or easy parts first.

Play the numbers. Pay attention to the number of points given to different questions and parts. Let's say a test has 25 multiple-choice questions worth 50 points and 2 essay questions worth 50 points. You know you can do the multiple-choice questions in about 20 minutes of the hour you're given. That leaves you 40 minutes for the essay questions. Obviously, it's best to do the multiple-choice part first.

Decide whether you will guess at answers. If no points are taken away for wrong answers, it's probably a good idea to guess. If points are taken off for wrong answers, figure the odds. For instance, with true-false tests, you have one chance out of 2 to get each answer right. Those odds are pretty good. With multiple-choice tests, there are usually 4 choices for each question. If you don't have any idea which is right, you have one chance in 4 of getting the right answer. Those are *not* good odds. It's best not to guess.

Keep in Mind . . .

Don't write down any old thing. Take the time to think. You know more than you think you do. However, don't spend time on what you don't know.

Let ideas and facts float into your mind. If you get stuck, shut your eyes for a few moments. Relax your brain. Say a nonsense word a couple of times. Go into low gear. Let answers come to you.

Don't stop to give yourself a pat on the back for a terrific answer. Keep working.

If you finish early, don't just rest. Go back and look for mistakes in your answers. Think again about questions you weren't sure of.

Essay Tests

Before answering an essay question, know what the question is really asking. Watch out for little words; they can trip you up. For example:

1. *Give* the *reasons the Ozonians lost the battle.*
2. *Give reasons the Ozonians lost the battle.*

The word *the* in the first sentence (before *reasons*) is more important than it might seem. It means you are being asked to give *all* the reasons. The second sentence allows a little more picking and choosing. You can decide to give the 2 or 3 reasons you think are most important and ignore the rest.

Look out, too, for words like *describe, compare,* and so forth. Give the answer that is asked for. Don't compare when you are asked to describe.

Time is all-important. Don't spend so much time on one question that you have little time to do the rest.

Before you answer a question, line up your facts and ideas in your mind. For example, if you're writing about the Ozonian downfall, you may know:

1. The Ozonians had no laser-Z guns. The Robos did.
2. There were more Robos than Ozonians.

Don't stop there. Do a little thinking. Why does any group lose a battle? A lack of spirit? A bad position from which to fight? Thinking like that helps you unearth another reason or two from your mind. It's like digging for treasure in your brain.

The good thing about essay tests is that you get a chance to parade what you do know. And to some extent you can cover up what you *don't* know. Make the most of what you have.

Fill-in Tests

Be careful in taking a test that requires you to supply the missing information to complete a series of statements. If you don't immediately know an answer, think a bit. If you're asked for the date on which something happened, a little thought may enable you to come up with a date that is *almost* the right one. Narrow things down.

Example: *The Zikkle Law was passed in* ___.

You know Congressman Zikkle was elected in 1976. Therefore, the law was passed sometime after that.

Multiple-Choice Tests

Watch out for tricks! Read the question and the answer you choose together to see if it makes sense.

Eliminate the choices you know are wrong. That usually leaves you with 2 possibly correct answers.

Example: *What is the capital of New York?*
  a) Albany
  b) New York City
  c) London
  d) Buffalo

You can forget London; you know it's in England. You may lean toward New York because it's such a big city, but you know that the largest city in a state is not always the capital. You may also know that the part of New York where Buffalo is was deep in the wilderness when the state capital was chosen. So you're left with 2 choices: Albany and New York City. Albany *seems* right. You choose it.

True-False Tests

Watch out for words like *always* and *never* in true-false tests. They usually appear in false statements.

Example: *A good driver never gets into an automobile accident.*

Obviously that statement is false. A good driver might get hit from behind by a car with failed brakes. His own car might go out of control. Examine statements for give-away clues. *There are exceptions.*

Example: The numerals 2, ¼, and ½ are fractions.

Since 2 is not a fraction, the statement is false, even though ¼ and ½ *are* fractions. Even if you don't know what a fraction looks like, you can see that ¼ and ½ have the same form, while 2 is a single number without that little line in the middle. Since all fractions would have the same form, you might then reason that at least one of the 3 numerals is not a fraction, and that therefore the statement is false.

Matching Tests

Before answering matching questions, count the number of items in each column. In some matching questions, the 2 columns have an equal number of items to be matched; in others, there are more items in one column than in the other.

Example:

A	B
race car	*information sources*
Barbie doll	*toys*
elm	*trees*
television	
kite	
newspaper	
baobab	
soothsayer	

In this case, it is clear that each item in column B will be matched to more than one item in column A.

First, match the items you are sure of, then use good sense on the others. Figure that baobab is probably a tree because the test-maker wouldn't use just one example of a tree. Figure that soothsayer is probably an information source because it contains the word *sayer*.

Math Tests

Especially on math tests, don't try to answer the questions you are unsure of until you have done the ones you know. Always check your work. More people fail math tests because of small mistakes than for any other reason. And those small mistakes are easy to fix.

Then take a stab at the problems you are unsure of.

Remember: Doing well on tests is a matter of knowing your stuff, not going into a panic, and being a little lucky.

How "Smart" Are I.Q. Tests?

I.Q. tests are supposed to measure how naturally intelligent people are. Intelligence is supposed to be something you're born with: your ability to learn. (All the experts do not agree about the "born" part of this.) If you grew up without going to school, you would still have your intelligence. However, intelligence can grow by being used, to some extent.

Most intelligence tests are not "pure." They almost always include a test of knowledge, and this can be unfair. Imagine being asked this question:

Defenestration is to frondescence as extirpation is to ___.

   a) teston   *c) barramunda*

   b) radix   *d) osculation*

This kind of question is supposed to measure your ability to see how one thing relates to another. It is not supposed to measure your knowledge of word meaning. It is taken for granted that the person being tested knows the meanings of the words in question. A kid who didn't know the words could fail this problem. Yet that same kid might understand the relationship the problem is testing for *if* he or she knew the meaning of the words. Thus the kid's wrong answer to this question would not mirror his or her intelligence.

Intelligence tests measure more than one kind of intelligence. Some kinds are the ability to use words, the ability to see

I.Q. tests can't measure how happy you are or how hard or successfully you work. *(Ulf Sjöstedt, Freelance Photographer's Guild)*

how things relate in space, and the ability to remember numbers.

Scores on intelligence tests for children are gotten by using this formula:

$$\frac{\text{mental age}}{\text{child's age}} \times 100 = \text{I.Q. score}$$

Let's say you get a score of 431 on an I.Q. test. That's the score an average 10-year-old would get, and so your mental age is 10. If you have lived for just 10 years, then your I.Q. score would be:

$$\frac{10 \text{ (mental age)}}{10 \text{ (your age)}} \times 100 = 100$$

If you were 5 years old and had a mental age of 10, then your I.Q. score would be:

$$\frac{10 \text{ (mental age)}}{5 \text{ (your age)}} \times 100 = 200$$

An I.Q. score of 100 means you are about as smart as the average kid your age. Anything above 100 means you're more intelligent. Anything less than 100 means you are less intelligent.

Only 3 people out of 100 have an I.Q. score of 130 or more. Many highly intelligent people were first-born children in a family or the only child in a family, and many were breast-fed as babies.

Intelligence tests should not be taken too seriously. They measure only one of the things that make people successful and happy. They don't measure how creative you are. Or how brave. Or how kind. Or how hard you work.

You can't change an I.Q. score very much, but you *can* keep learning, and in the end, that's what counts.

The Name Game

Are you terrible at remembering names? There is an easy way to improve your memory and, at the same time, impress your friends. You might even make some new friends. Aren't you happy when someone recalls your name? Other people feel the same way.

Some names are easy to remember. Would you forget the name of a person with the same name as your own? Probably not. Also, you might remember someone with a name that is the same as the name of a famous person. Who could forget someone with the name "Elvis"? Too bad all names aren't that easy to remember. Here are the 3 rules of The Name Game. Pretend you are meeting a Mr. Armstrong. He is a tall, skinny guy.

Rule 1: Pay attention to each person you meet. Make sure you hear the name right. Too many people don't do this. Look at Mr. Armstrong. Did you hear his name right? If not, ask to have the name repeated.

Rule 2: Say the name out loud. This is not too hard. Right away you might say, "Nice to meet you, Mr. Armstrong."

Rule 3: Form a cartoon in your mind. You have to link Mr. Armstrong's name with another idea in your mind. You might think it strange that such a tall, thin man has the name "Armstrong." The name sounds more like that of a strongman in a circus. You have just figured out your cartoon! Picture Mr. Armstrong in a circus. He has on a silly costume and is flexing his muscles. Look at the way he shows off his *strong arms*. His muscles are huge! The next time you see Mr. Armstrong you will remember his name. But don't make a mistake and call him "Mr. Strongarms."

Cartoons are the most important part of The Name Game. You should make them as crazy as possible. Try to get some action into the cartoon. Does the person's face give you any good ideas? Someone may have big eyes, a large dimple, or ears that stick out. You might want to exaggerate such features in the cartoon.

Suppose a girl's name is Fern Fadness. How will you remember her first name? Easy. You know what a fern looks like.

You can use a joke to remember Fern Fadness's name. *(Ming Chen)*

Imagine her wearing a big hat made out of ferns. She might even have a fern through her nose. What about her last name? That is a little harder. Break the name into syllables: Fad-ness. *Fad* makes you think of fads like the Hula Hoop. Picture her having a wild time with a Hula Hoop.

Can you imagine just one cartoon that will tell you the first and last names of a person? Usually that is too hard. But with Fern's name you can do it. Cartoon: She is wearing a hat made of *ferns*. She has a fern through her nose. And she is having a wonderful time with a *fad*—the Hula Hoop. Her name: Fern Fadness.

Here is one more person. His name is Doug Beagle. A cartoon for his last name is easy. A *beagle* is a dog. Look at Mr. Beagle's face. Notice his curly hair and mustache. Picture a beagle dog on his shoulder. The dog has curly hair and a mustache—just like Mr. Beagle! On your own, try to figure out a way to remember his first name. Is it possible to put his first name and last name into one cartoon? Try it.

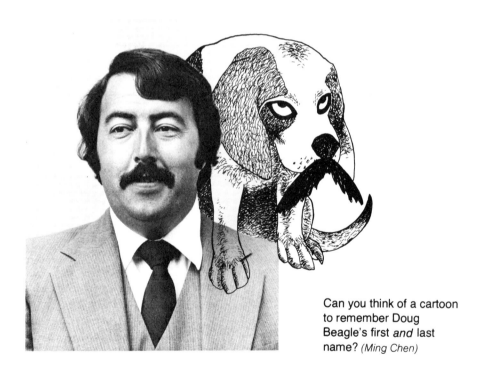

Can you think of a cartoon to remember Doug Beagle's first *and* last name? *(Ming Chen)*

Chapter 8

SPORTS, GAMES and CLUBS

Baseball

History

The earliest form of baseball, a game called "rounders," came from England. In the United States rounders grew into a game called "town ball," which in the 1830s became very popular in many towns and cities.

Town ball was very different from the baseball we know today. Wooden stakes or heavy stones were used for bases, and the shape of the playing field was square or oblong. The pitcher was called a "pecker" or "feeder." The batter was called a "striker." When the batter hit the ball, he ran *clockwise*—the opposite of the way the bases are run today. Nobody had a regular position to play. When a player in the field got the ball, he threw it at the runner. If the runner was hit, he was out. This was called "plugging" or "soaking." In those days the balls were made by winding yarn around a chunk of India rubber, and they were not very hard.

In 1845 the first regular baseball team, the Knickerbockers, was formed. The players were from New York City. They were mostly a "gentleman's club," playing for "health, recreation, and social enjoyment." However, they made big changes in baseball. First of all, they used a 9-man team, and each man had a regular position. Hitting runners with the ball was not allowed. The baseball field became diamond-shaped, and the bases were flat sacks instead of wooden stakes.

The Knickerbockers did not play games in innings. Instead, the first team to get 21 runs was the winner. They even fined players for breaking rules. Refusing to obey the captain of the team cost 50¢. The

In the first days of baseball players ran bases clockwise, the opposite way they run today.

They didn't even use gloves in the early days of the sport.

fine for arguing with the umpire was 25¢, and swearing was only 6¢!

The first "pro" team in the United States was formed in 1869. The team was called the Cincinnati Red Stockings, and its members were the first paid baseball players. At the time, the highest-paid player got $1,400 a year. The admission price of a game was 10¢.

The baseball used by the Red Stockings was almost as hard as the one we use today, yet the players used no gloves to catch it. Also, the catcher had no mask; he used only a rubber mouth protector. One writer made up a poem for the Red Stockings:

> We used no mattress on our hands,
> No cage upon our face;
> We stood right up and caught the ball
> With courage and with grace.

Many pro teams followed the Red Stockings, and baseball became one of America's favorite sports.

Equipment

Little League Baseball has certain rules about equipment. Here they are:

Baseball: It should weigh between 5 and 5¼ ounces. It should measure between 9 and 9½ inches around.

Bat: It must be a smooth, rounded stick that is made of wood. The bat can be no longer than 33 inches.

Glove: Fielders' gloves cannot be more than 12 inches long and 8 inches wide. The rules are different for the gloves of the catcher and the first baseman.

Helmet: Everyone must wear helmets for protection.

Shoes: Shoes with rubber cleats are allowed. Shoes with metal spikes or cleats are not allowed.

Tips for Improvement

Pete Rose, a top hitter, wrote a book called *Pete Rose's Winning Baseball.* In it he says: "Keep your eye on the ball. From the moment that baseball leaves the pitcher's hand until you have hit it, there is nothing else in the world. As a kid, this rule was drilled into me, so much so that when I take a pitch, I follow it all the way into the catcher's glove. It's something I advise. You can't take your eye off the ball too quickly if you follow it all the way to the catcher."

One of the greatest hitters in the major leagues was Hank Aaron. His book, *Hitting the Aaron Way,* is full of helpful advice. Here is one of them: "This may be a tough fact to swallow—you may never be able to hit for distance. It doesn't necessarily have anything to do with your size—relatively small men hit a lot of homers and some big players hit very few. If it turns out that you're not cut out for distance hitting, don't let it get you down. There are many ways you can help your team win games without hitting the long ball."

Pete Rose, one of today's top hitters, has written a book of baseball tips. *(Freelance Photographer's Guild)*

Fun Facts

Joe Nuxhall was the youngest major-league player in history. He began as a pitcher for Cincinnati in 1944. On the day he started his age was 15 years, 10 months, and 11 days.

Hank Aaron holds the U.S. home run record. He hit 755 homers in his major-league career.

Sadaharu Oh is the home-run king of the world. He hit over 850 home runs. Oh is Japanese and played baseball for the Yomiuri Giants.

People have always made fun of the umpires. Almost 100 years ago, kids chanted this:

Teamwork is important in baseball. *(Jack Zehrt, Freelance Photographer's Guild)*

Mother, may I plug the umpire,
  May I plug him right away?
So he cannot be here, mother,
  When the clubs begin to play?

Let me clasp his throat, dear mother,
  In a dear, delightful grip
With one hand, and with the other
  Bat him several in the lip.

Let me climb his frame, dear mother,
  While the happy people shout;
I'll not kill him, dearest mother,
  I will only knock him out.

Let me mop the ground up, mother,
  With his person, dearest do;
If the ground can stand it, mother,
  I don't see why you can't too.

Groups

About 3 million children play Little League baseball. You must be 9 to 12 years old to join. For more facts, write to:

Little League Baseball
P.O. Box 3485
Williamsport, Pennsylvania 17701

American Legion Baseball is a wonderful program for teenagers. Many major-league players once played in the program, and some even got elected to the Baseball Hall of Fame. They include Stan Musial, Roy Campanella, Yogi Berra, and Al Kaline. Call the American Legion in your area to see if it has a team. Or write to:

The American Legion
National Headquarters
700 N. Pennsylvania Street
Indianapolis, Indiana 46206

Magazine

Baseball Digest
P.O. Box 5031
Des Moines, Iowa 50347

Each year there's a Little League World Series. *(Vanucci, Freelance Photographer's Guild)*

Book

Official Little League Baseball Rules in Pictures (New York: Grosset & Dunlap, 1979).

Henry Walker, *Illustrated Baseball Dictionary for Young People* (Englewood Cliffs, N.J.: Prentice-Hall, Inc., 1978).

Basketball

History

An 1895 dictionary said this about basketball: "A game, resembling football, in which the goals are iron crates or baskets at the opposite ends of a gymnasium; played by girls." At that time basketball was 4 years old. It was first played in Springfield, Massachusetts. Credit for inventing the game goes to a man named James Naismith.

Naismith was born in Canada. An orphan, he was brought up by an uncle. In college he wanted to be a minister, but after finishing his studies he changed his mind and decided to devote himself to sports. He came to the United States to take some classes at the International YMCA Training School. (That school is now called Springfield College.) As a student, he played on the football team, which was called the "Stubby Christians." Soon he became a teacher at the college.

Naismith was asked to think up a good indoor game to play in the winter months. His idea for basketball came partly from a kids' game called "Duck on a Rock." He thought up 13 rules for his new game and got 2 teams together. The first game took place on December 21, 1891, in a YMCA gym. There were 9 men on each team, and a soccer ball was used. Peach baskets were nailed to the gym balcony. What happened when the ball went into the peach basket? A man with a ladder walked onto the court, climbed the ladder, and took the ball out of the basket. That sure could slow down a game. Luckily, the first game did not have much scoring—only one goal was made!

In the old days basketball was pretty rough. Many players wore padded pants, knee guards, and elbow pads. The stories that came out of Pennsylvania coal towns were shocking. Some miners came to games with nails. They heated the nails with mining lamps, then threw the hot nails at the players and referees. Some referees carried guns to protect themselves.

Basketball courts caused lots of problems. Some were just too small. The walls of the gym became the boundaries, and balls kept bouncing off the walls. So did the players! Also, stoves and radiators were often within the boundaries. Of course, they were turned on in the winter, and many players fell or were pushed onto them. It was easy to get a broken nose and a burned bottom in just one game.

Bigger courts had room between the boundary lines and the walls, and there was even space to put chairs for fans; but when the ball went out of bounds, there was still trouble. The first person to touch the ball out of bounds got to throw it back into play, so the players often charged out of bounds after the ball, racing right into

In the early days of basketball a peach basket was nailed up to serve as the hoop.

the crowd. Fans and their chairs were knocked over in the fight for the ball. The fans loved best of all, to see the ball go out of bounds and down a set of stairs. Down the stairs ran the players, and no one knew who would—and who would *not*— return.

Finally, some people got the bright idea to build fences around the court to keep the ball in bounds. However, some fans didn't like being left out of the game.

They brought hatpins to the games, and when a player got pushed up against the fence, a fan would stab him in the leg. The good old days of basketball were often not much fun for the players.

Girls have always been a big part of basketball. The very first school basketball game took place on November 18, 1892, between 2 girls' teams from schools in Berkeley, California. The final score was 6–5. The star of the game was

Some fans didn't like being kept out of the early basketball games, and jabbed players in protest.

described by a newspaper as "a tall young lady with Yum Yum features." Today, newspapers take girl basketball players more seriously, and high schools and colleges have good basketball programs for both boys and girls.

Equipment

All you need are a basketball and a basket. If you are on an indoor court, you must wear tennis shoes.

Tips for Improvement

The tips below come from the book *On Court With The Superstars of the NBA.*

Wilt Chamberlain (player): "If at first you don't succeed . . . get the rebound and try again. More than just scoring, rebounding affects other keys to a game, too. If a team is weak in shooting, weak in defense, not stocked with quick players,

it still has a chance to be a winner if it can do a job rebounding. A team that does lots of things well but can't hold its own on the boards will be a loser."

Jerry West (player and coach): "The big lesson for all players is this: Work on your shooting so you're as dangerous as possible, take your shot when you're open—but be sure the shot you take is a good one for you. Whether it's a good shot to take depends on a player's range, accuracy, and available time to get good balance and position."

Fun Facts

In 1963, 2 high schools in Alabama played a very unusual game. They were Glen Vocational High School and West End High School. West End won, 97–54. What was unusual? All of West End's 97 points were made by one player. His name was Walter Garrett.

The whole world's favorite basketball team is the Harlem Globetrotters. Their wonderful tricks make everyone laugh. So far, they have played in over 95 countries. Sometimes they play on strange courts. Once they played in a hayloft in Iowa. One Globetrotter got pushed out an open door, fell 25 feet, and landed in a mushy pile of cow manure.

One of basketball's great performers was Barney Sedran, who played from 1912 to 1926 and was elected to the Basketball Hall of Fame. Barney was only 5 feet 4 inches tall and weighed 118 pounds.

The tallest male basketball player is 7 feet 9¾ inches tall and lives in China. His name is Mu Tieh-Chu. The tallest woman player is Iuliana Semenova of Russia, who stands 7 feet 2 inches tall.

Magazine

Basketball Digest
P.O. Box 4852
Des Moines, Iowa 50340

Book

Gregory Morris, *Basketball Basics* (Englewood Cliffs, N.J.: Prentice-Hall, Inc., 1976).

Bowling

History

Bowling, one of the oldest sports in the world, has been around for more than 7,000 years. The earliest balls and pins were found in the tomb of a young Egyptian boy. The balls were rounded rocks and the pins were pointed stones. The game was buried with the boy when he died; it was probably his favorite sport. However, bowling goes back even farther in time. The cavemen probably played it.

Today's kind of bowling started in Germany. Believe it or not, it was first played in churches! The people used their war clubs, called "kegles," as pins. The kegle, which was supposed to stand for the devil, was set up at a certain place in the church. A man was given a rock or some sort of ball, and he tried to knock down the kegle. If he "knocked down the devil," it meant he was living a good life. If he missed, his life was full of too many sins.

Bowling moved out of the church and became a very popular sport in many countries. However, different kinds of bowling with different rules developed. In Germany the game used as little as 3 pins and as many as 17. The famous German religious leader, Martin Luther, was a big fan of bowling. It was Luther who came up with the "ninepin" bowling that spread throughout the United States.

Americans started bowling about 1626. By the 1830s the game had gained a very bad reputation—too many people were betting on the game. Big-time gamblers moved in. Some states made laws against ninepins. To get around the laws, the game of "tenpins" was invented, and it is the game we know today.

Over 40 million Americans enjoy bowling. About 14 million of them are under the age of 19.

At 10 years old, this girl bowled a 251 game.
(Courtesy American Junior Bowling Congress)

Bowling in colonial America: The sport came over from Europe.

Equipment

Using the right bowling ball is a must. Balls weigh from 8 to 16 pounds. Heavier balls cause the pins to "mix" better and more will fall down but you will get tired fast if the ball is too heavy for you. The rule is: Choose the heaviest one you can use *without straining yourself*. The 3 fingerholes on the ball should be comfortable for you. The thumbhole should be a little looser than the middle and ring finger holes. The "span" of the ball is important. The span is simply the distance from the thumbhole to each of the other 2 holes. To check the span, put your thumb into the thumbhole and spread your middle and ring fingers over the holes in which they belong. The knuckle of each finger should fall right over its hole. If you buy a bowling ball, the fingerholes will be drilled to fit your hand exactly.

All bowling alleys rent bowling balls and bowling shoes.

Tips for Improvement

Many kids have a lot of trouble with the 4-step approach. You should be 4½ walking steps away from the foul line to begin your approach. Here is the way to take your steps:

Step 1: Push away

Step 2: Pendulum backswing

Step 3: Top of backswing

Step 4 Releasing ball with sliding step

Fun Facts

Bowling has its own special language. Here are some words and their meanings:

Blowout—knocking down all the pins except one

Cheesecake—a lane on which it is easy to get strikes

Creeper—a slow ball

Dodo—a bowling ball that is more than the allowed weight

Kingpin—the head pin

Maples—the pins

Poodle—to roll a gutter ball

Sleeper—a pin hidden behind another pin

Splasher—a strike in which the pins fall down quickly

Turkey—3 strikes in a row

Group to Join

American Junior Bowling Congress
5301 South 76 Street
Greendale, Wisconsin 53129

Magazine

Junior Bowler
5301 South 76 Street
Greendale, Wisconsin 53129

Book

Edward F. Dolan, Jr., *The Complete Beginner's Guide to Bowling* (New York: Doubleday & Co., Inc., 1974).

Boxing

History

The first boxing match we know about happened over 3,000 years ago in Greece. Each boxer had strips of leather wrapped around his hands. Even so, the fight was a bloody one. The winner got a mule; the loser got a drinking cup.

After the Greek boxers came the Roman boxers. The Roman boxers were often prisoners who were forced to fight to entertain crowds of people. They were called gladiators. The gladiators, like the Greeks, wrapped leather strips around their hands and wrists, but they added one more thing: Metal spikes were pushed into the leather. It was like having a glove with built-in brass knuckles.

Modern boxing started in England. One of the first heroes was James Figg, who fought for "money, love, or a bellyful." The boxing matches were bare-knuckle: no gloves—not even leather strips—were used. Figg always kept his head shaved, for in those days a fighter could quickly grab his opponent's hair with one hand and slug him in the face with the other.

There were no rules—everything was allowed. Boxers pulled each other's ears, poked at each other's eyes, and kicked. They even wrestled. One favorite move was this: Trip the opponent. After he falls down, "accidentally" land on top of him. Make sure your knee or elbow gets shoved into his ribs.

When a fighter went down, his friends dragged him off to the side and poured whiskey down his throat. Sometimes a boxer could be brought back to life 15 or more times. The boxing matches seemed to last forever. In 1856 one bare-knuckle fight lasted 6 hours and 15 minutes.

Finally, 2 Englishmen—John Sholto Douglas and John Graham Chambers— wrote up a set of 12 rules for boxing. Each round was to last 3 minutes, and there would be a one-minute break between rounds. If a man was knocked down, he had 10 seconds to get up; if he could not, he lost the fight. No wrestling was allowed. And the most important rule: Each boxer had to wear gloves. Before gloves, boxers' hands were a mess.

In early days friends used to pour whiskey down a boxer's throat to revive him.

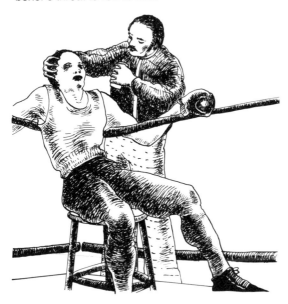

Sprained and broken fingers were common and knuckles were always covered with blood.

Rules made boxing a better sport, but the real thrills came from the boxers. There have been many exciting champions. Here are short stories about just a few.

JOHN L. SULLIVAN
Height: 5 feet 10½ inches
Weight: 200 pounds

They called him "the Boston Strong Boy." He loved to walk into a bar and brag, "I can lick any man in the house." And beat them he did. John L. Sullivan didn't have any fancy footwork, but his punch was powerful. "It was like being kicked in the head by a runaway horse," one boxer said. Another said, "It was like being hit in the face with the bottom of a telephone pole."

Before becoming a boxer, Sullivan went to Boston College. He was from an Irish Catholic family, and his mother wanted him to be a priest. It didn't work out, and he dropped out of school. Sullivan wore no gloves when he won the heavyweight title in 1882.

JOE LOUIS
Height: 6 feet 1½ inches
Weight: 198 pounds

Many experts pick Joe Louis as the all-time best boxer. He was born in Alabama, where his father picked cotton. The family moved to Detroit and lived in the slums. As a kid, he took violin lessons, but gave them up to spend more time on boxing. Called "the Brown Bomber," Louis punched fast and hard. "Louis had thunderbolts in his gloves," one reporter said. He was like a well-oiled fighting machine. He was only 23 when he won the heavyweight title. He kept the title for 11 years. In his whole career, Louis lost only 3 times.

MUHAMMAD ALI

Height: 6 feet 3 inches
Weight: 212 pounds

He is a man of power and poetry. Muhammad Ali loves attention. He always talks big and makes jokes. Born in Louisville, Kentucky, he has been called the "Louisville Lip." Ali loves to write poems. Here is one:

It all started 20 years past,
The greatest of them was born at last.
The very first words from his Louisville lips,
I'm pretty as a picture, and there's no one I can't whip.

Muhammad Ali, the Louisville Lip, has had a long, successful career. *(Marlene Karas)*

Ali started boxing at the age of 12. In 1960 he won a gold medal in the Olympics in Rome, Italy. He was only 18. People were amazed by his fast footwork and good reflexes. "Float like a butterfly, sting like a bee" is the way Ali described his style.

At 22 he won the heavyweight title from Sonny Liston. Then trouble entered his life. Ali refused to be a soldier and fight in the Vietnam War. He said his reasons were religious. When a court ruled that he had to join the Army, Ali again said no. Because he took this stand, his championship title was taken away in 1967 and he was told he could never again box in the United States. Years later, the court changed its mind and Ali made a comeback. In 1974 he won back the title by knocking out George Foreman in the eighth round. Ali had won boxing's highest honor twice.

Equipment

Kids learn to box in gyms and other training centers, and most of the important equipment will be there. However, you will probably have to buy some of the following:

Sweatsuit: This will be your workout outfit. It will help you sweat off any extra weight you want to lose.

Boxing trunks: Choose a color you like.

High-top boxing shoes: Tennis or gym shoes are okay in the beginning. If you like boxing and stick with it, you should buy proper shoes. They will protect your ankles.

Mouthpiece: It can be rubber or plastic. It protects your teeth and tongue.

Speed gloves: These are used for work on the speed bag and heavy bag. Your training center may provide them, so check first before you buy them.

Hand wrappings: Your training center may provide them. Ask before you buy them.

Skip ropes: The training center will have them, but lots of kids buy their own so they can practice at home.

Tips for Improvement

Chuck Bodak is the coach of Muhammad Ali's amateur boxing team in Santa Monica, California. In his book, *Boxing Basics,* he gives a lot of advice about how to defend yourself. Here are 2 helpful pointers:

1. Keep your hands high even though they are becoming weary from serving as your shield. Should you give in to the temptation to let your hands dip a little bit, your entire defense is likely to crumble.

2. Never slip punches by bending your head. It takes you off balance and puts you in danger.

Fun Facts

The saying "throw in the sponge" comes from boxing. In the early days, the sport was rough, and blood on the fighters' faces was wiped off with sponges. When a boxer was ready to give up, his friends threw the sponge into the ring. That ended the fight.

Wyatt Earp is remembered as the marshal of Tombstone, Arizona. However, he was once a boxing referee. In 1896 he took part in a fight between Bob Fitzsimmons and Tom Sharkey. Sharkey won. Many people thought that Earp fixed the fight. When Fitzsimmons stepped up to argue, Earp pulled out a gun. The argument ended.

In Duncanville, Texas, there is an all-girls boxing team called the Missy Junior Gloves. The girls are 6 to 16 years old, and they have a clubhouse and gym. Their coach, Doyle Weaver, has a lot of confidence in his team; he even matches the girls against boy boxers. "We pair boys against girls in fights but match them according to age, weight, and experience," he says. "When you do this the girls almost always win because they're better coordinated than boys their own age until they get to be teenagers. At age 9, a girl is 12 months ahead of a boy the same age in bone development. When they're 11, she's 18 months ahead of him in bone and teeth development. This has been proven medically."

How long was the shortest fight? Only 4 seconds. It happened in Minneapolis, Minnesota, on November 4, 1947, when a man named Collins threw one mighty punch at a man named Brownson. Brownson fell down. It was all over.

When paired for age and experience, girls 9 to 12 usually beat boys. *(Doyle Weaver)*

Groups To Join

Check the Yellow Pages for gyms or training centers in your area. Also, call your YMCA.

Magazines

The Ring
120 West 31st Street
New York, New York 10001

KO Magazine
TV Sports Inc.
Box 48
Rockville Centre, New York 11571

Books

Al Bernstein, *Boxing for Beginners* (Chicago: Contemporary Books, 1978).

Chuck Bodak with Neil Milbert, *Boxing Basics* (Chicago: Contemporary Books, 1979).

Figure Skating

History

The first ice skates were made of animal bones and tied to shoes with leather straps. People in Norway, Sweden, and Finland were skating over 2,000 years ago. The Netherlands (also called Holland) is the country that really made skating popular. In the Netherlands are many canals that become frozen highways during the cold winters, making it easy to skate to work, to church, and to school.

After the animal-bone skate came the wooden skate. Then came the wooden skate with iron blades. Following that was an all-metal skate with steel blades. Finally, steel blades were screwed on a boot, and the modern skate was invented. At last, there was a fast, safe skate.

Early skaters were very stiff. They often folded their arms across their chests, and movements were very simple. Then Jackson Haines, an American, put some excitement into ice skating.

Haines was a ballet teacher. Business was bad around the time of the Civil War, so he moved to Europe. While there, he got the idea of adding dance steps to ice skating. Haines dazzled people everywhere by performing spins and jumps as he glided and danced across the ice. He wore colorful, fancy costumes, and music played in the background. Before Haines, ice skating was pretty routine. After Haines, it was daring and thrilling.

There have been many superstars in figure skating Most people know of Sonja Henie (see the article later in this chapter), Peggy Fleming, Dick Button, Janet Lynn, and Dorothy Hamill. They all became famous in the Olympics and inspired people everywhere to learn the sport.

More than 20 million Americans skate, and there are over 1,500 ice rinks in the United States. It is an easy sport to learn. According to one teacher, "If you have a normal sense of balance and can walk, you can become an ice skater."

Equipment

Beginners should rent skates; good skates are pretty expensive. Be sure you

Jackson Haines added thrills to skating in the 1870s. *(Courtesy U.S. Figure Skating Assoc., Hall of Fame and Museum Collection)*

will be doing a lot of skating before you spend money on skates.

Your clothes should be comfortable. You don't have to buy a fancy figure-skating costume. Slacks, a shirt, socks, and a sweater will be enough for indoor skating. Many kids use gloves indoors to prevent ice burns on their hands when they fall. For outdoor skating, heavier clothing is needed. Wear tights or thermal underwear under your slacks, and get a hat for your head.

Tips for Improvement

Some people say they cannot skate well because of "weak ankles." That is not true. Most problems come from skates that do not fit well and are not laced properly. The Ice Skating Institute of America in Wilmette, Illinois, sends out a small booklet that tells how to buy skates. It also shows how to lace them. Here are the lacing rules:

- If you are a new skater, lacing should be tight.
- Lace tight up to the hooks, then put in a common knot or a couple of half twists.
- Put the knot a little below the ankle bend to prevent your ankle from getting sore.
- When the boot has been completely laced, the uppers should be at least an inch apart at the narrowest and tightest point in front of your ankle.

If you lace your ice skates properly, you won't have a problem with "weak ankles."

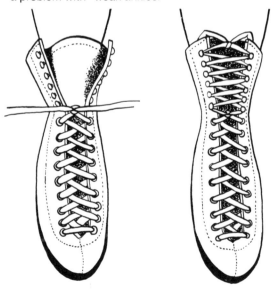

• Otherwise, the laces should be about 1½ inches apart.

• When lacing has been completed, you should have a snug feeling from the knot to the top of the boot.

• When the boot has been laced properly to get a hinge effect at the ankle forward and back, you should be able to insert 2 fingers at the back of your leg.

Proper lacing keeps your foot firm in the shoe and at the same time gives your ankle freedom for maneuvering.

Fun Facts

The first skating club was founded in-Scotland in 1742. To become a member, you had to pass a test. First, you had to be able to skate in a circle. Then you had to jump over one hat, then 2 hats, and finally 3 hats.

American skater Dick Button has won many honors. He has 2 Olympic gold medals, 5 world championships, 7 United States championships, and 3 North American championships. And he won them all by the age of 22!

Speed skating and racing are fun, too. *(Eugene Rosing, Freelance Photographer's Guild)*

Group to Join

United States Figure Skating
     Association
20 First Street
Colorado Springs, Colorado 80906

This group has programs in every kind of ice skating—figures, free, dance, and pairs. For more facts, write to the above address.

Magazine

Skating
c/o United States Figure Skating
     Association
20 First Street
Colorado Springs, Colorado 80906

Book

Peter Dunfield and Irwin J. Polk *Ice Skating for Everybody* (New York: David McKay Company, Inc., 1978).

Football

History

Most football fans have heard of Jim Thorpe and Red Grange. They know about Joe Namath and O. J. Simpson. And don't forget today's stars like Franco Harris and Terry Bradshaw. But have you ever heard of William Webb Ellis? Most people would say no.

Without Ellis there might never have been an American football game. He scored football's first touchdown. Here is how the story goes:

The year was 1823. Ellis, a student at Rugby School in England, was playing a game of soccer. The rules only allowed kicking and bouncing; players could not use their hands. All at once, the ball came straight at Ellis. Without thinking, he picked it up and ran toward the goal line. Touchdown! The other team got very angry and his team was very embarrassed. People were shocked to see Ellis disobey the rules.

But some people were impressed. They liked the idea of running with the ball; it made soccer more exciting. Soon more schools started to run with the ball. A new game was born. It was called "rugby" after the name of Ellis's school.

American football grew out of 2 games. One was soccer, the other was rugby. Until 1874 only soccer was played in the United States. In that year Harvard College played McGill University. Harvard, an important college in the United States, played football, but it was really a kind of soccer. McGill University, in Canada, played rugby. How could the 2 teams compete with each other when they played different games? They played one game under soccer rules, then switched to rugby rules for the second game. Harvard boys loved to run with the ball. For the first time, they were allowed to tackle. Other schools soon tried the new rules and American football was on its way.

In the early days, football was a killer sport. The players didn't wear any equipment—not even helmets—and some men let their hair grow long to help protect their heads. Many players were hurt. Numerous injuries were caused by the "flying wedge." In the wedge the players linked arms and stood in a V formation. Inside the V was the man with the ball, protected by the others. Down the field charged the group of men like a herd of stampeding cattle. When they crashed into the other team, there were lots of broken bones. In just one year, 1905, 18 people died of football injuries and 246 were hurt. President Theodore Roosevelt said the rules had to be changed to make football safer, and shortly afterwards the flying wedge was not allowed.

When the "flying wedge" charged down the field, a lot of opponents got hurt, so it was banned.

OUTLAWED

Some Common Football Signals

**Touchdown, Field goal
Successful attempt**

Time Out

Clipping

**Incomplete pass, Penalty refused,
No play, Missed goal**

**Offside, Encroaching,
Free kick violation**

**Interference with
pass or free kick**

**Start the clock,
No time outs**

First down

Holding

Unsportsmanlike conduct

Pulling face mask

Delay of game

224

In the last 75 years there have been many changes in football. One very important one happened in 1906, when teams started to use the forward pass. The game took to the air and became more open as players scattered all over the field. Another big change occurred about 1940, when the T-formation began to be used. Before then, football was called a "grab-it-and-run" game because it had no planned plays. The T-formation made a big difference. The offensive players lined up in the shape of a *T*, which allowed them to perform many different kinds of plays. Other formations came along after the T-formation and helped to make football a game of brains and strategy as well as muscle.

The first pro team was formed in 1895, and since then major-league football has become a big business. Every year the 2 top teams meet on "Super Sunday" in January in a championship game called the Super Bowl. Over 100 million people watch the game on TV.

Equipment

It is very important that your equipment fits properly. Use all of the following for tackle football.

For safety, wear the right equipment. For accuracy, use the right-sized ball!
(Jeffrey W. Myers, Freelance Photographer's Guild)

Helmet: Most kids use a "head suspension" type, which is cushioned inside to absorb shock.

   Shoulder pads
   Hip and kidney pads
   Thigh guards
   Knee pads
   Mouth guard
   Athletic supporter (male players only)
   Shoes: Sneakers or rubber-cleated shoes are okay.

Tips for Improvement

Bob Griese (quarterback) and Gale Sayers (running back) wrote a book called *Offensive Football.*

Bob Griese: "The problem many learning passers encounter is starting with a football too big to handle. If your hand isn't fully developed yet, don't practice with an official National Football League ball. It's too big. Find a football your size, one you can throw with your fingers. Master the art on this ball, and you'll be ready when the time comes to move up to the standard size."

Gale Sayers: "When running to the right, tuck the ball under your right arm, keeping it as far away from a tackler as possible. When running to the left, keep the ball under your left arm. This accomplishes two things: It frees your inside arm to ward off tacklers, and it puts the ball as far out of danger as possible. If you're running right and holding the ball under your left arm, you're giving that defensive man an open shot at causing a fumble."

And . . . a few words from running back O. J. Simpson: "Good runners,

when tackled, fall forward. That gets them extra yards."

Fun Facts

Some fans don't support their teams. One good example was the game between 2 college teams, Washington State and San Jose State, on November 12, 1955. Only one person paid to see the game!

Football is usually a low-scoring game, but that wasn't true on October 7, 1916, when Georgia Tech played Cumberland College. The final score was 222–0! Georgia Tech won.

Robert Carl Zuppe was a coach in the early days of bone-crushing football. He once said to a player, "Son, I don't look for tackles. I listen for them."

Group to Join

Pop Warner Football
Suite 606, 1315 Walnut Street Building
Philadelphia, Pennsylvania 19107

Pop Warner Football has been around for over 50 years. It is for boys and girls from 7 to 16. Write to the above address for the team nearest you.

Books

Bob Griese and Gale Sayers, *Offensive Football* (New York: Atheneum Publishers, 1972).

C. Paul Jackson, *How to Play Better Football* (New York: Thomas Y. Crowell Co., 1972).

Frisbee®

Hyper Hank watches Ashley Whippet catch a Frisbee. *(Alex Stein and Eldon McIntire, courtesy International Frisbee Disc Assoc.)*

History

Who would guess that throwing a plastic flying disc would become a big-time sport? Over 80 million kids and adults have thrown a Frisbee. There are many reasons why people love it. It's easy to play. It doesn't cost much. It's terrific fun. And it is great exercise.

Frisbee has been around for over 30 years. Inventor Fred Morrison made the flying disc after World War Two. As a kid, he had thrown pie tins into the air, and his idea was to make a pie tin into a toy that would sell. However, his early metal discs were too heavy and didn't fly very well. Then Morrison turned to plastic. What a difference!

Frisbee was not the first name for the disc. In the beginning it was called Morrison's Flyin' Saucer. In 1955 the toy was sold to a company named Wham-O in California. For a while the company called it Pluto Platter. Then 2 men from the company made a trip to some colleges in the East.

Students told the Wham-O men stories about a pie-tin game called "Frisbie-ing." The game had been played at different colleges for years. The tins came from the Frisbie Pie Company in Connecticut. The company men liked the sound of the name. They changed the spelling a little, and Frisbee became the name of their flying toy.

At first, Frisbee was a loser. Another Wham-O toy, the Hula Hoop, was getting all the attention. Nobody cared about the silly flying disc until, in 1964, an improved Frisbee came out. Called the Pro Model, it could really fly! Frisbee was not a toy anymore. It was a sport.

Throwing a Frisbee®

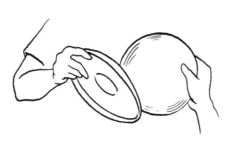

Basic grip
Hold Frisbee lightly, with thumb on top and index finger under rim.

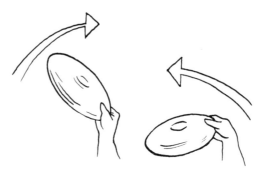

Backhand throw
Facing target, follow the famous rule: "Flat flip flies straight." Tilt the disc to curve left or right.

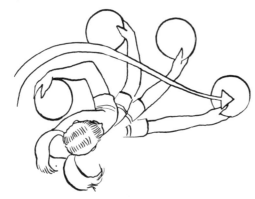

Backswing
Stand sideways. Coil wrist and forearm like a spring, then uncock smoothly.

Overhand
Facing forward, cock wrist and forearm behind back, then snap Frisbee forward, keeping arm straight, at shoulder level. Grip Frisbee with fingers on top, thumb underneath.

Skip
Use backhand throw, bouncing Frisbee edge forward about halfway to catcher.

Sidearm
Hold Frisbee with thumb on top, two fingers on bottom. Swing arm downward and throw like a baseball sidearm pitch.

Today there are Frisbee clubs all over the United States. Each year 2 million kids under 15 compete in the World Junior Frisbee disc Championships.

Equipment

There are 18 different kinds of Frisbees. They cost from $1 to $6.

Tips for Improvement

There are many kinds of throws. The most common are illustrated on the opposite page.

Fun Facts

There are many wonderful Frisbee games. One is Folf (Frisbee golf). Another is Basebee (Frisbee baseball). Still another if Frisball (Frisbee football).

Dogs are great Frisbee players. One champion named Ashley Whippet can leap 9 feet in the air! Some cities hold special contests for dogs called "Frisbee Catch and Fetch." Some of the best Frisbee dogs are German Shepherds, Whippets, Irish Setters, and Labrador Retrievers.

How far can you throw a Frisbee? Outdoors, some adults can throw the disc over 440 feet. Some kids (under 12) can throw it more than 215 feet.

Group to Join

International Frisbee Disc Association
P.O. Box 970
San Gabriel, California 91776

This club has over 110,000 members. About 300 of them are dogs!

Magazine

Frisbee World
P.O. Box 970
San Gabriel, California 91776

Books

Mark Danna and Dan Poynter, *Frisbee Player's Handbook* (Santa Barbara, Calif.: Parachuting Publications, 1978).

Charles Tips and Dan Roddick, *Frisbee Sports and Games* (Millbrae, Calif.: Celestial Arts, 1979).

Gymnastics

History

The words *gymnastics* and *gymnasium* were invented by the Greeks, who built the first gymnasiums about 2,500 years ago. They were special places for exercising. Strong, healthy bodies were very important to the Greeks.

Greek boys (teenagers) had to spend a lot of time at the gyms. They all wanted to win events at the Olympics, the great sports competition the Greeks started long ago. The boys took part in many kinds of exercises. They ran around the track, lifted weights, and climbed ropes. They threw the discus and the javelin. Jumping, tumbling, and wrestling were also part of the program. Each day they got an hour for recess. Girl friends waited outside for a chance to visit the boys. Most of the big cities in Greece had gyms.

Then the Romans conquered the Greeks. For a while, the Romans kept the gyms open and even added a new kind of exercise, one in which boys worked out on a wooden horse. But a Roman ruler decided to cancel the Olympics and said the boys no longer had to go to the gyms. Soon most of the gyms were closed.

For a long, long time gymnastics almost disappeared. Not until the 1800s did it return. Some men in Germany and the Scandinavian countries started the comeback. They said that gymnastics should be part of education; that the exercises would make children strong in mind and body. People started to listen. Schools started special programs, and other countries followed the lead.

Gymnastics is now a very big part of the sports world. Much of the popularity came from the television coverage of the last few Olympic Games competitions. Young and old people everywhere cheered for Olga Korbut, Nadia Com-

aneci, and Nelli Kim.

So far, most gymnastic champions come from Russia, and the United States is trying to catch up. About 500,000 American kids and teenagers are working hard. Some kids start as early as 5 years old!

Equipment

Comfortable shorts and shirts are what you need to begin. You can either be barefoot or wear socks and sneakers. Later on, you might want to buy some special clothes. Girls usually wear leotards made of stretch material. There are also special shoes for different events. A gym teacher or coach can tell you about them. Warm-up suits are also nice to have.

Leg stretch: Stand upright with arms on hips. Step forward on right leg, stretching out left leg behind. Return to a standing position and repeat with left leg forward, right stretched back.

Leg raise: Lying flat on your back, hands at sides, raise both legs together—keeping legs straight and lower back on the floor. Lower legs slowly. Variation: When lowering legs, keep them raised just off ground for a count of five.

Knee bend: Crouch, keeping feet apart, hands behind head. Jump straight up, then descend to starting position. Repeat.

Leg bend: From a standing position, raise right knee as high as possible. Repeat with left knee. Variation: Touch knee to chest and press it close for count of two.

Tips for Improvement

A gymnast has to be in good shape. Exercising at home will help. Just 5 minutes a day will make you stronger. You might want to try some of the following exercises.

Fun Facts

One of the greatest tumblers is James Chelich of Canada. On September 21, 1974, he did 8,450 forward rolls. That's a total of 8.3 miles!

In the 1972 Olympics Olga Korbut burst into tears in front of the crowd. She had made some bad mistakes on the Uneven Bars and her score was low. The crowd whistled and booed the judges. "Little Olga" was their favorite. That night she talked to some TV people. "I will not make any more blunders," she said. She didn't. The next day she won 3 gold medals.

Groups to Join

There are more than 10,000 gymnastics clubs in the United States. Check your phone book to see if any are in your area. Also, call your YMCA.

Magazine

International Gymnast
410 Broadway
Santa Monica, California 90406

Books

Michael Resnick, *Gymnastics and You* (New York: Rand McNally & Co., 1977).

George and June Szypula, *Contemporary Gymnastics* (Chicago: Contemporary Books, Inc., 1979).

Horseback Riding

History

The first horses were only 11 inches tall. It took millions and millions of years for them to grow bigger. Some experts say that horses have been around for 45 million years. Today's horses are giants compared to those early horses. Some horses, like the Percheron and the Clydesdale, can grow to be 7 feet tall!

Where did the early horses come from? They roamed the large, open plains on the continent of Asia. As the years went by, they became strong and tall enough to be ridden. In those days, groups of people wandered over the land. Called "nomads," they walked from place to place in search of food. They were the first people to try riding on the back of a horse. Soon, whole tribes of nomads could be seen riding across the plains.

At first, there weren't any saddles; people rode bareback. Then cloth or animal skins were thrown on the horse's back and fastened under the belly. Finally, someone (we don't know who) invented a saddle, which gave the rider better balance and helped the rider to stay on when the horse began to gallop.

Getting onto a horse was once a big problem. People used a pole or a spear to leap upon the animal, or stepped onto big blocks to get on. The stirrup changed all of that. Early stirrups came from India. In India the weather was warm and people rode barefoot. The stirrups were big enough for only one toe—the big toe. However, that stirrup didn't work in colder places, where people had to wear shoes and boots to keep their feet warm. Stirrups had to be made big enough for the whole foot.

The mare, Rare Medicine Hat, is learning to jump.
(Courtesy Wild Horses of America Registry, Inc.)

Down through history, horses have been used to fight wars and help in the hunt for food. In America they pulled stagecoaches and delivered mail. (Remember the Pony Express?) Today, horses are used mostly for sports, and horseback riding is one of the biggest. Thousands of kids are learning how to ride. Many riding stables and riding schools offer lessons. These places supply the horses and important equipment like saddles and bridles.

Equipment

Beginners need jeans, a shirt, and a pair of leather shoes. The shoes should be sturdy and have low heels. Later on, if you stick with the sport, you may want to buy a good pair of boots, gloves, and a hat.

Tips for Improvement

Follow these easy steps to learn how to lead a horse: Approach the horse along its left shoulder, walking slowly so that the horse doesn't get scared. Take the reins in your right hand below the bit, the part of the bridle that is in the horse's mouth. With your left hand, hold the end of the reins. You are now ready to lead the horse. Look straight ahead, walk straight ahead, and don't go too fast. Be sure to hold on to the reins. The horse will go with you.

Fun Facts

In 1976 a man named Walley Eaglesham wanted to find out how long he could stay in the saddle. Every 6 hours he changed horses. Altogether Wally rode for 245 hours and 15 minutes. He was very saddle sore!

In 1911, 2 boys from Texas rode horses from New York City to San Francisco. One kid was 9; the other was 11. It took them 62 days to cover 3,619 miles.

Groups to Join

Over 11,000 kids belong to The United States Pony Clubs, Inc. "Pony" refers to the age of the members, not the size of the horse. There are 320 Pony Clubs around the United States, and any person under 21 can join. To find out if one is near you, write to:

The United States Pony Clubs, Inc.
303 S. High Street
West Chester, Pennsylvania 19380

Also, many 4-H Clubs have special programs for horseback riding. Check with the 4-H Club nearest you.

Magazines

Horseman
5314 Bingle Road
Houston, Texas 77092

Western Horseman
P.O. Box 7980
Colorado Springs, Colorado 80933

Book

Jane Sholinsky, *In the Saddle* (New York: Julian Messner, 1977).

Kites

History

Kites are more than 2,500 years old and were probably first made in China. In the beginning, kites were simply large leaves. They didn't have string in those days, so the kites were flown from lines of twisted vines.

Kites have not been used just for fun. In the twelfth century in Korea, kites were used in times of war. Burning torches were hung from kites and flown over enemy villages. Then the kite strings were cut and the burning bombs fell from the sky. Many years later kites played a part in a war in Africa called the Boer War. A man named Captain Baden-Powell, fighting for England in that war, flew 6 kites on one string and attached a basket underneath them. In the basket was a man called a "spotter," who glided over the treetops and spied on the enemy. Baden-Powell later became the founder of the Boy Scouts.

Kites have been important in gathering facts about the weather, carrying special instruments high into the sky to measure wind pressure and air temperature. Weather kites also help us to learn about clouds and storms.

In 1825 an English schoolteacher attracted a lot of attention. He tied 2 8-foot kites to a carriage and drove around country roads in England. It was a strange

Flying kites is fun, but only on a windy day! *(Jeffrey W. Myers, Freelance Photographer's Guild)*

sight! With the kites helping to pull his carriage he was able to go 25 miles an hour. The teacher—Mr. Pocock—did use a brake, but it was not the kind we know today. It was a big iron spike, and it had to dig right into the road to stop the carriage!

Some well-known Americans have used kites in their work. Benjamin Franklin helped to make the kite very popular when he used one in a famous experiment. During a storm he and his son used a kite to prove that lightning was a kind of electricity. There was a key at the end of the kite string. When lightning traveled down the string and hit the key, Franklin could feel the electricity. It is surprising that Franklin did not get himself killed, because the kite line was not grounded. Other people tried the same experiment and were knocked out. Franklin certainly did enjoy kites. He would float on his back in a pond with a kite tied to him, allowing the kite to gently pull his body across the water.

Alexander Graham Bell, who invented the telephone, built huge kites. They were made of many triangle-like cells called "tetrahedral cells." Some of his kites had over 3,000 of these cells and were large enough to lift a person into the air.

The Wright brothers flew the first airplane in Kitty Hawk, North Carolina, in 1903. Their airplane was really more of a box kite than an airplane. For years they had experimented with kites, and what they learned helped them build the first airplane.

Equipment

There are many kinds of kites. The most common are the flat kite, the bowed kite, and the box kite. Newer kinds include the delta kite and the parafoil kite. Animal kites, including one that looks like a dragon, are very popular. Thre are even some kites that look like sailing ships and airplanes. You can buy a kite for as little as 59¢. Most people spend between $6 and $10 for one. Many kids make their own kites at a cost of $1 to $3. Good string costs about $2.

Tips for Improvement

1. The best winds for flying kites have a speed of 2 to 15 miles an hour. The best time of the year for these winds is the fall.

2. The strings on your kite must be the right length and must be in the right places. Be sure to read the instructions that come with your kite.

3. Dacron or nylon test line (20- to 30-pound strength) is good for flying kites and will last a long time. Also, it will not burn your hands too much.

4. Using a kite with a tail? If so, make the tail about 10 to 12 feet in length. It should be an inch wide.

Fun Facts

The most kites flown on one line is 1,050.
The largest kite in the world weighed 9½ tons.
The longest flight of a kite is 169 hours.

Book

Wyatt Brummitt, *Kites* (New York: Golden Press, 1971).

Monopoly®

History

"Pass Go, Collect $200." Is there anyone who doesn't know that phrase? It comes from one of the world's favorite board games—MONOPOLY. The game has been around for almost 50 years, and over 80 million sets have been sold. It all started with a man named Charles Darrow.

The year was 1932, and Darrow was 43 years old and out of work. He lived in a small town near Philadelphia and had been a salesman for a heating equipment company before the Great Depression caused him to lose his job. He had plenty of time to kill, so he invented things. Many of his inventions were fun, like jigsaw puzzles and beach toys.

One day he dreamed up the idea of a game that used the street names of Atlantic City, where he and his wife had spent their vacations. He drew the outline of the playing board on a plastic-like kitchen tablecloth. With some different paints he added a little color, then built little houses and hotels from scraps of wood.

C. B. Darrow invented it, and the world has been playing MONOPOLY® ever since. *(MONOPOLY® game equipment © 1935, 1946, 1961 Parker Brothers, Beverly, Massachusetts 01915. Used by permission)*

Colored buttons became tokens, and pieces of cardboard became deeds to the properties. Then he bought some play money and a pair of dice. Presto! The very first MONOPOLY game was ready to be played.

Darrow's friends loved the board game. Everyone wanted a set, and soon he started making them by hand. Each day he was able to turn out 2 sets. He sold the game for $2.50. As more and more people wanted the game, Darrow had a tough time keeping up with the demand. In 1934 he tried to sell MONOPOLY to Parker Brothers, a big company that makes and sells games.

The most important people at Parker Brothers sat down to play MONOPOLY. They liked it but they rejected it. Why? It took too long to play a game. No game, they said, should last more than 45 minutes. In addition, the rules were too hard to understand; nobody would read all those rules. Kids would never play

MONOPOLY! Altogether, the company came up with 52 fundamental playing errors.

Darrow didn't give up. He made a deal with a friend of his, a printer, to make 5,000 games and sell them to local stores. More orders poured in. Meanwhile, Parker Brothers heard what was happening, changed its mind, and bought the game.

The popularity of MONOPOLY has been amazing. Over 250 million people in 46 countries play the game, and the rules are printed in 18 different languages. No matter how you say it, everyone likes to "Pass Go, Collect $200."

Equipment

You may have a hand-me-down set in your family. If not, you'll find MONOPOLY in most toy stores.

Tips for Improvement

1. The square that people land on most is Illinois Avenue. Keep that in mind if you get the chance to buy it.

2. A big pile of money will not win the game for you. Don't keep saving your money; use it to put buildings on the squares that you own.

3. If you have a lot of money, put houses and hotels on your expensive properties—like Boardwalk and Park Place.

4. If you have just a little money, use it to put houses and hotels on your cheap properties—like Vermont and Oriental.

5. Do you own all 4 railroads? If you do, you get $200 every time another player lands on any one of them. However, owning all of them is more important in the beginning of the game than later on, so don't get upset if you have to sell one or two toward the end of the game.

Fun Facts

Printing presses for MONOPOLY make more "money" than the United States government. In one year, 1975, $40 billion in fake money was printed for the game. The government printed $22 billion in real money in that year.

The little green houses are an important part of the game. Guess how many of them have been made. Over 2,560,000,000.

People everywhere try to set world records in playing MONOPOLY. The longest game ever played lasted 1,416 hours, or 59 days in a row. Students in St. Louis, Missouri, took turns playing to set the record. The longest game played in a moving elevator went on for 384 hours. The longest game in a bathtub lasted 99 hours. The longest game played on a ceiling ended after 36 hours.

What is the only property whose name does *not* come from Atlantic City? Answer: Marvin Gardens. It is in the nearby town of Margate. The correct name is Marven Gardens; Darrow made a spelling mistake.

There is a special MONOPOLY set that allows people to play underwater. It was made in 1967 by Parker Brothers. The board is backed with steel and weighs 95 pounds. Houses and hotels are weighed down so they won't float away, and the paper parts are covered with cellophane to keep them from coming apart in the water.

Book

Maxine Brady, *The Monopoly Book* (New York: David McKay Company, Inc., 1974).

Roller Skating

History

In Belgium in 1760, a man named Joseph Merlin, a musician, made the first pair of roller skates. When he moved to London, England, Merlin tried to sell his skates, but didn't have much luck.

One day he was invited to a very fancy party where everyone was dressed in costumes. Merlin went to the party on his skates and took along a violin. While rolling along through the crowd, Merlin played music. Suddenly, he was moving too fast, and moments later crashed into a $1,300 mirror. The mirror broke, so did the violin, and Merlin's body was full of cuts and bruises. Why didn't he stop? He couldn't. Merlin had never figured out a way to make his skates turn or stop!

Down through the years, many people tried to make a better skate. One kind had 5 wheels, all in a row. Another type had only 2 wheels. One of the funniest-looking skates had 8 wheels on it. However, none of them worked very well.

Funny as it seems, roller skating started to get popular because of opera shows. In 1849 an opera in Paris, France, had an ice skating scene. At that time, there was no way to make fake ice on stage so that the actors could ice skate. Instead, they used roller skates. Often they got carried away and rolled right off the stage.

An American named James Plimpton invented the kind of skate that we use today. It had 4 wheels and was at first called a "rocking skate." At last it was easy to make turns; leaning the body weight to one side or the other would do it. Before that, skaters had to lift their wheels off the ground to turn.

At times roller skating was an "in" sport, but then people would get bored with it. However, in the 1960s there was a big improvement when a new kind of wheel made of polyurethane was put on skates. The new wheels made skating smoother and quieter.

Equipment

Roller skates: Skating at a rink is cheap. Admission and rented skates together cost from $2 to $4. Buying skates can be very expensive. Skates that fit on regular shoes sell for about $20, but boot

Roller skating can be a very fast sport. The speed record of 25.78 miles per hour was set in 1963. *(Ted Kirk, UPI)*

skates can cost from $50 to $400.

Safety equipment: Everybody falls down, especialy when learning to skate, so it is important to wear knee and elbow pads. Another good idea is a mouthpiece to protect your teeth, and some kids like to wear helmets when they skate.

For tips on skating safety, write for a small book called *Wheels.* It is free from the government. It also gives facts on skateboards and bicycles. Write to Wheels, Consumer Product Safety Commission, Washington, D.C. 20207.

Fun Facts

The longest trip made on roller skates is 5,193 miles. It was skated by Theodore J. Coombs of Hermosa Beach, California, in 1979. He traveled from Los Angeles to New York City and then back to Yates Center, Kansas.

The world's speed record for roller skating is 25.78 miles per hour. It was set by Giuseppe Cantarella of Italy in 1963. Many TV and movie stars love to skate, among them Jerry Lewis, Dustin Hoffman, Cher, Kate Jackson, Penny Marshall, Olivia Newton-John, and Linda Ronstadt.

Groups to Join

Roller skating is popular with Girl Scout troops, Camp Fire clubs, Boy Scouts, and Cub Scouts. Check with your local groups to see if they have special programs.

Every year The United States Amateur Confederation of Roller Skating holds contests for skaters, and over 35,000 skaters take part. Some kids are as young as 6 years old. For more facts, write to:

The United States Amateur Confederation of Roller Skating
7700 "A" Street
P.O. Box 83067
Lincoln, Nebraska 68501

Starting and Stroking

Stand with feet close together

Shift weight to right foot.

Push off with left.

Lean forward on right.

Glide, lifting left foot.

Bring skates together.

Shift weight to left foot.

Push off with right.

Magazines

Roller News
7700 "A" Street
Lincoln, Nebraska 68501

Skate
7700 "A" Street
Lincoln, Nebraska 68501

Books

Hal Straus and Marilou Sturges, *Roller Skating Guide* (Mountain View, Calif.: World Publications, Inc., 1979).

Carol Ann Waugh and Judith LaBell Larsen, *Roller Skating: The Sport of a Lifetime.* (New York: Macmillan Publishing Co., Inc., 1979).

Skateboarding

History

No one knows who made the first homemade skateboard from a set of metal skate wheels and a board. It was probably a surfer, though, who very likely built the thing on a day when the waves weren't very good, hoping to practice surfing moves on land.

After a while, skateboarding became popular with many people. "Sidewalk Surfin'" was a hit song. By then, clay wheels, which were better than the metal ones, were being used. Still, skateboards were dangerous. When they hit a stone they would stop dead, and the rider would "take a header." On a turn, the wheels could slip, causing the board to spin out from under the skater.

Show-offs, including more adults than you might think, were ending up in hospitals. Doctors were coming out against skateboards, and so were the car drivers who had come close to hitting skateboarders on the streets. Parents wouldn't let their children have skateboards, and towns started to ban them. It looked as if skateboarding was just a fad that died.

Then, in 1973, plastic skate wheels were invented. The plastic wheels gripped the ground far better than the clay ones, so the rider was not as likely to get dumped. Riders began wearing helmets and padding to keep from getting hurt when they fell. Skateboarding became far safer than it had been, and what had been a fad began to turn into a real sport.

Equipment

If you skateboard at all, you should have this equipment:

Helmet (A head injury can kill you.)
Elbow pads
Knee pads
Padded gloves

Skate parks always make riders wear this gear, since it can prevent you from breaking a bone, hurting your head, or losing a lot of skin.

The kind of board, trucks, and wheels you use depends on the kind of skateboarding you do. Beginners will find it best to buy boards made for people who are just starting to skateboard.

Boards: Boards are made of wood, plastic, or metal. Some bend more easily than

Whether you're an expert skateboarder like this, or just a beginner, always wear safety equipment.
(Marlene Karas)

others, allowing you to take bumps better. Long boards are used for downhill skateboarding (going straight down a hill); medium-size boards are best for slalom (zigzagging down a hill); and short boards, which turn easily, are used for tricks.

Trucks: Trucks attach the wheels to the board. Make sure they are put on so they won't come loose.

Wheels: Wide wheels are for speed skateboarding, thin wheels (less than an inch wide) for tricks. The best are made of very good plastic.

Tips for Improvement

1. If you are just learning, get someone who knows how to teach you.

2. Don't try to push yourself too far too fast. That's a good way to get hurt.

3. Don't let other people talk you into trying tricks you know are too dangerous for you.

4. Always use a helmet, elbow pads, knee pads, and padded gloves.

5. Learn to fall.

6. If you skateboard on the street, watch out for cars. Better yet, don't skateboard on the street—go to a skate park. If there is no skate park around, maybe you and your friends can get the local public playground people to set one up for you.

7. Before you skateboard in parking lots or other public places, make sure there is no law in your town against it.

8. Check your equipment to make sure it is working right.

Fun Facts

Skate boards with motors are becoming very popular. Called "motoboards," some can cruise at 20 miles per hour for about a half hour. Each board has a tiny 12-ounce gas tank attached at the rear.

Skateboard freestyle tricks have crazy, wonderful names like: Hang Ten, Coffin, Daffy, Spinner, and Handstand Wheelie.

Groups to Join:

California Skateboard Amateur League
P.O. Box 1325
Upland, California 91786

National Skateboard Association
P.O. Box 1325
Upland, California 91786

United States Skateboard Association
2236 Pacific Avenue
San Pedro, California 90731

Magazines

Thrasher Magazine
P.O. Box 24592
San Francisco, California 94124

Trans World Skateboarding
P.O. Box 6
Cardiff-by-the-Sea, California 92007

Books

Jack Grant, *Skateboarding* (Millbrae, Calif.: Celestial Arts, 1976).

Ben Davidson, *The Skateboard Book* (New York, Grosset & Dunlap, 1976).

Soccer

History

When did the first human kick a ball? Nobody knows. We do know that the early Greeks and Romans each had a special kind of soccer game, and that 2,000 years ago the Chinese were playing *tsu chu*. In that game the players kicked around a leather ball filled with hair. But the game of soccer really began in England.

In early England soccer was a wild game. There were hardly any rules. Kicking other players was allowed, along with scratching, elbowing, tripping, pushing, and pulling hair. Any number of people could play, and sometimes hundreds took part in one game. The playing field could be miles long. Often, the ball was the blown-up bladder (a bag-like organ of the body that holds urine) of a dead animal, or a hog's head. The game lasted for hours and hours, and many times ended only because all the players were too beaten up to go on.

Villages played other villages. Towns played other towns. People ran through the fields and streets. Everyone was caught up in the excitement of the game. Afterwards, arguments and fights broke out. One person called the game "a bloody and murderous practice." In the fourteenth century 3 kings of England tried to stop soccer. One outlawed it be-

A fast, exciting sport, soccer is rapidly growing in popularity here. *(Harold Krauth, Freelance Photographer's Guild)*

cause it caused too much noise; the other 2 were against it because too many men played soccer instead of practicing archery. In those days, archery was important in defending the country against enemies. However, nothing could stop the popularity of the game.

The first rules for the game were written in 1863 in London, England, and since then the game has spread all over the world. But there is one very confusing fact. In all countries but the United States, soccer is called "football"! Only in the United States is the game called "soccer." The game is the same, but the names are different. American football (with teams like the Pittsburgh Steelers) did grow out of the football of England, but they are very different sports.

For many years soccer has been the Number One sport in the world. The world championship game in soccer is called the World Cup, and it is played every 4 years. Over 140 countries have teams that compete, and more than a bil-

lion people around the world watch the game on TV.

In the last 20 years soccer has taken off in the United States. Before that, it was just a second-rate sport. Kids helped the game to grow, and today about a million American kids play soccer.

Why do kids love soccer? First, it is a very exciting game. There are no time-outs; the game is all action! Second, it is not a power game, so you don't have to be big and strong to play. There are skills to learn, but anyone who can run and kick a ball can be a good player. Third, all players are equally important. In football the quarterback gets much of the attention, and in baseball the pitcher is the hero; but everyone counts in soccer.

Equipment

It is easy to get ready for soccer. Here is all you need:

Shirt: Wear a lightweight jersey or T-shirt.

Shorts: Gym shorts will work. They should fit loosely.

Socks: Any knee socks will do.

Shoes: You can buy soccer shoes with special studs on the bottom, but lots of kids just wear tennis shoes or gym shoes.

Ball: The official ball weighs between 14 and 16 ounces and is smaller than a basketball. Kids under 13 sometimes use a 10- to 14-ounce ball.

Shin guards: These pads are placed under the socks to protect your shins.

Tips for Improvement

In soccer the team with the most goals is the winner. Here is how to shoot the ball:

Basic soccer kick: As you run up to the ball, plant your pivot foot next to the ball. Swing through with your kicking foot, toes down, ankle rigid. Kick the ball solidly in the center.

REMEMBER:

1. Don't waste time. Scoring chances often last no more than a split second. When you have a chance, shoot.

2. It's best to be in balance when you shoot, but if you're off balance and have a scoring chance, shoot anyway.

3. Don't just shoot blindly into the goal. Try to put the ball out of the goalkeeper's reach.

4. To get more power, put all your weight into the shot. Good shooters are almost airborne at the moment of ball contact.

5. Before the kick, keep your eyes on the center of the ball. Keep your eyes there during the kick. After the kick, follow through with your foot.

These tips are from *Soccer Tips: How to Improve Your Skills.* For a copy, send $1 to The U.S. Soccer Federation, 350 Fifth Avenue, Suite 4010, New York, NY 10001.

Fun Facts

Everyone loves to watch the goalkeepers. One of the best was Bill ("Fatty") Foulke of England, who was 6 feet tall and weighed 300 pounds. When Fatty got mad, he picked up players by their shorts and threw them into the back of the net. If they made fun of his weight, he chased them all over the field. One day, after a game, Fatty ran wildly through the team dressing room. He was very angry and wanted to find the referee. He had no clothes on. What a sight! Luckily, the referee got away.

One of soccer's best referees was Arthur Ellis of England. Every year he received lots of presents at Christmas.

Almost always he got eyeglasses, white canes, and books containing the addresses of seeing-eye dog trainers.

Groups to Join

The American Youth Soccer Organization has been around for over 16 years. It sponsors more than 6,500 teams in 25 states, and its motto is "Everyone plays." For more facts, write to:

American Youth Soccer Organization
5403 W. 138th Street
Hawthorne, California 90250

Another wonderful group is:

United States Youth Soccer Association.
350 Fifth Avenue, Suite 4010
New York, New York 10118

Books

C. Paul Jackson, *How to Play Better Soccer* (New York: Thomas Y. Crowell, 1978).

Osvaldo S. Garcia, *Soccer Games for Kids* (San Francisco: Chronicle Books, 1979).

Swimming

History

Thousands and thousands of years ago people watched animals swim and learned the "dog paddle." Early swimmers didn't have much style and it took a long time to swim from one place to another. The dog paddle was not a speedy stroke.

At first, swimming was not a sport. It was used mainly to save people from drowning. Swimming was also useful in time of war. Soldiers could surprise the enemy with an attack from the water, or might make a fast escape by swimming out to sea.

Not until the nineteenth century did swimming become a sport. It happened in England, and the first contests were held about 1837. For a long time, swimmers used only the breaststroke. Except for the head, all parts of the body stayed under the water.

Then along came J. Arthur Trudgen, an English swimmer who had visited South America. While there, he carefully studied how the natives swam. They lifted their hands and arms out of the water, a technique he called the "double-overhead stroke." When Trudgen returned home, he taught everyone the new stroke. It improved swimming and became very popular.

Being able to save a drowning victim is an important skill to know.

The Australian crawl is the most common and efficient swim stroke. *(Vanucci Photos, Freelance Photographer's Guild)*

The biggest and best changes in swimming happened about 1879. A family named Cavill moved to Australia from England. The father, named Frederick, built a pool and taught swimming. One day he took his 6 sons on a vacation to the South Sea Islands. The Cavills were surprised at how fast the natives could swim. The natives used the same double-overhead stroke that J. Arthur Trudgen had seen in South America, but they did one other thing—they used their feet to kick them forward. This leg action added speed to the stroke.

The Cavills went back to Australia and spread the word. The new stroke was called the "splash stroke," and later became the Australian Crawl. American swimming teachers learned about the crawl. They made a few changes and called it the American Crawl. Today it is often called the freestyle stroke.

Equipment

All you really need is a bathing suit. It should fit well and be made of a material that dries quickly. You have to be able to move easily in it. Most girls like tank suits. Boys can pick from a number of different kinds of trunks. A warm-up jacket or sweatsuit is a good idea; it will keep your muscles and body warm when you are out of the water.

Tips for Improvement

Mark Spitz won 7 gold medals in swimming in the 1972 Olympics. He learned to swim at the age of 6, and at 10 he set his first swimming record. Here are 2 tips from *The Mark Spitz Complete Book of Swimming:*

"In learning how to float on your back, try to keep the waist stiff at all times, but not rigid. If you try too hard to keep yourself still while you are floating, you'll drive your legs down and then you've lost the balance you need to float freely."

"Treading water is an important skill to learn, for it allows you to rest, change strokes, and look around to get your bearings in the water. It is also an enjoyable skill, for it will let you stand still in the water and talk to friends."

Fun Facts

People are always trying to swim across the English Channel, a distance of 21

Kids enjoy the local pool to cool off in hot weather.
(Freelance Photographer's Guild)

miles. The first man to do it was Matthew Webb of England, who used the breast stroke for 21 hours and 45 minutes. The first woman to swim the Channel was Gertrude Ederle of the United States. In 1926 she did the crawl for 14 hours and 39 minutes to make the crossing. The youngest person to win honors is Marcus Hooper of England, who in 1979 swam the Channel in 14 hours and 37 minutes. His age: 12 years, 53 days.

The world's record for treading water belongs to Norman Albert, a student at Pennsylvania State University. In 1978 he didn't stop for 64 hours

Groups to Join

YMCAs have wonderful swimming programs. Call your local YMCA and ask when classes begin.

Book

The Diagram Group, *Enjoying Swimming and Diving* (New York: Paddington Press Ltd. 1979).

Tennis

History

How far back in time does tennis go? An old form of tennis was played in France as early as the twelfth century. The game was called "le jeu de paume," which in our language means "the game of the palm." There were no rackets at that time; players hit the ball with the palm of their hands. The ball was made of pieces of cloth sewed into a round shape, and did not bounce very well. The net was either a rope or a pile of dirt. In time, players started to wear gloves, and finally the racket was invented.

Modern tennis began in England. Everyone gives credit to Major Walter Clopton Wingfield, called "the father of tennis." Before 1873 tennis was mostly played indoors. In that year Major Wingfield moved the game outside. Players used a plain rubber ball and a spoon-shaped racket, and played on a grass court shaped like an hourglass. Major Wingfield called his game "sphairistike," the Greek word for ball game. The name didn't stick—nobody could remember it! The name was changed to "lawn tennis."

How did tennis get to the United States? We owe it all to a girl from New York City, Mary Ewing Outerbridge. In 1874 she was on vacation on the island of Bermuda, and for days she watched British soldiers play lawn tennis. She played the game, too, and loved it. After buying some equipment, Mary returned home, and she and her brother built a court on Staten Island. At first, hardly anyone would play. Women said the game was "unladylike." Men said only a sissy would play a game that used the word *love* to keep score!

There are many championship contests in tennis. Almost everyone's favorite is called Wimbledon, a contest held every year in England. The best players from all over the world hope to win at Wimbledon. The first Wimbledon was held in 1877, when only 22 players—none of them women—took part in the games. There was only one prize. Only 200 fans came out to watch. They were all dressed up and acted very proper. There were no stands for the fans to sit in, so they sat on the ground or in their horse-drawn carriages. In the finals, Spencer William Gore played William Marshall. At that time the overhead serve was not in use. Both men served the ball in a side-arm style. Gore kept reaching over the net to hit the ball, which made the judges angry, but there was no rule against it. In the end, Gore was the winner. "Lawn tennis is a bit boring," he said. "It will never catch on." Gore was very wrong!

Equipment

Racket: Most rackets are 27 inches long. If you are under 13 years old, that may be too long for you. Get a junior-length racket. It is 25 to 25½ inches long. Rackets are made of many different materials, including wood and metal, and come in many different weights. Choose one that will be easy for you to control. The grip size is marked near the handle. Most kids use 4⅜, 4½, or 4⅝.

Tennis balls
Tennis shoes
Shorts
Short-sleeved shirt
Socks

Tips for Improvement

Billie Jean King has written a tennis book—*Billie Jean King's Secrets of Winning Tennis*. In it she says: "The forehand and backhand should be taught, learned, and practiced together. What usually happens is that the beginner first learns the forehand drive and, having reached the point where he or she can hit that shot fairly well, he or she avoids the backhand out of fear or distrust. Don't make that mistake. If you spend a half-hour on your forehand, spend a half-hour on your backhand and never, never run around either shot."

Getting Started in Tennis by Arthur Ashe is an ideal book for beginners. Here is one of his pointers: "When you get into a rally, get the ball back into the court four times before you even think about winning the point. If you will do that at your age against opponents of about the same age, I firmly believe you will win almost every match you play. It sounds simple, but remember this: Most people,

May Sutton caused a stir at Wimbledon in 1905 by showing her ankles! *(Courtesy Wimbledon Lawn Tennis Museum)*

especially juniors and beginners, tend to make an error within the first three shots."

Fun Facts

Rules for tennis clothing were once very strict. Men wore long pants, and women wore long skirts, long-sleeved blouses, and sometimes even hats! In 1905 May Sutton, a 17-year-old American, was in the women's singles match at Wimbledon. One player complained about May's outfit. Why? Because a little bit of her ankles could be seen, and she was wearing a short-sleeved blouse. She was ordered to lower the hem on her dress. Then the match went on. May won.

Chris Evert won at Wimbledon in 1972. The prize was $50,000 but she could not collect it because she was not yet 18 years old.

The youngest Wimbledon winner was 15 years and 9 months old. Her name was Charlotte Dod. She won in 1887.

Chris Evert, in today's tennis dress, swept Wimbledon while still a teenager. *(Carson Baldwin, Freelance Photographer's Guild)*

A volley is a return of the ball before it hits the ground. On January 7, 1936, 2 tennis players volleyed for 78 straight minutes. They were Helen Moody and Howard Kinsey. Without stopping, they hit the ball 2,001 times. They quit because Kinsey had to leave for a tennis lesson!

Group to Join

United States Tennis Association (junior division)
51 East 42nd Street
New York, New York 10017

This group holds contests throughout the country. Junior players are put into 4 groups: 18-and-under, 16-and-under, 14-and-under, and 12-and-under.

Books

Arthur Ashe, *Getting Started in Tennis* (New York: Atheneum, 1979)

Karen O'Conner Sweeney, *Illustrated Tennis Dictionary for Young People* (Englewood Cliffs, N.J.: Prentice-Hall, Inc., 1979).

Yo-Yo

History

"It looked like a potato on a string. It didn't do anything. It just went up and down." That is what Donald F. Duncan said when he first saw a yo-yo in 1927. However, he did change his mind! Before too long, Duncan yo-yos were in the hands of almost every kid in the country.

The word yo-yo means "come-come" or "to return." The word—and the toy—was brought to America by Pedro Flores of the Philippines. Kids in the Philippines had played with yo-yos for many years. When he moved to California, Flores carved yo-yos out of wood and started his own company. His yo-yos were much better than the one Donald Duncan saw.

Duncan liked Flores's yo-yo. He bought Flores's company and the name "Yo-Yo," then set out to make a better toy. First, he smoothed out the edges, which were rough and could scratch your hand. Then he attached a stronger string, called a "slip-string." The slip-string was great

for doing tricks. Kids could throw the yo-yo down and make it "sleep" at the bottom of the string.

The next problem: How to sell it? Ads in newspapers was one way. The first Duncan yo-yo was called "O-Boy Yo-Yo Top." The ad read, "The Toy with a Big Kick for All Ages." Another smart idea was to use big-name stars. Duncan took lots of pictures of movie stars playing with yo-yos. He took pictures of mayors, dancers, baseball players, singers—all with yo-yos. Even the famous Our Gang Kids helped out.

To top everything off, yo-yo experts traveled the country and taught tricks to kids. Some of the most popular tricks were Walking the Dog and Sky Rocket. Soon there were contests. Kids—and their parents—were wild about the new toy, and yo-yos were selling like crazy!

World War Two slowed down the yo-yo fad. During the war it was hard to get wood and other things to make the toy.

When the war was over, the yo-yo was back in full swing. The 1950s were booming with contests. Bicycles, radios, sweaters, yo-yo patches, and trophies were only some of the prizes. Then came plastic yo-yos—heavier than wooden ones, longer-lasting, and better for tricks.

Equipment

Duncan makes many kinds of yo-yos. Experts say that beginners have good luck with the "Special," the "Butterfly," and the "Imperial."

Another company called Festival makes yo-yos, and it also has many different kinds. Some are shaped like footballs and baseballs; others have Disney characters on them, like Mickey Mouse and Donald Duck. A good model for beginners is "Chuck 'n' Joy."

Donald F. Duncan Jr. (son of Donald Duncan) has his own yo-yo company. His yo-yo, called the "Pro-Yo," spins longer than other yo-yos. Duncan Jr. gets lots of fan mail from kids. One girl wrote, "I am very satisfied with your Pro-Yo. It works so much better than my old yo-yo that I am learning tricks much faster."

Tips for Improvement

Make sure the yo-yo string is the right length. Put the yo-yo between your feet and pull the string up to a point 4 inches above your waist. Cut it there.

Here are 2 favorite yo-yo tricks.

The sleeper: Throw the yo-yo downward, stopping your hand as soon as you release it. The yo-yo will "sleep" at the bottom of the string. If you turn your palm downward, and tug on the string, the yo-yo will climb back up.

Walk the dog: After the yo-yo is sleeping, swing the yo-yo forward and let it walk along the ground. A tug will return it to your hand.

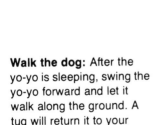   

Fun Facts

In the Philippines yo-yos were first used as weapons. Jungle soldiers made yo-yos out of stone, and each weighed about 4 pounds. The soldiers used thick ropes about 20 feet long. The poor enemy really took a beating!

For a long time, Duncan yo-yos came from Luck, Wisconsin. It was called "the Yo-Yo Capital of the World." Every hour, 3,600 yo-yos were made.

To become a Duncan Grand Master you have to do many tricks. The hardest ones are Shoot for the Moon, Ferris Wheel, Lindy Loops, Splitting the Atom, Whirlybird, and Interlocking Astro Loops.

In 1977, a man from Virginia, John Winslow, played with a yo-yo for 120 hours without stopping.

Group to Join

Yo-Yo Players International
801 Lynn Avenue
Baraboo, Wisconsin 53913

This group holds many contests every year. You can buy a book from them called *Duncan Yo-Yo Trick Book* for $1.

Books

Helane Zeiger, *World on a String* (Chicago: Contemporary Books, Inc., 1979).

George Malko, *The One and Only Yo-Yo Book* (New York: Avon Books, 1978).

Odds and Ends

Badminton

Badminton "birdies" were once pieces of cork with feathers stuck into them and didn't fly very well. Today's birdies can travel as fast as 100 miles per hour.

Chess

More and more kids are learning to play chess. Some start as early as 6 years old. Some kids become experts and get to compete in contests in other countries. One 7-year-old got to play in Iceland. In 1979 a group of junior high school students traveled to Yugoslavia for a tournament. Move over Bobby Fischer! For more information about chess clubs and contests, write to U.S. Chess Federation, 186 Rt. 9W, New Windsor, New York 12550.

Fishing

The biggest fish ever caught on a fishing rod was a man-eating shark that weighed 2,664 pounds. The fisherman was Alf Dean, who made the giant catch off the coast of Australia in 1959.

Golf

On March 8, 1968, Tommy Moore was playing golf in Martinsburg, West Virginia. He got a hole-in-one on the fourth hole. The hole was 145 yards. Tommy was 6 years old!

Golf balls used to be little leather bags stuffed with goose feathers.

One of golf's funniest moments happened in 1912. A ladies' golf tournament was held in Shawnee-on-Delaware, Pennsylvania. One woman needed 166 strokes for just one hole! And the hole was a short one—only 130 yards. Her ball often ended up in the nearby river. Once as it floated on the water, the woman and her husband rowed out in a boat and kept playing. Today, nobody knows the woman's name. Of course, she wanted to keep it a secret!

Ice Hockey

Bobby Orr is one of hockey's biggest superstars. Born in Canada, he played team hockey as a "Minor Squirt" when he was only 6 years old.

Hockey's fastest skater is Bobby Hull, who can fly across the ice at 29.7 miles per hour.

Ice hockey got its start in Canada. Some people think it grew out of a kid's game called "shinny." In that game kids used broomsticks to push stones across the ice.

Juggling

Juggling is the favorite pastime of girls in Tonga, a group of 150 little islands in the Pacific Ocean. For hundreds of years juggling has been a custom there. Only girls juggle, not boys. Many contests are held, and sometimes they last so long that everyone is finally called a winner. The girls can juggle as many as 7 limes or tui tui nuts (a kind of chestnut).

Junior Olympics

All kid athletes dream of winning a medal in the Junior Olympics. It is a great honor. Many winners in these games go on to compete in the international Olympic Games. One such winner was Mark Spitz. Anyone from 6 to 18 can take part in the program. There are 17 sports to choose from, including basket-ball, boxing, diving, gymnastics, judo, swimming, and volleyball. If you want to take part in the contests, write to Junior Olympics, AAU House, 3400 West 86th Street, Indianapolis, Indiana 46268.

Jumping Rope

Jumping rope used to be a boy's game; adults thought it was "unladylike" for girls. Then boys turned to baseball and girls took over. There are many rhymes that go with jumping rope. One goes like this:

Johnny on the ocean,
Johnny on the sea,
Johnny broke a milk bottle
  and blamed it on me.
I told Ma, Ma told Pa,
Johnny got a licking,
  and ha, ha, ha.
How many lickings did he get?
1, 2, 3 . . .

Karate

Several years ago 15 karate experts went to Bradford, England, to try to destroy a house. Using only their hands and feet, they "chopped" apart a 6-room home. Boards and bricks flew through the air, and before long, the house was in ruins. The men bowed gracefully to the house, then turned and walked away.

Marbles

Kids in Turkey and Iran play marbles with the knucklebones of sheep.

There are many different kinds of marbles. Some are called alleys, aggies, and commies. Others are glassies, stonies, steelies, and marrididdles.

American kids love to play marble games. Some favorites are Chasies, Holy Bang, Potsies, Killer, Last Clams, and Rockies.

Four U.S. presidents were good marble players—George Washington, Thomas Jefferson, John Quincy Adams, and Abraham Lincoln. Lincoln was very good at a game called "Old Bowler."

Rodeo

Little Britches Rodeo Association is open to boys and girls from 8 to 18. The group holds rodeos in 20 states. Little Britches has all the rugged events of adult rodeos, including steer-bull riding, calf roping, goat tying, and bareback riding. A newspaper, *Little Britches Rodeo News,* tells members all about the rodeos and where they will be held. To join, write to:

National Little Britches Rodeo Association
411 Lakewood Circle, Suite C205A
Colorado Springs, Colorado 80910

Running

Wesley Paul, age 8, took part in the 1977 New York City Marathon. He ran 26 miles, 285 yards in 3 hours, no minutes, 31 seconds, setting an age group world record. Wesley's home town is Columbia, Missouri.

Marathon runner Jim Fixx says running is a good sport for young people. His advice: "Don't go too far at first. Young people in average condition can usually run a mile or more without difficulty but it's smart, just the same, to break it up with some walking."

Surfing

Surfing started in Hawaii. In the beginning, it was a very serious sport. Contests took place and people gambled. One bet was 16 war canoes against 4,000 wild pigs. In some contests a surfer might even give up his life if he lost the contest.

The first wooden surfboards weighed as much as 150 pounds.

Table Tennis

In 1907 the world table-tennis tournament was held in Vienna, Austria. One of the rules was very strange: Male players had to wear tuxedos and women players had to wear evening gowns. But that wasn't all. The people in the audience had to dress the same way!

The youngest table-tennis champion was Joy Foster, age 8. She won an international title in Jamaica in 1958.

Table tennis has been called many other names. The most popular is Ping-Pong. Other names are Whiff-Whaff and Flim-Flam.

Tiddlywinks

Tiddlywinks started in England in the late 1700s. At that time they were made of wood or ivory; today they are plastic. "Potting" means flipping the winks into a cup. In 1966 a college student potted 10,000 winks in 3 hours, 51 minutes, and 46 seconds.

Tops

The Japanese make many wonderful kinds of tops. One is called a "childbearing top." In it are little tops. As the big top turns, the little tops spin out of it. Another popular kind can be balanced on a string—while spinning.

Wrestling

History's heaviest wrestler was William J. Cobb of Macon, Georgia, who weighed 802 pounds. People called him "Happy Humphrey." Cobb went on a diet for 3 years and lost 570 pounds.

Special Olympics

Let me win,
but if I cannot win,
let me be brave in the attempt.
— Oath of the Special Olympics

Roberta Cameron, running first in a race, stopped to pick up a friend who had fallen. Two young men in the lead in a mile race joined hands and finished together. Mike Baker, who has only one leg, won a gold medal in gymnastics. These are the special competitors of the Special Olympics, in which all the athletes are heroes.

Special Olympics is a sports program for mentally retarded people over 8 years old. No one is thought to be too handicapped to join. The sponsor is the Joseph P. Kennedy, Jr. Foundation. People everywhere help with Special Olympics —boxer Muhammad Ali, skier Suzy Chaffee, runner Rafer Johnson, and many other sport figures, television and movie-stars, high school athletes, and groups like the YMCA, YWCA, and Camp Fire Clubs.

The Special Olympics athletes start in local training programs. Some are in wheelchairs with handicaps like cerebral palsy. Many come into the program thinking they can do almost nothing. Soon they find out they can do far more than they had dreamed.

Thousands of athletes qualify through state Special Olympics Games for the International Special Olympics held every 4 years. The International Special Olympics is a big event. Thousands of spectators come, and the stands in the stadium, usually at a college, are packed. Flags fly, and a band plays. A special Olympics athlete carries the torch into the stadium, and the Flame of Hope is lit.

In the Special Olympics all the competitors are heroes. *(Special Olympics, Inc.)*

Balloons are set free to soar in the sky in colored flocks. The athletes parade around the stadium, some of them on crutches or in wheelchairs. The cheering begins. For 4 days it goes on as the athletes compete in a number of events. While winning is important, courage and determination are *more important*. Every competitor receives an award, and at the finish line of races, people wait to hug the athletes as they cross.

In Special Olympic Games, athletes are divided into classes according to age and how well they can do. The Official Sports of the Special Olympics are:

Basketball—Team play. Individual run, dribble, and shoot competition.

Bowling—American Bowling Congress rules.

Diving—1 meter. Each athlete does 2 or 3 different dives.

Floor Hockey—Teams of 11 players. Six players involved in play at all times during the games.

Frisbee-Disc—Like the Olympic discus event.

Gymnastics—Free exercise, tumbling, balance beam.

Ice Skating—Speed skating and figure skating.

Poly Hockey—Like floor hockey.

Skiing—Downhill and cross country.

Soccer—Team play. Individual competition in dribbling, passing, shooting, and juggling.

Swimming—Relay events, 25-meter freestyle, 50-meter freestyle, 25-meter backstroke, 25-meter breaststroke, 25-meter butterfly, 100-meter freestyle relay.

Track and Field—50-meter dash, 200-meter dash, 400-meter dash, mile run, softball throw, 400-meter relay, standing long jump, pentathlon, high jump.

Volleyball—Teams.

Wheelchair Events—25-meter race, 30-meter slalom, 100-meter relay.

If you want to help with Special Olympics, get your club to sponsor a team. As an individual, you can make phone calls, raise money, or be a hugger. To contact your local Special Olympics group, look in the white pages of your phone book for "Special Olympics." If there is no Special Olympics program in your area, you can work to get one started. Write to:

Eunice Kennedy Shriver
Special Olympics, Inc.
1701 K Street, NW, Suite 203
Washington, D.C. 20006

Sports Greats

Sesame Street Soccer

TRACY AUSTIN, tennis player

Born: 1962, in California.

Her Record: At age 10, won the National Junior Tournament for 12 and under.

At ages 12 and 13, won the National Junior Tournament for 14 and under.

At age 14, played Wimbledon—the youngest player ever to do so. Was champion of players 18 and under.

At age 16, won the U.S. Open Tournament at Forest Hills. Was ranked fifth in the world in women's tennis.

At age 17, was ranked first in the world in women's tennis. Was youngest woman player to make a million dollars.

Her Life: Tracy Austin, at age 14, wore her blond hair in pigtails. Her teeth were in braces. And she was famous—the youngest player ever to qualify for Wimbledon, the biggest and best tennis tournament in the world. She flew from California, her home, to England for the tournament. Twenty reporters met the plane in London. Before the tournament started, she went to Wimbledon for a preview. She peeked through a hole in the fence around Centre Court, where the big matches are played. "It holds no terror for me," she said. "I would love to play on it." Tracy did not win the tournament. She was beaten in the third round by Chris Evert.

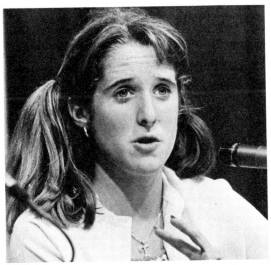

Tracy Austin, a 14-year-old tennis superstar.
(Danilo Nardi, Freelance Photographer's Guild)

In September of that year, Tracy played in the U.S. Open at Forest Hills. She made it to the quarter-finals, the youngest player ever to get that far. Betty Stove, a foot taller than she, beat her.

In 1979, at age 15, Tracy turned pro. She won between $200,000 and $300,000 that year. She also won a red Porsche at a tournament in Germany, where she beat Betty Stove.

At 16, she won the U.S. Open in a match against Chris Evert-Lloyd, 6–4, 6–3. She also reached the semifinals at Wimbledon, where she beat Billie Jean King. Billie Jean called her Babycakes and said, "She's just too cute."

Tracy has been playing tennis since she was 3. She is the youngest in a tennis-playing family. Her 2 brothers and her sister have also played tournament tennis.

Tennis has been her life. She works at it, practicing at least 3 hours a day. Her workouts are tougher than a match, her coach, Robert Landsdorp, has said.

Tracy has powerful strokes and likes to charge the net. She is famous for her 2-handed backhand. Most important, she is tough-minded. She doesn't choke up on big points. "I really think I was born mentally tough," she once said. Between games, she thinks about strategy.

What She Is Like: Tracy is a person who loves people. It shows in her big smile. She emphasizes the bright side of life.

Yet she knows how to be tough. When she started ninth grade at Rolling Hills High School in California, she found reporters and cameramen waiting for her at school. They wanted to ask her about her matches at the U.S. Open. One reporter asked her what her biggest problem was. Her answer was, "You."

By the time Tracy was 16, the braces were gone and she was wearing nail polish and earrings. "No longer is she the little girl in pigtails and pinafores," wrote Barry McDermott, in *Sports Illustrated* magazine. "She's sweet 16, and a killer."

And Tracy herself said that year, after Wimbledon, "I was always doing things younger, and it hasn't hurt me so far."

Bug Boy Winner

STEVE CAUTHEN, jockey

Born: 1960, in Kentucky.

His Record: At age 16, rode nearly 300 winning horses.

At age 17, named Sportsman of the Year by *Sports Illustrated.*

At age 18, won the Triple Crown, riding Affirmed.

His Life: Holding reins hung from a nail on the barn wall, 12-year-old Steve whipped a hay bale. Crazy? Just play-acting? Not really. It was serious work— practice for horse racing. Placing the whip is an art. Once Steve's father watched him whipping the hay and wondered out loud if it was worth it. Would Steve ever earn enough money to make up for what the slashed bales cost?

The answer is yes. In 1977, Steve was the first jockey to bring in $6,000,000 in prize money in one year.

Steve grew up on a farm in Walton, Kentucky. He is the oldest of 3 boys. His father and mother both work with horses, and Steve began to ride ponies when he was 2.

It wasn't until he was 12 that he decided to be a "race rider." Making that decision was risky. Jockeys have to be small, under 116 pounds. Though Steve was small for his age then, there was no way to tell if he would grow. Plenty of small 12-year-olds turn out to be big adults.

Steve knew what he wanted. He has said, "I knew I didn't want to grow up like the other guys. I didn't like riding around

in cars or going to the movies. I didn't enjoy dances or listening to records. All the guys did was run in a pack. I got bored with them and bored with school."

Steve practiced, kept slicing at the hay bales. He could place the whip within an eighth of an inch of where he wanted it. With his father, he watched movies of races over and over again. They figured out what the winners did to win.

At 16, Steve could apply for a jockey's license. (Kids under 16 can't be jockeys.) He was a "bug boy," like all first-year jockeys. The name comes from the stars (*) that follow their names in the official listing. The weight allowance for rider and saddle for a regular jockey is 120 pounds. For a bug boy with 3 stars (***) it is 110 pounds. Carrying less weight, the horse can run faster. The bug boy keeps this advantage until he wins his fifth race. Then his weight allowance is 113 pounds. Two stars follow his name. After his

Steve Cauthen was the most successful apprentice jockey ever. *(Danilo Nardi, Freelance Photographer's Guild)*

thirty-fifth win, the allowance goes up to 115 pounds.

Steve rode a horse named King of Swat in his first race. The horse came in last. A week later, he brought in his first winner—Red Pipe. Soon he was down to one bug. By October he was riding at an important track—Aqueduct, in New York. He became the most successful apprentice in racing history. In his first year he won more races and made more money than any other first-year jockey ever had. In 1977 he was named Sportsman of the Year by *Sports Illustrated*. At age 18, riding a horse named Affirmed, he won the 3 most important races in the United States—the Kentucky Derby, the Belmont Stakes, and the Preakness.

How does he do it? He "talks" to the horse through the reins. He knows the horse's rhythm. He thinks about strategies. He may be one of the finest riders of all time.

What He Is Like: Steve weighs a little over 100 pounds and stands just over 5 feet tall. He is brown-eyed and pale, with big hands and feet. Not much of a talker, he admits to the bad habit of "cussin." For fun he plays gin rummy and table tennis and goes to Broadway shows.

When Steve said he wanted to be a jockey, his mother said it was okay if he didn't get too big or develop a swelled head. He has done neither.

Winner of 7 Perfect 10s

NADIA COMANECI, gymnastics champion

Born: 1961, in Romania.

Her Record: At age 7, came in thirteenth in National Junior Championships of Romania.

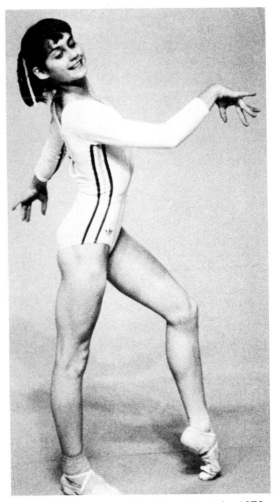

Nadia Comaneci won 7 gold medals at the 1976 Olympics. *(Glenn Sundby, International GYMNAST)*

At age 13, was European all-around gymnastics champion.

At age 14, broke a record by getting 6 perfect scores out of 10 at international meet.

Received 7 gold medals, with perfect scores, at the 1976 World Olympics in Montreal.

Her Life: Nadia was 6 years old, in kindergarten, when her coach found her.

She was playing at gymnastics with a friend in the courtyard of her school. "I saw nothing fantastic in her on the first day," her coach has said. "But in a couple of years she became very serious. Her mental attitude is her great plus. She likes to work. She is always the first to warm up."

When Nadia was only 14 she became a world champion. Not only that—she was better at what she did in gymnastics than anyone had ever been before. She was the first female gymnast to do 3 back hand-springs in a row on the balance beam. She was also the first to do 3 hip circles and a handstand on the higher of the un-even bars.

At the 1976 World Olympics, she scored a 10—a perfect score. No one had ever done that before. The scoreboards, which could only go as high as 9.99, had to be fixed to show 10. Then Nadia scored 6 more 10s! Four were for work on the bar, and 3 were for performances on the bal-ance beam.

Nadia lives with her family in a city in Romania. Her father fixes cars for a liv-ing, and her mother works in a hospital. She has a brother, Adrian, 4 years younger than she. For 4 hours a day she practices gymnastics.

What She Is Like: Nadia says what she thinks. She is so sure of herself that sometimes it sounds as if she is bragging. Before the 1976 Olympics she said on television, "I want for myself gold med-als."

"How many?" someone asked.

"Five," she replied. Then she went ahead and won 7!

For fun, brown-eyed Nadia skis, swims, bicycles, and reads. She collects dolls, too, and now has more than 200 of them. When she came in thirteenth at a meet, her coach bought her an Eskimo doll. He said it was to remind her not to place as low as thirteenth again. She never has. The doll is her lucky piece.

But gymnastics means more to her than anything else. Her secret? "I am so good," she said once, "because I work very hard for it."

Queen of the Ice

SONJA HENIE, figure skater

Born: 1912

Died: 1969

Her Record: At age 10, won National Figure Skating Championship of Nor-way.

At age 14, won World Figure Skating Championship.

At age 15, won gold medal in figure skating at 1928 Winter Olympics in St. Moritz.

Came in first in World Figure Skating Championships 9 more times; received 2 more gold medals in Winter Olympics in 1932 and 1936.

Her Life: Sonja Henie, an 11-year-old with a dimpled smile, competed in the solo figure skating event in the 1924 Winter Olympics. She probably expected to win. After all, only a year after her first skating lesson from her older brother, Leif, she had become a winner. Sonja was 9 when she won the junior championship in her city, Oslo, Norway. At 10, she came in first in Norway's National Figure Skating Championship. But there was no gold medal for her (not even a silver) at the 1924 Olympics.

It didn't stop her. When Leif told her she should burn her skates, she paid no attention. Instead, she started practicing skating 7 hours a day. She also took ballet lessons. It paid off. In 1927 Sonja won the

At 10 Sonja Henie won her first championship.
(Courtesy U.S. Figure Skating Assoc. Hall of Fame and Museum Collection)

World Figure Skating Championship. She was 14. And in the 1928 Winter Olympics, she was awarded the gold medal for figure skating. From then on, there was no stopping her.

Sonja turned skating into an art. She did things that had never been done before. Her costume—white silk and ermine—was different. But, more important, she made major changes in free skating.

In the first half of most competitions, skaters show their skill in doing "school figures," like figure eights. In the second half, they do free skating. Sonja's free skating was dramatic and different. One

of her famous free skating acts was the Dying Swan, adapted from a solo in the ballet *Swan Lake*. She invented 19 kinds of spins. In some, she spun in a complete circle 80 times before stopping.

Sonja won the World Figure Skating Championship 9 more times. In the 1932 and 1936 Winter Olympics, she won the gold medal. Then she turned pro.

Ice skating became popular in the United States in the 1930s. The main reason for this was Sonja Henie. She moved here to star in ice shows and movies. Her ice shows were spectacular, and huge crowds came to see her and the members of her group perform. The acts were beautiful and tricky. Sometimes Sonja was traveling on skates at 35 miles an hour. Skaters were not allowed to wear hairpins. If the pins fell on the ice, they could catch in a performer's skate. Falling at great speeds is, of course, very dangerous.

Between 1938 and 1960, Sonja starred in 11 movies. When she was 26 she was making nearly a million dollars a year. Her legs were insured for $260,000.

What She Was Like: As a child, Sonja said, "Almost always, I win." She was right. All her life she was a winner. Not only was she a champion skater, she also was an expert skier and tennis player. And a money-maker. *And* a movie star. Her death was tragic. At the age of 57 she was traveling in a plane to go for treatments for cancer. The plane crashed, and she was killed.

Camping and Hiking

Mosquito bites. Smoke smell in your clothes. Sore feet. Wild country seen from a mountaintop, and no signs of humans.

Singing around the campfire. Eating potatoes cooked in the embers, ashes and all. Getting lost. A bear track. Water run-

Hiking along the Appalachian Trail in the East is an increasingly popular activity. (For trails in the Northwest, see the map on page 265)
(Courtesy National Park Service)

ning over rocks in a stream. Camping and hiking are wonderful, often uncomfortable, and sometimes dangerous. You can make them less uncomfortable through planning, though getting away from a soft life is part of the fun. And you can avoid danger and still have adventures by following a few rules.

Rules for Safety, Et Cetera

1. Never hike or camp alone. On long hikes and overnight camping trips, you need an adult along. Don't wade or swim alone.

2. Know where you are going. Bring a map and know how to read it. Don't take shortcuts.

3. Use fallen branches for firewood. Don't cut down trees. Build your fire on bare ground, and keep it small. When you break camp, make sure your fire is out. *Completely out.*

4. Don't leave food or open food cans around; the smell may bring animals to your camp. (Not all animals are little and cute. Some are big and dangerous, like bears.) Hang your pack on a tree limb if you have to leave it for a while. Bury or burn all your garbage.

5. Eat or pick only the plants and berries you know are safe.

6. Avoid snakes. Always wear shoes—snakes strike at foot level. Bring a snakebite kit, and read the instructions in it before starting out.

7. Don't put your hands in hollow trees or other hidden places. You might get a surprise—like a set of sharp teeth attached to your fingers.

8. Be careful around baby animals—a big, not-so-cute mother may be around, and animal mothers don't like humans to pick up their children. They may attack.

9. Make sure your boots fit and have been "broken in." To break them in, wear

them around for a few days. Take short hikes in them. Change your socks every night. Always have a clean pair handy.

10. In the morning, shake out your clothes. Something that bites might have decided your hat would make a nice house, and moved in.

11. Enjoy yourself! Racking up a score of miles covered is not the real purpose of hiking. See things. Take along books you can use to identify birds and plants, rocks and shells. Rest when you feel like it. Plan on covering about 2 miles an hour when hiking. Allow enough time to get back. Plan to hike no more than 6 to 10 hours a day. Know when sunset is!

Pack Up Your Troubles?

Don't pack your troubles! Leave them at home, along with other unnecessary things. Keep the weight of your pack under 30 pounds if you're under 14. Lay what you plan to take on the floor before you pack. Decide what's *really* necessary and put the rest away. Put light things on the bottom of the pack, along with items you won't need often or fast. On top, put heavier things. Items you may need in a hurry—like lunch or first-aid kit—go in pockets or on top. While you're still home, try the full pack on. Walk around with it. Make sure it balances right.

Checklist of Things to Pack for a One-Day Trip

map flashlight compass matches
signal whistle first-aid kit snakebite kit
insect repellent poncho
extra shirt or sweatshirt
lunch canteen

Checklist of Things to Add for an Overnight Trip

☐ sleeping bag
☐ ground cover
☐ string
☐ stove and fuel
☐ soap, toothpaste, toothbrush, comb and brush
☐ tube tent
☐ sun cream
☐ pots to cook with
☐ fish line and hooks
☐ food
☐ knife, fork, dish
☐ toilet paper
☐ Band-Aids, adhesive tape, moleskin
☐ spare shirt and pants
☐ socks
☐ down vest
☐ hat

Trail Mix Recipe

Trail mix is a good snack that gives you energy on a hike. Use any combination of the following:
nuts
raisins
dried apricots
dried prunes (not *too* many)
sunflower seeds
pumpkin seeds
Pack the mix in plastic baggies in half-cup batches.

Walk Like an Indian

The way you walk can make a difference in how many miles you cover and how tired you get. Walk like an Indian. Come down on your heel. Push off with your toes. Your tracks should look like this:

See next page for the wrong way to walk.

Not like this:

If You Get Lost

Most of the time, when you think you're lost, you aren't. The main thing to remember is THINK. Keep calm. Other hints:

1. Climb to a high place, so you can see distances. Look for a landmark you can head for.

2. If you can't figure a way out, stay where you are. On high ground, build a fire. Feed it with green branches and leaves to make smoke. Searchers may then be able to spot you. If you can find a clearing, make a distress signal. That way searchers in planes will know where you are. You can stamp out the signal in snow, if there is some. Otherwise, use bright cloth or scratch in the dirt. Make the signal as big as you can.

Another distress signal: 3 whistles, 3 shouts, or 3 flashes from a flashlight.

3. If you decide to walk out, follow a road or trail made by humans. Or follow a power line. Or travel downstream.

4. Never travel at night.

Where to Go

You can hike in a city park or woods near your house. You can camp in your backyard. Other places are national forests, national parks, and wilderness regions.

For information, write to the government agency in charge.

National Forest System. In the United States there are 154 national forests, threaded with roads and trails. Picnic and camping areas are provided. Write to:

Forest Service
Department of Agriculture
Washington, D.C. 20250

Distress Signals

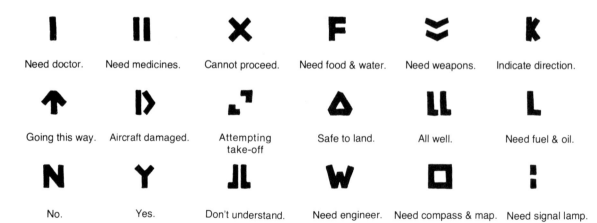

National Trail System. Many long trials are maintained by the Forest Service. Some have been important in the history of our country. Though you may not be able to travel the entire length of a trail, you may want to hike on part of it. Here's a sample map of the Northwest.

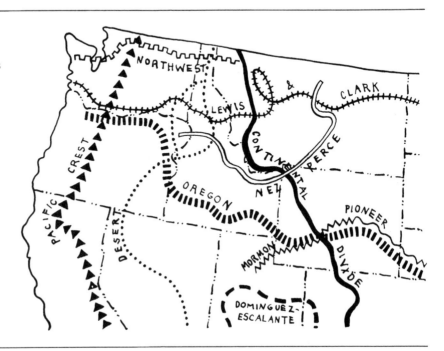

The Forest Service maintains many long trails for hiking and camping. Which of these in the Pacific Northwest would you like to hike? *(U.S. Department of the Interior, Heritage Conservation and Recreation Service)*

National Parks. Our national parks are managed by the National Park Service. Rangers often offer nature hikes for people who visit. There are also programs like the NESA (National Environmental Study Area) program and the NEED (National Environmental Education Development) program. Write to:

Office of Public Affairs
National Park Service
Department of the Interior
Washington, D.C. 20240

You can request a "Guide and Map of National Parks of the United States" from the Research and Scientific Services Division of the National Park Service at the same address.

Clubs to Join

Many hiking clubs have been formed in the United States. Some are local. Major national clubs are, of course, the Boy Scouts and Girl Scouts. Also, write to the following groups for information:

Sierra Club. Children under 14 can be members if their parents are. Until you are 16, you can't go on outings unless a responsible adult goes with you. Sierra Club outings include short hikes as well as long backpacking trips, canoe trips, rafting, and more. Address: Sierra Club,

530 Bush Street, San Francisco, California 94108.

United States Orienteering Federation. Some of the clubs in this group accept children. Orienteering is a sport. You learn to find your way with a map and compass through a course in the countryside. Class A meets (competitions) have events for children. Boy Scouts of America offers a merit badge in orienteering. Address: United States Orienteering Federation, P.O. Box 1039, Ballwin, Missouri 63011.

Bicycle Safety: Rules of the Road

1. Obey all traffic laws and signals.
2. Don't ride double or try stunts.
3. Ride near the curb in the same direction as traffic.
4. Try not to ride through busy streets or high-speed traffic.
5. Walk—don't ride—your bike across busy intersections and left-turn corners.
6. Don't ride in wet weather. When wet, handbrakes need a long distance to stop.
7. Try not to ride at night. Most bad accidents happen at night. If you must, then wear white or light-colored clothes. Be sure your bike has reflectors. You can even buy reflector tape to sew onto your clothes. Some people strap front-back flashlights on their legs and arms.
8. Don't wear loose clothing or long coats. They can get caught in pedals or wheels.
9. Watch out for pot holes, big rocks, sewer grates, and other trouble spots.
10. Keep your bike in good working condition (see drawing).

Biking is great with a friend, but avoid heavy traffic.
(Bill Price, Freelance Photographer's Guild)

Have your bicycle checked twice a year by a reliable serviceman.

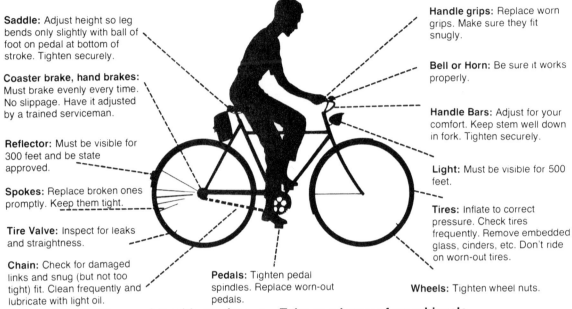

Saddle: Adjust height so leg bends only slightly with ball of foot on pedal at bottom of stroke. Tighten securely.

Coaster brake, hand brakes: Must brake evenly every time. No slippage. Have it adjusted by a trained serviceman.

Reflector: Must be visible for 300 feet and be state approved.

Spokes: Replace broken ones promptly. Keep them tight.

Tire Valve: Inspect for leaks and straightness.

Chain: Check for damaged links and snug (but not too tight) fit. Clean frequently and lubricate with light oil.

Pedals: Tighten pedal spindles. Replace worn-out pedals.

Handle grips: Replace worn grips. Make sure they fit snugly.

Bell or Horn: Be sure it works properly.

Handle Bars: Adjust for your comfort. Keep stem well down in fork. Tighten securely.

Light: Must be visible for 500 feet.

Tires: Inflate to correct pressure. Check tires frequently. Remove embedded glass, cinders, etc. Don't ride on worn-out tires.

Wheels: Tighten wheel nuts.

Always ride with caution • Take good care of your bicycle

(Courtesy Bicycle Manufacturers' Association of America, Inc.)

Get Involved! Clubs to Join

Many of these groups like the Boy Scouts and Girl Scouts, have local clubs. Look in your phone book for the clubs that are in your area. If you have any problems, write to the addresses that are given below. The addresses are for the national headquarters of the clubs.

Academy of Model Aeronautics
815 15th Street, N.W.
Washington, D.C. 20005

Flying model airplanes has always been an exciting sport. This group has a special "cub" program for kids from 8 to 13. The program offers easy-to-understand kits on how to build good models. There are more than 1,200 clubs across the country. There is probably one near you. Write to the main headquarters. Ask for a list of clubs in your area.

Boys' Clubs of America
771 First Avenue
New York, New York 10017

What do Joe DiMaggio, O. J. Simpson, and Neil Diamond have in common? They all belonged to Boys' Clubs. Today over a million boys belong to 1,100 of these clubs in the United States. They are 6 to 18 years old. The clubs have programs in sports, arts and crafts, and many other fields. One kid from New Jersey said, "I always liked sports a lot. I started coming to the club because they had nice basketball courts and a swimming pool. Now I do a lot of other things, too. And I think there are a lot more things I can do."

Boy Scouts of America
P.O. Box 61030
Dallas/Fort Worth Airport, Texas 75261

The Boy Scouts is made up of 3 groups: Cub Scouts (ages 8 to 10), Boy Scouts (ages 11 to 17), and Explorers (ages 15 to 20). Since the club began in 1910, over 62 million people have joined. Some of them—like President John F. Kennedy, Reggie Jackson, and Muhammad Ali—have become famous. Earning merit badges is an important part of the scouting program. There are more than 100 areas in which you can get a merit badge. Some of them are camping, coin collecting, hiking, pets, horsemanship, and photography.

Camp Fire Clubs
4601 Madison Avenue
Kansas City, Missouri 64112

This club used to be called Camp Fire Girls. However, boys can now join, so the name has been changed. Fourth, fifth, and sixth graders are members of the Camp Fire Adventure Club. They go on camping trips, play games, and do many other things. Seventh and eighth graders can join the Discovery Club. Members hold parties, dances, carnivals, and hikes. Both age groups learn about conservation, safety, and health.

4-H Clubs
United States Department of Agriculture
Washington, D.C. 20250

These scouts are practicing with semaphore flags. See page 419 for a semaphore chart. *(Courtesy Boy Scouts of America)*

The 4-H is for young people in both the country and in the city. More than 5 million kids from 9 to 19 take part in many wonderful activities. Most people know about the animal and farming programs. However, the 4-H is also interested in gardening, photography, horseback riding, bicycle safety, and karate. And that is only a short list of what 4-H clubs have to offer. There are more than 93,000 clubs.

Girls' Clubs of America, Inc.
205 Lexington Avenue
New York, New York 10016

Girls from 6 to 18 can join. Over 220,000 girls belong to 250 local clubs. Local clubs have sports programs and classes in art, health, and homemaking.

Girl Scouts
830 Third Avenue
New York, New York 10022

These girls have raised the sheep themselves as part of a 4-H Club project.
(Courtesy 4-H-Youth Programs, Cooperative Extension Service, USDA)

Everybody knows about the Girl Scouts. The group has been around for over 65 years. Today, more than 3 million girls belong.

There are 4 different kinds of Girl Scouts: Brownies (ages 6 to 8), Juniors (ages 9 to 11), Cadettes (ages 12 to 14), and Seniors (ages 14 to 17). The groups sponsor many activities, especially in science, the arts, and the out-of-doors.

Puppeteers of America
5 Cricklewood Path
Pasadena, California 91107

If you love puppets, this is the club for you. Members get a magazine that gives all the latest news about puppets. It will also tell you when puppet carnivals will be held in your area. Special worksheets will be sent to you, providing tips on how to become a good puppeteer.

Ranger Rick's Nature Club
1412 16th Street, N.W.
Washington, D.C. 20036

There are more than 2,500 local chapters of this group. This is the club pledge:

I give my pledge as a member of
Ranger Rick's Nature Club
To use my eyes to see the beauty
of all outdoors.
To train my mind to learn the
importance of nature.
To use my hands to help protect
our soil, water, woods and wildlife.
And, by my good example, to
show others how to respect,
properly use and enjoy our
natural resources.

Local clubs have many exciting projects. Here are just a few of the things they do:

1. Go on nature hikes and other field trips.
2. Put together ecology fairs.
3. Start recycling centers for paper or aluminum cans.
4. Plant trees in areas that need them.
5. Plan bike-a-thons and walks for wildlife.

6. Hold poster or photography contests. If there is no club in your neighborhood, start one. All you need is an adult to be the club sponsor. Write to the above address for more facts.

Star Trek Welcommittee
Box 12
Saranac, Michigan 48881

This group will answer any questions you have about *Star Trek*. Also, they can send you a list of other fans in your area. Want to start a club of your own? They will tell you how to do it. When you write to the club, send along a self-addressed, stamped envelope.

World Pen Pals
1690 Como Avenue
Saint Paul, Minnesota 55108

World Pen Pals has matched up over 40,000 young people in 175 countries. It is a great way to make new friends and learn about other places. You have to be 12 to get a pen pal. Write to the group and they will send you a form to fill out. Be sure to send a self-addressed, stamped envelope.

YMCA
101 N. Wacker Drive
Chicago, Illinois 60606

There are YMCAs all around the country. They have wonderful sports programs—like swimming and basketball—plus great camping and hiking activities. Almost 600 million boys and girls belong to YMCAs.

Girls enjoy a game of pogo stick at a summer camp.
(Syd Greenberg, Freelance Photographer's Guild)

Chapter *9*
MONEY AND WORK

Money Didn't Always Jingle or Fold—
Facts About Money

Stone money was used on the Caroline Islands until World War Two. The stones were round, with holes in the middle. Some pieces were so heavy they had to be strung on a pole and carried by 2 men. Other kinds were as big as doughnuts.

In the New Hebrides, feathers were used for money.

The obol, in ancient Greece, was a small coin about the size of a pinhead. People carried obols in their mouths to keep them from getting lost.

The Chinese invented metal money nearly 4,000 years ago. At first they used gold cubes. Later the coins had holes in the middle so they could be carried on a string. They were called *cash*.

The Chinese also had folding money. At first it was made of deerskin. Later it was made of paper. The larger the piece of paper, the more it was worth. One piece 8½ by 13½ inches was worth 1,000 copper coins. The government forced people to use it. If they refused, they could lose their heads.

From 1050 to 1108, some French money was made of leather.

Once the money in England was made of wood.

The American Indians cut clam shells into pieces to make money. They called it "wampum." The purple wampum was worth more than the white wampum, because less of the shell was purple. (Usually, the rarer something is, the more it is worth.) Some people cheated by painting the white wampum purple.

On the Franklin cent of 200 years ago was written "Mind Your Own Business."

Skulls were money in Borneo.

Some American Indians used wampum (strings of clamshell pieces) as money.

Even today, the Masai in Africa consider cattle to be money.

When the government was short of money in Quebec in 1685, playing cards were used. The cards were cut into 4 parts and stamped with the crown and lily. Their value was written on them, and they were signed by 2 government officials.

In Germany, after World War One, money lost its value. Paper money was cheaper to burn than firewood. In 1923, it took 4,200 billion German marks to equal one U.S. dollar.

After World War I, German money was so worthless people needed wheelbarrows for it.

Collectibles: For Fun—and Maybe Money

Collecting things has always been a wonderful hobby. The list of collectibles is endless. People save toys, postcards, banks, and tools. They keep buttons, bottles, and music boxes. Some people collect barbed wire, beer cans, bubble gum wrappers, and bear traps. One man in the Midwest has a collection of 735 oil rags!

Making money should not be the reason to start a collection. You want to have fun, find new interests, and make new friends. Perhaps you will also make a little money. Maybe you won't. It shouldn't matter.

Here are some collectibles that are among kids' favorites. Remember: The prices given can change from day to day.

Autographs

What is an autograph? It can be just a signed name. It might be a signed picture or letter. It could be a signed "document"—like a telegram or a military paper. It can also be a signed poem or speech. Collecting autographs is easy and fun, and it doesn't cost much.

To begin, you have to decide what autographs you want. Some ideas: movie stars, TV stars, writers, famous children, sports heroes, famous women, artists. Don't collect too many different kinds. About 3 or 4 areas is enough.

Make a list of people and write to them. Your letter should be friendly and polite. You can ask for a signed picture, or else enclose a special card for them to sign. However, the very best autographs are letters. A man named Charles Hamilton, an autograph dealer in New York City makes a living by collecting autographs. He says, "In the long run, those letters that tell us something about the person's thoughts are especially valuable."

How do you get someone to write you a letter? First of all, make your letter interesting and thoughtful. Do a little homework on the celebrity. Maybe you and the celebrity have something in common.

For example, suppose you are writing to a famous senator. While reading about him, you learn he was once very shy. He must have overcome it because he makes

Signatures of the Declaration of Independence signers are precious collectibles. Can you find Button Gwinnett's autograph? *(Charles Hamilton Galleries)*

speeches all the time. Maybe you are shy. Tell him so and ask him how he got over his shyness. Letters don't have to be about problems. You and the celebrity may share the same hobby. Maybe you both come from the same hometown.

Besides a letter, there are other good kinds of autographs. Are you writing to a favorite author? Do you have a favorite paragraph from one of the author's books? If so, get it typed up and send it to the author. Ask to have it signed. Maybe you are good at drawing. You might draw a picture of the person and try to get it signed. Use your imagination. There are many ways to get a good autograph.

Getting addresses for celebrities is easy. Check *Who's Who in America, International Who's Who,* and *Current Biography.* All libraries have these books. Ask the librarian for help if you need it.

Very important: Be sure to send the celebrity a self-addressed, stamped envelope. Your chances of getting an answer are much better if you do. Then you can sit back and wait. It is very thrilling when the mail comes and there is a letter for you!

Take good care of your collection. The best way is to put your autographs between cellulose acetate leaves, available at all stationery stores. Or put each one in a separate manila envelope. Keep them out of very warm and very damp places. *Never* use glue, Scotch tape, staples, or paper clips on your autographs.

Someday your autographs may be worth some money. The autographs of celebrities of the past are worth money today. An autograph from Clark Gable is worth about $100. One from Humphrey Bogart is worth $300. President Harry Truman's autograph sells for $40. The artist Pierre Auguste Renoir's autograph can bring as much as $150. The

highest-priced autograph is the signature of Button Gwinnett, one of the men who signed the Declaration of Independence. Altogether, there are only 40 of his autographs around. Recently, a collector paid $100,000 for Gwinnett's autograph.

Sometimes very popular people don't have time to answer letters. They have a secretary sign their letters or they buy a special machine that does the signing. This kind of signature is worth nothing. You won't be able to tell if the signature is fake, but an autograph dealer can. Look for an autograph dealer near you. The Yellow Pages lists dealers. Visit a dealer's store. It will be great fun to see what is for sale. You will also learn about prices. If there are no dealers near you, ask your library for the address of some dealers and write to them. Ask for a catalog to find out what is for sale. Sometimes, autographs sell for as little as $3. Once you get a collection underway, you may want to buy a few autographs.

If you want to know more, read *Big Name Hunting* by Charles and Diane Hamilton (New York: Simon and Schuster, 1973). It is a great book for beginners.

Coins

Collecting coins has been called "the hobby of kings." Coins have been around for over 2,500 years. At first, only kings and rich people were collectors, but it wasn't long before everyone got interested. Today, over 5 million Americans take part in the hobby.

All you need are a few coins and a desire to collect. Most kids like to start with penny collections. You try to get one penny for each date that is in a penny coin folder. The folders are made of cardboard and have holes to hold the coins. You can buy them in coin stores and hobby stores.

Different folders have different years. Get as many folders as you want.

You don't have to start with pennies. Some kids like Jefferson nickels. Some like Roosevelt dimes. Also very popular are "proof sets." They are made especially for collectors and are never used as spending money. They are very shiny and nice-looking.

The condition of a coin is very important. Always try to get coins that are not too worn out. The design, letters, and numbers should be clear. Coin collectors rate all coins. One of the best ratings is "extremely fine." Another rating is "good." One of your pennies in "good" condition might be worth 6¢. If it were in "extremely fine" condition, it would be worth 25¢.

Coins should *not* be cleaned. Old coins should look old. If a coin is covered with dirt, you might use a little soap and water on it. Don't rub it dry; just pat it with a towel. Never use polish on a coin and never rub it with a cloth. You don't want to destroy the coin by wearing down the surface. Also, pick coins up by the edges. Try not to touch the face.

Always be on the lookout for coins. Go through pocket change every night. Do you have an attic? If so, maybe some old coins have been packed away up there. Check pockets of old clothes. Check under cushions of sofas and chairs. Go to

Old coins can be quite valuable. Pictured here are the front or obverse (left) and reverse sides (right) of ancient coins: Top, coins from Tyre (126 B.C.–A.D. 57); center, a gold coin of Tiberius; bottom, an Augustine penny and a Hebrew sheckel. *(Ewing Galloway)*

Obverse   **Reverse**

U.S. silver coins before 1965 are also valuable.
(Ewing Galloway)

the bank and get a roll of whatever kind of coin you are collecting.

Will your coins ever be worth much money? Probably not. You'll never get rich with a coin collection. They will be worth a little money, but not a lot. The coins worth money are hard to find, but you might get lucky! A taxi cab driver once found a penny worth $115!

No matter what you collect, remember this: "Pure silver" coins are worth money. Any dimes, quarters, or half dollars with dates *before* 1965 are valuable. Don't spend them. Hold on to them and ask a dealer what they are worth.

It is a good idea to join a coin club. A wonderful club is the American Numismatic Association. (Numismatics means the study and collecting of money.) You

have to be 11 years old to join. Write to the club:

American Numismatic Association
P.O. Box 2366
Colorado Springs, Colorado 80901

There are many good books on coins; check your nearest bookstore. Many of the books are paperbacks. Most books give price lists of what different coins are worth. Also, your library has books on how to start a coin collection.

Comic Books

Finding *Marvel Comics #1* would make a collector turn cartwheels. It's almost impossible to find one. Buying one is even worse. When the first issue came out in 1939, it cost a dime. Today it is worth about $18,000!

Action Comics #1 is another important comic book. It came out in 1938, and in it was the very first story about Superman. The story told all about how Superman came to Earth, and said he could run "faster than an express train." That first issue is worth about $16,000.

Comic books from the "Golden Age" are worth big money. They were published from 1938 to 1945. However, kids have a slim chance of finding one, and they cost too much money to buy. But you might get lucky and find some good comics books from the 1960s on. Some are worth $1, or $5, or much more. Old comics might be hiding in family attics, Goodwill stores, or garage sales.

Your best bet is to start a new collection. Comic books don't cost very much. They might be valuable in the future. Nobody knows exactly which comic books to save. However, there are a few "good bets":

Number One Issues: The first issue of any new comic book is a good bet. Buy a copy.

First Appearance Issues: This refers to the first time a new character shows up in a comic book. It doesn't matter which comic book. Superman first appeared in *Action Comics #1*. Later on, Superman got his very own comic book. Spiderman got started in *Amazing Fantasy #15*. That issue is now worth about $1,400.

Origin Issues: Origin means how the character was born or "came into being." Sometimes the "origin" issue and the "first appearance" issue are the same comic book. That is true of Superman. On the other hand, that's not true of the Black Panther. He showed up in *Fantastic Four #52* and his origin was not told until *Fantastic Four #53*.

Cross-over Issues: Cross-over refers to a popular character's "visit" to the comic book of another popular character. For instance, Batman visited Superman in *Superman #76*. Watch out for this kind of comic book.

Comic books are made of cheap paper and need special care. Comic book dealers keep them in special plastic bags. (Baggies and Glad Bags are *not* good.) Usually a dealer will be happy to sell you some of the plastic bags. Keep comic books in a dark, cool place. *Do not* put them in cardboard boxes.

Have an old comic book? Want to know what it is worth? Go to the library and ask for the *The Comic Book Price Guide* by Robert Overstreet. Prices for most comic books are listed. They are retail prices; if you sell to a dealer, you usually only get half of the retail price.

There are other ways to sell comic books. One way is through special magazines. Lots of people buy and sell this way. Here are 2 addresses to write to:

Comics Buyers' Guide
700 E. State Street
Iola, Wisconsin 54990

Comics Collector
700 E. State Street
Iola, Wisconsin 54990

Every year special comic book conventions are held in cities like New York, San Diego, Chicago, and Portland. Be sure to go if one is held near you.

Rock Records

In the 1950s and 1960s, rock 'n' roll music blasted its way across America. Kids loved it, adults hated it. Today thousands of people are collecting those early records.

The big names in those days were Chuck Berry, Little Richard, Fats Domino, and Buddy Holly. And the biggest name of all was Elvis Presley. Their early records are worth the most money. They might sell for $2 to $25 each.

Prices for old 45 rpm records and albums change a great deal. A book called *Official Price Guide to Records* by Thomas E. Hudgeons gives today's prices, as well as a big list of people and stores that buy and sell records. Ask for the book at your library. Or write to:

House of Collectibles
1900 Premier Row
Orlando, Florida 32809

Some record dealers make up lists of records and mail them to collectors. The collectors bid on the records. You might write to a few of those places. Ask for their past lists. Tell them you are a new collector and want to know what different records are worth. Two good lists to write for:

Record Exchanger
Box 6144
Orange, California 92667

Goldmine
700 E. State Street
Iola, Wisconsin 54990

Are today's records good to collect? Sure! Watch for the *early* recordings of singers like Linda Ronstadt, Elton John, and Fleetwood Mac. *Early* records are those done before the singer became a star. Someday those records may be valuable.

Compared to lots of hobbies, record collecting is pretty new. That means you have a good chance of finding some old records for a pretty cheap price. Check out swap meets and garage sales. Also, look in thrift stores. You could pay as little as a dime or 50¢ for a record. Keep your eyes open!

Once you get some records, take good care of them. Scratches hurt the value of records. The records should stay inside the paper liner. An album will also have a jacket. Both singles and albums should *not* be stacked, but should stand upright. Always keep the records away from heat.

A Number One Find: One album that is hard to find is a first edition of "Yesterday and Today," an early Beatles album. The cover is important. It should have the Beatles dressed in white butcher's outfits. If you ever find that album, get in touch with a good record dealer. It could pay off!

Sports Cards

The earliest sports cards came out in the 1880s. Tobacco companies put them in cigarette packages. These "give-away" cards help to sell cigarettes. Since then, many different companies have used the same idea. It is a good way to sell products. Sports cards helped to sell candy, popcorn, and ice cream. They were packed with cereal, meat, donuts, and soft drinks. People even found cards with dog food, beer, and macaroni!

Collecting cards became big-time in 1951 when Topps Chewing Gum included cards with their bubble gum. Today the company is still making cards. They cover 4 sports: baseball, football, basketball, and hockey. Baseball cards have always been the most popular. But who knows? That could change.

Every year Topps puts out a series of

The Honus Wagner card was issued in 1910. Only 24 are still around now.

TY COBB
OUTFIELDER—DETROIT TIGERS

1927 NEW YORK YANKEES

BABE RUTH
OUTFIELDER—NEW YORK YANKEES

BRANCH RICKEY
MANAGER—ST. LOUIS BROWNS

SAD SAM JONES
PITCHER—BOSTON RED SOX

ROGERS HORNSBY
SECOND BASEMAN—ST. LOUIS CARDINALS

133

BOB MEUSEL
Outfielder—N.Y. Yankees

Long Bob Meusel was a star outfielder for the great
Yankee teams of the 1920's. His best year was in
1925 when he led the American League in RBI's with
138 and 33 home runs. His career lasted 11 years, in
which he collected 1693 hits for a solid .309 average.

BOB MEUSEL
OUTFIELDER—N.Y. YANKEES

RENATA GALASSO Inc.

WORLD'S LARGEST
HOBBY CARD DEALER

1170 75th STREET
BROOKLYN, NEW YORK 11228

1980 TCMA

Old baseball cards. *(Courtesy Renata Galasso, Inc.)*

cards for each sport. Some kids like to collect the whole series. For example, the 1977 baseball set had 660 cards. Each one is worth about 8¢. The whole set is worth about $60. Older sets can be more valuable. The 1956 baseball set might sell for $530. It has 340 cards.

Everybody likes to collect star cards. The value, of course, depends on how hard they are to get. When Willie Mays started playing baseball, Topps wasn't sure that he would be a star. They printed some cards for Mays but not many. Those early cards are great to have. A 1955 Mays card sells for $125. Topps put out the first Mickey Mantle card in 1952. It is now worth $800! Most recent cards are worth about 4¢ each, but someday they could be worth more.

The king of all cards is a 1910 Honus Wagner. He played for the Pittsburgh Pirates. A tobacco company, Sweet Caporal, printed the card. Wagner didn't like smoking and told the company to get rid of the card. They did, and less than 24 of those cards are still around. Today one of them is worth more than $20,000!

Want to collect cards with mistakes on them? In 1969 the card of Aurelio Rodriguez (third baseman for the Angels) carried his name but not his picture. It had the batboy's picture. Topps made another big goof in 1967 on the card for Philadelphia Phillies' pitcher Dave Bennett. The card read, "The 19-year-old fireballer is only 18 years old." In 1959 pitcher Lew Burdette played a trick on the Topps people. He was a right-handed pitcher, but he posed for his card picture as if he were a left-handed pitcher. Topps didn't catch the mistake. In addition, Topps spelled his name Lou, not Lew.

The condition of the card is important. "Mint" condition is the best. It has no wear and tear on it; not even the edges are bent. Other conditons are excellent, very good, good, and poor. Trade and flip cards with your friends—that's the easiest way to get the cards you want. Ask relatives whether they saved any of their cards. Check garage sales and swap meets. You might find an old card.

For current prices, check *The Sports Collector's Bible* by Bert Randolph Sugar. It also gives lists of players in every set of cards. Here are 2 magazines for collectors:

Sports Collector's Digest
700 E. State Street
Iola, Wisconsin 54990

Baseball Hobby News
4540 Kearny Villa Road, Suite 215
San Diego, California 92123

Stamps

Over 20 million Americans collect stamps. Those little pieces of gummed paper can tell you a lot about the past. Pictures of famous people, buildings, and animals are on stamps, as well as airplanes, boats, and birds. Special events—like the Boston Tea Party—are also shown on stamps. The list of different kinds of stamps goes on and on.

To start, save the stamps from the mail sent to your house. Ask friends to save their stamps for you. Buy a big bag of used stamps at a hobby store or toy store. A big bag of stamps is low in cost. It gives beginners a good idea of how many kinds of stamps are around.

What kind of stamps would you like to collect? Some people like to collect stamps from foreign countries. Some like to collect air-mail or special-delivery stamps. Collecting stamps on different subjects is very popular with kids. Your

This is one of America's great stamp mistakes—the 1918 "inverted airmail."

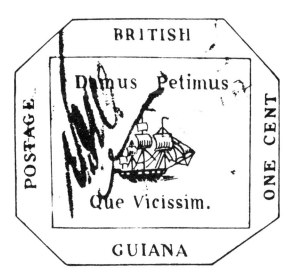

This penny stamp, now worth over $850,000, is the world's most valuable stamp.

local post office can help. The post office sells "starter kits," each on a different topic—like travel, sports, outer space, and so on. The post office also sells a terrific book called *Stamps and Stories*. It tells how to start a collection and gives the latest prices of stamps. Full of beautiful colored pictures, the book also tells stories about each American stamp.

Beginners should have a good stamp album. To put stamps in the album you will need special hinges and mounts. Mounts (little plastic envelopes) should be used for your most important stamps. Hinges are okay for all other stamps. An important tool to get is a pair of tongs. You should use tongs, instead of your fingers, to pick up stamps. As you build a collection, there are other tools to buy. All good stamp books will tell you about different kinds of equipment. Taking care of your stamps is important. A stamp in "superb" condition is much better than one in "good condition."

Finding a rare stamp would be a miracle—don't expect it to happen. The most talked-about stamp is the 1856 British Guiana one-cent magenta (a purplish-red color). There is only one copy in the whole world. In 1873 a 12-year-old boy in England found it. He sold it for $1.50. Today it is worth over $850,000!

One of the most famous American stamps is the 1918 "inverted airmail" stamp. It has on it a picture of a Curtiss "Jenny" airplane—flying upside down. The government usually catches that kind of mistake, but somebody in the post office goofed, and one sheet of 100 "Jenny" stamps slipped by. It was sent to a post office in Washington, D.C., where a customer named William T. Robey bought the whole sheet. He paid 24¢ for each stamp. Each one is now worth over $100,000.

Every new collector needs a good guidebook. *Stamps and Stories* is one.

There are many good paperbacks. Look in your local bookstore or ask a stamp dealer to suggest a beginner's book.

Joining a stamp club is a good idea. The United States Post Office sponsors one called the Benjamin Franklin Stamp Club. This club is in thousands of schools around the country.

Another club is the Junior Philatelists of America. (A "philatelist" is a stamp collector.) Members can borrow films and records about stamps. The club has a pen pal department and a department for members who want to exchange stamps. If you write to the club, send a self-addressed, stamped envelope. The address:

Junior Philatelists of America
1018 Foster Street
Evanston, Illinois 60201

Kids and Work

"To See the Men at Play" — What Led up to Child Labor Laws

Chimneys were small in the 1800s; some were only 7 inches across. And chimneys had to be cleaned. If they weren't, the soot that formed could start a fire. The best people to clean small chimneys? Small people. Children.

Children as young as 4 were chimney sweeps in England and America. If they refused to climb up the chimney, they were forced to do it. Pins were stuck in their feet or lighted matches were held under them. Chimney sweepers' bones grew crooked from the work they did. Some got chimney sweeper's cancer.

In the 1800s children worked 12 hours a day hauling carts in the coal mines.

When they became too big for the job, they were let go. They had no education, and they knew no other skills.

Kids worked in the mines, too. Very small children opened and shut doors that let the coal wagons through. They worked far below the surface of the earth. After their candles burned out, it was very dark. One child, 8, told a group of English adults what mining was like for him:

"I am a trapper in the . . . pit. I have to trap without a light, and I'm scared. I never go to sleep. Sometimes I sing when I have a light, but not in the dark. I dare not sing then."

Older children pulled the coal trucks. All they wore, boy or girl, was a pair of pants. Around their waists they wore a belt, and attached to the belt were chains. The chains went between their legs to the coal truck, and they crawled along hauling the cart. Children worked 12 hours a day doing this.

Children worked in the mills, too. In glass factories they stood 12 hours a day in front of fiery furnaces making glass. Girls worked in sweat shops, sewing clothes. They spun silk, made cigarettes by hand, and worked on fake flowers.

A poem from the time goes:

> The golf links lie so near the mill
> That almost every day
> The laboring children can look out
> To see the men at play.

And of course children worked long hours at farming.

In the late 1800s, laws were passed so that children need not work so long and so hard. In 1890, though, 1,750,000 children from 10 to 15 were working full-time in the United States. It was not until 1938 that child labor was largely stopped.

Some American kids still work long hours in the fields. Their families are migrants who travel to the places where the farmwork is.

The Kids of the Pioneer Railway

Kids do it all on the Pioneer Railway of Budapest, Hungary. The stationmaster is 11 years old. The girl train conductor is 10. The engineer apprentice is a teenager. Others sell tickets, run the telegraph, operate control stations. There are 700 of them aged 10 to 14.

The Pioneer Railway is not a toy railroad or a ride in an amusement park. It's full-sized. It runs on 7 miles of track through the country. It has sidings, tunnels, depots. Each year, thousands of people ride in its cars. Trains go from early in the morning until late in the evening. They travel to the ski slopes at Elore Station. To Csilléberc Station, where the kids' camping headquarters are. To Normafa Station, by the big, 100-year-old beech tree, where open-air operas are staged. In the more than 30 years kids have run the Pioneer Railway, there has never been an accident.

About 50 young people, in dark blue uniforms and red hats, are on duty at one time. Each gets a chance to try several jobs. To qualify to work for Pioneer Railway, they have to do well in school and pass oral and written tests. They receive 4 months of classes and several years' experience. And when they grow up, they can work full-time for other railroads in Hungary.

"All aboard! . . ."

Turn the page to see the many kids of the Pioneer Railway at work keeping the trains running well.

The Pioneer Railway of Hungary, where kids do everything...

Kids aged 10 to 14 do all the work of running the Pioneer Railway in Budapest, Hungary. Read the previous page for more of the story.
(Courtesy Tourist Information Service of Hungary)

Getting a Job—No, You Can't Mine Coal for 12 Hours a Day, Poor Kid!

Because of child labor laws, you probably will have a hard time finding a full-time job. This is especially true if you are under 14. By law, the number of hours you can work is limited. You can't do anything dangerous. You can't work in factories, on boats, or for the railroad. Places that sell liquor can't hire you. (For a list of rules, see "Laws About Working," pages 127–128.)

You must be paid the legal minimum wage (more for overtime) if you work for a company that does business across state lines.

Some jobs are open to children:

You can be an actor or singer in television, movies, and radio. Your parents have to agree to it.

You can work for your family in a family-owned business, if the job is not dangerous.

You probably can do farm work, but not during school hours.

And you can work for yourself.

Getting a Work Permit

For many jobs, you need to get a work permit. You don't need one for babysitting, delivering papers, mowing lawns, and doing other odd jobs. But if you want to bag groceries at a market, you *will* need one.

Ask your teacher or principal how to get a work permit in your community. Rules vary from place to place. You will probably need written permission from your parent or guardian. The person who wants to hire you must promise the job in writing. You may also need proof of your age (a birth certificate), and you may need to have a physical.

In many places, the schools give out work permits. And if not, someone at the school can tell you where to go to get one.

Social Security

For many jobs, you must get a Social Security number. To find out about it, call the United States Social Security Administration. The number is in your phone book under "United States Government." Then look for "Social Security Administration" in the *S* section.

Who'd Hire a Kid?
Tips for Getting a Job

1. Find out what places hire young people in your area. Ask other kids. Check the newspaper classified section under "Jobs" or "Employment." Read bulletin board notices.

2. If you want a summer job, start looking early—in March or April.

3. Be careful in filling out application blanks. Think over your answers before writing anything. Make sure you're putting the information in the right place. Watch your handwriting and spelling.

4. Dress carefully for an interview. Be sure you look neat and clean. Be on time.

5. When the person interviewing you asks a question, speak up. Act excited about the work. Show that you want to do it. Ask questions about it. *But* don't hog the interview. Let the interviewer talk.

Income Tax

The person who hires you must take tax money out of your pay and give it to the government. This is called "withholding tax." If you make over $3,300 a year, you must file a tax form. The Internal Revenue Service, which collects United States income tax, says it is a good idea to file even if you make less than that. You will probably get some of your money back. Call to find out more. You will find the Internal Revenue Service listed under "United States Government." (Ask about state income taxes, too. Some states have income tax, but others don't.)

Starting Your Own Business

You may be too young to get a job doing what you want to do. In fact, you may be too young to get a job at all. *But,* you are not too young to make money. How? By going into business for yourself.

Let's say you like working with animals. You can't be a wild animal trainer or zoo keeper or veterinarian. But you *can* make money in your own animal business. You can run a service—walking or washing dogs, for example. You can raise animals to sell.

What if you just want to earn money and don't care how you do it? You may make more working for yourself than for someone else.

Making Kloppers ... or What?

The time you spend making up your mind about what business to start is not wasted. Neither is the time you spend in planning wasted. Here are some questions to ask yourself:

1. What do I like to do?
2. How can I make money doing it?
3. Is another person doing the same thing to make money?
4. Can I compete with that person?
5. Do people need what I plan to sell?
6. What money do I need to start?
7. What equipment, if any, do I need to start?

8. Will the price I ask be one that people are willing to pay?

Some products can be made more cheaply in factories than you can make them by hand. Also, though, some products are worth more if they're handmade than if they're machine made.

Write out a plan. Let's say you've decided to go into business making Kloppers. (Don't bother to look up *klopper;* there is no such thing.) You've already decided you like making them. People are willing to buy them. The neighbors are interested. Most have agreed to take 2 kloppers each a week. The nearest klopper maker lives 20 miles away.

Figure your costs. You plan to make 100 kloppers to start:

Equipment
   klopper flipper-upper $25.00
Materials (to make 100 kloppers)
   Raw klops   5.00
   Glue (1 quart, enough for
   100 kloppers)   1.00
Advertising
   Copying 25 flyers   2.50
Labor (to make and sell 100 kloppers)
   You can make 4 kloppers an hour, so making 100 will take 25 hours. You want to earn $4 an hour. Multiply 25 × 4. Labor cost: $100   100.00
                  $133.50
          for 100 kloppers

The cost for each is $1.33. Tack on something for profit—say, 17¢. Your price is then $1.50 each. Since the other klopper maker charges $1.65, your price is reasonable.

Legal Stuff

Before you start, check on government rules. Your best way to find out about them is to call the government agency in charge. Government rules vary according to where you live. For example, in some places you don't need a license to sell door to door; in other places, you do. Start at your local library. Tell the librarian what you plan to do. Ask what the government rules are concerning it. If the librarian cannot find the information, he or she will send you to someone who does. Or you might call the Small Business Administration. It is listed under "United States Government" in the white pages of your phone book.

You should be aware of:

1. *Income tax.* If you make more than $400 in your own business, you have to file an income tax form with the U.S. government. In some states, you may have to file a state tax form. Ask someone at the Internal Revenue Service by calling 1 (800) 242-4500.

2. *Sales tax.* If you sell anything, you may have to pay state or city sales tax. Ask the Small Business Administration.

3. *Child care rules.* In some places, you cannot take care of children in your house on a regular basis without following strict rules. Ask the Small Business Administration.

4. *Sales permits.* If you sell door to door or from a stand in front of your house, you may need to get a permit. Ask the Chamber of Commerce in your community, or ask the Small Business Administration.

5. *Food and drug laws.* If you make up a mixture of anything and sell it, you may be breaking a law. The government rules are strict. Why? Because what you make may be harmful to people. The Food and Drug Administration of the U.S. has rules. So do many states. County health departments watch out for unclean con-

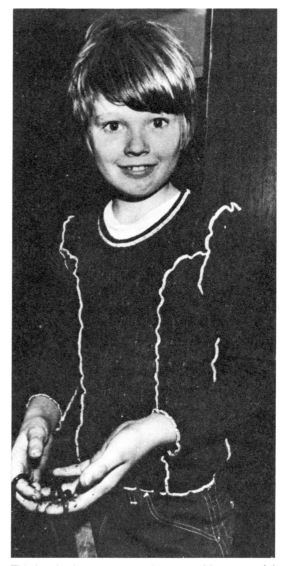

This boy had to pay state sales tax on his successful backyard business selling worms to fishermen. *(Wide World Photos)*

ditions. So before you sell any homemade mixture, check with one of these agencies. If you have no luck getting information, ask at your library or the Small

Business Administration or your community Chamber of Commerce.

6. *Zoning laws.* Your county may have laws against raising animals in your area. Look in the white pages for the name of your county, then for a phone number for the zoning commission. If you can't find the number, try the general information number.

7. *Laws against performing in public.* Call the Chamber of Commerce in your community.

Advertising

At first, word-of-mouth advertising around the neighborhood may bring you enough customers. But if you want your business to grow or have many things to sell, you may need to advertise.

Cards. You can make business cards from $3'' \times 5''$ index cards. Be sure to include all information:

Your name	Cindy O'Reilly
Name of your business and/or	Green Thumb Services
What you offer	Lawn mowing/hedge clipping/ weeding/raking/plant care
How you can be reached	(714) 555-0009 8 A.M–9 A.M. 6 P.M–7 P.M.

You can have cards printed by a local printer. Ask for costs.

You can tack cards up on bulletin boards in supermarkets, libraries, laundromats, and schools. Ask yourself where your customers go. For instance, if you fix bike tires, your customers may go to a bicycle store. Ask the owner if you can leave a stack of cards. The owner may suggest that customers call you. (This won't work if the store performs the same service you do.)

Posters and flyers. Posters are for posting (tacking up) and flyers are for handing out. Both are best for advertising events. A good size is $8\frac{1}{2}'' \times 11''$. Use stenciled letters, letters cut from magazines, or careful hand lettering. Use very large letters for the main message: GARAGE SALE, or LET ME UP—A TWO-ACT PLAY.

Be sure to include what the event is, the place, date, time, cost, and how to get there.

If you like, make one master poster or flyer, then run off copies on a copying machine. It's possible, too, to have posters printed. Unless you need 100 or more, the cost per poster is high.

Always ask before you put up posters. Try stores, libraries, laundromats, and schools. Put flyers under doors or pass them out in places where people gather (parking lots of supermarkets, for example).

Newspaper advertisements. You can advertise your service or product in the classified section of the local newspaper. Costs vary according to newspaper circulation (number sold) and the number of words in your ad. Don't advertise in a paper that reaches people who live too far away to buy from you. That costs more and won't bring you more business. In wording your ad, put the most important thing first. Example:

Clown Act for Parties.
Reasonable. Experienced.
Call Joe at (714) 431–0009, 7 P.M. to 9 P.M.

Consider advertising in advertising supplements and free newspapers.

Radio. Some radio stations will make announcements free. Usually, these can go on for no more than 30 seconds. Keep your announcements to 20 seconds. Write it first, then say it slowly while someone times you with the second hand of a watch. Get the main points in first.

Making Phone Calls

Sometimes adults you don't know may be hard to talk to. They aren't used to answering children's questions. If an adult at a government agency tries to put you off, keep talking. Be polite, but firm. Your questions are as serious as anyone else's questions. Don't be shy. Stick with it. Once the adult realizes you are serious, he or she will probably pay attention.

Some Tips About Running a Business

1. Stay small at first. Don't spend a lot on fancy equipment. For instance, if you want to make money mowing lawns, rent, don't buy, a lawnmower at first. Your parents might rent you theirs. When you start making money, you can buy your own.

2. If other people are involved in your business, decide on important things right away—when to hold meetings, how to split the money, who does what.

3. Keep records. Always be able to look up how much you spent and how much you made. You can do this in a notebook. Example:

Income	Amount	Expense	Amount
5 kloppers sold to Mrs. Haldane	$7.50	Repairs on machine	$4.95
		50 kloppers	2.50

4. Give receipts for what you sell. You can get a receipt book at a stationery store.

It's a good idea to get adult help with things like record keeping or tax problems.

5. If you need help from adults, ask for it. An adult can help you with record-keeping or tax problems. Grown-ups who have businesses get outside help all the time; no reason you shouldn't, too!

6. Keep your promises. If you say you will deliver 9 kloppers on Friday, *do it*.

7. If you get tired of the business, quit or let someone else take over.

Starting a Kid Job Agency

If you and several friends want to earn money, consider starting a job agency. That way you can offer several services at once. What will pay off depends on where you live. If tourists come to your town, offering tours is a good idea. If your town seldom sees a stranger, forget it.

Here are some ideas. (You can do them alone, too.)

1. *House chores:* Washing windows,

polishing silver or brass, taking out garbage, taking cans or glass or newspaper to the recycling center, shampooing rugs, providing after-the-party clean-up.

2. *Animal care:* Walking dogs (not more than 2 at once), bathing dogs, taking care of pets while owners are away.

Bathing dogs can be a messy but profitable way to make money.

Taking out the garbage is a chore many people will pay to have done.

3. *Vacation service:* While people are away on vacation, feeding fish or cats, bringing in the mail, watering plants, mowing lawn, weeding garden.

4. *Yard chores:* Mowing lawns, shoveling snow, weeding, clipping hedges, painting the fence, sweeping walks, cleaning out sheds and garages.

5. *Child care:* Taking little children to school or to the park or library, holding a neighborhood story hour, running children's birthday parties, baby-sitting, being a mother's helper.

6. *Performing:* Acts for rent—clown, magician, rock band, Santa, mime. Good for parties, store-openings, parades. Provide a local "singing telegram" service—rhymed messages delivered by someone in costume.

Being a clown at a party or store opening is a fun money-maker, if you're good at it.

7. *Teaching:* Tutoring school subjects; teaching piano or guitar, a language, knitting, macramé, tennis, dancing, how to program a home computer.

And: Typing, taking pictures on special

occasions, making home movies or videotapes of special occasions. Home movies? Teenager Brad Pelo of Orem, Utah, videotaped houses for real estate agents. The agents were then able to show houses to customers without leaving their offices. They saved time and money. Brad made money.

And more: Gift-wrapping, shopping, painting and repairing toys and bicycles, changing bicycle tires, giving tours of the community for tourists, running nature walks, washing car windshields, washing cars or trucks or boats, watching a person's wash in a laundromat while the person shops, sitting with grandparents (make sure you know them), picking produce for farmers . . .

One member of your job agency group should be available to answer the phone and send people out on jobs. That person should be paid.

You need a card for each worker and each customer. On the workers' cards, keep track of what they are willing to do, the people they have worked for, the money they have made. On the customers' cards, write the work done, when, and by whom.

For example:

Customer: Florence Goodly

Worker	Work Done	Date	Time	Hourly Rate	Total
Jane B.	Dog walking	1/9/82	2 hr.	$3.50	$ 7
T.J. Brown	Window washing	2/3/82	5 hr.	$4	$20

Make sure your workers are aware of rules set up by your group. For example:
1. Be polite.
2. Be on time.
3. Tell the customer when you begin the job and when you finish it.
4. Keep track of your hours.

Deciding What to Charge

Many children are afraid to ask for what they think they're worth. They're afraid adults will laugh. *Don't be shy.* Tell the customer what you expect to get for the job. Never say, "Just give me what you think I'm worth." That's not fair to the customer, and if you get a skinflint, it's not fair to you.

Don't undersell yourself. If you can work nearly as well and fast as an adult, then you should get nearly what an adult gets. And, of course, boys and girls should get equal pay for equal work.

By the hour: Find out what the minimum wage is. Ask for it. Ask for more if the work you do is skilled.

By the job: Estimate how long it will take. Multiply by the hourly rate you want. Find out what others charge for jobs like it. If you need to, go home and figure your price, then come back to the customer with it. Some children like to give the customer a written estimate.

If you use materials (like gas for your mower), include those costs in your price.

Give a full hour's work for a full hour's pay.

How to Be a Super Babysitter

1. Before you start the job, let the parents know what you charge per hour. You don't want to argue about money when it's time to be paid.

2. Ask what your privileges are. Can you use the TV and stereo? Is it okay to have a can of soda from the refrigerator? What rooms can you use?

3. Make up a list of emergency phone numbers. (See chart.) Put them next to the telephone.

4. Know about "danger" places in the house. Where are electrical outlets and small appliances? Medicines, bleaches, and household cleaners should be locked away in a safe place. Beware of stairs. Little kids love to play on them.

5. Lock doors and windows after the parents leave. *Never open the door to strangers.*

6. Know where the emergency exits are in the house. In case of fire, you can get the child out of the house safely—and fast.

7. Be sure you ask about the child's habits. What time does the child go to

Babysitting is a common way to earn money. It carries a serious responsibility, too.

THE SUPER SITTERS

VERY IMPORTANT
PHONE NUMBERS

Post these names and phone numbers by the telephone. Then you'll have them when and if you need them.

Where parents will be: _____

Nearby friend _____

or relative _____

or neighbor _____

Children's doctor _____

Fire Department _____

Police Department _____

Poison Control Center _____

Hospital _____

Using a form like this one when you babysit shows you're both helpful and have a sense of responsibility. *(U.S. Government Printing Office)* sleep? Are snacks allowed? Any TV rules? Does the child have any special problems?

8. Watch out for unsafe toys. They are toys that have sharp edges, small parts, or sharp points. Toys that send things flying in the air can also be dangerous.

9. *Never leave a young child alone, not even for a minute.*

10. Play with the child. No matter what their age, all kids love to play. Many baby-sitters take along their own "bag of tricks." Some of the things you might want to take with you: a deck of cards, yarn, rubber animals, a couple of story-books, crayons, balloons, small plastic toys.

11. Don't stay on the telephone for a long time. The parents might be trying to call you.

12. Call for help if the child gets ill or has an accident. Usually, you can take care of small cuts or bruises. But you are not a doctor. Get help when you need it.

13. Remember: You are not a parent. You cannot punish the child.

14. Keep a notebook on your baby-sitting jobs. Write down all the facts about each family. Put down your hours and the money you earned. This record book will become an important part of your baby-sitting business.

Garage Sales

Aunt Millie's weird lamp with the ruffled apple-green shade and the elephant base may be just what your neighbor always wanted. What you don't want is not always junk; someone else may be able to use it. Old things can be worth money, and a good way to make money from them is to hold a garage sale. (Other names for the garage sale are tag sale, yard sale, and attic sale.)

Gather the stuff you and your family don't want anymore. Offer to clean out garages and attics for people. Then ask which of their things you found that they don't want. Offer to sell their unwanted stuff for them at your garage sale. You can make a deal on how much you will get, say, one-quarter of the money paid for their things. Or you can hold a group sale with your friends. Each person can sell his or her own stuff, or you may decide to split the profits equally.

Good items for garage sales are toys, clothes, books, comics, records, and furniture. Make sure your parents and other people give their okay for you to sell their things. Don't fix things up too much, but make sure they are clean.

When should you hold a garage sale? Weekends are best. Don't hold a garage sale on a holiday weekend, though.

Advertising should start a week before your sale. Put up posters in laundromats, schools, markets, and so on. Give the dates, times, and address.

Sample

BIG GIANT HUGE GARAGE SALE
By the Marconi Kids
Saturday and Sunday, April 2–3
9 A.M. to 5 P.M.
5771 Leacock Road, Kidsville
(Turn right off Billings Road)

If directions to your house are complicated, draw a map showing how to get there.

Newspaper ads should appear one to 3 days before the sale. Most local papers have a garage sale section in the classified section.

On the day before, put up signs on telephone poles. Use arrows to point the way.

A day or two before the sale, gather all the items together. Price them. If the

If you give a garage sale, be sure to group things together and label each item with a price.

stuff is in good shape, you can probably get one-quarter to one-half of what it is worth new. (A mail order catalog is a good source for prices.) If something is broken or torn, put a very low price on it. You can use gummed labels, chalk, or a piece of paper attached with pins to show prices. If several of you will be collecting separately for items, use a code on the labels to show that. Initials are good.

Make sure you have boxes, tables, hangers and a rope for hanging clothes, paper and pencil for receipts, and at least $10 in change.

Early on the day of the sale, arrange things in groups—toys in one, furniture in another, and so on. Don't put out what you don't want to sell. Everything should be ready at least half an hour before the sale begins. People tend to show up early for garage sales to get the best bargains.

As things are sold, put their labels in a box. The labels are your record of the money you make. Give receipts to people who ask for them. When the time is almost up, you might want to lower your prices.

When the sale is over, divvy up the money. Be sure you clean up, put unsold things away, and take down your signs.

Selling Things

Being a Salesman

Some companies will let you sell their products for part of the profits. Examples are greeting cards, seeds, magazines, and newspapers.

To get a newspaper route, ask the circulation manager of your local paper for one. (You must be 12 or older in most states to have a route.)

Selling magazines, seeds, greeting cards: Check back sections of magazines for offers.

Making Things to Sell

You can't sell snowshoes in Florida. (Not unless you convince people that snowshoes make good wall decorations.) *Sell what people want to buy.* Possible items are cookies, candy, bread, pot holders, macramé, batik, and newspaper logs. Once you decide what you want to make, look up directions on how to make it. The library has lots of books on cooking and crafts.

Animals and Plants

If you have a magic touch with living things, try growing plants or raising animals to sell. Again, make sure people want to buy them. Imagine a stock of 100 white mice and more on the way . . . and no one to buy.

Plants to grow include vegetables, fruits, house plants, and flowers. Neighbors make good customers. Health food stores like to buy produce grown without artificial fertilizers or insecticides.

If you raise animals, make sure it's allowed in your part of town. For help in raising them, write to the United States Department of Agriculture, Washington, D.C. 20250. Ask for their Publications List. Some animals you might consider raising are dogs, cats, tropical fish, pigeons, chickens, geese, ducks, rabbits, and worms (for fishing).

WARNING: Be careful of get-rich-quick offers in magazines and newspapers. Sometimes the promises are overblown;

If you raise animals to sell, make sure there's a market for them.

you'll make money, but not a fortune. And sometimes the offers are fake. Envelope-stuffing offers are among these.

The third grade at St. Louise School in Bellevue, Washington, went into the pumpkin business. They borrowed $100 from the bank to buy pumpkins, then they sold the pumpkins on Halloween. After paying back the bank, they had a profit of $25.

How to Start Your Own Newspaper

by Lisa Ann Powell

Have you ever dreamed of starting your own newspaper? Lots of kids have done it. Some have even made money at it.

Here are a few tips that may come in handy if you decide to go into the newspaper business.

How big should the paper be? How often should it come out? The answers will depend on the amount of money, if any, that you have to begin with. Your best bet would be to start out with a small publication that comes out once or twice a month. Then you won't need a lot of people working with you at first. Once you get the paper rolling, you can try to get other people involved. They can help with stories, handing out papers, and selling advertising space to merchants.

You can have either a tight or a loose structure for running your paper. In a tight structure, specific duties are assigned to different kids. You, as publisher, make the main decisions. In a loose structure, each person has a chance to try everything. Decisions are made by the group. Of course, kids will be more committed to the paper if they have a say in matters. It's always a good practice to talk over new suggestions and ideas before going to press.

How well the paper sells will depend in part on what the paper says. Writing about neighborhood people or events will certainly help sell a local paper. Readers are interested in people they know, especially themselves. You might try tape-recording interviews with interesting people in the community. Other subjects might include the weather, editorial opinions, news, and humor. Newspapers by children have included verses from the Bible, English lessons, a children's column, poems, and serials.

A newspaper at the University of Michigan Hospital in Ann Arbor has a different angle altogether. The writers are young patients at the hospital. They deal with the pain and discomfort of being in a hospital by composing editorials, poems, and jokes for the paper. Some draw cartoons. The children's suggestions have helped the hospital staff to improve hospital conditions and to plan new facilities. This shows that a small newspaper written by children can have power.

Once you have your collection of stories, articles, and other material, you'll need a plan for compiling everything. This is called a layout. Naturally, you'll want eye-catching, important news on the front page. Study other papers to see how news is arranged. How many columns? What kind of headlines?

It's important at this point to warn about libel. You can be charged with libel if you write or say anything tending to injure a person's reputation unjustly. As publisher, you should make certain all nonfiction material can be supported with facts. The last thing you want to do is start a rumor about one of your subscribers—or anyone else. You might lose several subscriptions and also come up against legal problems.

Once the stories are typed and laid out, you'll need to make copies of your paper. There are 4 basic ways it can be done: ditto, mimeograph, photocopy, and offset. For small print runs, mimeograph or ditto methods have the lowest per-copy cost. For both, you need to type a special master copy.

Almost every school has a ditto machine. Maybe a deal with a sympathetic teacher can be worked out. One group of students gave a share of their profits to the school in exchange for use of the ditto machine. The mimeograph works something like a stencil. Many offices, churches, and schools have mimeograph machines; you may be allowed to use one of them. Another possibility is to buy your own ditto or mimeograph machine. They're often sold at auctions and secondhand sales. Just be sure the one you buy is in working order.

The paper sizes for printing machines vary. One popular size is 11 × 17 inches. That's double the size of a standard piece of typing paper.

When you have your newspaper organized and ready to print, you'll have to make plans to sell it. You can try selling it to neighbors in your area and to teachers and friends at school. You can offer subscriptions at special rates.

Advertising can be another way to make money. Any place where young people go would be likely to advertise in your paper, especially if your rates are low. Try fast-food restaurants, record stores, local radio stations, and bowling alleys.

Another way to raise money is to get sponsors. List the names of people who make donations in a Sponsors column.

The money from ads, donations, and subscriptions should add up to more than what you spend to print the paper—at least after a trial period. With the right planning, you can soon be on the way to owning your own profitable little business. And maybe to making a difference in the world.

Found Money

Panning for Gold

Gold travels in fast-moving water. Bits are loosened from gold veins by a stream's current, and the current carries the gold downstream. When the water slows, the bits drop to the bed of the stream. This goes on all the time. Someone may take all the gold from a stream bed on Tuesday, and on Wednesday more gold flows down.

That's why you can (maybe) find gold if you pan for it. You may not find much, and you may not get rich, but you will have fun.

Gold is found everywhere in the United States. There is more in the western states and in Tennessee, North Carolina, South Carolina, Georgia, and Vermont,

You may not get rich panning for gold, but you can have fun trying it.

than elsewhere. The best streams to pan are those where gold was found before.

You'll need a pan. You can buy one if you like. They come in 9-inch, 12-inch, and 15-inch sizes. Buy the biggest one you can handle easily. You can also use a heavy pie plate or a salad bowl. You will need a shovel to dig with and something to put your gold into. A tweezers is a nice thing to have.

Before you start panning, ask permission from the owner of the land. Don't be a claim-jumper; if you see a sign claiming a spot, don't look for gold there.

After you have chosen a stream, look for a good place to start. Drop a stick into the water. The place where it slows down may be a good spot for panning. Gold is heavy. It falls to the bottom where the force of the stream is too weak to carry it.

Dig deep into your spot with your shovel. Bring up a panful of gravel. Put the pan back into the water. Stir to get rid of the dirt and light bits of gravel. (Gold is heavier than dirt or gravel, and sinks to the bottom of your pan.) Pick out the big stones and gravel pieces.

Carefully put more water in the pan. Swirl so the water spins. Let anything that spins go over the edge of your pan. Keep doing this until only black sand is left. Black sand goes with gold. If you have no black sand in your pan, go to another spot. If you do have black sand, look for "color" in it. The color is tiny grains of gold. Pick them out with the tweezer and check to see if they are gold. Pinch them. If they don't break, they may be gold. If they flatten, they may be gold.

How can you know for sure? Ask at the United States Government Gold Assay Office. (Ask the U.S. Government Information Center for the telephone number, if "Gold Assay Office" is not listed under "United States Government" in your phone book.)

If you do find gold, stake a claim. To do this, put a sign on a stick. On the sign write something like: *This is my gold claim. Harry Ellis, Prop., June 6, 1982.*

You may find gold on land owned by a person, the state, or the country. If owned by a person, you can make your own deal to keep at least part of the gold. If owned by the state, write to the person in charge of state lands at the state capital. If owned by the United States government, write to:

Bureau of Land Management
Department of the Interior
Washington, D.C. 20240

And Other "Found" Money

After a carnival or game, check the place where it was held. You may find lots of change people dropped from their pockets.

Collect pop bottles, aluminum cans, and other glass and metal objects from streets, the beach, and anywhere else people go. If you live in a place where a deposit is required on bottles, you can get the deposit. If not, you can take them to a junk dealer or recycling center.* (Ask your fire station where the recycling center is.) Aluminum can collecting trucks come to supermarket parking lots on certain days during the week. They pay for cans by the pound.

Pick up discarded wood. Ask where houses are being built for scrap lumber. Package it with twigs, pine cones, other scrap wood. Sell for kindling.

Gather and sell nuts, field flowers, and wild berries.

---

*Some recycling centers don't pay for glass, but the glass will be re-used. You're being a good citizen, even if you're not making money.

How Not to Get Ripped Off

Think Before You Shell Out Your Money

If you want something that costs a lot, think before buying it. Do you need it? Will something else do? Will you be tired of it before you've gotten your money's worth?

When you have decided to buy, make sure you get the best deal.

1. Check prices at several stores. Sometimes fancy stores in high-priced locations charge more. Make sure you're getting prices on the same item. Make sure stores give guarantees.

2. Find out if the item is what you have been led to believe it is. Will it do everything the ads say it will? How long will it last?

3. Might you get the thing on sale at a later date? Can you wait until then? (See "When to Buy," page 302).

Money doesn't grow on trees like this make-believe one. Be a smart consumer. *(Ewing Galloway)*

4. Is the huge economy size or the small size the better deal? Generally, buy the huge size if you can use it up before it goes bad (*if* it goes bad). The more sheets in a pack of paper, the less the paper will cost per sheet. A 12-pencil package is usually a better buy than a one-pencil package. Do a little arithmetic to see if you can get a better deal with the larger package.

Complaining

What if what you buy falls apart or is missing something or is no good? You can complain. It's best to work your way up from store clerk to president of the manufacturing company when you complain. Here are some general rules:

1. Be sure you have something to complain about.

2. Get your facts together. What's wrong with what you bought? When did you buy it? What did it cost? Who sold it to you? What do you want—a new one? Repair? Your money back?

3. Check the guarantee or warranty. (*Guarantee* and *warranty* mean about the same thing—that the manufacturer or seller promises to fix what you bought or give you your money back if anything goes wrong with it.) Is there a time limit? Some guarantees are good for only a certain time. What does the guarantee cover? Parts? Labor? Both? Remember, though, that if what you buy doesn't work as it should, you should still get satisfaction from the store.

4. Keep records of your complaints. Be pleasant, but act as if you expect something to be done.

5. Complain first to the person who

sold the item to you. Then speak to the manager.

6. *Then* complain to the president of the company who makes the item. You can find the address at your library.

If Complaining Doesn't Work

Try one of these agencies:

1. Office of Consumer Affairs. (Look in the white pages under "United States Government.") Some states have consumer affairs departments, too.

2. A newspaper consumer column. Also radio and television consumer shows.

3. Better Business Bureau. (See the white pages.)

4. Chamber of Commerce in your town.

Mail Orders

People who buy by mail are protected by law against getting ripped off. If a company sends you something you did not order, you can legally keep it without paying for it. When ordering by mail, you should:

1. Read the description of the item in the ad to be sure it is what you want.

2. Write your full name and address on the order. Include the name of the item, its order number, and its price.

3. Pay with a check or money order. (You can buy a money order at your post office.) Never send cash through the mail.

4. If you send an item back, write a letter telling why and paste it on the package. Again, include your name and address, along with the name, description, and cost of the item.

5. If you have a complaint about anything ordered by mail, write to:

Postal Inspection Service
U.S. Postal Service
Washington, D.C. 20260

and/or

Direct Mail Marketing Association
Consumer Service Director
6 East 43rd Street
New York, New York 10017

If Something Can Hurt You or Another Kid

The 1966 Child Protection Act and the 1970 Toy Safety Act prevent the sale of dangerous products to children. If you come across a toy or something else that is dangerous, call the Consumer Product Safety Commission at 1 (800) 638-2772. If you live in Maryland, call 1 (800) 492-8363. For Alaska, Hawaii, Puerto Rico, and the Virgin Islands, call 1 (800) 638-8333. Be ready to tell the name of the toy, who makes it, and its model number.

Should You Believe the Whizzer Will Fly Into the Black Hole?

Many ads are honest. *Still, it's a good idea to pay careful attention to what ads say and show.* Watch with critical eyes, and listen with critical ears. Ask yourself what is really being said. What does "up to $10" mean? "Pennies a day"? (What's a thousand pennies? A million?) If your favorite television actor says that Sweeto Cereal is just great, should you believe him? Should your teeth believe him? Do you need something every other kid on the block is going to have? What if it's measles?

An article in a magazine for people who write ads recently said: "Eager minds can be molded to want your products! In the grade schools throughout America are nearly 23,000,000 young girls and boys. These children eat food, wear out clothes, use soap. They are consumers today and will be the buyers of tomorrow. . . . Sell these children on your brand name and they will insist that their parents buy no other."

That's how they think. So be prepared to think, too.

Your Money Is as Good as Anyone's—Don't Be Pushed Around

Sometimes rude people shove ahead of kids in lines. They think kids don't matter or are too small to speak up. If someone does this to you, say, "Excuse me, but I think I am ahead of you in line." If the person pays no attention to you, others probably will, and chances are they will be on your side. The rude person will be put in his place—behind you in line.

Sales clerks can be rude to children, too. Remember, your money is as good as anyone's. Don't let yourself be hurried. If the clerk doesn't give you enough time to make up your mind, be polite about it but say, "I'm sorry, I haven't made up my mind yet."

If a clerk is rude to you, be nice at first. If that doesn't work, complain to the manager of the store. And if *that* doesn't work, you might consider getting a group together. Chances are that if the clerk was rude to you, he or she has been rude to others. Write a letter to the store manager. Explain why you are complaining. Make sure you have your facts straight. Remind the store manager that you spend quite a bit of money in the store. Then have everyone in the group sign the letter.

There is another side to this story. If someone is very nice to you, thank that person. You might even tell the store manager if a clerk has been especially helpful.

When to Buy

Buy Christmas cards in January? Yes, if you want the best price. Things are often on sale after their "season." This list, adapted from *Sylvia Porter's Money Book*, tells the best time of year to buy certain things.

Art supplies	January, February
Bathing suits	After July 4, August
Bikes	January, February, September, October, November
Books	January
Camping equipment	August
Clothes	July, September, November, December
Christmas gifts	Anytime but the Christmas season
Fishing equipment	October
Radios and phonographs	January, February, July
School clothes	August, October
School supplies	August, October
Shoes	January, March, July
Skates	March
Ski equipment	March
Stereo equipment	January, February, July
Summer sports equipment	July
Television sets	May, June
Toys	January, February

How to Ask for a Raise in Your Allowance

First ask yourself if you really *need* a raise. Maybe you don't. It's easy to think you should have as much as your friends, but maybe your friends' parents are richer than yours and can afford more. Also, your friends may have to buy more things for themselves than you. Kids who buy their own clothes, for instance, usually need bigger allowances than kids who don't.

Before you ask, keep track of what you spend during a week. It may give you some idea of what you need. Make up a statement showing your expenses. For instance:

Weekly Expenses

5 school lunches at $1.50 each	$ 7.50
School supplies	1.00
Movies	2.00
Saving for a bike	2.00
Miscellaneous (snacks, etc.)	1.50
Charity	1.00
	$15.00

Write down your reasons for wanting more allowance. Some you might think of are:

1. P.J. gets more.
2. I'm older.
3. School lunches cost more than last year.
4. I want to save up for a 10-speed.
5. I need to learn to handle money by paying for more of my expenses.

The first reason probably won't impress your parents. (It shouldn't.) The second and fifth reasons have something to do with each other. Older children are able to take more responsibility for their expenses.

Present your case. Use your Weekly Expenses sheet and your best reasons. Ask your parents if they wouldn't prefer to give you a larger amount rather than always having to dole out small extra amounts. Offer to keep a record to show where the money is going. If you use the "I'm older" argument, say that you will take on more of the household chores. (An allowance isn't payment for chores, but being responsible for more work *shows* you are more grown-up, and the more grown-up you are, the better you should be able to handle money.) Perhaps, too, it's time for you to handle more of your own expenses.

Give your parents time to think over their answer. If they say no, don't argue. Maybe they can't afford to give you more.

Banks—Piggy and Other

Piggy banks are for saving small amounts of money. The money is there when you need it. But it doesn't grow. And money can grow—if you put it in a bank savings account.

The bank pays to use your money. It lends your money to people who need it. In return, the bank receives interest—the money people pay to borrow money. And the bank pays you interest, too.

How much interest? That depends on how long you agree to leave your money in the bank. It also depends on the rate of interest your bank pays.

With a passbook savings account, you can take your money out whenever you

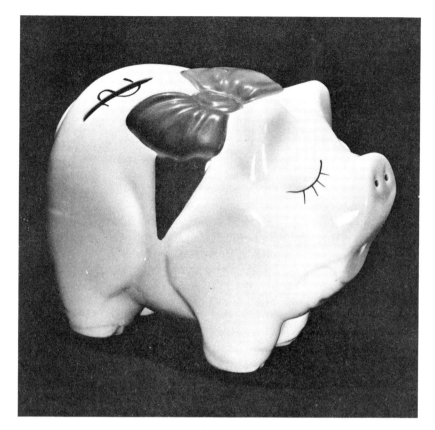

Piggy banks are fine for keeping pocket money, but money to be saved belongs in a real bank. *(Ewing Galloway)*

want it. You don't need much to start a passbook account. Even $1 is usually enough. You may need to have a parent sign your bank application form. When your account is opened, you will get a little book called a passbook. In it are your name and account number. The teller will record amounts that you deposit (put in) and withdraw (take out). You will draw interest on your balance (the amount in your account).

Interest is stated in percent. If you get 5 percent simple interest on your money, that means you will make 5¢ for every dollar over a year's time. If the interest is compounded, you'll make more. The more often it is compounded during the year, the more you will make.

If you won't need to use your money right away, you might want to put it in another kind of account. Some accounts require that you leave your money in over a certain period of time. If you do, you will make more on it. The rate of interest will be higher.

You might want to compare the rates of interest at different banks, then pick the best one.

In any case, you will do better than if you keep your money in your dresser drawer. Or under your mattress. Or even in a piggy bank.

The Stock Market

When you put money in the stock market, you buy a part of a company. Your money goes to pay workers and to buy materials and equipment. If the company makes a profit, you usually get part of it. The price of your stock may go up. You can sell the stock and make more money. Of course, it can work the other way too. The company may lose money. If it does, the price of your stock may go down.

If you are under 21, you may need your parents to help you buy stock. Stock is bought through stockbrokers.

NOTE: If you make more than $1,000 in interest or from stocks, you have to file a federal tax form. The Internal Revenue Service, listed under "United States Government" in the white pages, can tell you about this.

Chapter *10*
ANIMALS

Weird and Wonderful Animals

They seem weird because they're so different from us. How do we look to them? Maybe even weirder.

Flashlight fish. Two lights like green headlights move in the dark ocean. You could read your watch by them. The lights come from a flashlight fish, a creature about as big as a goldfish. The fish itself doesn't make the lights. Tiny bacteria, billions of them, live in 2 organs under the fish's eyes and produce the light from the fish's blood. Flashlight fish use the lights to see by and to attract the tiny fish they eat. They blink the lights in what may be a kind of code used to talk to one another. When an enemy comes near, the flashlight fish may blink and run; or it may come closer to the enemy, *then* blink and run.

Duck-billed platypus. It has a bill and webbed feet like a duck. It lays eggs as a

The duck-billed platypus, which looks about as strange as its name, lives in Australia.

duck does. But the duck-billed platypus has fur, and it isn't a bird. It's a mammal, like you. It lives in Australia, partly on land, partly in the water. With its bill, the platypus digs in the mud on the river bottom to find food. It also eats giant earthworms as big around as a hose. On each hind leg, the platypus has a hollow bone containing a fang that shoots poison.

Baby seahorses hatch in a pouch on the father's body, not the mother's.

Sea horse. The sea horse has a head like a horse's. Its tail resembles a monkey's and it has a pouch like a kangaroo's. Because each eye can move without the other, it can look ahead and behind at the same time. It changes color to match the color of its surroundings. The mother sea horse puts her eggs into the father's pouch, where they stay until they hatch into baby sea horses. Sea horses make clicking noises to talk to each other.

Bombardier beetle. This insect, only half an inch long, makes a chemical bomb in its body. When the bomb shoots out at an enemy, it is boiling hot. How can the beetle keep the bomb in its body without killing itself? We don't know.

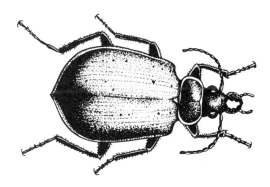

The bombardier beetle shoots a hot bomb at its enemies.

Water ouzel. A western mountain bird, the water ouzel can run *under the water*, where it pokes its beak among the stones in its search for worms and insects to eat. Water ouzels often make their nests in rocks behind waterfalls. Because the falls are noisy, the birds can't hear each other sing, and so they blink their white-lidded eyes to send messages to one another.

Elephant. The elephant's trunk is really a big nose containing 40,000 muscles. That's more muscles than there are in the

The elephant's trunk is actually a very big nose. It is a useful thing to have.

whole body of a human being. With its nose, an elephant can pull a tree out of the ground, untie a knot, or pick up a thread from the floor. Elephants have been trained to throw a baseball and shoot a gun. One elephant in England swept paths with a broom and watered plants with a watering can. She could also pull the cork from a wine bottle by holding the bottle at an angle with her foot and then twisting the cork with her trunk. She would then drink the wine and give her keeper the empty bottle.

Walking catfish. Walking catfish can live in or out of the water. When on land, they walk on their fins and use organs that can breathe air.

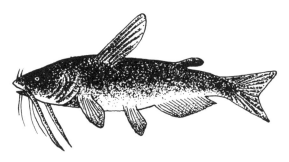

Some catfish can live either in the water or on land.

Anteater. The anteater, big as a bear, eats only ants. To keep itself going, it has to eat thousands of them a day. It has a thin sticky tongue inside a long, tube-like mouth that has no jaws. The anteater tears apart an anthill with its strong claws and then lashes its tongue on the ground to catch the ants, hundreds at a time.

Anglerfish. The anglerfish "fishes" for its food. On top of its nose is a strange fin that looks like a fishing pole and line. On the end of the line is a blob that looks like bait. Some deep-water anglerfish have

glowing bait. One kind of anglerfish has bait that looks like a tiny fish, complete with eyes. It wiggles this "fish" through the water so that it seems to be swimming. Smaller fish see the bait, swim close to eat it, and *get* eaten instead.

Slime mold. The slime mold is a tiny plant-animal. During one part of its life it lives as one cell. At another time it joins with hundreds of other cells to form a body. (Imagine that you could combine with hundreds of other people to make one very large person—a giant blob.) The slime mold cells live separately until they

Slime mold starts out life as a single cell (top), later joining other cells to form a body.

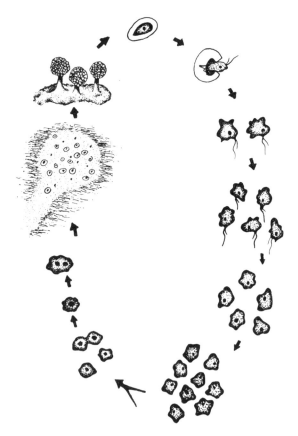

run out of bacteria to eat. They then move together into a cigar-shaped mass of cells. This mass is small; it's never much bigger than one of the letters in one of the words on this page. The slime body crawls slowly toward light and heat. If the air is dry and hot enough, it starts to grow a stalk, like a plant. On top of the stalk is a ball containing spores, and inside the spores are slime mold cells. Soon the ball bursts and the spores float off. If a spore lands in a good spot, the cells inside are set free and start eating. Then the whole process begins again.

Flatfish. Flatfish, like sole and halibut, end up with both eyes on one side of their heads. They start life with an eye on each side of their heads like other fish. Slowly they turn over to swim on their sides. As they do, the bottom eye slowly moves to the top.

Bola Spider. The bola spider is a South American "cowboy." It spins a long thread with a sticky ball on the end and then twirls the thread like a bola, a kind of lariat. The thread wraps itself around a

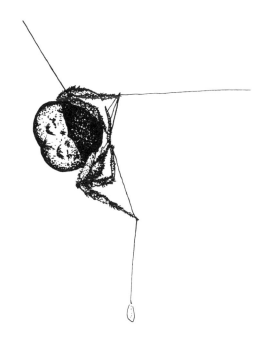

The bola spider spins a lasso to catch its next meal.

The flat fish starts out with eyes on both sides of its head, but they slowly move to the top.

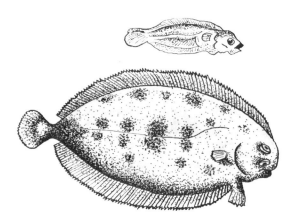

moth or other insect, which the spider eats.

Narwhal. No one knows why the narwhal, a kind of whale, has one long, spiraled tooth on the left side of its jaw and none on the right side. It is the only animal in the world that has a long tooth, or tusk, on only one side of its body. The narwhal disobeys a law of nature—that animals are shaped the same on one side as they are on the other. (If you could flatten any animal, even an octopus, then fold it in half lengthwise, the sides would roughly match. This law holds only for animals bigger than amoebas.) The narwhal's tooth is as long as eight feet and sticks out in front of its head like a spear. When explorers brought some narwhal teeth back to Europe 400 years ago, they started the myth of the unicorn. People thought the teeth were horns belonging to a horse-like animal, a creature with a horn growing out of the middle of its head. (There is no such thing as a unicorn.) Nobody knows what the tooth is for. It may be used as a giant ice pick to break through the ice in the cold lands where the narwhal lives. It could be a weapon used to hurt the narwhal's enemies. It could act as a kind of prod employed to keep members of a group of narwhals in line.

Seventeen-year locust. For 17 years, the larvae of the 17-year locust live underground. In late May of the seventeenth year, they come to the surface. As many as 40,000 locusts may come up out of the roots of one tree. The locusts sit on branches for a couple of hours. They become winged creatures that can fly. After that, they live for only a month, and during that time they lay eggs that turn into larvae. The larvae go underground to live for 17 years. Then . . .

Vampire bats. Vampire bats bite animals and drink their blood in the night. In the day, they hang upside down from the ceilings of caves. They live in South America.

Electric Eels–Power Plants
That Can Light Signs or Kill

The electric eel hurls death rays at its enemies. These rays, bolts of electricity made in the eel's body, can knock down a human being. Only one-fifth of the electric eel's body holds its stomach, lungs, and other organs; the rest makes electricity. (Some other fish can make electricity, too, but their electricity is weaker.)

Electric eels are really long, skinny fish. They live in South American rivers. When grown, they are about 6 feet long.

Some Facts and Stories
About Electric Eels

A dog in the New York Aquarium tried to make friends with an electric eel by licking it. The electricity made it fly up in the air and spin around. It was the shock of the dog's life. After that the dog was more careful about picking its friends.

Power from an electric eel has been used to light a sign saying ELECTRIC EEL.

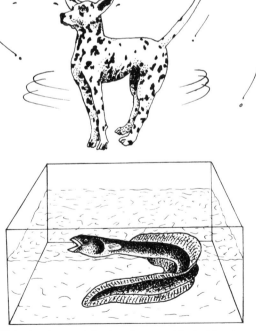

This dog learned the hard way not to befriend an electric eel by licking it.

It has started a boat engine. It has even turned on a searchlight on top of a skyscraper.

If an electric eel is put in salt water, it will short-circuit itself.

An electric eel bitten by another electric eel won't die for a whole day.

Electric eels can grow new electric tissue all their lives.

Indians in South America eat electric eels to cure some diseases.

Scientists made an antidote for nerve gas using what they found out by studying electric eels.

Leeches can suck blood from electric eels without getting hurt. As many as 2,000 leeches have been taken off just one electric eel.

Dinosaurs ("Terrible Lizards")

Dinosaurs were the kings of the earth before human beings existed. Some dinosaurs were bigger than houses, while others were as small as turkeys. Many walked on 2 legs and used their hands to hold things, like people do. Dinosaurs may have seen the world in color. We don't know if they made noise. We *do* know that their brains were tiny—often no bigger than a nut. To help their tiny brains move their big bodies, some dinosaurs had a kind of second brain close to their tails. Baby dinosaurs came from eggs. The biggest dinosaur egg was about the size of a football.

We know about dinosaurs from fossils. By studying fossil dinosaur teeth, we can tell if they ate meat or plants. From fossil dinosaur footprints, we can tell how they moved. (Try walking or running in soft dirt, then "reading" your footprints.)

Dinosaur experts don't agree about some things. Were dinosaurs warm-blooded (like you) or cold-blooded (like snakes)? Did they really die out, or do birds come from a dinosaur line? The answers may come with time. After all, we have known about dinosaurs for only about 150 years, and new fossils are being discovered all the time.

On the following pages appears a "rogues' gallery" of some of the more famous dinosaurs we know about.

This footprint of a brontosaurus is large enough to make a fine chair. *(American Museum of Natural History)*

DINOSAURS THAT LIVED 225 TO 195 MILLION YEARS AGO

NAME	SIZE	SOME FACTS
Procompsognathus	As big as a turkey.	One of the first dinosaurs.
Syntarsus	Tall as a toddler and long as a car.	The first syntarsus bones were found in 1964 by a group of boys in Africa. May have been warm-blooded. May have had feathers—for keeping warm, not for flying. Food: other animals.
Coelophysis	8 feet long; shorter than an 8-year-old child.	Light bones and feet like a bird's. Sharp teeth with saw edges. Long tail for balance and for sitting on. Food: other animals, even its own kind.
Heterodontosaurus	3 to 4 feet long; 2 feet high.	May have been warm-blooded. Had 3 kinds of teeth—for biting, tearing, chewing. Food: plants.
Plateosaurus	Big as a room.	Small head and big body. Luckily, was a plant-eater. Otherwise it might have eaten other little dinosaurs.

DINOSAURS THAT LIVED 195 TO 135 MILLION YEARS AGO

NAME	SIZE	SOME FACTS
Megalosaurus	20 feet long; 8 feet high.	Second dinosaur ever found, in England. Teeth like knives. Name means "big lizard."
Allosaurus	Long as 3 rooms; tall as a one-story house. Heavy as an elephant.	Looked like large lizard with big mouth. Food: other dinosaurs and food other animals left behind.

Plateosaurus
(big as a room)

Allosaurus
(tall as a one-story house)

Diplodocus	87 feet long—longer than a railroad car. Weighed 11 tons.	The longest dinosaur. Food: plants growing in ponds and swamps.
Stegosaurus	About 20 feet long (2 rooms). Weighed 2 tons, as much as a small car.	Tiny brain weighed a little more than a candy bar. The man who named this dinosaur thought the big plates on its back looked like shingles, so he called it a name that means "roofed lizard." Puzzle: What were the plates for? To make it look leafy so other animals would think it was a tree and not try to kill it? For cooling? Did the plates lie flat, then rise up when the animal was in danger to make it look fierce?
Apatosaurus (or Brontosaurus)	Long as a railroad car; higher than a house. Weighed 30 to 40 tons.	Looked like a steam shovel. Brain as big as a baseball. Nose on top of head. Stood in deep water to get away from other dinosaurs who wanted to eat it. Sometimes lived on land. Slow mover.
Camptosaurus	5 feet high; 4 to 15 feet long.	Walked on hind legs.
Ornitholestes	Big as a pony.	Ran on 2 feet. No teeth. Probably ate fruit.
Compsognathus	Chicken-size	Smallest dinosaur. Food: other animals. Story: Inside a big compsognathus skeleton a tiny one was found; the big one had eaten a baby whole.
Brachiosaurus	60 to 80 feet long; tall as a 3- or 4-story building. Weighed 50 to 80 tons.	Once thought to be heaviest land animal ever. Brain as big as hen's egg. Front legs longer than back legs. Puzzle: Why was its nose on top of its head?
"Supersaurus"	Perhaps bigger than any dinosaur found before.	Discovered in 1973 by James A. Jensen, amateur dinosaur hunter, at Dry Creek Mesa Quarry in Colorado. Children call Jensen "Dinosaur Jim" and write him hundreds of letters. Jensen likes them, too—children are his favorite audience. He keeps his dinosaur bones under a football stadium.
"Ultrasaurus"	Probably the biggest dinosaur yet. 50 to 60 feet tall. Weighed about 80 tons.	A shoulder blade of this huge creature was found in 1979 at Dry Creek Mesa Quarry by Jensen. The bone is 9 feet long. The "ultrasaurus" was probably a plant-eater.

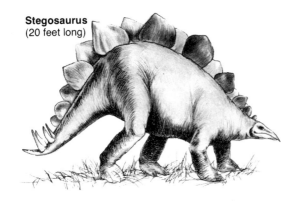

Stegosaurus
(20 feet long)

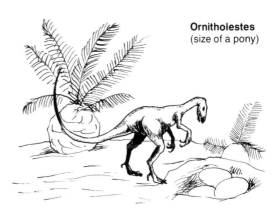

Ornitholestes
(size of a pony)

DINOSAURS THAT LIVED 135 TO 65 MILLION YEARS AGO

NAME	SIZE	SOME FACTS
Iguanodon	About 30 feet long and 15 feet high. Weighed a little more than an elephant.	Had spiked thumb for attacking enemies or digging for food. Feet like a bird's. Story: The first dinosaur bones, found in 1822, belonged to an iguanodon. A model of its skeleton was made, then 22 people had a dinner party inside it.
Deinocheirus	45 feet long; 25 feet tall.	The biggest meat-eating land dinosaur. Name means "terrible hand." Fossils found in desert in 1965.
Deinonychus	Long as a small room; high as a short adult.	First bones found in Montana in 1964. Had 3-fingered hand. Name means "terrible claw" for ripping, knife-like claws on hind feet. Sharp teeth. Looked like roadrunner. May have hunted in packs, running down animals to kill and eat.
Hypsilophodon	7 feet long; 5 feet high.	Walked around eating fruit, leaves, and insects from trees.
Velociraptor	5 feet long; 2 to 3 feet high.	Name means "fast robber." Meat-eater.
Protoceratops	Long as a man is tall.	Ran on 4 legs and had a beak like a turtle. Story: In 1923, 70 protoceratops eggs the size of baked potatoes were found in the desert. For the first time, people knew how baby dinosaurs were born
Tarbosaurus	25 feet long; 15 feet high.	Sharp teeth and little arms.
Ankylosaurus	15 feet long; high as a big child.	Lived in swamps and watery places. Built like an army tank—covered with bony rings. When attacked, sank down like turtle so enemy could not get teeth in. Tail like a club with round bone at the end.
Triceratops	About 20 feet long; high as low house.	Moved in herds. Walked on 4 legs. Three horns—one over each eye and one on nose. Fought like deer, using its horns.
Anatosaurus	Long as 3 rooms; high as 2 men.	Duck-like bill to shovel for plants in the mud. Swam in water, tail acting like an oar. As teeth grew old, new ones grew in—as many as 2,000 in a lifetime.
Tyrannosaurus rex	Longer than a box car; high as 2-story house.	Once thought to be largest meat-eater. Big, grinning mouth opened very wide to show 60 curved teeth like saw-toothed knives. Food: other dinosaurs and other animals' leftovers.
Parasaurolophus	About 30 feet long and 12 feet high.	Duck bill and long, hollow horn on head. What was the horn for? An air hose so it could breathe under water? A noise-maker?
Torosaurus	30 feet long and 10 feet high.	Name means "bull lizard." Had 3 horns.
Corythosaurus	18 feet long; 8 feet high.	Air could travel through bill, up into head, and out the back of mouth. Why? So it could eat and breathe at the same time? So it could smell more easily? Food: plants.
Struthiomimus	20 feet long; tall as a low house.	Looked like an ostrich except for its long arms and tail. Ran fast on 2 legs. No teeth—ate everything whole. Food: eggs, lizards, plants.

Ankylosaurus
(15 feet long, 3 feet high)

Anatosaurus
(50 feet long, 10 feet tall)

Triceratops
(20 feet long)

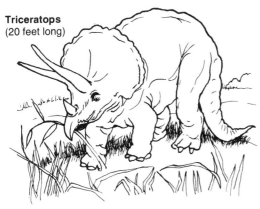

Struthiomimus
(20 feet long, 15 feet tall)

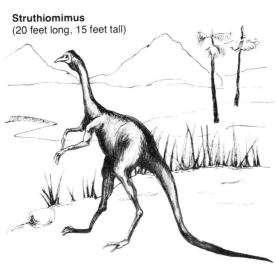

Tyrannosaurus rex
(tall as a two-story house)

If you want to learn more, try ALBUM OF DINOSAURS by
Tom McGowen.

How can you tell a bird from a dinosaur?
A bird has a wishbone.

WHO Came to Dinner?

The Prince del Drago

The Prince del Drago? No one *knew* him. In fact, no one had even laid eyes on him or read about him in the newspapers. But who doesn't want to meet a prince? When rich Harry Lehr invited his friends to a dinner party to meet the prince, they accepted. In that time—the 1890s—and place—Newport, Rhode Island—rich people were bored and restless, and always looking for excitement. One of the ways they found it was in the weird parties they gave. Harry gave some of the best ones. He outdid everyone.

The prince came late the night of the dinner. When he arrived he was wearing a full dress suit and black tie. That wasn't so strange. What *was* strange was the fact that he was a monkey.

The prince-monkey in the full dress suit took his place at the table. At first he behaved very well. Like everyone else he ate his food. His conversation was not so interesting, but how could it be? Then the Prince del Drago grew bored and restless. Rich, restless people are boring to monkeys. So he climbed up on the chandelier (a ceiling light fixture) and started unscrewing the light bulbs to throw them at the guests. That was the end of *that* party.

The Dinner for One Hundred WHAT?

One hundred guests were invited to another of Harry's parties. The males wore black ties and the females gauzy scarves. They all looked very dressed up as they gathered around the dinner table, which was one foot high. Why such a low

Would you like to have the Prince del Drago come to your birthday party?

table? The guests were all dogs. The menu was stewed liver and rice, stewed bones, and dog biscuits. One dog ate so much he passed out at his plate and had to be taken home.

A reporter sneaked into what became known as the Dog Dinner. He had a poodle with a ruffle as his ticket. However, someone found him out, and he was told to leave. To get even, he wrote a story for the newspapers saying the dogs were served very expensive food—like roast chicken and goose liver. The story got many readers up in arms. How dare those rich people feed expensive food to dogs when people were starving?

The guests at this famous dinner party in Newport, Rhode Island, were dogs.

In the 1970s, a television show was created by the British Broadcasting System. The subject was rich people in Newport in the 1800s. Of course, part of the show was a dog dinner like the first. Twenty dog actors took their places at the table. A dog named Baron started eating from the other dogs' bowls. Polly, dressed in pink, licked up what he left behind. Joshua burped. Were dogs more polite in the olden days?

Apes That "Speak" English

In the eighteenth century, a doctor, Julien Offroy de La Mettrie, believed apes could be taught to speak French. Most people thought he was wrong. In fact, according to a book written in 1954, "Apes have proved to be highly unteachable as far as language goes."

Scientists thought apes could not be language learners. Apes just weren't smart enough, they said, just didn't have the brains for it. Brains, it turns out, are probably not the problem. The fact is that apes just don't have the speech organs to make language sounds.

Since the mid-1960s, several apes—chimpanzees and gorillas—appear to have been taught to "speak." Most use American Sign Language, Ameslan for short—the sign language of the deaf.

Sarah, a chimpanzee, "talks" with plastic tokens arranged in a certain order; and Lana, another chimp, types what she wants to say.

The teachers of apes have had some surprises. As the teachers expected, the apes learned to ask and answer questions. (Some experts think they were just mimicking their teachers.) As they *didn't* expect, the apes seem to use language to swear, lie, and call their enemies names. And also as they didn't expect, the apes appear to make up their own names for things. It all began with Washoe . . .

Washoe, born 1965, chimpanzee

Allen and Beatrice Gardner started teaching Washoe Ameslan when she was a year old. Washoe's first word was "more." Soon she was asking for things and starting conversations with people. By the time she was 6, she could use more than 200 signs. Raised like a human child, Washoe thought she *was* human for a long time. Other chimpanzees were "bugs" to her. Now she lives in a chimpanzee colony in Oklahoma, where some of the other chimps speak Ameslan, too. So she's not too lonely.

Lucy, born 1966, chimpanzee

Raised by Jane and Maurice Temerlin, Lucy learned Ameslan very fast. When she was little, she would sit by herself and practice words. Now grown, she still lives with the Temerlins. In the evening, before dinner, she has a martini.

Lana, born 1970, chimpanzee

Lana lives in a cage with a computer. Each key on the computer keyboard stands for something in a language called Yerkish. By typing on the keyboard, Lana can ask to see movies, look at pictures, get something to eat, or listen to music. Her favorite music is rock. The computer is attached to a machine that records what she says. Sometimes at night when no one is there, Lana types anyway. One night she typed, "Please machine come play with Lana."

Sarah, born 1964, chimpanzee

Sarah uses plastic tokens to communicate with her teacher, David Premack. A blue triangle, for example, stands for "apple." To get what she wants, she has to put down the tokens in the right order. For instance, David will give her chocolate only if she asks with "Give Sarah chocolate." "Sarah chocolate give" won't work. Sarah understands sentences with the word *not* in them. She also under-stands sentences like, "If you choose the apple, then you will get the chocolate."

Koko, born 1971, gorilla

Koko was born on the Fourth of July. Her real name is Hanabi-Ko, Japanese for "fireworks child." Like Washoe and Lucy, she lives like a human. She even helps to clean her room, though she tears up the sponge when she's through wiping the floor. By the time she was 7, Koko had learned 375 Ameslan signs from her teacher, Penny Patterson. Among them were "airplane," "bellybutton," and "friend." Koko's favorite foods are corn on the cob and tomatoes. She rides in the car with Penny and Michael, another gorilla. Koko uses Ameslan to lie. Once, after breaking a sink, she used Ameslan to blame the accident on someone else. She also uses Ameslan to insult people. Some of her insult words are "stink," "rotten," and "nut." When she's bad, Penny makes her sit in a corner.

And then there are other apes who "speak"—Ally, Booie, Bruno, Neam Chimpsky . . .

Koko, a gorilla, has been taught how to "speak" by using Ameslan, a sign language.

Ape Dictionary

The chimpanzees and gorillas that are learning language seem to make up their own words for things. Here are some examples:

Brazil nut	*rock berry* (Washoe)
enemy	*dirty Jack* (Washoe)
mask	*eye hat* (Koko)
orange drink	*drink which is orange* (Lana)
radish	*cry hurt fruit* (Lucy)
swan	*water bird* (Washoe)
watermelon	*drink fruit* (Washoe)
	candy drink fruit (Lucy)
zebra	*white tiger* (Koko)

Dolphins—Kind Hearts and Big Brains

In a legend, the Greeks talked of a boy riding a dolphin. They were so fond of dolphins that they named temples for them and said they once were men. The Greek Plutarch said that the dolphin was the "only creature who loves man for his own sake." That seems to be true. Dolphins are big enough to hurt us, but they never do. In fact, they have saved people who were drowning and have rescued lost divers.

Though dolphins live in the water, they are mammals like us. Every few minutes they need to breathe air. If a dolphin passes out while it's under water, its friends bring it to the surface to save its life. Otherwise, it would drown.

We don't know how smart dolphins are.

Dolphins live in the sea, but they must surface to breathe air. *(U.S. National Marine Fisheries Service)*

They learn very fast when humans teach them. But then, they are playing by our rules, not theirs. It isn't natural for dolphins to play basketball and put on shows for humans. It isn't natural for them to speak English, either. There are those who say they can, but it's never been proved. Perhaps instead we should try to learn to speak "dolphin." Dolphins talk to each other with clicks, squeaks, and other noises, some of which are out of human hearing range and can only be heard on machines. Some people say we might use dolphins to translate for us if creatures from UFOs ever land on Earth.

Dolphin sounds are part of a wonderful dolphin sonar system. When a dolphin clicks very fast, the clicks come together in a sound like a rusty hinge. That sound bounces off things, and the dolphin who made it listens to the echoes. From those echoes it can tell what a thing is, where it is, and how big it is. With their sonar, dolphins can find a tiny pellet in a pool of water. They can tell one metal from another. They may be even able to beam into another dolphin's body to tell how it feels. Our sonar equipment is very crude compared to the dolphin's.

The Navy uses dolphins to carry tools and messages to deep-sea divers. A dolphin's body can adjust to deep ocean water pressure, while human bodies can't. If a human moves up or down in deep water too fast, he or she will get sick with something called "the bends."

Unless humans have gotten hold of them and put them to work, dolphins live a pretty easy life. They spend a good deal of time just playing in the water.

So who's smarter—a dolphin or a human? According to Ashley Montagu, a scientist, "Dolphins have large brains. Possibly they will someday be able to teach us what brains are for."

Some Facts About Dolphins

Dolphins can swim from 26 to 50 miles an hour.

There are 500 species of dolphins. The 2 commonest are the common dolphin and the bottlenose dolphin. The bottlenose dolphin is the one with the built-in smile. The killer whale is a dolphin.

The difference between a dolphin and a porpoise lies in the nose. The one with the longer nose is a dolphin.

It is against the law for a United States citizen to capture a dolphin without a permit.

See the stories about Pelorus Jack and Opo (page 341). Both were famous dolphins.

The Great Escape of the Killer Bees

The scientists in Brazil knew that killer bees were fierce and mean. They also knew that killer bees make more honey per bee than European ones. It seemed worth the chance to fly in some killer bees from Africa. If they could be crossed with European bees, the result might be gentle bees that make lots of honey.

The African bees were kept in guarded hives. Only the worker bees could get out through the holes in the hives—the queens and drones, which were bigger, didn't fit. It would be a disaster if the queens got out—the whole group might swarm and go wild. As long as the queens were locked up in the hives, though, the workers would come home to them.

Accidents happen. In 1957, a beekeeper

who didn't know about the killer bees took the grids off the hives. Twenty-six queens escaped, and with them went all their workers and drones.

The killer bees did go wild. Swarms frightened whole towns. When soccer games were held, the killer bees would often show up. The shouting of the crowds got them excited, and that would be the end of the soccer games. Many animals and more than 150 people died from bee stings.

It isn't that killer bees go looking for trouble. When they sting people, they are defending their hives. If they lose their stingers in a person, they die. But the stinger leaves a smell, and that smell makes other bees attack. So if a person gets stung by one bee, chances are he or she will be stung by more.

The wild killer bees have been moving north at about 200 miles a year. By the early 1990s, they may reach the United States. Should you be worried? Most experts say no. As the bees mix with other kinds of bees, they become gentler. Besides, killer bees can't live through cold winters. Still, be careful about how loudly you shout at soccer games.

Wild Ponies of Chincoteague

Down a watery lane lined with boats, the wild ponies swim the quarter-mile from their island home of Assateague to the shores of Chincoteague. One hundred or more ponies' heads bob in the water. Even the colts swim. On the shore, crowds, which grow larger every year, are cheering.

It is a day in late July—time for the Pony Penning. The Pony Penning has been held every year for 200 years, and since 1925 Chincoteague's volunteer firemen have been in charge of it. They herd the ponies, which run wild on the island the rest of the year, into the water. The day after the swim, some young colts are auctioned off. If they weren't sold, the island would be overrun with ponies, and some would die from lack of food. Many of the ponies are sold to families as pets for their children. This was true even in colonial days.

After the auction, the ponies swim back to Assateague for another year of freedom.

How did the ponies get on the island in the first place? It may be that they came from Spanish horses that swam to Assateague after a shipwreck in the 1700s. It is known that the *San Lorenzo*, a ship carrying a herd of horses to America, *was* wrecked then. But where the ponies came from is not known for sure.

Misty of Chincoteague, by Marguerite Henry, is a story about one of the ponies. Children have loved it for years.

Croaker College

Every year in California, people enter their pet frogs in the Calaveras County Frog Jumping Contest. The writer Mark Twain started the whole thing with a funny article he wrote in 1865 called "The Celebrated Jumping Frog of

Calaveras County." Twain got the idea for the article from a California folk tale. In the tale, Dan'l Webster, a jumping frog, lost a contest because he was too heavy to jump. The reason? Someone made him swallow bird shot, tiny pellets like BBs.

After the Twain article appeared, real frog-jumping contests began to be held every year in several parts of the country. Each frog is given 15 seconds to jump 3 times. The distance is measured from the starting point in a straight line to where the frog lands on the third jump, like this:

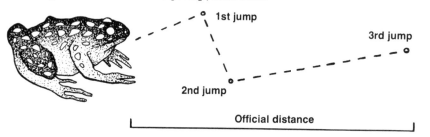

A winning frog usually jumps straight, not zigzag.

Some people who enter frog-jumping contests are so serious about winning that they send their frogs to school. The most famous school is Bill Steed's Croaker College, started in 1970. One of Steed's first students was Grim Leaper, owned by the governor of Arkansas. After Croaker training, the frog won a contest, and since then Steed has trained the frogs of some famous and not-so-famous people. Among them are:

- Evil Green Evil, a frog that rides a toy motorcycle and is owned by stunt rider Evel Knievel.
- Jelly Bean, a frog owned by President Ronald Reagan.

- Rhinestone Cowboy, owned by singer Glen Campbell. Rhinestone rides a toy horse and travels in a fur-lined case.
- Old Cantankerous, a frog that couldn't be trained. Owner comedian Don Rickles.
- Dolly Do, owned by singer Dolly Parton.

The frog-training course lasts 240 hours. Steed stars by hypnotizing the frogs. "You must win. You can win. You will win," he croons. "A relaxed frog is a happy frog and a better athlete," says Steed. The frogs work out in a pool, lift tiny weights, do chin-ups and high dives. According to Steed, they eat "centipede soup, ladybug salad, and filet of dragonfly." A special treat is "bumblebees dipped in honey."

While the frogs are resting, they listen to tape recordings that give them positive

These are some of the illustrious graduates of Bill Steed's Croaker College.

thoughts about winning. "You have to know how to talk frog," Steed says. He suggests that stroking a frog's stomach will make him jump. That's kinder than stamping your feet or yelling.

How serious is frog training? Well, if you know how to talk frog . . .

Bill Steed says that stroking a frog's stomach will make it jump better.

Pet Motel

At American Pet Hotel in Prairie View, Illinois, pets sleep in little brass beds with mattresses and sheets. Their rooms are carpeted with fake grass. They get 3 meals and 2 cookie breaks a day.

A Saint Bernard had a special diet at the motel that would have pleased anyone. It consisted of:

breakfast: 6 slices of bacon, 3 scrambled eggs, bowl of milk with frosted flakes.

Lunch: roast beef, bowl of milk.

Dinner: ravioli, bowl of milk.

Some of the guests at the motel have been snakes, birds, raccoons, and foxes. And cats and dogs, of course.

This motel is for the dogs . . . and cats and other pets. They treat the animals royally and put up signs to protect them. *(Courtesy American Pet Motels, Inc.)*

Animals in the City

Raccoons are good at tipping over your garbage can to dine on your leftovers.

Coyotes howl along with the music at concerts in Los Angeles. Alligators show up on front lawns in Florida towns. There are beavers in the Potomac River near Washington, D.C., and blackbirds sing in the brightly lit London nights. For a while, a fox lived under the bleachers in New York's Yankee Stadium.

In most cities, raccoons are very clever at tipping over garbage cans and raiding them for food. Falcons live high on skyscrapers and eat pigeons to stay alive. More animals live in the center strips of highways, in the grass and bushes. There are field mice and voles, and hawks that eat mice and voles.

This cute, mostly nocturnal animal is such a stinker too. (Nobody crosses a skunk twice!)

If you go to an outdoor concert in Los Angeles, you may hear coyotes howling to the music.

And there are:

bats	sparrows
rats	starlings
swifts	opossums
nighthawks	skunks
weasels	

And don't forget our old friend the cockroach, which has been around for 350 million years.

And that's not all. There are . . .

An Orphanage for Elephants

In the dry season, elephants sometimes leave the jungle to look for food, and the food they find often is in farmers' fields. When the farmers scare the elephants away, the young elephants sometimes panic and fall into mudholes or wells. By the time they are rescued, their parents are gone. Other baby elephants are orphaned when their parents die.

In Sri Lanka, an Asian country, baby elephants that have lost their parents are ·sent to Pinnewala, a 28-acre elephant orphanage that was opened in 1975.

The babies at the orphanage are fed with rubber hoses attached to beer bottles full of milk. Leaves are also given to them. When a gong sounds in the morning, the elephants know it is time to go to the river and start walking down the path. Children from the village join them in a kind of parade. At the river, the

Elephants like to drink, play, and have baths at the orphanage for elephants.

elephants drink, play, and have baths.

When the elephants are big enough, some are sold to zoos. One elephant, Shanti, was recently chosen to go to the National Zoo in Washington, D.C.

Brainy Creatures

Some animals are born knowing how to do things. Spiders, for example, do not have to learn how to make webs. Other animals learn as they go. There are songbirds whose parents teach them songs. But no matter how they come by what they know, animals can be smarter than we humans think!

Tool-users

Sea otters, weasels that live in the ocean, love to eat shellfish. Lying on their

Sea otters use a rock to smash open shellfish. Then they lie back and enjoy their dinner.

Bowerbirds are the "interior decorators" of the bird world.

backs, they hold the unopened shells on their chests and smash them open with a rock. Sea otters often float in groups on rafts of seaweed, winding pieces of seaweed around themsleves to keep from drifting away.

Termites don't like sun. Some termites make paper umbrellas to hold over their heads when they leave the mound.

Chimpanzees chew the ends of sticks to make brushes, then use the brushes to dig termites out of mounds.

An elephant will take a stick in its trunk and use it as a back-scratcher.

The Egyptian vulture picks up a rock in its beak and throws it at an ostrich egg to break it open so that it can be eaten.

The woodpecker finch takes a cactus spine in its beak and digs insects out of tree bark with it.

Bowerbirds like to make fancy avenues. They decorate them with wings, shells, leaves, even blue clothespins. (Bowerbirds love blue.) Some paint their bowers with plant juice. They use leaves as brushes.

Fakers

A kind of weevil (a bug) has a garden of tiny plants on its back. Thus it looks like

what it walks on, and its enemies aren't so likely to see it.

The aphid lion (another bug) kills aphids by sucking out their insides, then hangs the empty bodies on hooks on its skin. The more bodies, the better luck it has hunting. It looks like a gang of aphids out for a stroll.

There is a butterfly in India that looks like a dead leaf. Another kind of butterfly looks like a bird dropping, and still another looks like a thorn. What butterfly enemy wants to eat dead leaves, bird droppings, or thorns?

If scared, opossums play dead to fool their enemies. Opossums prefer the nighttime.

Some birds can "throw" their voices to fool their enemies.

A bird called the killdeer lures an enemy away from her nest by pretending she has a broken wing. The intruder, thinking she is crippled and therefore will be easily caught for a meal, follows her as she limps away from her nest, dragging her wing on the ground. That way her enemies don't know where her babies are.

Opossums play dead to fool their enemies. They go into a trance, their eyes turn glassy, and their tongues hang out of their mouths.

Bee Dance

Bees use light to find their way to food. They see the world as flat, broken designs. When they go back to the hive, they do a dance to tell the other bees where the food is. The dance is in the shape of a figure 8, the middle line of the 8 showing the direction to travel in and how far to go.

This bee is doing a dance to show the others where good food can be found.

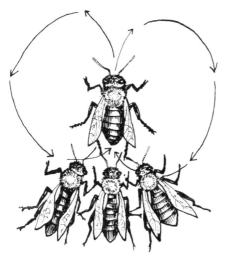

Fish That Learn

Triggerfish like to eat sea urchins, but sea urchins are covered with sharp spines, except underneath. Some triggerfish shoot a fast stream of water out of their mouths to knock the urchins over so they have a spine-free meal. Others snap the spines off with their teeth. Hans W. Fricke, who studies ocean life in the Red Sea, has been watching triggerfish. Fricke put a sea urchin in a jar with a piece of glass on top as a lid, then put the jar in an aquarium with a triggerfish. The triggerfish took the lid in its mouth and moved it off the jar to get at the sea urchin. Which shows triggerfish can learn something new.

Singing Whales

The humpback whale sings long, beautiful songs, and each season its song changes. Scientists have recorded the songs in order to study them and so that others can enjoy listening, too.

If your library has a record of the songs of the humpback whale, listen to it . . . beautiful.

Barnacle Glue

The barnacle, a kind of shellfish, makes a glue stronger than any humans have come up with. It uses the glue to attach itself to ship bottoms and other places.

Light-makers

Fireflies make cold light. It has been said that once a doctor did an operation using a bottle of fireflies for light.

Bat Echo-location

Bats fly at night and have poor eyesight. They figure out where things are and how big they are by bouncing sound off them. The sounds a bat constantly makes as it flies around are too high for the human ear to hear. In 1937 a

Bats find their way around by listening to sounds bounced off things—an animal radar set.

scientist put some bats in front of a big horn that could pick up supersonic sounds. He was the first human to hear a bat's echo-location squeaks.

Quake Sensing

A long time before earthquakes start, animals seem to know they are coming.

The Chinese, who have studied this, wrote a verse about what animals do befor a quake:

> Cattle, sheep, mules, and horses do not enter corrals,
> Rats leave their homes and flee.
> Hibernating snakes leave their burrows early,
> Frightened pigeons continuously fly and do not return to nests.
> Rabbits raise their ears, jump aimlessly and bump things,
> Fish are frightened, jump above water surface.

Pigeon Messengers

In ancient Rome, soldiers used carrier pigeons to send messages. A message was put into a little tube that was attached to the bird's leg, and the bird flew the message to the place it thought of as home. In World War One, an English pigeon named Cher Ami saved a group of

People have sent messages by birds like this carrier pigeon throughout history. We still do in National Parks.

American soldiers who were lost somewhere in France. The soldiers sent a message on the bird's leg, telling where they were. During its flight the bird's leg was shattered by pieces of flying metal from guns, and a piece also hit its heart. But Cher Ami got the message through.

Today, pigeons carry messages from campers in far-flung parts of U.S. National Parks. The pigeons are taken in by muleback in containers. The mules don't like it because the pigeons are noisy.

Flying Instructors

Back in the early 1900s, before airplanes were invented, scientist Samuel P. Langley bought 12 vultures for $3 each. Wanting to study how they fly, he put them in 2 high towers so he could watch them. With what he learned he built a flying machine, which he nicknamed Buzzard. However, Buzzard crashed. The Wright brothers, who later built a plane that *did* fly, asked Langley for advice, and he told them what he had learned from the vultures.

Toothpicks

Certain birds go inside the mouths of hippos and alligators . . . and aren't eaten. Why? They do a service for the big animals—they pick insects and leeches out of their teeth. Hippos yawn as a signal they want their teeth picked. Sometimes a crocodile shuts its mouth on a toothpicking bird, but it doesn't swallow. It always opens its mouth again . . . and out walks the bird, unharmed.

Ant Farmers

Some ants keep herds of aphids and "milk" them for honeydew, sugar left over from the food the aphids eat. The black lawn ant builds little mud houses for the aphids so that they will have somewhere to go to hide from their enemies.

The ant is a smart creature. Some ants keep herds of aphids, which they "milk."

Animal First Aid

Before anything happens, put 3 phone numbers close to your telephone:

- Your veterinarian's number.
- Emergency veterinarian service number. (Ask your veterinarian for it.)
- Poison Control Center's number.

Be careful around hurt animals. They may bite. If your dog is hurt, tie its mouth shut gently with a piece of soft cloth. Throw a towel over a hurt cat or bird, *then* pick it up.

Broken bones (dislocations, sprains): Don't move the pet unless you have to. If you do have to, change its position as little as possible. Use a flat board as a stretcher. Use a splint only if the lower part of leg dangles. Don't splint over the break. Take the animal to the veterinarian.

Bleeding: If you can, put a bandage over the part that is bleeding. Tie it firmly, but not too tight. Take the animal to the veterinarian.

Bites: Clip hair from around the wound with scissors. Wash with water and mild soap. Take the animal to the veterinarian.

Burns: Put ice or cloths dipped in cold water against the burn for 20 minutes—no longer. If the animal was burned with acid or alkali, flush with water. Take the animal to a veterinarian.

Drowning: If you can, grasp the animal's hind legs above the joint and lift them up to let the water run out. Do mouth-to-nose resuscitation.

Mouth-to-Nose Resuscitation
Close the animal's mouth. Take a breath and put your mouth over the animal's nose. Breathe into the pet. Let the pet breathe the air out. Repeat. Do 10 to 15 breaths a minute.

Convulsions: Hold pet down until they stop. Take the animal to a veterinarian.

Heat stroke: Watch for fast breathing, weakness, and staggering. Put the animal in a cool place and hose it down with cool water. Take it to a veterinarian.

Poisoning: Find out what the poison is. Call the veterinarian for directions on what to do, or call the Poison Control Center. After emergency care, take the pet and the poison to the veterinarian.

Choking: Use your fingers to try to get the object out. If that doesn't work, hold the animal upside down and shake gently.

Diarrhea: You can give medicine for human diarrhea. First figure out how much your pet weighs compared to a human. A medium-size (60 pounds) dog weighs about half what a human does, so give half as much medicine as the label says.

Vomiting: If it keeps up, call the veterinarian.

Snake bite: Tie a flat piece of cloth above the wound, not too tight. Keep it on only an hour. Hold the leg or other bitten part in a position level with the heart. Get the animal to the veterinarian as fast as you can.

Remember the doctor's rule: Do no harm.

Some Numbers You Should Know

	Dog	Cat
Heartbeat rate	80–100 beats/min.	100–130 beats/min.
Breathing rate (while resting and cool)	12–14 breaths/min.	20–30 breaths/min.
Temperature (while resting)	100.5°–102.5°F.	100.5°–102.5°F

No Horses Allowed in Your Highrise?
All Is Not Lost . . .

A CHART FOR CHOOSING A PET

What if the rules of your apartment building say "no pets"? That might not include fish in a bowl. Your sister has an allergy? Choose a pet without fur. Some other things to consider when choosing a pet are:

Money. The chart gives you an idea what it costs to keep each pet. The cost of buying a pet in the first place varies. For example, an alley cat can cost nothing, but a Siamese may cost a lot. Generally, though, mice are cheaper than horses, and bugs are cheaper than cats.

The Rest of the Family. After you've chosen, ask the rest of your family what they think. You may find out that your brother hates spiders, even though you love them.

Wild Pets? Animals taken out of the wild usually do not make good pets. Some are okay—they're on the chart. But small mammals, no. When they grow up, they have gotten too big to be pets and don't know enough to survive in the wild. The same goes for alligators and crocodiles.

Pet	Cost to Keep	Care Needed	Space Needed	Facts
Horse, pony, burro	high	a lot	stall and yard	You can get a burro or wild horse free. See page 333.
Dog	medium to high	quite a bit	run of house, place to exercise	Friend to humans for 12,000 years. Choose according to size and personality.
Cat	low to medium	some	run of house	Related to the big cats in the zoo.
Rat, mouse, guinea pig, hamster, gerbil	low	some	cage (size depends on size of animal)	Rats can learn tricks. Mice need toys. Fun to watch.
Rabbit	low	some	yard or cage	Can be housebroken. Watch out for thumpers and biters! Don't pick up by the ears.
Caged birds: parrot, canary, finch, parakeet, budgie, cockateel, lovebirds	low to medium	some	cage (size depends on size of bird); let out of cage once in a while; shut windows!	Keep warm—not hot or cold. Canaries sing. Parakeets and parrots talk—teach by using only a few words a few minutes a day.
Chicken	low to medium	some	cage or pen	Can't be kept in many cities.
Duck, goose	low to medium	some	yard	Can't be kept in many cities. Goose can be a watchbird.
Pigeon	low to medium	some	cage	Homing pigeons can carry messages.
Salamander, newt, frog, toad	low	not much	terrarium (see page 334)	Toads easiest to tame. Watch frogs go from egg to tadpole to frog. Newts can grow new legs if they lose them.

Pet	Cost to Keep	Care Needed	Space Needed	Facts
Lizard, snake	low	not much	terrarium, reptile cage	Keep cannibals alone. Some sleep through winter; if so, keep in cool basement or set free before winter.
Turtle, tortoise	low	not much	terrarium or yard; *don't keep in water*	Provide a little swimming pool with steps.
Fish	low to medium	depends on kind	aquarium	Read up on fish if you get into fancy kinds. Learn to balance aquarium. Fun if you like science and gadgets. Non-allergic.
Spiders, insects	low	not much	jar—dirt and plants from where found	See "Bug Zoo," page 335.
Hermit crab	low	not much	terrarium with sand and rocks	Hermit crab needs snail shell to live in.

Taking Care of Pets

Study up on care for your pet before you bring it home. Ask your veterinarian, read a book, or talk to the people in the pet store. Find our what, how much, and when to feed it. Check on what doctor's care it will need, including regular shots.

Some general rules:

1. Don't take animals out of the wild. It's cruel to do so. If you find a wild animal that is hurt or sick, call your local humane society to find out what to do. It will be listed in the Yellow Pages of your phone book under "Animal Shelters" or "Humane Societies." If you find a baby animal, wait a while to see if its mother is coming back. If the baby turns out to be an orphan, call the humane society for advice on what to do.

2. Choose the right pet for you and your situation. Don't try to keep a huge dog in a tiny city apartment.

3. Use a soft voice when talking to your pet. Move slowly when you are near it. Be gentle.

4. Pick your pet up properly. Always support its feet. Don't pick it up by its ears, tail, or legs.

5. Don't handle your pet too much. Don't tease it.

6. Feed your pet according to directions. Don't give it too much food. Feed it at the same time (or times) every day.

7. Make sure your pet always has fresh water (unless it's a saltwater fish).

8. Don't give your pet splintery bones.

9. Groom your pet regularly.

10. Don't leave animals in parked cars in hot weather, even with windows open.

11. Give your pet the exercise it needs. Don't let it run outside without you. It could get hurt.

12. Make sure your pet has identifica-

tion. Put a tag on its collar. Put only elastic collars on cats.

13. Watch out for danger in the house. Example: dangling electric cords. Cats love to play with them and can get zapped.

14. Provide proper medical care. If your pet gets sick, take it to a veterinarian.

15. Make sure your pet doesn't have unwanted babies. If your pet has babies, make sure you have homes for them.

16. Most of all, love your pet!

Adopt a Horse or Burro

In the West, wild horses and burros live on open government land. (The burros are called "Rocky Mountain canaries.") Because there are too many for the amount of land they live on, the government gives some away free. To get one, you must:

- prove you have enough space for it.
- prove you aren't going to try to make money from it.
- pick it up from its holding corral.

To find out more, write to:

International Society for the Protection of Mustangs and Burros
11790 Deodar Way
Reno, NV 89506
     or
Adopt-a-Horse Program
Bureau of Land Management
Post Office Box 25047
Denver, CO 80225

Ferrying wild burros for adoption in Arizona.
(Courtesy International Society for the Protection of Mustangs and Burros)

Be sure to include your name and address in your letter.

WARNING: Wild horses and burros, especially if grown, may be very hard to tame.

Wild horses enjoy freedom in California. *(Courtesy International Society for Protection of Mustangs and Burros)*

Toad in a Bowl

Toads, lizards, praying mantises, and other small animals can be kept in a terrarium. To make one, you first need a jar, bottle, or aquarium. Fill it as described in the drawing.

You can keep a toad in a bowl if you wish. Follow the directions on the left.

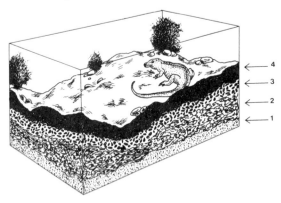

To make your terrarium, first you put down a layer of soil, one part dirt, one part sand, one part peat moss (**1**). Then add a thin layer of charcoal chips (**2**). Next goes a layer of peat moss or sphagnum moss or dead leaves (**3**). Top it off with an inch or two of sand (**4**).

Make the soil layer somewhat bumpy, with a few hills and valleys. Add a few stones, pieces of wood, and plants. Use tiny plants you find in the woods: ferns, moss, violets or cactus plants. Plant carefully. Give roots room and cover with dirt. Water, but not too much. Put a glass lid on top. If, after a while, the water makes so much of a fog on the glass that you can't see inside, take the lid off and let it dry out. Don't keep the terrarium in strong sunlight—or in the dark, either.

Be a "Wild Animal" Hunter

The Smithsonian Institution in Washington, D.C., keeps an insect zoo. In the zoo are, among other things, crickets and tarantulas. The zoo is always looking for more animals. If you want to catch and send some, write to:

Insect Zoo
NHB Stop 101
Washington, D.C. 20560

Include your name and address. In the mail, you will get a list of what animals the zoo needs, mailing labels, and instructions.

Bug Zoo

To make a bug zoo, first catch the bug. To accomplish this, put a jar over it, mouth down. Then slide a piece of thin cardboard under the bug and jar. Then make a "cage" from a canning jar with a screw lid. Put a screen in the lid or punch holes in it. Keep a piece of the plant you found the bug on in the jar. Spray the plant with water first. Some good bugs to keep are:

stink beetle

click beetle (Flip it on its back. It will play dead at first. Then—click!—it will snap in the air and land on its feet.)

cricket

caterpillar (will turn into a butterfly or moth)

pillbug or sowbug

praying mantis

ants

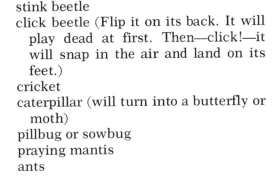

Bugs like this praying mantis and caterpillar in a bug zoo need air, water, and plants.

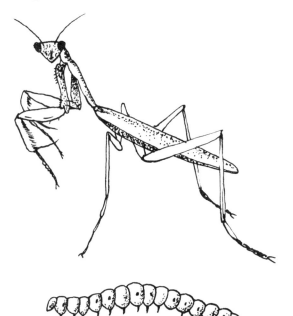

Endangered Animals

Since the 1600s more than 130 species of animals have died out. That means they have ceased to be—not one exists in the world. Among them is the passenger pigeon. Once there were millions of passenger pigeons in North America. The skies were black with them when flocks flew from place to place. The last passenger pigeon died in the Cincinnati Zoo in 1914.

Quagga
extinct 1883

Labrador Duck
extinct 1875

Cape Lion
extinct 1860

Longtailed
Ground Roller
population
rare

Giant Otter
population
unknown,
declining

Northern Kit Fox
extinct 1938?

Passenger Pigeon
extinct 1914

Galapagos Giant Tortoise
population unknown, declining

Aye-Aye
population 50?

Giant Panda
population rare

Kirtland's Warbler
population 1,000

Volcano Rabbit
population 1,200

Siberian Tiger
population 60–70?

Black-Footed Ferret
population unknown, declining

American Bald Eagle
population 800 nesting pairs

Extinct is forever.

Some animals become extinct in the course of time, like dinosaurs. But man is killing off these creatures. *(Courtesy Friends of Animals)*

Why do animal species die out? It is partly the fault of human beings. Too much hunting or pollution can kill them off. Animal habitats are destroyed by human activities. Purses and coats are made from animal skins. Feathers are taken for hats.

Governments are beginning to protect animal species in danger of being killed off. In the United States, the Fish and Wildlife Service is in charge. Their list of nearly 200 endangered species in North America includes some of the following:

Some Endangered Species in North America

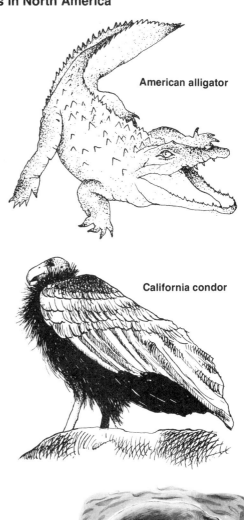

American alligator

California condor

Manatee (sea cow)

Fishes

Blue pike
Shortnose sturgeon
Gila trout

Reptiles and Amphibians

American alligator
American crocodile
4 species of sea turtle

Mammals

3 species of bat
Eastern cougar
2 species of deer
Black-footed ferret
2 species of fox
Manatee (sea cow)
Utah prairie dog
Hawaiian monk seal
8 species of whale
Gray wolf
Red wolf

Birds

California condor
Whooping crane
Bald eagle
American peregrine falcon
Aleutian Canada goose
Brown pelican
Attwater's greater prairie chicken
California least tern
2 species of wood warbler
2 species of woodpecker

Insects

6 species of butterfly

Endangered Animals in Other Parts of the World

Fishes
  Catfish

Reptiles and Amphibians
  Chinese alligator
  11 species of crocodile
  3 species of frog
  Galapagos tortoise
  16 species of turtle

Mammals
  2 species of wild ass
  5 species of bandicoot
  Bactrian camel
  Asian elephant
  Gorilla
  Leopard
  12 species of monkey
  Ocelot
  Orangutan

4 species of rhinoceros
Tiger
8 species of whale

Birds
  Short-tailed albatross
  Abbott's booby
  Great Indian bustard
  Japanese crane
  Japanese crested ibis

What You Can Do to Help Save Endangered Animals

Write to government officials about endangered animals. Get people to sign petitions to save endangered animals. Don't disturb the places wild animals live. Don't trap or hunt or fish for endangered animals.

A Dictionary of Some Famous Animals

Barry—Lifesaver. Swiss Saint Bernard. Back in the early 1800s, Barry worked with the rescue corps of the Saint Bernard Hospice. In his lifetime he saved more than 40 travelers who were lost in the snow.

Bucephalus—Warrior. Macedonian horse. In 343 B.C. the leader of Macedonia, Philip, was looking for a new war horse. A trader brought some for him to look at. Philip and his son, Alexander, then 13, watched the horses parade in front of them. One horse was very large and wild, and Alexander bet his father he could ride it. His father thought he couldn't and took the bet. Alexander turned the horse facing the sun so it

wouldn't shy at its own shadow Then he leaped on its back and galloped down the field and back. The horse was his. He named it Bucephalus, which means Oxhead in Greek, for the shape of a white spot on its forehead. Riding Bucephalus, Alexander won many battles. (He rode some other horses, too.) In fact, he won so many battles that he conquered most of the world then known.

Chips—War Hero. American dog. In World War Two, Chips was an Army watchdog. One night he got loose and captured 5 enemy soldiers all by himself.

Clever Hans—Smart Mind Reader? Russian horse. Clever Hans lived in Elberfeld, Germany. He could answer questions by pawing with his hoofs, and he could do arithmetic. How? No one was sure. Some people thought he was "reading" his master's face and gestures. But whatever the reason, he became famous in his time—the late 1800s. Children named their toy horses after him and people flocked to see him perform.

Comanche—Last One Left. American horse. At the Battle of the Little Big Horn (1876), 265 Army soldiers fought 2,500 Sioux Indians. The Army lost. All the men and horses were killed except one—a mustang named Comanche. After Comanche died he was stuffed and put on display.

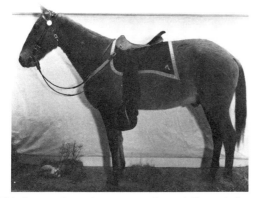

This horse, the only army survivor of Custer's last stand, was stuffed and put on display! *(University of Kansas Museum of Natural History)*

Hachi—The Faithful. Japanese dog. It was back in the 1920s. Every morning, Hachi went with his master to the station and watched him board the train to the city. Every night, Hachi met the 5 P.M. train that brought his master home. But one evening his master did not get off the train. He had died in the city. Hachi went sadly home. For the next 10 years

he met every 5 P.M. train. And every night, no master appeared. When Hachi died, the Japanese government put a statue of him at the place where he waited.

(Courtesy Japan National Tourist Organization)

Harvey—Attack Animal. American rabbit. Harvey was very tough. He'd bite and thump anyone who came too close to him because he had been abused by the people who had him when he was young. The American Society for the Prevention of Cruelty to Animals used him as guard rabbit for their offices. He became a symbol of animal abuse. The ASPCA sent him on tour and sold T-shirts with his picture on them.

Harvey the Attack Rabbit patrolled an ASPCA office just like a guard dog. He disliked people because he was once mistreated. *(Paul Duckworth)*

For 9 years, Jack, the African baboon, never made a mistake helping to set railway signals and switches.

Jack—Signalman. African baboon. In a wooden shack, Jack lived with James Wide. Wide, who had lost his legs, was in charge of railroad signals. Every morning, Jack pushed Wide to work on a trolley that ran on the tracks. The animal could work the levers that set signals and opened and closed switches. In the 9 years he worked for the railroad, he never made a mistake.

Lampo—Traveler. Italian dog. Lampo, traveling alone, made 3,000 railroad journeys. He seemed to know the schedules, for he never got lost. Every night he came back to his home station. After he died, a statue of him was put near the station. Travelers say it barks when trains come in late.

Lassie—Actor. American collie. Pal barked, chased cars, and chewed things up. A real sinner. Pal was so bad, his owner brought him to a training school for reform. The Weatherwax brothers, who owned the school, took Pal to try out for a part in the movies. The role was Lassie, and Pal got it. After that, he was called Lassie, even though he was male.

(Male dogs have better coats than females, so a male dog had to be chosen.) The movie was *Lassie Come Home* (1943). Since then, there have been 7 Lassies. Lassie's son was the second, his grandson was the third, and so on down the line. There are tricks to Lassie's tricks. For instance, to make Lassie lick his master's face, the movie-maker puts ice cream on the boy's cheek.

Lizzie—Talking Animal? American dolphin. Scientist John Lilly was trying to teach Lizzie and other dolphins to speak English. Lizzie died in her tank after speaking what some people think was an English sentence. The sentence may have been "It's six o'clock." It might also have been, "It's a trick."

Monster—Lover. American tortoise. He's kept at the Utah Zoo and he's been looking for a girl friend. So far, he's been in love with a garbage can lid, a food dish, and a big rock.

Monster, a lonely American tortoise at a Utah zoo, fell in love with a big rock—among other things.

Morocco—Genius. English horse. Back in the late 1500s, Morocco amazed the world. He could answer questions by pawing with his hoof and could even tell how old people were by looking at them.

According to one story, Morocco saved his master's life. The master had been sentenced to die for witchcraft, and Morocco begged for his life by kneeling down before an official. The official gave in and let the master live.

Old Abe—Battle Screamer. American eagle. In the Civil War, Old Abe was a Yankee soldier. He wore red, white, and blue ribbons around his neck. Once he took the American flag in his beak and held it out so it could be seen in all its glory. During battles, he flew above the troops screaming a battle cry. Though his tail feathers were shot off, he lived through 36 battles. When the war ended, Old Abe went on tour to raise money for soldiers.

Opononi ("Opo")—Friend to Children. New Zealand dolphin. About 1955, some children were playing on a New Zealand beach. A wild dolphin came up to play with them every day. The children called it Opononi, or Opo for short. Later, one of the children, Jill Baker, wrote a story about the dolphin.

Pelorus Jack—Ship's Pilot. New Zealand porpoise. For 40 years, beginning in 1872, a porpoise guided ships through a tricky channel in New Zealand waters. His name was Pelorus Jack. In 1903, while Jack was piloting the ship Penguin, a passenger shot the dolphin. Jack left for 2 weeks, then came back healed up, but he never piloted the *Penguin* again. In 1909 the *Penguin* was wrecked in the channel.

Rin Tin Tin—Actor. German dog. Rin Tin Tin was left behind by his owners, the German army, after World War One. His mother was a war dog. By the 1920s he had become a star in American movies. In one week he received 12,000 fan letters.

Rotten Ralph—Bad Cat. American cat. He was the meanest cat in the Glamor Kitty contest—he bit a judge. Ralph was also the star of a play, *Dick Whittington and His Cat.* Each night, wearing a red, white, and blue suit, he came on stage in a pony cart. His co-owner said, "Rotten doesn't bite the hand that feeds him except once in a while."

Sandy—Annie's Sidekick. American mixed-breed dog. He was at the dog pound, scheduled to be put to sleep the next day. But that night a talent scout discovered him and sprung him for $8. It was his luck to look like Sandy, the dog in the cartoon "Little Orphan Annie." His

Sandy stars in the Broadway hit show *Annie*.
(Martha Swope, courtesy of Dave Powers)

wiry hair was the right color—sandy. A musical play, *Annie*, based on the cartoon, was being put on in New York City, and a dog actor was needed. Guess who got the part. Now Sandy is famous. His main speech in the play is "Arf." Sandy's understudy, named Arf, was rescued from a dog pound, too.

Secretariat—Wonder Horse. American race horse. In 1973 Secretariat won the 3 biggest races in the country. Those wins made him a Triple Crown winner, the first in 25 years, and he was named Athlete of the Year, too. Big and golden-red, Secretariat looks like a war horse. His co-owner said he was like a "big kid." When he retired, 2 little girls unfolded a sheet that read, "Goodbye, Secretariat. We Love You." It was true. Children loved the big horse.

Smokey the Bear—Firefighter. American black bear. The first Smokey was on Forest Service posters for 25 years. He is now retired and lives in the National Zoo in Washington, D.C. The new Smokey was found as a small orphan in the forest. He is on posters, too, and children send him 5,000 letters a week. You can write to Smokey to get a Junior Forest Ranger Kit, with badge, membership card, photo of Smokey, bookmark, and 4 stamps. The address is:

Smokey Bear Headquarters
Washington, D.C. 20252

Texas Tailwaggers—Square Dancers. American dogs. Eight of the 16 tailwaggers in this square-dance team are dogs. Though they work on leashes, they could do the steps alone. They perform in "Irish Washerwoman" and "Cotton-Eye Joe." Their favorite part is the grand march. "Them dogs is not dancin'," one old lady said. "Them people's dancin'. Them dogs is just followin'."

Ziggy—Prisoner. Indian elephant brought to America. In 1920 baby Ziggy was bought as a present for a little girl and was taken to his new home in a taxi. However, he was too hard for a little girl to handle, so he was given to a circus, where he learned to do tricks. He played "Yes, Sir, That's My Baby" on the harmonica and smoked a cigarette in a long holder. Then he was sent to the zoo. He turned mean and tried to kill his keeper. As punishment, he spent the next 30 years in a lonely, dark cage. Children saved him. They raised enough money to get him a proper cage in the sun in 1970. There, life was better for Ziggy. He played trunksies over the fence with 3 female elephants.

Rogues' Gallery of (Alleged) Monsters

Monster: LOCH NESS MONSTER, nicknamed Nessie (probably more than one, some males and some females).

Where It Lives: Loch Ness, a deep, narrow lake in Scotland, in murky water the color of coffee.

What It Is Like: A water animal, from 15 to 30 feet long (one-fourth to one-half the distance from home plate to first base on a Little League baseball field). Breathes air. Big body, with 2 to 12 humps seen when swimming. Tiny head sits on top of a long neck. Has flippers. Fast swimmer.

First Seen: About A.D. 565 by St. Columba. Described then as "a very old beastie, something like a huge frog."

Number of Sightings: About 10,000.

Some Interesting Sightings and Searches: 1880: Diver Donald Mac-Donald, in the water's depths to look at a sunken ship, saw the monster. "I was underwater about my work," he said, "when all of a sudden the monster swam by me as cool and calm as you please."

1933: A married couple saw Nessie walking across a road. They said it looked like a big snail with a long neck. The first photograph and film (now lost) were taken of Nessie. A newspaper printed a story saying that Nessie's footprint had been found. The footprint turned out to be a doctored hippo print. The whole thing was a hoax.

1934: A London doctor took a photograph of Nessie's head and neck. In addition, Captain James Fraser captured the monster on film. Some experts thought his movie showed only a seal at play.

1954: Some people on a bus watched Nessie for 10 minutes.

1960: A man named Tim Dinsdale filmed Nessie.

1966: Experts said the Dinsdale film showed something alive.

1969: A tiny submarine with divers in it went down to look for Nessie.

1970: Sonar was used to look for Nessie. It tracked a large, moving body.

1972: Triggered by sonar, an underwater camera took a photograph of something that looked like a big flipper.

1975: Another sonar-camera photograph, this time of a body and some neck, was taken.

1976: A manned balloon trailed a line with bacon bait to catch Nessie. No luck.

A big campaign was begun to find the monster. Camera-sonar systems called "monster pots" were lowered into the lake. Photographers, divers, and scientists all worked on the problem. They tried to attract Nessie with fish sounds, bait, and light. Murky results.

What It Could Be: A plesiosaur—a large, sea-going dinosaur thought to have died out 70 million years ago. A giant relative of a newt. A whale. A huge sea slug. A big worm. A snake, salamander, sea cow, or eel. A crocodile. A large frog. An elephant. Part of a sunken Viking ship (the oars look like flippers). A mirage.

Evidence says there is something big down there. Sonar has found a sunken airplane, pots, tires, and shoes. One scientist joked: "I've solved the mystery. Nessie is nothing but a big Florsheim."

What Next?: Nessie is protected under British law. To make the monster official, it was given a scientific name: *Nessiteras rhomboteryx*. This means "Ness wonder with diamond-shaped fins." There has been talk of trapping her in a big box trap and of sending down dolphins to search for her.

Some Relatives of Nessie

Monster: FLATHEAD LAKE MONSTER, a USO (Unidentified Swimming Object).

Where It Lives: Flathead Lake, Montana.

What It Is Like: About 10 feet long with 3 humps.

What It Could Be: A big fish, a homemade submarine, a fat skin-diver, a dinosaur.

Monster: OGOPOGO (English name) or NAITAKA (Indian name).

Where It lives: Lake Okanagan, British Columbia.

What It Is Like: According to a woman named Erin Neely, who saw it while water skiing: "A huge garden hose thrashing about in the water."

A Little History: 1854: The monster reached up and grabbed a team of horses crossing the partly frozen lake.

Monster: CHAMP
Where It Lives: Lake Champlain (New York, Vermont, Canada).
What It Is Like: Has a huge head with horns and mane, and one to 3 humps. Is about 40 feet long. Travels at 15 miles an hour.
A Story: P. T. Barnum, a great showman of the 1800s, offered $15,000 for Champ's hide. No one ever collected.

Monster: PONIK THE TERRIBLE (English name) or LA BÊTE (French name—means "the beast").
Where It Lives: Lake Pohenegamook, Canada.
What It Is Like: Has 3 humps. Is 85 to 90 feet long.

Monster: SKRIMSL
Where It Lives: Lagerflot, a lake in Iceland.
What It is Like: About 50 feet long and looks like Nessie.

Monster: SASQUATCH (Indian name) or BIG FOOT (English name).
Where It Lives: The Pacific Northwest of the United States and Canada, in thick forest.
What It Is Like: A creature something like an ape. Thick fur, long arms. Walks on 2 feet, upright. Height: 7 to 12 feet (taller than a tall man). Weight: 600 to 900 pounds. Footprints 12 to 22 inches long, 6 inches wide. Sometimes sticks out its tongue at people who have sighted it.
First Seen: Indian stories go very far back. The Chehalis say the monsters descended from 2 groups of giants.
Number of Sightings: About 750.
Some Interesting Sightings and Searches: 1811: Explorer and trader David Thompson saw a set of Sasquatch footprints.

1884: A Canadian newspaper reported that a train crew had captured a Sasquatch. It supposedly was put on display. Then it was sold to the circus.

1910: A double murder of prospectors was blamed on Sasquatch.

1918: A Sasquatch attacked a prospector's shack in Washington. A newspaper story said it was 8 feet tall. The story also said the Sasquatch could hypnotize people, throw its voice, and make itself invisible.

1924: A group of Sasquatch threw stones at a coal miner's cabin in Ape Canyon, Washington.

1924: Albert Ostman, according to a story he told in 1957, was captured by 4 Sasquatch. While camping out, he had fallen asleep in his sleeping bag and woke to find himself carried, still in his sleeping bag, by a huge creature. The creature was the father in a family of 4 Sasquatch. They kept him in a valley for a week. The Sasquatch ate plants, Ostman said. He escaped, but did not tell his story then. He thought no one would believe him.

1967: A film was made of a creature walking through a forest. The filmmakers said it was a Sasquatch. Some people think it was a human in an ape suit.

1969: Big footprints, more than 1,000 of them, were found in an area in Bossburg, Washington. The creature that made them had a crippled right foot. A Sasquatch?

1970: A man named Frank White and his wife were sitting on a log in the woods, eating sandwiches. "There's a bear," the wife said. It was a Sasquatch, and White made a film of it.

What It Could Be: A creature brought by a UFO. A kind of ape. A kind of early human. A bear. A hallucination.

Celebrations: Go to the "Big Foot Daze" carnival held each year in Willow Creek, California. You can look at an 8-foot statue of Big Foot and buy a Big Foot ring.

Monster: ABOMINABLE SNOWMAN (English name) or YETI (Tibetan name—means "magical creature").

Where It Lives: High in the Himalaya Mountains.

What It Looks Like: Squat, no tail, body covered with hair. Flat-faced, with big teeth and a big mouth. Head comes to a point. Walks on 2 legs. Awake mostly at night, sleeps in the day.

First Seen: Stories by Tibetans go back a long way, more than 300 years.

Number of Sightings: More than 40.

Some Interesting Sightings and Searches: 1832: Explorer B. H. Hodgson said some of the people working for him saw a "hairy apelike creature" in the mountains of Nepal.

1887: A scientist saw a huge creature. Strange footprints were found.

1921: More footprints were found.

1937: The first photographs of footprints were taken.

1938: An Englishman said he was kidnapped by a yeti when on vacation in Sikkim. The yeti kept him in a cave, then let him go.

1951: Mountain climber Eric Shipton found yeti footprints on Mt. Everest.

1952–1960: Expeditions to find yeti didn't come up with much.

1958: Nepal listed the yeti as protected species.

1970: An expedition leader saw "something between a gorilla and a bear."

1972: Plaster casts were made of yeti footprints.

1975: A Polish hiker said a yeti came up to him near Everest.

1978: Forest ranger said he was attacked by a yeti. Yetis were seen in Siberia.

What It Could Be: An ape-like creature. An early human. A giant bear.

Evidence: Footprints. A scalp found in a monastery, said to be of a yeti. Scalp later proved to be made of skin of a serow (a goat antelope).

Extra Facts: The country of Bhutan lists the yeti as its national animal and has issued stamps with pictures of the yeti on them.

Some Relatives of the Sasquatch and Yeti

Monster: ALMAS or CHUCHUNAA.

Where It Lives: Soviet Union.

What It Is Like: Ape-like creature with low forehead and a flat nose. Shrieks and steals food. Footprints 12 inches long.

Monster: MOUNT VERNON MONSTER.

Where It Lives: Virginia.

What It Is Like: Makes noise "ooah-kra-ah" or "eeveakgoo-agh" or "aa-aoohauoa-ah-o".

What It Could Be: Big Foot, frog, owl, ghosts of George Washington's pigs, peacock.

Monster: SKUNK APE.

Where It Lives: Florida swamps.

What It Is Like: Sasquatch. Smells terrible. Policeman Charles Stoeckman saw it in the 1970s. He said, "It stunk awful, like a dog that hasn't been bathed in a year and suddenly gets rained on." His wife, Leslie, saw it in the yard at night. She said its "bright, colorless eyes . . . evil-staring" reflected the light. "I could see the silhouette of its huge shoulder and head above an 8-foot bush she said."

Monster: GOATMAN.

Where It Lives: Prince Georges County, Maryland.

What It Is Like: Size of human male, covered with fur, human face. Walks on hind legs. Some say its lower body is like that of a goat.

A Story: Some say Goatman was once a scientist. He was doing experiments on goats, then went crazy. Now, according to this story, he lives in a shack, has a hairy body, and attacks cars with an axe. Maybe he eats dogs.

Bird-like Monsters

Monster: MOTHMAN.

Where It Lives: Point Pleasant, West Virginia.

What It Is Like: A creature with huge wings. Flies like a helicopter (goes straight up). Red eyes. Makes sound like a big mouse.

When Seen: 1966–1967.

Number of Sightings: About 100.

Relative: "Big Bird," who lives in Texas. About 5 feet 8 inches tall. Monkey-like face. 12-foot wings.

Are these monsters real? Who knows?

How Fast Some Animals Travel

The following animals are listed from the speediest to the slowest.

Animal	Miles per Hour
Cheetah	70
Dragonfly	60
Pronghorn	60
Lion	50
Quarter horse	47
Coyote	43
Gray fox	42
Zebra	40
Greyhound	40
Rabbit	35
Wolf	35
Cougar	35
Giraffe	32
White-tailed deer	30

Animal	Miles per Hour
Grizzly bear	30
Cat (house)	30
Human	28
Elephant	25
Black mamba (snake)	20
Squirrel	12
Pig	11
Chicken	9
Spider	1
Giant Tortoise	0.17 (about 15 feet a minute)
Snail	0.03 (about 2 or 3 feet a minute)

NOTE: Some numbers are rounded off.

How Long Some Animals Live

This list tells the *average* number of years each animal lives. Dogs, for example, live to be 12 years old, on the average. Some dogs live fewer years, and some live far more. (One dog lived to be 22.) The figures for wild animals are from studies of those kept in zoos. Those that live in the wild don't last as long.

Animal	Number of Years
Galapagos tortoise	150
European catfish	60
condor	52
Asian elephant	40
African elephant	35
black bear	32
hippopotamus	25
English sparrow	23
horse	20
gorilla	20
tiger	16
zebra	15
rhinoceros	15
monkey (rhesus)	15
cow	15
lion	13

Animal	Number of Years
house cat	12–14
leopard	12
moose	12
sheep	12
dog	12
sea lion (California)	12
giraffe	10
pig	10
gray squirrel	10
white-tailed deer	8
goat	8
kangaroo	7
red fox	7
chipmunk	6
white rabbit	5
guinea pig	4
white mouse	3
opossum	1
fruit fly	1/25 (about 2 weeks)

A human being born in 1973 can expect to live about 71 years. That puts the human higher than the European catfish but lower than the Galapagos tortoise.

Animal Watching

Zoos. In the United States there are more than 250 zoos and wildlife parks. See the telephone book's Yellow Pages under "Zoological Gardens."

Whale-watching. If you live near the ocean, watch your local newspaper for stories about whale-watching tours. These usually take place in spring and fall, when the whales migrate.

Bird-watching. Put out a bird feeder with seeds, suet, apples, and raisins. Watch who comes to dinner. Visit the

You might see a rare African chevrotain at the zoo.
(American Museum of Natural History)

The flamingo pool is always a popular spot at the zoo. *(Courtesy Jerusalem Biblical Zoo)*

This is a zonkey—a cross between a donkey and a zebra. *(Courtesy Jerusalem Biblical Zoo)*

Safari parks, where the animals roam freely, are popular now. *(National Parks Service)*

woods and fields early in the morning. Join a bird walk. To know who's who among the birds, get a book that will help identify them. Look for: size, shape, coloring, markings, behavior, songs.

Nature Creep. Take a hand lens and get down on your hands and knees in a field or forest. Look at what's there. If you don't see much, dig a little hole and watch what crawls around. In one square foot of dirt are more than 1,000 animals. (Some are too small to see, of course.)

Environmental Education Centers. You can take a nature course at one of these centers. You might even get to camp out. To find out where they are, write to:

National Park Service
Washington, D.C. 20240

Can you find the anhinga (a water bird) here? Spotting animals that blend in with the background is challenging. *(Richard Frear, courtesy National Parks Service)*

Chapter 11
SCIENCE TIDBITS

Wild and Crazy Inventions

*E*very year thousands of inventions are recorded with the U.S. government, but only a small number ever catch on and make a lot of money. Here are some inventions that have almost been forgotten.

Eyeglasses for Chickens. Chickens peck each other. These special glasses would protect their eyes. The frames go all the way around the back of the chicken's neck. The lenses are made of glass. They are easy to put on and easy to take off.

Bicycle Seat to Stop a Thief. One or more sharp needles are built into the seat of a bicycle. The owner of the bicycle keeps the needles "down" when riding it. When the bicycle is left alone, the needles are put in the "up" position. Any thief who jumps onto the bike is in for a big shock!

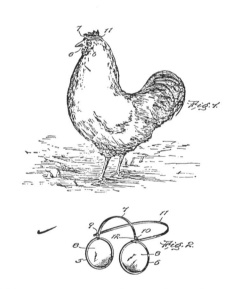

Chickens peck at each other. So these glasses could protect their eyes. *(Courtesy U.S. Patent Office)*

Spanking Paddle with Safety Feature. Parents using this paddle will never spank their children too hard. Part of the handle has a joint made with special pieces of metal. The handle will break if the blow is too strong.

Lots of us have trouble getting up in the morning. This alarm clock will hit you in the head! *(Courtesy U.S. Patent Office)*

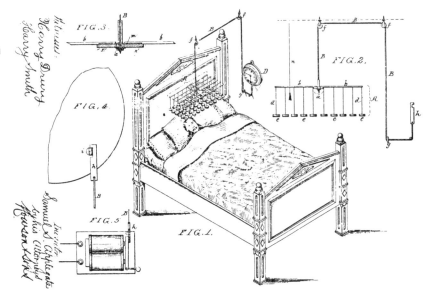

An Alarm Clock That Hits Your Head. This clock was invented for people who have a hard time getting up in the morning. It has 60 little wooden blocks that hang over a person's head. At the proper time, they drop down and hit the sleeping person on the head. It will wake you up but won't hurt you.

A Flying Fire Escape. This wacky invention allows a person to jump out the window of a burning building. A parachute and hat are attached under the chin, letting the person float safely to the ground. There are also big thickly padded shoes that cushion the fall when the person lands.

Fake Tooth for Good Breath. This false tooth is filled with a material like cotton that can soak up a liquid. The liquid both tastes good and smells good. No more bad breath!

This wacky fire escape was patented in 1879, but nothing ever came of it. *(Courtesy U.S. Patent Office)*

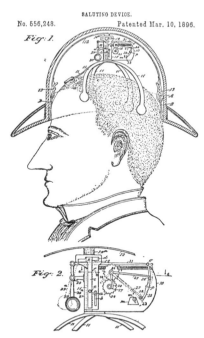

This gismo, a self-tipping hat, is just the thing for men with their hands full. *(Courtesy U.S. Patent Office)*

The Self-tipping Hat. How can a gentleman tip his hat to a lady if his arms and hands are full of packages? This hat solves the problem. When a man bows to a lady, gears and springs built into the hat make the front brim tip upward. Then the whole hat quickly spins around once and settles back on the man's head. And it all happens without the use of the hands.

A Locket for Chewing Gum. This locket can be put on a chain and worn around the neck. After chewing gum, just put it in the locket until you want to chew again. The locket will keep the gum safe and clean.

The Twirling Spaghetti Fork. This fork makes spaghetti simple to eat. It has a small wheel in the handle that you move with your thumb. That makes the fork spin around and roll up the spaghetti.

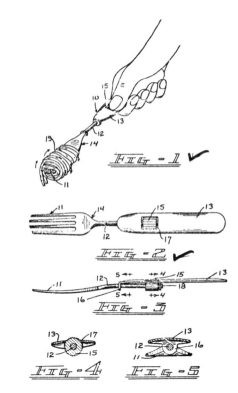

We all like spaghetti, yet somehow this twirling fork never caught on. *(Courtesy U.S. Patent Office)*

Robots Never Make Mistakes, Mistakes, Mistakes . . .

In the Olden Days

People have been making robots for a couple hundred years. Some of the early ones looked like animals or humans. However, they were pretty dumb. They worked like clocks and did the same things over and over.

The Quacking, Eating Duck. A French toymaker, Jacques de Vaucanson, built a mechanical duck in the 1700s. The duck ate and drank. When food was offered to it, it stretched out its neck. It quacked and paddled in the water. The duck was a star in a show at the opera house in Milan, Italy.

The Writing Boy. Another Frenchman of the 1700s made a 3-foot-high boy. When a spring was sprung, the boy started writing. His eyes followed the pen. After a line was finished, the boy's hand came back to cross the *t*'s and dot the *i*'s. One of the things this robot wrote was "Welcome to Neuchâtel."

The Breathing Organist. About the same time in Europe, a woman organ player was built. The woman seemed to breathe, her eyes and hands moved as she played, and sometimes she looked down at the keyboard. When she was through playing, she bowed.

The Fake Chess Player. A robot of the early 1800s seemed to play and win chess games. It may even have beaten some kings of Europe. The robot looked like a full-size man in a headdress. It smoked a pipe. Though it seemed smart, it had no brains. The chess-playing brains belonged to a human chess player, who was hidden under the robot's table. He moved levers which moved the chess pieces, and the robot got all the glory.

A famous chess-playing robot had a person hidden in the box. *(Courtesy New York Public Library)*

The Illustrated London News/New York Public Library Picture Collection

37

Now—Smart Robots

Modern robots don't always look like people. Some are walking junk piles; others are nothing but long arms attached to boxy bodies. However, modern robots are smart. Some can solve problems on their own. Their brains are computers and their eyes are sensors. Motors help them move.

Robots weld metal, deliver mail, teach children. They work where it is dangerous for people to work—deep in mines and oceans, out in space, in power plants.

Long-armed Monster. Clyde is a Unimate robot, one of about 2,000 of his kind. He weighs 2 tons and his long arm can reach 10 feet. Clyde can pick up red-hot things without getting burned. He'll work a 24-hour day if asked to. When Clyde broke down, his fellow human workers sent him flowers, and after he was fixed he was welcomed back with a party.

Squee, the Robot Squirrel. Made in 1951 by scientist Edmund C. Berkeley, Squee did nothing but find nuts. But that was a breakthrough in robots. With its photocell eyes, Squee would spot a nut. Then he'd roll over to the nut, pick it up, and take it to his "nest." That was all Squee did, but it was pretty amazing.

CORA, Brain on Wheels. Like Squee, CORA rolled around, looking at the world through photocell eyes. CORA could keep from bumping into things. When she began to run out of power, she could recharge her batteries. CORA answered whistles. She learned not to do things when her shell was tapped.

Theseus, Maze-runner Mouse. He ran the maze from "Start" to "Cheese." If he went up a dead end, he learned from his mistake. Theseus was one of the first of many electronic mice. In 1978 an Amaz-

Today's robots, like this Unimate welder, don't look like people. *(Courtesy Unimation®, Inc., a Condec Company)*

ing MicroMouse Maze contest was held to find the world's smartest robot mouse.

Beetle, Robot Truck. Beetle weighs 85 tons and stands 25 feet tall. Its big body moves on tank treads. A human operator sits inside and operates Beetle's 16-foot-long arms. With the jaws at the end of the arms, Beetle can pick up an egg, yet the arm is strong enough to punch through concrete. Four hundred miles of wires make up its nervous system. Its eyes are television cameras. Beetle is a worker. It can work in dangerous places where humans can be hurt.

Arok, Homemade Dog-walker and Show-off. It took Ben Skora more than 4 years to make Arok. (Arok is Skora spelled backwards without the *S*.) Arok runs on wheels, weighs 275 pounds, and has 2 car batteries for power. He looks human enough, with his Frankenstein mask face and football helmet skull. Inside he has thousands of circuits and 15 electric motors. Many of the things Arok does are set in motion by Ben Skora with a remote-control device. However, Arok can do some things on his own. Skora likes to play jokes with Arok. Once he had Arok take out the trash just as the garbage truck drove up. The garbage men were so shocked that they just sat in the truck. Arok places Skora's orders at McDonald's. Once, in a restaurant, Skora had him ask for a salad with 3-in-1 Oil dressing. Arok can run the vacuum cleaner, bring in the mail, and walk the dog. When Skora has a party, Arok answers the door and serves the drinks. Skora also shows Arok at exhibitions as a way to make money. The robot has been on television. Once he took a little boy for a ride on his huge shoes (size 60 EEEE). He got out of radio range and Skora couldn't control him. Arok went crazy. He wrecked the scenery and broke in half. The boy said, "Can you do that again?" Arok tells jokes. One is: "You can be replaced by a robot because robots never made mistakes, mistakes, mistakes . . ."

DA II, the Robot Maid. DA II is 5 feet 4 inches tall and weighs 240 pounds. You might call her stocky. She can do 12 household jobs. Among them are mopping the floor, mowing the lawn, and washing the dishes.

Century I, Security Guard. Century I is bulletproof and weighs 650 pounds. His sensors can pick up on body heat, movement, and noise. When he's on duty and senses someone breaking in, he locks in on the person. Never tired, he follows the intruder at 20 miles an hour. When he gets close, he tells the intruder to stop. If the intruder doesn't, Century I can hurt the intruder's ears with a high sound, blind him with a light, or shock him with electricity.

Mark VII, Brave Cop. Mark VII is English. He looks like a little tank on tracks. On an arm in front he carries a television camera and a gun. Mark VII can climb stairs, disarm bombs, shoot his way into buildings. He can also open a car trunk and break windows.

Harvey, the Patient. Harvey has blue eyes and looks like a person. His heart beats and his chest moves as if he were breathing. Harvey is a heart patient robot. Students at the University of Miami study him to learn about heart disease.

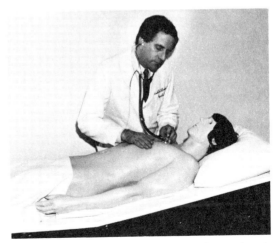

Harvey the heart patient robot helps doctors teach about heart disease. *(Courtesy Jackson Memorial Hospital, Medical Center Communications)*

Clarence, Lawn Mower. All by himself, Clarence mows the lawn. He looks like a vacuum cleaner with a bubble on top. Directed by a tape recording, he knows how to avoid trees and flower beds. If a child gets in his way, he shuts off. When he's through mowing, he goes back into his garage and turns off his motor.

Bobby, Mailman. Bobby, a moving box on wheels, brings the mail in a large office building in Washington, D.C. When he comes to an office, he rings a bell. Someone comes out in the hall and collects the mail for that office. He's only one of 250 robot mailmen in the U.S.

Viking 1 and 2 Landers, Astronauts. Launched in 1975, the Viking Landers touched down on the planet Mars in 1976. They picked up rocks, did tests, sent photographs back to Earth. One of their tasks was to see if there was life on Mars. The answer? Probably nothing lives on Mars.

Mr. Leachim, Fourth-Grade Teacher. Mr. Leachim weighs 200 pounds and is 6 feet tall. In his front is a display board called a tableau, and in his computer brain is stored a lot of information. The names of all the children he teaches. What the children know. What they need to know. The names of each child's parents and pets. The children's hobbies. When a child comes to Mr. Leachim for a lesson, the child says, "I am So-and-So." She dials her identification number on Mr. Leachim. Mr. Leachim matches the sound of her voice with her number. Then he begins a lesson. While he talks, other material shows up on the tableau. The child can ask for more time by moving switches. She can answer questions by punching buttons on Mr. Leachim's chest. If she does a good job with her lesson, Mr. Leachim might give her some interesting tips about her hobby. When the lesson is over, the child shuts Mr. Leachim off.

Robots in the Future

In the future, robots will learn from their mistakes more than they do now. They will be smarter. It's possible we will have robot judges, robot household workers, and robot factory workers.

Viking I's cameras took this photo of sand dunes and rocks on Mars. *(Courtesy NASA)*

Rover, Astronaut. Due to land on Mars in 1986 is Rover, a robot like the Viking 2 Lander. Rover will be small, the size of a compact car. It will have 2 cameras for eyes. Carrying instruments and computers, it will collect information. If it comes across an unexpected problem, it will probably be able to solve the problem on its own.

Space Spider. A robot spider in space would spin a solid metal web from the center outward. The web would look something like a huge phonograph record. Why spin from the center outward? Because there are no skyhooks in space, says one of the spider's makers. Moving at a foot a minute, the spider could spin a web nearly half a mile wide in 6 months. When all the thread is spun out of its body box, the box could be a place for spacemen to live. The spider's web might be the base for a solar reflector.

Funny, Fantastic, and True Science Short Stories

Blowing Up—Including the Tale of the Exploding Apron

People have been blowing things up for a long time. The Chinese invented firecrackers about 1,000 years ago. Later people in other parts of the world invented gunpowder. In the 1200s a scientist named Roger Bacon discovered how to make gunpowder. He knew it could kill people, so he hid his discovery, writing the formula for it in code. The code wasn't "broken" until 1904. Others found out how to make gunpowder on their own long before then, though.

In 1846 Professor Christian Schoenbein was working on experiments with acids. One night he was fooling with them in the kitchen at home. When he spilled some acids he was mixing, he mopped them up with his wife's cotton apron, then hung the apron to dry by the stove. It exploded from the heat. The exploding apron was the start of a new invention in explosives. Schoenbein proved that cotton treated with acid could blow up like gunpowder.

A lot of scientific discoveries happen by accident, like the case of the exploding apron.

Space Garbage

Since 1957 spaceships have been zooming up into space from Earth. Astronauts have thrown out their trash. The

With all the rocket launchings, there is a lot of trash even in space now.

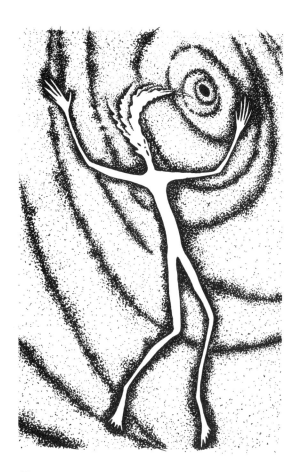

Black holes—if they exist—would twist and distort anything that went into them.

trash is spinning around out there, including a lost glove, food wrappers, and a camera.

Black Holes in Space

When a star dies, if it's big enough, a black hole may be formed. A black hole has such strong gravity that even light is pulled inside it. The light can't escape. That's why it's called a *black* hole. The black hole shrinks until it seems not to exist. If you were to fall into a black hole (not a good idea), you'd become long and thin like a piece of spaghetti. You might go into another world in another time.

Googols

Mathematician Edward Kasner wanted a name for this number:
10000000000000000000000000000000 00000000000000000000000000000000 00000000000000000000000000000000 00. (The number is a 1 followed by 100 zeroes.) His 9-year-old nephew came up with a perfect name: *googol.* And that's the name mathematicians use. The boy also thought of a name for an even larger number: *googolplex.* At first he said that it was 1 followed by as many zeroes as you could write before you got tired. In the end, it was decided that a googolplex is 1 with a googol of zeroes. It's so big that you couldn't take the time to write it.

The Nation's Attic

The Smithsonian Institution keeps lots of old stuff. In 1980 a show of some of those things was held. The show was called *Nation's Attic.* It included items like the following:

. . . General Tom Thumb's tiny piano, a silk purse made from a sow's ear, and a chest of false teeth that can be made to chatter all at once when you pull a wire.

The Rubber Suit

Rubber used to be made of gum from rubber trees. At first there were real problems with rubber. Things made from it melted in summer and smelled so bad they had to be buried. In winter they became stiff and cracked. Charles Goodyear decided to solve the problems. *His* problem was that he wasn't really a scientist, but he went ahead anyway. Some of his ideas that didn't work were: Mixing the rubber with salt, with soup, and with cream cheese. A process using an acid worked better. (It still wasn't quite right.) No one wanted to buy rubber. Goodyear wasn't making any money. So he decided to advertise. He made himself a rubber suit and wore the suit everywhere. People started telling this joke: Question: How do you know who Goodyear is? Answer: If you see a man in a rubber coat, rubber shoes, a rubber hat, and in his pocket a rubber purse, and in that rubber purse not one cent, that's Goodyear. Finally in 1841 Goodyear discovered a way to treat rubber by using heat. It's called vulcanization. He was a big success and didn't have to wear the suit anymore.

Pedal That Plane!

In 1959 a prize was offered to anyone who could fly a heavier-than-air, human-powered plane in the air for a mile and a half. The course the plane had to fly was shaped like an 8. It was not until 1977 that the prize—$85,000—was won. The winners were an engineer, Dr. Paul MacCready, and a bicycle rider, Bryan Allen. Their plane was the *Gossamer Condor.* It was light and strong. There was no motor. The power came from Allen, who pedaled the plane to make it fly. His leg power was sent over a bicycle chain to the propeller.

In 1979, the 2 men had another plane, the *Gossamer Albatross,* ready to fly. It weighed about 70 pounds and its wingspread was 96 feet. Again, Allen supplied the power by pedaling—across the English Channel! The English Channel is an arm of the sea between England and France, 22 miles wide. Allen almost gave up once during his flight. He got

Solar Challenger, built by Dr. MacCready, gets its power from solar cells. It really flew across the English Channel. *(Randa Bishop 1981/Contact)*

tired and the plane began to sink too close to the waves. But somehow he got more energy and pedaled on. Later on he saw a shark in the water. After nearly 3 hours of pedaling, he reached the shore of France. "Wow . . . wow!" was all he could say. For that feat, MacCready and Allen received $21,000.

Their motto is: "If the wind don't blow and the chain don't break, we'll make it across."

Dr. MacCready has developed two solar-powered planes—the *Gossamer Penguin* and the *Solar Challenger*. Both use solar cells for energy.

Iceberg Ship

A serious plan has been created to tow icebergs thousands of miles from the Antarctic to hot desert countries. The water from the melting iceberg would then irrigate the land. To make the plan worthwhile, the iceberg would have to be very large. How large? Maybe as big as the island of Manhattan. Or at least 5 miles long and 2 miles wide. The iceberg itself would be a kind of ship. It would be powered by Freon gas, used over and over again in a heat-exchanger engine. The crew would live onboard the iceberg in solar-heated living spaces. When the "ship" had crossed the oceans, it would be put in a giant plastic bag. As it melted, the water would be piped to the fields. Sound crazy? Not when you realize that more than half the world's fresh water is in icebergs. One iceberg would supply a trillion gallons. That's a lot of water!

Nine-year-old Discovers Dinosaur Bones

In 1979, 9-year-old Warren Hofmann of Sioux Falls, South Dakota, said that bones his father brought home from a

construction site were from a dinosaur. No, his father replied, the bones were from a cow. It turned out that Warren was right. His bones were from a dinosaur that died 110 million years ago. He gave the bones to a museum. His grandmother said, "I'm proud of that boy—he certainly knows his bones!"

Holography—Real "Ghosts"

A hologram is a "photograph" that can project a 3-D image made of light. Seeing one of these images is like seeing a ghost, and you can put your hand right through it. The principle was discovered in 1948, and one of the first images was of a toy train. Laser beams are used in making the image. Just imagine! You might be able to have a hologram made of yourself. It would be like your ghost, and you could scare yourself with it.

Old Mold and Hippo Fat

To cure disease, Egyptians thousands of years ago mixed hippo fat and moldy bread crumbs. They used this mess as a medicine, and it worked. Even 500 years ago, people kept old bread on their ceiling beams. If someone was cut, this moldy bread was put on the wound to keep it from becoming infected. The moldy bread contained what is now a modern medicine—penicillin.

Penicillin was discovered almost by accident in 1928. Alexander Fleming, a scientist, was growing some bacteria for an experiment. His helper forgot to cover the dish where the bacteria were growing. Some mold blew in a window, fell on the dish, and killed the bacteria. Fleming found the part of the mold that killed the bacteria and called it penicillin. One of his friends said penicillin was only good for making cheese. (Lots of cheese has

Penicillin was discovered almost by accident. Some mold blew in and killed the bacteria.

mold in it.) It was good for lots more. In World War Two, millions of soldiers' lives were saved with penicillin. Penicillin kills about 90 kinds of bacteria.

Some Odd Short Facts

When X rays were discovered, many people were afraid they could be used to see through their clothes. One smart clothing maker advertised clothes that he claimed were "X ray proof."

The Model-T Ford, one of the most popular cars ever made, came only in black. It was 7 feet high.

Blue whales are the biggest animals the world has ever known. They are even bigger than dinosaurs were.

People today are taller, on the average, than people were 100 years ago.

In one teaspoon of dirt are 5 billion bacteria.

It's not true that lightning doesn't strike the same place twice. Lightning usually strikes a very tall building many times in one thunderstorm.

Benjamin Franklin invented bifocal glasses when he was 83 years old.

Famous Scientists

MARIE CURIE
Born: November 7, 1867
Died: July 4, 1934

"We must believe that we are gifted for something, and that this thing, at whatever cost, must be obtained." Those are the words of Marie Curie, and they guided her life. She became a famous scientist and was the first person ever to win 2 Nobel Prizes.

Born in Warsaw, Poland, Marie Sklodowska had 3 sisters and a brother. Her mother and father were schoolteachers. The family was very close, but growing up was not easy for Marie. The family was poor and always struggling for money. Worst of all, Marie's mother was very sick. Mrs. Sklodowska suffered from tuberculosis, a disease of the lungs. In those days little was known about curing the disease. Marie's mother was afraid she would give the disease to her children, and so she never hugged or kissed them. Marie knew that her mother loved her, but she did not understand why her mother never hugged or kissed her. When Marie was 10, Mrs. Sklodowska died.

In school Marie was smarter than all of her classmates. When she graduated she

Marie Curie was a great scientist—the first to win 2 Nobel Prizes. *(Courtesy AIP Neils Bohr Library, W.F. Meggers Collection)*

won a gold medal, the highest honor for a Polish student. For many years she dreamed of going to college, but only men went to college in Poland; women were not allowed.

In Paris, France, there is a college called the Sorbonne. Marie's older sister, Bronya, wanted to go to the school and so did Marie. There was not enough money to send both girls, and Marie said that Bronya should go. For the next few years Marie worked as a teacher and sent much of her earnings to Bronya in Paris.

Finally, Marie's dream came true. At age 24 she too enrolled at the Sorbonne. At first she lived with Bronya, who had married a doctor. But it was hard for Marie to study with other people around, and she decided to get a place of her own. It was a tiny attic room in a house near the school. She had to climb 6 flights of stairs to get to it. The room had no lights, no water, and no heat, but it was cheap. For weeks at a time, Marie ate very little. Sometimes, all she could afford was buttered bread and tea.

Marie loved her classes at the Sorbonne. All she did was study. Other students liked her but she was hard to get to know. Marie was very shy. "She is always in the first row in the science classes," one boy said. "Doesn't talk much."

At 27, Marie met Pierre Curie and her whole life changed. They got married a year later. Pierre was also a scientist. They worked side by side for many years.

The Curies discovered 2 elements, radium and polonium. Both elements give off rays; they are "radioactive" elements. The powerful rays of radium can kill diseased cells in the body, allowing healthy cells to grow in their place. Doctors use radium rays to treat cancer, a treatment called radiation therapy. For the discovery of "radioactivity" the Curies won a Nobel Prize—one of the highest awards a scientist can win.

When Marie was 39, Pierre died after he accidentally stepped in front of a heavy wagon pulled by 2 horses. After that, Marie's life had little joy but she continued with her work. In 1911 she won another Nobel Prize.

Marie could have become rich from her discoveries but she turned down a lot of money and never asked special favors of anyone. Albert Einstein, another famous scientist, once said, "Marie Curie is, of all celebrated beings, the only one whom fame has not corrupted."

CHARLES DARWIN

Born: February 12, 1809
Died: April 19, 1882

Charles Darwin was always collecting

things. As a boy, he saved shells, coins, and minerals. Later on he collected and studied plants and animals. This hobby turned into his life's work.

Born in Shrewsbury, England, Darwin

Charles Darwin, a British scientist who developed the theory of evolution, always loved to collect things. *(Photoworld/FPG)*

had 5 brothers and sisters. His father was a successful doctor and wanted his son to follow in his footsteps. However, Charles had a tough time in school. He was always daydreaming and his grades were poor. After school, Charles and his brother Erasmus loved to do chemistry experiments, and they set up their own laboratory in the family tool shed. Because of this, Charles got a nickname. His friends called him "Gas."

"Gas" Darwin had a terrible time deciding what to do with his life. First, he went to school to become a doctor but soon learned that he hated the sight of blood. Also, in those days patients suffered a lot during operations because there were no medicines to numb the pain. Darwin saw 2 horrible operations and that was enough for him. He knew he could never be a doctor.

Darwin turned from medicine to religion. For 3 years he went to Cambridge University and studied to be a minister. But he just wasn't cut out to be a clergyman.

While thinking over his future, Darwin got a lucky break. He received an offer to travel around the world on a boat called the H.M.S. *Beagle.* The ship and its crew were hired by the government to survey a number of different lands, and Darwin became the ship's naturalist, the crew member assigned to study the plants and animals found on the journey. The trip lasted for 5 years and the *Beagle* went to many places, including South America and Australia.

Years later, Darwin said, "The voyage of the *Beagle* has been by far the most important event in my life, and has determined my whole career." It was quite an adventure. In Brazil, Darwin walked through a tropical forest. In Chile, he lived through an earthquake. For Darwin, everything was new and wonderful—except seasickness. He was seasick every single day he was on the ship, yet he never once complained.

Traveling on the *Beagle,* Darwin kept collecting—insects, birds, seashells, plants, small animals. He packed many of them in boxes and shipped them home. One shipment would contain as many as 1,500 different items! When he returned to England, Darwin spent many years sorting out and studying all of the plants and animals he had gathered. Then he wrote *The Origin of Species.*

In that book Darwin discussed

Thomas Edison at 14 was a newsboy on the Grand Trunk Railroad. *(Courtesy Edison National Historic Site, National Park Service, U.S. Dept. of Interior)*

"evolution"—the idea that today's plants and animals all came from earlier and simpler kinds of life. It took millions of years, he said, for this to happen. Over the years each kind (or "species") of plant and animal went through a lot of changes. For example, a horse of long ago "evloved"—or changed—into the horse we know today.

Before Darwin's book, most scientists had other thoughts about living things. They believed that God made each different kind of plant and animal, and that today's horse had nothing to do with the horse of long ago.

Darwin's book made scientists change their minds. His ideas about evolution, however, made some people very angry. Religious people said Darwin didn't believe in God. Darwin said that wasn't true; that he never meant for evolution to take the place of God.

Charles Darwin lived to be 73 years old. Altogether, he wrote 8 books about plants and animals. His last book, one of his favorites, was about earthworms!

THOMAS ALVA EDISON
Born: February 11, 1847
Died: October 18, 1931

When Thomas Edison was 7, he came home crying because the teacher called him stupid. He was not popular at his school in Port Huron, Michigan. He was puny and could not play games well. Sometimes the kids made fun of him because his head was a little too big for his body. Also, Tom was sick much of the time. Tom's mother took him out of school even though he had only been there for 3 months. From then on, she taught him lessons at home. After reading his first science book—when he was

10—Tom built a chemical laboratory in the basement of his home.

At age 12 Tom started his own business. He worked on a train that ran between the cities of Port Huron and Detroit, Michigan. Each day he sold newspapers and candy. It was hard work and Tom got up at 6:00 every morning. Quitting time was 8:00 at night. He got to bed at 11:00. But Tom still had time to publish his own one-page paper called the *Grand Trunk Herald*. It sold for 3¢ a copy. Sometimes his job was difficult because a childhood sickness had made Tom deaf. But he did not complain. Even when he grew up and became rich, Tom said that the happiest time of his life was on the railroad.

At 16 he learned Morse code and got a job in a telegraph office. The pay was $25 a month. When he was not busy, Tom did chemical experiments at work. One day, he accidentally blew up the office and lost his job. After that, Tom traveled a lot. In 3 years he lived in 8 different cities.

Tom became an inventor at 16. His early inventions helped the men who worked on the telegraph lines. But they were only the beginning. Altogether he had over 1,000 inventions. The most important are the electric light bulb and the phonograph.

No matter how old he was, Tom worked long hours. As an adult, he usually slept 5 or 6 hours a day. And often he got into bed with all of his clothes on. But he did have a habit of taking naps. Once he even fell asleep in a closet. And another time he dozed off in a dog coop at his office. The only game his children could talk him into playing was Parcheesi.

Thomas Edison became a millionaire. He wasn't afraid to take chances and one time he almost lost all of his money. He had 9 cars. Seven ran on gasoline and 2 on electricity. People from all over the world came to see him. One man wrote Edison a letter and left out the address. Instead, the man pasted a picture of Tom on the envelope. Tom was so fa-

Thomas Edison invented the phonograph, plus much more. *(National Portrait Gallery, Smithsonian Institution)*

mous that the letter was delivered. When he was 84, Tom was so ill that he had to use a wheelchair. But he still tried to go to work each day. He always told his friends, "The brain that isn't used rusts."

ALBERT EINSTEIN
Born: March 14, 1879
Died: April 18, 1955

Experts say Einstein is one of the 8 greatest scientists who ever lived. His "theory of relativity" changed the way we think about the universe.

In many ways Albert Einstein was a very simple man. He cared little about the clothes he wore or the food he ate. He didn't drive a car. His only hobbies were sailing and playing the violin. Einstein couldn't be bothered with the ordinary things of life. To him, science was more important.

Einstein was born in Ulm, Germany. When he was 5, Albert saw his first compass. No matter how he turned the compass, the needle always pointed in the same direction. What made the needle move? The boy looked but couldn't see anything. Whatever made the needle move was there—in space. But space was empty! It was the first time that the boy started to think about the mysteries of the universe.

Nobody would have guessed that the young Einstein would grow up to become a genius. First of all, he had trouble learning how to talk, and his parents were scared that something was wrong with him. He did learn to speak well but that didn't help him in school. His grades were low. Hermann Einstein, Albert's father, worried about the boy's future. When he asked Albert's teacher for advice, the teacher replied, "It doesn't mat-

Albert Einstein, one of the greatest scientists, loved sailing. *(Courtesy AIP Neils Bohr Library)*

ter; he'll never make a success of anything." However, Albert was good at math and science. He went to college and became a teacher himself.

Einstein's "theory of relativity" shook up the science world. People everywhere were excited about his new ideas, but even scientists had a hard time understanding what Einstein had to say. The ideas were very complicated. Einstein presented new ways of thinking about time and space. Other things he talked about were gravity, energy, and matter.

Einstein suddenly became famous. He traveled to many countries around the world. Everywhere he went, people asked the same question: "Can you explain the theory of relativity in a few easy sentences?" The scientist replied, "If you will not take the answer too seriously and consider it only as a kind of joke, then I can explain it as follows. It was formerly believed that if all material things disappeared out of the universe, time and space would be left. According to the relativity theory, however, time and space disappear together with the material things."

In 1933 Einstein gave up his German citizenship and left Germany. Why? A man named Adolf Hitler had taken over the government. Hitler hated Jews, and Einstein, a Jew, had a difficult time for several years. Finally, the scientist left Germany and came to the United States. For the next 22 years Einstein worked at the Institute for Advanced Study in Princeton, New Jersey.

The people of Princeton were thrilled to have Einstein in their town. Every time the great man went for a walk, people would gather in the streets. He was easy to recognize—long white hair, wrinkled clothes, no socks. He was always friendly and never "talked down" to anyone.

Einstein didn't care that people called him the "absentminded professor." He would laugh and say that his mind was usually too full of science to think about much else. Once he used a $1,500 check for a bookmark—and lost the book! Einstein's wife, Elsa, sometimes packed his suitcase when he went on a trip. When he came home, Elsa was always shocked to see that the suitcase had never been opened. Einstein either forgot he had a suitcase or didn't have time to open it!

Everyone in Princeton had a favorite Einstein story. One of the best was about what happened shortly after the brilliant scientist moved to Princeton. A man called the school's main office and a secretary answered the phone. The caller asked for Einstein's address. The secretary said that the address was a secret, that she wasn't allowed to give it to strangers. The caller then whispered, "Please do not tell anybody, but I am Einstein. I am on my way home and have forgotten where my house is."

In his lifetime Einstein received many awards and honors, including the Nobel Prize. Yet he was a very humble man. "What I have done personally is much exaggerated," he once said. "What is really beautiful is science! It is a great gift if one is permitted to work in science for his whole life."

KARL FRIEDRICH GAUSS
Born: April 30, 1777
Died: February 23, 1855

Karl Gauss's teacher was tough and mean. Most of the students were afraid of him. One day, when Karl was 10, the teacher gave his class a math problem. It was supposed to take a long time to do. The teacher knew the shortcuts to the answer but all the students except one didn't. The problem: Add up all the numbers from 1 to 100.

In just a few seconds, Karl wrote an answer on his slate. "There it lies," he said, using the standard way students in those days announced they had finished a problem. The other boys kept working. A long time went by. The teacher didn't say anything. He probably figured that Karl had written down just any old number.

At the end of the class, when the teacher saw what Karl had written, he was amazed. Karl was right. The teacher asked him to explain how he had done the problem. Karl told him. He had arranged the numbers in pairs in his head this way:

Karl Gauss was a child genius, who grew up to become a great mathematician *(From Betlex The Discovery of Nature, Simon and Schuster, 1965/ Courtesy AIP Neils Bohr Library)*

$$100 + 1 = 101$$
$$99 + 2 + 101$$
$$98 + 3 + 101$$
. . . and so on.

He had realized that there would be 50 pairs like that. The problem could be stated as 50×101. The answer: 5050.

Karl hadn't come up with anything new. He had stumbled on a way of doing such problems that mathematicians had figured out a long time before. But even so, it was amazing that Karl had seen it.

The mean teacher became friendly. He bought Karl a book on arithmetic. Karl went through the book very fast and was ready for more. The teacher admitted that Karl was beyond him.

Karl's father, a poor laborer, didn't want his son to be educated. Luckily, his mother did. So did his uncle Friedrich, a weaver. Uncle Friedrich taught Karl a great deal.

At the age of 13, Karl entered a new mathematics class. When his professor read Karl's first exercise, he told him not to come back to class. Karl was so smart, he said, that he could teach him nothing.

The Duke of Brunswick, who heard about the boy's genius, paid for Karl's education from the time he was 14. That was lucky, because in Germany at that time only rich students got to college.

Karl became one of the greatest mathematicians of all time. He solved problems no one before him had been able to solve. At age 18, he figured out a formula for dividing a circle into 17 parts.

Karl liked to do things right. His seal, with which he marked things he wrote, featured a tree with a few pieces of fruit hanging on it. Next to the tree were the words *Pauca sed matura*. That's Latin for "Few, but ripe."

Volcanoes

A volcano is one of nature's greatest forces. Today there are between 500 and 600 active volcanoes in the world. Many volcanoes are pretty tame; even when they erupt, little damage is done. But volcanoes can be very violent and can kill many people. Mount St. Helens in Washington State, for example, without much warning erupted violently in early 1980, devastating a large area. From the past, here are the stories of 3 explosive volcanoes.

On May 18, 1980, Mt. St. Helen's erupted in an awesome spew of ash. *(Courtesy U.S. Geological Survey)*

MT. VESUVIUS
THE DATE: August 24, A.D. 79

August 24 started out as a busy day in Pompeii, a beautiful city in Italy. Over 20,000 people lived there. Everyone was talking about the sports contests that would be held that evening. But the contests never took place.

Around noon there was a loud explosion. The nearby volcano, Mt. Vesuvius, had erupted. For 1,500 years the volcano had been asleep, but now it woke up with a mighty explosion. The volcano's mouth opened up and out came an enormous amount of ash, smoke, and poisonous gases. Then came another explosion. Hot rocks and ash fell like rain from the sky. No longer could anyone see the sun.

For 8 days and nights the volcano erupted. People thought they would be safe indoors, but that wasn't true. The falling rocks and ash caved in the walls and roofs of buildings. Many people were crushed to death in their own homes. Others died from breathing the poisonous gases.

Finally, the volcano became quiet. The city of Pompeii lay buried under 20 feet of ash and rock. The nearby city of Herculaneum was also destroyed. Altogether, about 25,000 people died.

The ancient city of Pompeii was buried by Mt. Vesuvius, which is still active. *(Wide World Photos)*

Today, Mt. Vesuvius is considered an active volcano. It has erupted many times since that disastrous day in Pompeii.

Science Facts

A giant earthquake helped Mt. Vesuvius to explode. The earthquake happened 16 years earlier, in the year 63. It caused great cracks in the earth inside the volcano. Steam, lava, and gases deep within the earth then had a way to escape and everything came upward through the volcano.

Soil formed on top of all the ash and rock that buried Pompeii. The volcanic soil was very rich and farmers came and planted crops. Thousands of years went by. No one knew that a city was underneath. In 1748 scientists began to dig at Pompeii. Today much of the city has been uncovered.

In most volcanic eruptions it is not lava (hot, melted, flowing rock) that kills people. Many volcanoes, like Mt. Vesuvius, send out very little lava. Poisonous, super-hot, gases are more dangerous than lava.

KRAKATOA
THE DATE: August 27, 1883

Krakatoa was a small island in the Indian Ocean. Nobody lived there. On the island were 3 volcanoes. In May 1883, one of them started to erupt, and in a few months the other 2 followed. For months, sailors at sea watched the island. They saw a high cloud—6 miles high—over Krakatoa, and heard explosions and saw flashes of light.

Then on August 27 the whole island blew itself apart. The sound was the loudest noise ever heard in history. The explosions shook the earth and caused giant waves in the ocean. These waves rushed over hundreds of villages on nearby islands, and more than 36,000 people drowned.

Later on, a group of people went to explore Krakatoa. Three-fourths of the island was gone and all of the trees and plants were dead. The explorers found only one living thing—a red spider, spinning a web.

Krakatoa was probably the worst disaster ever caused by a volcano.

Science Facts

The noise of Krakatoa exploding reached one island, Rodriguez, that was 3,000 miles away. It took the sound 4 hours to get to Rodriguez.

The giant waves at Krakatoa are called *tsunami*, a Japanese word. Some of the killer waves caused by the great explosion were as high as 120 feet. Billions of tons of water swept over the little islands around Krakatoa.

During the explosions, huge amounts of ash and bits of volcanic rock were thrown into the air. The wind blew tiny pieces of ash (like red dust) 50 miles high. The dust circled the world for 2 years and caused many blood-red sunsets.

Today, Krakatoa is called Anak Krakatoa (child of Krakatoa). It last erupted in 1969.

MT. PELEE
THE DATE: May 8, 1902

Mt. Pelee is only 4 miles from the town of St. Pierre on the island of Martinique. Martinique is part of a group of islands called the West Indies. Most people thought Mt. Pelee was an "extinct"—or dead—volcano.

At the end of April, ash and gases started to come from the volcano. Soon brown clouds hung over St. Pierre. Birds breathed the gases and started to fall dead into the streets. Then came an explosion on May 5. It caused a mudslide that killed 150 people. The next few days brought more and more explosions. Ash and cinders filled the air. At night the town had a red glow.

On May 8, Mt. Pelee let loose. The side of the mountain blew open and a huge cloud of dust, steam, and gas came out. The "glowing cloud" was so thick that it was almost like a liquid. The deadly cloud rolled down the mountain like a wall of fire, covering St. Pierre. It was all over in just 3 minutes. Almost 30,000 people were dead. Only 2 men lived. One, a shoemaker, was badly burned but was able to run out of the town. The other was a criminal confined in an underground prison cell.

Science Facts

The cloud moved fast. It came down the mountain at 100 miles per hour.

The super-hot "glowing cloud" was about 1500°F. It was able to melt even glass.

Some people died from breathing the gases from the cloud, but most of the volcano's victims were burned to death.

Great Characters of The Plant World

1. **Stinkers.** The elephant tree shoots a mist of awful-smelling oil from holes in its bark. The oil flies as far as 3 feet. Animals stay away from this tree.

The durian, a plant that grows in hot places, grows a stinky fruit. The fruit's outer part smells like onions, old drains, and coal gas. Inside, though, it has another part that tastes wonderful. Tigers, elephants, monkeys, humans, and ants love to eat it.

Some cactuses bloom at night. Their flowers do not smell flowery to human noses. They may smell like an old cellar, sour milk, or cucumbers. The smell attracts bats, which fly in to eat the nectar and pollen in the flowers. The pollen of the cactus flower sticks to the bat's body, and when it goes on to the next flower, some pollen drops off, giving the flower the pollen it needs to make seeds. The vampire bat eats from the "Queen of the Night" cactus. The long-nosed bat visits the century plant, which blooms only once in its life. Luckily, the century plants bloom at different times, so the bats don't go hungry waiting. Some bats like the sausage tree. It smells like mice, and its fruits look like giant hot dogs.

2.   **Meat-eaters—Venus Flytrap and Friends.** Over 500 species of plants eat bugs. The Venus flytrap has some leaves that end in little traps. They give out sweet smells that attract insects. On each flap of each trap are 3 hairs. If an insect touches one hair, it's okay, but if it touches 2 hairs or the same one twice, it's in trouble. The trap snaps shut in about one-fourth of a second and the insect's body is crushed. Acid from the Venus flytrap eats the insect's body. Venus flytraps have caught small animals like frogs, too.

Other plants catch insects on their leaves. One has leaves with sticky red hairs, and people in Portugal hang the leaves up as flypaper. The leaves of another plant have hairs that ooze liquid when an insect walks on them. The insect is glued down by the liquid.

3.   **The Chocolate Tree.** Chocolate and cocoa come from a tree that grows in Mexico and other parts of Central America. The Aztecs, who lived there a long time ago, made a drink with the chocolate beans. The beans were ground up, mixed with spices, and whipped up like cotton candy. The Aztecs drank it cold. Sound good? There is one thing missing—sugar! One ruler of the Aztecs, it is said, ate 50 jars of whipped chocolate a day, using a golden spoon and a golden bowl. The Aztecs used chocolate beans as money. They paid their taxes in chocolate.

4.   **Old Giants.** Redwood trees, which grow on the West Coast of the United States, live for a long time. The oldest known redwood has lived for more than 3,000 years. Redwood bark is almost fireproof and resists insects. Redwoods seem to die only when chopped down or when not enough dirt is around their roots. A redwood about 300 feet tall was cut down in 1853 and its stump, 25 feet across, was used as a giant dance floor. More than 40 people could dance on it at one time.

How can you tell the age of a tree? By its rings. Each year the tree grows a new ring of cells on the outer layer of its trunk. The cells grow bigger in spring and summer, so the space from one layer of big cells to another—a ring—is a year's growth. By looking at a tree's rings after it is cut down, experts can find out a lot. They can tell what the weather was like a long time ago, for example. The tree's history is written in its rings. This picture of a tree's rings gives some idea of how old trees can grow.

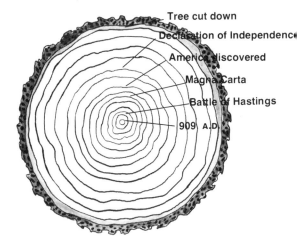

The number of rings in a tree tells how old the tree is.

5. **Supermarket Plants.** From the papyrus plant, the ancient Egyptians made paper. They also made ropes, sandals, and boats from it. And if times were bad, the papyrus could be used as food. It was like a supermarket on a trunk.

Bamboo also has many uses. From bamboo, people make houses, roofs, cups and pots, weapons, farm tools, even musical instruments.

And one writer of ancient times said the date palm had 360 uses, though he didn't name them all.

In Mali, today, there is a tree that is like a drugstore. Its name is gardenia micranthum, and its bark is ground up to cure a disease called hepatitis. The fruit and roots are used to treat 2 other diseases.

6. **Squirters.** The squirting cucumber plant has fruits that look like little pickles. The little fruit's inside skin is stretched as it grows. Pressure builds inside the fruit. When the fruit is ripe it falls off the stem, and this opens a hole in the end of it. From that hole the fruit squirts seeds as far as 25 feet.

7. **Stingers.** The nettle has needle-like stingers that operate like hypodermic needles. If you brush a nettle as you pass, it sticks stingers in you that force liquid out into your body. The chemicals in the liquid make your skin itch and burn. It has been said that people have stung themselves with nettles to keep warm in cold places.

8. **Poison Apple?** People in Europe

The squirting cucumber plant can send seeds flying as far as 25 feet.

called it the golden apple. It was yellow then, not red. One scientist said that eating it would chill your body. Others said it would make you sick. One Latin name for it means "unhealthy apple." (The French called it love apple.) Still, it was planted in gardens because it was pretty to look at. What was it? The tomato. It was not until the early 1800s that Americans and Europeans began to eat tomatoes. But people in South America, where the tomato came from, had been eating them all along.

Soap Bubbles

Blowing beautiful bubbles is easy. You can buy bubble kits at toy stores, but it's more fun to make your own soapy water and bubble tools. It takes very little time and practice. Get your friends to join you. See who can make the biggest bubble. How long can you make a bubble last? How high can you get a bubble to float?

Here are a few bubble experiments. First you have to mix up some soapy water and gather together a few tools.

BUBBLE SOAP

4 cups water
8 tablespoons of
  dishwashing liquid
1–2 tablespoons of glycerine

Mix the water and dishwashing liquid in a jar. You may want to add some glycerine; some people think glycerine makes the bubbles last longer.

TOOLS

straws
a tray
masking tape
3 5-ounce Dixie Cups

Experiment 1—Tray Bubbles

Pour some of the bubble mixture into a tray. The bigger the tray, the bigger the bubbles you can blow. Wet the end of your straw by dipping it into the soapy water. Then hold the straw just a tiny bit above the surface of the water. Blow in an easy, steady way to produce the bubble. When you are finished, gently pull the straw away.

Experiment 2—Dixie Cup Bubbles

Cut out the bottoms of 2 5-ounce Dixie Cups. Using masking tape, tape the bottoms together. Poke a hole in the bottom of a third cup, then put a straw into the hole you poked. Tape the third cup to the other 2 cups. You now have a 3-story tube. Dip the open end into your bubble mixture. You will get a thin film—a soapy window—on the end. Now you are ready

to blow. Go. After you get a good-size bubble, twist your tube to let the bubble float away.

You can have fun blowing bubbles with some Dixie cups.

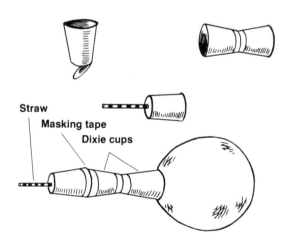

Straw
Masking tape
Dixie cups

SPECIAL NOTE: Want to become a bubble-blowing expert? Get a paperback book called *Bubbles* by Bernie Zubrowski (Little, Brown and Company, 1979). It will tell you how to make very big bubbles as well as many different-shaped bubbles. It will even tell you how to build bubble houses.

Bang, Crash, and Boom:
Noise and Your Health

Noise is any unwanted sound. Too much noise can be harmful. It causes pain in the ears and gives you a headache. It makes people angry and upset. Worst of all, it makes some people lose their hearing.

Loud sounds can hurt the tiny hair cells in your inner ear. It's like walking on grass over and over again. At first, the blades of grass spring back. But what happens if you keep walking on them? Soon the blades will no longer spring back. They will die. If you lose some of your hearing because of noise, there is no way to get it back; the hearing is gone forever. Medicines or operations will not help. More than 3 million kids have some kind of hearing problem.

Noise is measured in units called decibels. The sound of rustling leaves are about 10 decibels. People talking (not shouting) creates about 60 decibels. Rock music is at about 110 decibels. Any noise over 70 decibels can be dangerous. Remember: The louder the noise and the longer you listen to it, the more harmful it can be.

The government is working to stamp out loud noises. A group called the Environmental Protection Agency is trying hard to tell people about the dangers of noise. Soon many things—from hair dryers to toys to motorcycles—will have noise labels on them.

There are many things you can do to protect your hearing. Here are just a few:

1. Turn down loud TVs and radios.
2. Don't listen to loud music too long.
3. Complain when something is too loud.
4. Wear earmuffs or earplugs when working or playing around very loud noise.
5. Teach others about noise. Many people don't know how bad noise is for them.

The Environmental Protection Agency puts out some free booklets about noise. Write to this organization, give your age, and ask for some booklets. Here is their address:

U.S. Environmental Protection Agency
Office of Noise Abatement and Control
Washington, DC 20460

Fingerprints on the Exhibits Are Welcome!—
Museums for Kids

I hear and I forget
I see and I remember
I do and I understand
         --Popular children's museum slogan

Get inside a giant crystal to see its shape. Put on a turtle shell to feel as a turtle feels. Listen to an old-time radio the way your grandparents did. Make an animated film. Play with a computer. Put on a television news show. Pet an opossum. Watch the inside workings of a human body in motion. Wear shoes from your grandmother's time. Join an astronomy club.

Where? At a children's museum where the word is not "hands off" but "hands on." In fact, some people call the "new" museums "Hands-on Museums." The word *new* is in quotation marks because the first hands-on children's museum was begun in 1899! In that year a nature study teacher named Anna Billings Gallup was made curator (person in charge) of the Brooklyn Children's Museum. One of the first things she did was take kids around the museum. As they made their tour, she took things out of their locked cases and put them in kids' hands. It was unheard of! Museums were supposed to be for looking, not touching! She changed all that.

Now there are nearly 100 children's museums and hands-on museums in the United States. Other names for them are nature centers, discovery centers, and science museums. One in San Francisco is called The Exploratorium.

Most of these museums have special programs for kids. You can sign up to learn to make tools, bread, and other things. You might become a junior curator and learn to prepare specimens. You can go on field trips.

Here are some famous children's museums and what they offer:

The Brooklyn Children's Museum, Brooklyn, New York. Old skeletons and old dolls. A giant model of a crystal. A working water mill that grinds grain for flour. Workshops for kids. More.

The Children's Museum of Boston, Boston, Massachusetts. Grandmother's Attic. A television newsroom for kids. A gas pump to operate. A computer to experiment on. An assembly line making Spree Spinners (toys)—kid workers get a Spree Spinner free. A Japanese house. Live entertainment at night—a puppeteer, clown, music. Programs in which kids invent things and build things. More.

The Los Angeles Children's Museum, Los Angeles, California. City Streets—to show

These kids are having fun on the spree spinner assembly line. *(Tad Goodale, courtesy Boston Children's Museum)*

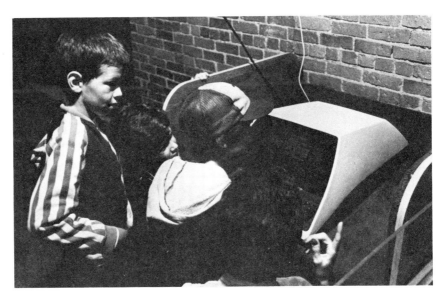

You can play with a computer at some museums. *(Tad Goodale, courtesy Boston Children's Museum)*

kids what it's like to live in a city. Sticky City, where big foam shapes stick to everything. A working model of the KNXT newsroom (Channel 2). The underground city, showing what it's like *under* city streets. "How Would I Feel?"—trying out a Braille typewriter, among other things. More.

Charlotte Nature Museum, Charlotte, North Carolina. A mini-zoo with animals to play with. A nature trail. A see-through model of the human body. Discovery Place. A planetarium with shows like "Captain Cosmos and the Space Puzzles Affair." Workshops such as "Squirmies," "Volts and Jolts," and so on. More.

Children's Museum, Indianapolis, Indiana. A limestone cave. A train station and wood-burning locomotive. An old carousel to ride. A race car from the Indy 500—you can sit in it. A mummy in a tomb. Dinosaurs. A space module. "The Decision Shop" with 4 computer games about economics—"Sell Robots," "Carnival," "Kingdom," and "Star Trader." A theater with plays, music, puppet shows, dance. More.

Corpus Christi Museum, Corpus Christi, Texas. "Front Porch," where you can show off your talents. Japanese giant crabs. Fossils and shells. Animals to touch. Help with school science projects. A television show. More.

The Exploratorium, San Francisco, California. Giant Echo Tube. A room with crazy proportions where adults can seem smaller than kids. Blocks from which you can make an arch. Vidium—an exhibit where you can draw designs with sound. Shadow Box, which "freezes" your shadow on a screen as you turn a somersault or act in a goofy way.

Jacksonville Museum of Arts and Sciences, Jacksonville, Florida. A country store. Mummies 3,000 years old. Birds and animals. A giant microscope. An aquarium. A planetarium. A pioneer house, tobacco barn, corn crib, and sugar mill. A computer to work with. Old toys. Shows and workshops. More.

The Ontario Science Centre, Toronto, Canada. A beehive behind glass. A television newsroom. A computer. A space vehicle model you can pretend to fly. A bike

Would you like to bounce on this giant telephone?
(Tad Goodale, courtesy Boston Children's Museum)

to ride hitched to a generator that runs a television set—pedal your own television show. Workshops. More.

These are only a few of the children's museums around. To find out the one nearest you, go to your library and ask the reference librarian for *The Official Museum Directory*. The directory is put out every year by The American Association of Museums. States, cities, and towns are listed alphabetically. Look within your state listing for the name of your city or town, or the city nearest your town. One of the museums listed there may be a hands-on museum; you will probably be able to tell by the description. If not, ask the librarian. The directory does not list *all* children's museums *as* children's museums. The following list gives you some of the others.

List of Children's Museums (Alphabetically, by State)

Arkansas
Museum of Science & Natural History, MacArthur Park, Little Rock, AR 72202.

California
Exploratorium, 3601 Lyon Street, San Francisco, CA 94123.

Josephine Randall Junior Museum, 199 Museum Way, San Francisco, CA 94114.

Junior Art Center, 4814 Hollywood Boulevard, Los Angeles, CA 90027.

Los Angeles Children's Museum, 310 North Main Street, Los Angeles, CA 90012.

Nature and Science Administration, 250 Hamilton Avenue, Palo Alto, CA 94301.

Colorado
Children's Museum of Denver, Inc., 931 Bannock Street, Denver, CO 80204.

Connecticut
Children's Museum of Hartford, 950 Trout Brook Drive, West Hartford, CT 06119.

Lutz Junior Museum, Inc., 126 Cedar Street, Manchester, CT 06040.

New Britain Youth Museum, 28 High Street, New Britain, CT 06051.

Youthmobile Museum, Inc., Old Ponsitte Road, Haddam, CT 06438.

District of Columbia

Capitol Children's Museum, 800 3rd Street, N.E. Washington, DC 20002.

Smithsonian Institution, A & I Building, Washington, DC 20560.

Florida

Jacksonville Museum of Arts and Sciences, 1025 Gulf Line Drive, Jacksonville, FL 32207.

Tallahassee Junior Museum, 3945 Museum Drive, Tallahassee, FL 32311.

Georgia

Museum of Arts and Science, 4882 Forsythe Road, Macon, GA 31204.

Indiana

Children's Museum of Indianapolis, 3010 North Meridian Street, Indianapolis, IN 46208.

Kentucky

Junior Art Gallery, 301 York Street, Louisville, KY 40230.

Louisiana

Louisiana Arts and Science Center, P.O. Box 3373, Baton Rouge, LA 70821.

New Orleans Museum of Art, P.O. Box 19123, City Park, New Orleans, LA 70179.

Massachusetts

The Children's Museum, 300 Congress Street, Boston, MA 02210.

Wistariahurst Museum, 238 Cabot Street, Holyoke, MA 01040.

Michigan

Children's Museum—Detroit Public Schools, 67 East Kirby Street, Detroit, MI 48202.

Minnesota

A. M. Chisholm Museum, 506 West Michigan Street, Duluth, MN 55802.

Junior Gallery and Creative Arts Center, Nelson Gallery of Atkins Museum of Fine Arts, 4525 Oak Street, Kansas City, MO 64111.

New Jersey

Morris Museum of Arts and Sciences, Box 125 Convent, Morristown, NJ 07961.

Newark Museum, P.O. Box 540/43 Washington, Newark, NJ 07102.

New York

Brooklyn Children's Museum, 145 Brooklyn Avenue, Brooklyn, NY 11213.

Metropolitan Museum of Art Junior Museum, 5th Avenue at 82nd Street, New York, NY 10028.

North Carolina

Charlotte Nature Museum Discovery Place, 3610 South Boulevard, Charlotte, NC 20209.

Nature and Science Center, Museum Drive, Winston-Salem, NC 27105.

Rocky Mount Children's Museum, Sunset Park, Rocky Mount, NC 27801.

Ohio

Lake Erie Junior Nature and Science Center, 28728 Wolf Road, Bay Village, OH 44140.

Oregon

Washington Park Zoo, 4001 S.W. Canyon Road, Portland, OR 97221.

Rhode Island

The Children's Museum, Inc., 58 Walcott Street, Pawtucket, RI 02860.

Tennessee

Children's Museum of Oak Ridge, Inc., P.O. Box 3066, Oak Ridge, TN 37830.

Cumberland Museum and Science Center, 800 Ridley Avenue, Nashville, TN 37210.

Students Museum, Inc., 516 Beaman Street, Chilhowee Park, P.O. Box 6108, Knoxville, TN 37914.

Texas

The Corpus Christi Museum, 1919 North Water Street, Corpus Christi, TX 78401.

Dallas Health and Science Museum, Box 26407, Dallas, TX 75226.

Fort Worth Museum of Science, 1501 Montgomery Street, Fort Worth, TX 76107.

McAllen International Museum, P.O. Box 2495, McAllen, TX 78501.

Virginia

Peninsula Nature and Science Center, 524 J. Clyde Morris Boulevard, Newport News, VA 23601.

West Virginia

Sunrise Foundation, Inc., Children's Museum Department, 746 Myrtle Road, Charleston, WV 25314.

List courtesy of American Association of Youth Museums

The Edmund Scientific Catalog

Are you interested in telescopes and microscopes? Do you like photography? Would you like to have your own weather station kit? Like to see a solar music box or a UFO Invader Turbo Kite? Do you like crafts and hobbies? Are you a do-it-yourselfer? If you answered yes to any of those questions, you'll love the Edmund Scientific Catalog!

There are more than 4,000 products in this catalog. Students all over the country have used these products in Science Fair projects. Some things, like toy parachutes, cost as little as $2. Other things, like the Voyager 6001 telescope, cost hundreds of dollars.

One part of the catalog is called "Science Fun." Here are a few products in that section:

GIANT ANT FARM: Ants work inside of a big plastic case. You can watch them build rooms and tunnels, and see how they store food. With the farm you get an "Ant Watcher's Book." The Edmund Company will even send you a supply of live ants!

POLLUTION TEST KIT: You can do more than 30 experiments with this kit. Test your air, water, and soil. You get test tubes and special testing papers. Also, you get safe chemicals and an instruction book.

THE AMAZING SKY ROCKET: Using a special kind of slingshot, you launch the sky rocket high into the air. Then a parachute pops out of the rocket and glides back to earth. In a few minutes you can be ready to blast off again!

JUMPING DISCS: These tiny discs are great fun. They are paper thin and can jump 2½ feet high. First you click the disc between your fingers. Then you lay it down on a smooth surface, like a table. Pop! It goes soaring into the air. Your friends will think you are a magician.

That's only the start. There are many exciting things to choose from. Be sure to look at the games part of the catalog. There you will find "Space Hop," "Pit Stop," and "Star City." Maybe you will like some of the kites, paper airplanes, or Star Trek action ships. Girls will like the "Make Your Own Perfume" kit.

Here's the best news: The catalog is free. All you have to do is send a letter or postcard to the Edmund Company. Write to:

Edmund Scientific Company
101 E. Gloucester Pike
Barrington, NJ 08007

Chapter *12*
ARTS AND COMMUNICATIONS

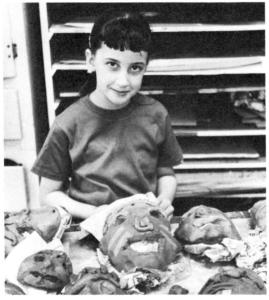

A young sculptor displaying her clay masks. *(James Durrell, Freelance Photographer's Guild)*

A young painter at work on a still life of bottles. *Vanucci Foto-Services; Freelance Photographer's Guild)*

National High School Art Exhibition

Since 1927 *Scholastic Magazine* has been running an art contest for children in secondary schools. Many of the winners have been between 12 and 14. To enter the contest you must ask your art teacher.

Art teachers submit children's art to a central group in a region. There are about 60 of these regions in the United States. In February a regional exhibit is held. It is sponsored by a business—newspaper, bank, shopping center, television station.

Pieces of art that win are sent to New York. They are judged in the national contest in March, then go on exhibit. National winners receive scholarships, medals, and special awards. The prizes are presented in May.

Categories are:

1. Oils
2. Acrylics
3. Watercolors
4. Pencil Drawing
5. Ink Drawing
6. Pastels, Crayon, Charcoal
7. Mixed Media
8. Printmaking
9. Graphic Design
10. Textile Design
11. Sculpture
12. Pottery
13. Jewelry
14. Three-dimensional Design
15. Photography

If your school is not in one of the regions set up by *Scholastic,* your teacher can send your art to the national committee. Write to:

Scholastic Art Awards
Scholastic Magazines, Inc.
730 Broadway
New York, NY 10003

All these Scholastic Art Awards medal winners are budding young artists. *(Photographs were supplied courtesy of Scholastic Art Awards, © 1980 Scholastic, Inc. All rights reserved)*

Print by Charles Lively, 14, Wichita, Kansas.

"Friends," pencil drawing by Lon Peterson, 15, Joliet, Illinois.

"Portrait of Lisa," mixed media, by Mik Young Oh, 15, Mesa, Arizona.

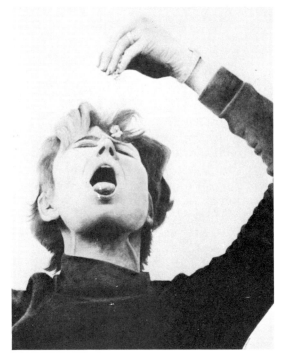

Pencil drawing by Becca Smith, 14, Memphis, Tennessee.

Pencil drawing by Mark Yamada, 14, Honolulu, Hawaii.

The Flying Giant Rat, the Masked Dancer, Ballooning in Colombia . . .

On the first greeting card by UNICEF was a painting by a child. The child lived in Czechoslovakia, in Europe. The time was after World War Two. Because of the war, many children in Europe were poor and homeless. UNICEF, a group formed by the United Nations, helped them. In return, children drew pictures that showed how they lived.

Now UNICEF has a collection of 10,000 pieces of children's art from countries all over the world. UNICEF uses the art on calendars and placemats. It is also printed in books, on slides, and in films. The money from the sale of these things goes to help more of the world's children.

UNICEF children's art includes paintings done in oil, watercolor, and tempera. There are pictures in crayon and ink. Some are collages made up of bits of paper and cloth pasted on a background. The art tells a great deal about holidays, sports, music, and working.

One painting shows lions from Africa. Another is of an elephant working. There are masked dancers on stilts and a Dragon and Lion Dance. One fanciful child drew a giant rat flying over the roofs of her village. Sports? Boxing in Thailand. Ballooning in Colombia. Cricket in England. Football in the United States. Anita, from Sweden, painted "The Most Fun Thing I Know Is Puddles."

From time to time, collections of UNICEF art travel around the United States for people to look at. If you'd like a peek into other kids' lives, visit a UNICEF art exhibit when it comes to your hometown.

A Children's Art Exchange

UNICEF suggests that American children share their art with children from other countries. It's a way to give other children a window on our world. In return, you learn about their way of life.

Setting up an exchange takes some work and planning. It's probably best to work with a club or class—a group of some kind. Here's how to go about it:

1. Make sure you have many months for the project. Mail across oceans takes time.

2. To find a group in another country, ask a Peace Corps volunteer who has returned to the United States. Or ask students from another country at a local college. Or write to:

Information Center on Children's Cultures
The U.S. Committee for UNICEF
331 East 38th Street
New York, NY 10016

Ask for "Pen Pals and Other Exchanges."

3. When you've found a group, write and ask if they want to exchange art with you. If the group is in a country where

English is not spoken, have your letter translated into their language. Set up some rules about the number of art pieces to be sent, deadlines, and so on. Give a date by which the group must reply with a yes or no. If you don't hear from them or if they say no, try another group.

4. For groups in poor countries, raise money to send art supplies. Don't send more than $20 worth. If you do, the kids will have to pay to receive it. Send paper, paint, brushes, and other art supplies. Include some international postal reply coupons so they won't have to pay for postage. You can get the coupons at your post office. Mark your package "Educational Art Supplies." Ask your school or an art supply company to send it for you.

5. Send your art to them. Choose it carefully to show what your lives are like. Include a photograph of your group if you like.

6. When art arrives from the foreign country, arrange a show. Try to find a public place—a library, your school, a shopping center. You might add some objects from the foreign country or show a film. A speaker who knows something about the country may be willing to talk.

7. Take pictures of the show and send them to your exchange group. In the package put any stories about the exhibit that have been in the local paper.

Music Greats

Here are the stories of 3 people who became famous as kids—and stayed famous even when they grew up. The first is from the distant past. The second is from the not-so-far-away past. The third is still playing music today.

Wolfgang Amadeus Mozart (1756–1791)

Born in Austria, Mozart was a musical genius. At the age of 4 he began taking music lessons. The teacher was Leopold Mozart, his father. The little boy had an amazing memory and learned very fast. A year later, Wolfgang was making up his very own music. One day the 5-year-old wrote a piece of music to be played on the piano. At first, everyone laughed. Wolfgang's piece of paper was a mess. He had accidentally dripped ink all over it, then had written the music notes over the ink blots. But his father carefully studied the boy's work. Leopold was so happy that he almost cried. The piano music was wonderful. But it was very difficult to play. Could anyone play it? Wolfgang said yes. All it took was a lot of practice!

Leopold wanted his son to be a great musician. They set out on a trip to many countries in Europe. Wolfgang was only 6 years old. Marianne, Wolfgang's older sister, was also a musician and she went along. Together, the 2 kids played for kings and queens and many other important people. On and off, Wolfgang was "on the road" for 15 years.

People everywhere couldn't believe their eyes—and ears! How could a boy so young have so much talent? Wolfgang loved all the attention and knew he was a very special person. However, music was a serious subject with him. If anyone interrupted his program, Wolfgang would burst into tears.

A drawing of the great composer Mozart, painted around 1786. *(Freelance Photographer's Guild)*

One day, the boy, age 7, picked up a violin for the first time. Without any training, he started to play. The sounds were beautiful. When he was only 12, Wolfgang wrote an opera! He was always surprising everyone—even his father.

There was no end to his talent. He worked hard—and fast. Many ideas were always bouncing around in his head. That's why his music, like his letters, was always so messy—he couldn't write fast enough to keep up with his mind!

While he lived, Wolfgang Mozart received many honors. He wrote many great operas, symphonies, and concertos (the popular music of his time). Today, experts still say he is one of the world's greatest composers.

Judy Garland (1922–1969)

She played the part of Dorothy in *The Wizard of Oz*. In that movie she sang "Over the Rainbow," a song that became a big hit. But "Dorothy" became a much bigger hit. Her name was Judy Garland.

She was born in Minnesota, and her real name was Frances Ethel Gumm. Adults called her Baby Gumm, and Frances always hated that nickname. She had 2 older sisters, Virginia and Mary Jane. The older girls were a singing act—the Gumm Sisters.

Baby Gumm first sang in front of an audience when she was 2½. Her sisters were singing in a movie theater in December, around Christmas time, and Frances wanted to join them. Her parents said no because she was too little. But when her sisters finished singing, Frances marched out on the stage. She knew only one song—"Jingle Bells"—but she sang out loud and clear. Frances had a little bell that she shook as she sang. The audience was crazy for the tiny girl with the big voice, and Baby Gumm didn't want to leave the stage. So she sang "Jingle Bells" again. And again. After 6 times, her father came out and threw her over his shoulder. Even as he carried her away, she kept singing and ringing her bell. From then on, Frances was a part of the act.

Hoping that the singing sisters would become stars, the family moved to California. The girls sang in movie theaters, hotels, churches, and on the radio. Frances was always the favorite. When she was 6, people called her "Little Miss Leather Lungs." Her voice was rich, beautiful, and loud. It was so powerful that she didn't need a microphone.

The Gumms went to the World's Fair in

The scarecrow, Dorothy (Judy Garland), and the Tin Man on the way to see the Wizard of Oz. *(From the MGM release* The Wizard of Oz, © *1939 Loew's Inc. Copyright renewed 1966, MGM/Inc.)*

Chicago in 1934. They sang at the Oriental Theater. Someone made a big mistake on the sign outside the theater, which read "The Glum Sisters." For years people had made jokes about the family name. It was easy to rhyme with bum, rum, crumb, and dumb. It was time to come up with a better name. They picked Garland. Frances Ethel Gumm became Judy Garland.

In Los Angeles, Judy went to acting school. When she was 13 a big movie studio, MGM, hired her. Soon she started to sing and act in movies. Right from the start, it looked like Judy would be a big star. But Judy wasn't so sure. She was always worrying about her looks. On the movie set there were always many beautiful girls. They made her feel short, fat, and ugly. After seeing one of her first movies, Judy almost cried. "I was frightful," she said. "I was fat—a fat little pig in pigtails. My acting was terrible. It was just little Kick-the-Can Baby Gumm—just dreadful.".

Judy Garland became a superstar. In movies and in concerts, her voice was unforgettable. Audiences could never get enough of her. They always screamed for more. But Judy's life was not happy. She took too many pills—some to go to sleep, some to wake up, and some to lose weight. And she drank too much alcohol. She died when she was only 47.

Stevie Wonder (1950–)

Stevie Wonder is a music magician. He writes songs. He sings songs. And he plays the piano, drums, organ, and harmonica. For more than 20 years he has been thrilling audiences with his own special kind of talent.

His real name is Steve Judkins and he comes from Michigan. He was born blind. At first, the blindness confused Stevie—he couldn't understand why he was always bumping into things. His brothers and sisters tried to treat him like a regular kid. With their help, Stevie learned how to ride a bike and climb trees. Sometimes his brothers went around the neighborhood and jumped from one woodshed roof to the other. Stevie joined in. He couldn't see the roofs but he could "hear" them. Before jumping he would call out from one rooftop, then listen for the sound to bounce off the next one. Different distances sounded different. After a lot of practice, he got very good at judging how far he had to jump.

Music has always been the most important part of Stevie's life. At age 2 he pounded a tin pan with a spoon. Soon his mother bought him a cardboard drum. (The family had very little money and couldn't afford a real drum.) After the drum came a harmonica. It had only 4 holes, so Stevie could only play 4 notes. That didn't bother him. The harmonica came on a chain and Stevie wore it around his neck. Friends and family were stunned by the sounds he could make with those 4 notes. When he was about 5, Stevie got his first transistor radio. He often put it under his pillow when he went to sleep.

Stevie grew up in a poor section of Detroit. He went to public school but attended special classes for the blind. Being around kids who could see made him realize how different he was. He also started to learn that he was special in another way—he was black. Stevie knew his skin was black, but he had no idea what his skin color looked like or why it mattered. His family had to tell him about the hardships that black people had to face. At times, Stevie was very self-conscious when he rode the bus to school. He was the only blind kid, and he was the only black kid among his classmates.

At 10, the boy "wonder" was entertaining all around the neighborhood. People would gather on somebody's porch and everybody would sing. Stevie played the music and his voice always stood out in the singing. Friends said he "played his voice" as if it were an instrument. The music was mostly rhythm and blues. Another favorite pastime was singing in the church choir, but he got thrown out of the choir because church members didn't like him singing "worldly" music!

In 1960 Stevie was hired by Motown Records. At 12 he had his first big hit— "Fingertips." Motown called him "Little Stevie Wonder." He went to a new school—the Michigan School for the Blind. There Stevie studied music by using Braille books and song sheets.

His career moved very fast and his popularity has lasted a long time. The list of his hit singles and albums is very long. "Superstition," "Uptight," and "You Are the Sunshine of My Life" are just a few of them. He has sold more than 25 million records.

He has done many kinds of music— rhythm and blues, rock, and ballads. Stevie's music is always changing. He sets the pace for other performers.

Today Stevie can still bring an audience to its feet, and he is always reaching out for new sounds. He breaks into song in cars, elevators, bathrooms, airplanes—anywhere. Stevie's friends always carry a tape recorder when they are with him. At any time, the music magician might feel inspired and start singing another hit song!

JAZZ IS . . .
by Marge Curson

"What is jazz?" a music teacher asked her class of beginning students.

"It's fast, loud music," said one student.

"Black music," said another.

"Music played by guys who wear sunglasses indoors and use words like dig and cool all the time," said a third student.

Can you see why none of these definitions is any good?

Here is a better answer to the teacher's question:

The music we call jazz began sometime between 1865 (the end of the Civil War) and 1900. At that time there were no records or tapes, no radio, and no TV, so it's impossible to say exactly when and where jazz was first played.

There is, however, no doubt that jazz was created by black people living in the southern part of the United States. It has been called the only original American art form. Today jazz is known and played all over the world. It has influenced almost any other kind of music you can name.

Although the parents or grandparents of the first jazz musicians were brought to this country from Africa, they did not bring jazz music with them. And jazz didn't develop in the islands of the West Indies or in South America, even though African people were enslaved there, too.

SOURCE: "Jazz Is . . ." by Marge Curson, *New York Amsterdam News*, Nov. 10, 1979, © 1979 Curriculum Concepts, Inc.

Jazz has been called America's original art form. Here Ted Curson, jazz trumpeter and band leader, carries on the tradition. *(Courtesy Ted Curson)*

Jazz grew out of the experience of one people living in one place.

What makes jazz sound different from other kinds of music? Here are 4 features of jazz:

Improvisation, both group and solo
A rhythm section playing behind a soloist
A steady, underlying beat
Emphasis on the performer, not the composer

Some parts of jazz are memorized or written down. Other parts are improvised—made up right on the spot—by the musicians. Don't expect to hear the melody of a tune over and over again, as you do in a popular song. Do expect to hear difficult and dazzling, startling, funny, beautiful lines of music that are completely fresh and new.

The soloist is important in jazz. Behind him or her you will hear the rhythm section. Often, the musicians use a call-and-response pattern in which a leader, the soloist, plays a musical idea that is answered by the other players.

Certain instruments are popular in jazz bands. The soloists in the "front line" often play cornets and trumpets, trombones, saxophones, clarinets, or flutes. Members of the rhythm section play piano, bass, and drums. (Other rhythm-section instruments are guitar, banjo, and tuba.) In some bands, of course, everyone gets a chance to solo.

Rhythm is very important in jazz—even more important than the melody. Have you ever heard this line from a famous song: "It don't mean a thing if it ain't got that swing"? Any jazz lover will tell you this is quite true. But what is swing? One musician of the 1920s said swing was "feeling an increase in tempo though you're still playing at the same tempo." Listen to jazz and see if you can understand what he was saying.

Most jazz music has a steady, underlying pulse: the beat. In the past, the beat was usually 4 quarter notes to a bar, but jazz has grown much more complicated with age. Today's musicians are using rhythmic patterns that are actually more closely related to African drumming than the rhythm of early jazz.

Syncopation—putting an accent in an unexpected place—is often a feature of jazz. Listen to the wonderful ragtime jazz of Scott Joplin (Remember the music in the movie *The Sting?*) and you'll begin to understand syncopation.

Finally, jazz has always been a music shaped by the personal feelings of the musicians who play it. Even when a musician plays a tune written by such a famous composer as Duke Ellington, the musician plays it "his or her way." No 2 performances of a jazz tune are alike, even if you are hearing the same song played by the same band. On Saturday it won't sound the same as it sounded on Friday. You might say freedom is another word for jazz, especially the new jazz that is being played by young musicians today. (Who created jazz? People newly freed from slavery.)

Do you have to study jazz in order to appreciate it? Probably. But one person may study by reading jazz books and magazines, while another studies by listening to the radio for hours on end. Why don't you give both methods a try?

And listen to all different kinds of jazz. You can learn from all of them: the blues, ragtime, classic jazz (also known as traditional jazz or New Orleans Dixieland), swing, boogie-woogie, bebop, progressive jazz, funk, and free jazz. Soon you'll be able to write your own definition of this original American art form.

Drums and Kids in Africa

Drums are an important part of life in all countries of Africa. Different tribes have different kinds of drums and different customs. One very interesting tribe is the Dagomba, a group that lives in the northern part of Ghana in Africa.

A Dagomba boy gets his first drum when he is 3 years old. Usually it is small and simple—a tin can covered by a skin. When he gets older, a boy helps his father plant crops on the family farm. Sometimes, adults build special treehouses on the fields and Dagomba boys sit there all day and beat on their drums to drive away any monkeys that might eat the crops.

The "talking drums" of Africa are known around the world. They are used on special occasions, like holidays and weddings. The Dagombas call their talking drum a *lunga*. The talking drum is shaped like an hourglass. A drummer hangs it from his shoulder and holds it under his armpit. When squeezed, the drum makes different sounds. The drummer can beat on the drum with his

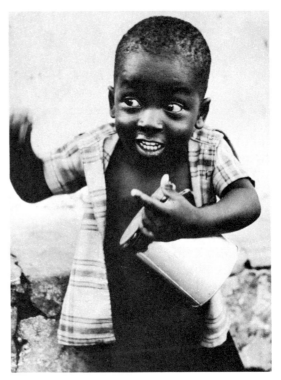

Dagomba boys in Ghana start drumming at age 3.
(John Chernoff)

fingers or hand, or he might use a stick. In this way, he makes the drum "talk."

Dagomba children first learn to beat the names of people in their families. Then they learn to beat the names of all the chiefs in their tribe. Later on, they are able to beat out whole sentences and tell stories.

Dagomba drummers have spent their whole lives learning the art of drumming. You cannot become a drummer for the tribe unless your father is one. Even so, it takes many, many years of hard practice.

Learning to drum isn't all fun. Sometimes the teachers get angry with young drummers who are lazy. Many young drummers have been hit on the head with heavy drumsticks, and they have the scars to prove it!

Dagomba children love music and dancing. One of the most popular dances is the Atikatika. Young boys from 4 to 8 years old do the dancing. Girls form a chorus and do the singing. Usually, special metal drums are used, played by boys from 8 to 10. The kids make up all the songs, music, and dance steps. The songs often criticize certain leaders and tell of problems that need to be solved. Or the songs talk of "children's rights." Some adults get mad when they hear the "modern" music. The adults forbid certain songs, but the kids just go ahead and write more of the same. They speak out with their songs—and with their drums.

Presto Chango! Magic Tricks

Magic is very old. American Indians were doing magic before the white man came. Africans have known magic for thousands of years. So have the Chinese.

When you learn magic tricks, it is important that you practice. Practice until you can do the trick without thinking about it. Learn to move your eyes to the spot you want the audience to watch. That way, the audience is not so likely to see you doing hidden things. Talking is important, too. Practice what you say as much as what you do.

Don't give away the secrets of your tricks!

Escaping Washers

This is an old trick created by the Chinese. They used money as props. But their money had holes in it then, and holes are necessary to do the trick. So use washers instead.

You need 6 washers, a piece of string about 3 feet long, and a piece of cloth (a handkerchief will do).

Practice

1. Tying the knot. Hold the string like this:

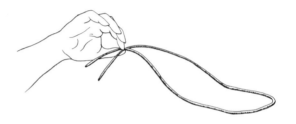

Thread the first washer on the 2 ends of the string.

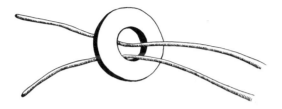

Take hold of the ends of the string and pull through the loop. Pull tight.

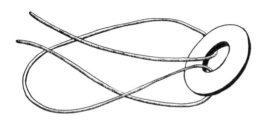

2. Untying the knot. Hold the washer. Pull up on the middle of the string to make a loop. Bring the loop over the coin to free it.

The Trick

Show the audience the string, the washers, and the handkerchief. Give them to someone. Ask, "Is there anything funny about the string? The washers? The handkerchief? No, they are ordinary. But they have magic power to escape."

After the person has agreed that the props aren't tricks, take them back. Say,

"I'm going to tie these washers on this string. We want to be sure they don't slide off. Let's put one in place first." As you talk, bring the ends of the string together. Then tie the first washer in the middle of the string with the special knot (1). Say, "Now I'll thread on the rest of the washers." Do this. Then shake the string by the ends so it jingles. "See? All secure," you say.

Pull the ends of the string out. Let 2 people in the audience hold them. "Hold them loosely now, but don't let go," you tell them.

Drop the cloth over the washers. Say, "Now the washers are ready to do their secret escape." Reach under the cloth and untie the knot. Don't let anyone see what you are doing. Then slide the washers into your hand. As you do this, keep talking, "They're getting loose. Almost . . . Not quite . . . Just a little longer . . ."

Pick up the cloth with your other hand. Show the washers and say, "Presto chango!"

Beans Away!

The Trick

Put 3 beans on the table. Give your friend one and put the other 2 in your hand. Close your hand, open it—there are 3 beans in it. Do it again. With this trick, you fool them twice.

1. **DO NOT SHOW:** First, get 5 beans. Put 3 in your left-hand pocket, one in your right pocket, and the other between the first and second fingers of your right hand like this:

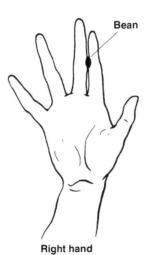

Bean

Right hand

2. **DO NOT SHOW:** Hold your right hand so that people see the *back* of it. Here's a good way to hide the bean. *Cover it with your thumb.* That way, you can move your hand in any direction and nobody knows you've got a bean between your first and second fingers. Of course, you can move your thumb away from the hidden bean if you want to pick up the beans on the table with your right hand (Step 4).

3. Begin the trick by taking the 3 beans from your pocket. Drop them on the table.

Say, "I'll give you this one," and hand somebody one bean.

4. Then, using one hand, pick up the other 2 beans and put them into your left hand. Say, "Just 2 beans," and let everyone see them.

5. Close your right hand around your left. Then shake both hands together. **DO NOT SHOW:** Let the bean between the first and second fingers of your right hand drop into your left with the other 2 beans.

6. Open your left hand and show 3 beans.

7. While people are thinking over what happened, put the 3 beans on the table. Raise your left hand, look up at it, and say, "I'll do that one again."

8. While you and your friends are staring at your left hand, **DO NOT SHOW** that you reach into your right pocket with your right hand. Take a bean and hide it between your first and second fingers, just as you did at the beginning (Step 1).

9. At the same time say, "Watch everything I do from now on, so you can tell why there *has* to be a three some." Do the trick over again. It's hard for people to follow this one, so you fool them twice.

Tips for the Magician: Of course, there are lots of other small objects you can use instead of beans. Magicians like sponge. Buy a big kitchen sponge or ask someone at home if you can have one. Cut it into little squares and snip off the corners until you have small balls. Or cut paper napkins, paper towels, or newspapers into 2-inch squares; fold the corners into the center a couple of times and then roll each one into a little wad.

Which Hand? If you are left-handed, you'll want to hide the bean in your left hand and use your right hand for showing the beans to your friends.

What You Need: At least 5 small, dried beans; pockets on both sides that are easy to get at. Ask someone at home for some dried beans. The small white ones are especially good, but any kind will work.

The Two-Sided Trick Book has other tricks and tricks for doing tricks. It was written by Robert Heger and Marianne Polachek. It is sold by Academic Therapy Publications, 20 Commercial Boulevard, Novato, California 94947.

The ABCs of Picture-taking

1. Keep your fingers off the camera lens. Many people forget this simple rule. Their pictures are filled with blurry globs.

2. You must hold the camera steady. Also, it should be level, not tilted.

3. Gently squeeze the shutter release instead of punching it. You don't want to jerk the camera at the last minute and ruin the picture.

4. When taking people pictures, get close to the people. Beginners often stand too far away and later they can't recognize who is in the picture! With most cameras you can get as close as 5 feet. Check your camera instruction book for the proper distance.

5. Don't take pictures of people when they are facing the sun; everybody will squint and the picture will look terrible. Turn everyone around so that their backs are to the sun.

6. The best people pictures are "candid" ones—photographs taken of people when they are not aware of what you are doing. This kind of picture catches expressions and actions that are natural, not posed. You have to be alert—and fast—to take good candid pictures.

7. When taking flash pictures, watch out for shiny surfaces. Eyeglasses or mirrors are good examples. These shiny surfaces reflect the flash and can leave glare spots on your pictures. To avoid that, stand at an angle to the shiny surface instead of facing it head-on.

8. Be aware of the background for people pictures. It is usually best to keep the background simple so that the person will stand out better in the picture. Before you snap, check to see that an unwanted person or object didn't stray into the picture. You might miss seeing the person or object, but your camera won't!

9. Simple, less expensive cameras have trouble with fast-action shots. These cameras aren't fast enough to stop the speed of people running or moving fast. When developed, the pictures are blurred. However, there is one thing you can do if you have a slow-shutter-speed camera: Take the picture when the action is at a peak. For example, if a girl is swinging back and forth on a swing, snap the picture at the top of the swing—just before the girl starts to go back in the other direction. At that instant she is almost stopped and your camera can catch that slow action.

10. Read the instruction book that comes with your camera. It will give you important tips on lighting, distance, special equipment, and much more. These tips will make the difference between a good and a bad picture.

Award-winning Photographs

There are many photography contests for kids. Three of the best are held by Scholastic Magazines, the Girl Scouts, and the Boy Scouts. The Eastman Kodak Company is the sponsor of all 3 of these contests. Here are some of the recent winners:

"Ballerina," by Nancy Peterson, Wahiawa, Hawaii.

"Farmer," by Michael Springer, Pierre, South Dakota.

"Zebras," by George Skrbin, Victorville, California.

The 1979 Scholastic/Kodak Photography Awards winners were made available courtesy of the Eastman Kodak Company.

"Shoes and Scarf," by Brenda Magnuson, Cypress, California.

"Peek-a-boo," by Janet Edwards, Cypress, California.

"Cups," by Lynn Easley, Burbank, California.

"Old Man," by Sarah Skeen, Barrington, Illinois.

"Children in the Door of a Hut," by Mark Carpenter, San Antonio, Texas.

The Magazine Rack

The newstands carry many good magazines for kids. Here are just some of the most popular. Interested in a year's subscription to a certain magazine? Check a recent copy for the current price. If the magazine is not sold in your area, write to the address given below.

ANIMAL KINGDOM
New York Zoological Park
Bronx, NY 10460

Animal lovers will enjoy this magazine, which presents articles on wildlife around the world. Other subjects covered are ecology and conservation. Color pho-tographs are usually included. Published 6 times a year.

ART & MAN
730 Broadway
New York, NY 10003

Every issue has a full-size poster. Usually, it is a painting or a photograph. Student artists and their works are always included. Anyone who likes art will love this magazine. Published 6 times a year.

BANANAS
730 Broadway
New York, NY 10003

Fun and laughs—that's what you'll get in every issue. Cartoons, puzzles, and jokes are everywhere. There are also interviews with stars like Erik Estrada. Published 9 times a year.

BITTERSWEET
Lebanon High School
777 Brice Street
Lebanon, MO 65536

"Our pages contain the secrets of the Ozarks, such as the making of maple syrup, blackberry wine, cheese, and china dolls." These are the words of the high school students at Lebanon High School. They do *all* of the work for this magazine. It tells about the history and customs of the people who live in the Ozark Mountains. Published 4 times a year.

BOYS' LIFE
1325 Walnut Hill Lane
Irving, TX 75062

Lots of action articles fill these pages. Sports, hobbies, and hiking are just a few of the subjects included. There are special columns on fishing, nature, and books. *Boys' Life* is the official magazine of the Boy Scouts. Published every month.

CHILD LIFE
P.O. Box 6500
Bergenfield, NJ 07621

Do you write stories or poetry? *Child Life* publishes many articles and poems by kids. Favorite topics are mystery, adventure, and science fiction. Puzzles, recipes, and jokes are also found in this wonderful magazine. Published 10 times a year.

CHILDREN'S DIGEST
P.O. Box 6500
Bergenfield, NJ 07621

Like to read an article on "Famous Cowboys and Their Horses"? How about "How to Cope with Teasing"? Or you might like "Special Effects in the Movies." These are the kinds of articles that are included in this magazine. Also there are cartoons plus an "activities" section. Published 9 times a year.

CRICKET
P.O. Box 2672
Boulder, CO 80321

This magazine has something for everyone. There are science fiction and fairy tale stories. There are science, geography, and travel articles. For fun, toss in some riddles, jokes, and rhymes. The photographs and drawings are beautiful. Published every month.

CURIOUS NATURALIST
c/o Massachusetts Audubon Society
South Great Road
Lincoln, MA 01773

Your whole family will love this nature magazine. Every page is packed with facts and drawings. One issue had this: "Make Your Own Raisins," "Poison Ivy," "Shooting Seeds," "The Striped Skunk," and much more. Published 4 times a year.

CURRENT SCIENCE
c/o Xerox Education Publications
1250 Fairwood Avenue
Columbus, OH 43216

You don't have to be a scientist to enjoy articles like "Niagara Falls is Falling Down." Each issue of this magazine covers the latest facts and happenings in science. Regular features include "Take-a-Break" (fun projects) and "Would You Believe?" (odd facts in science). Published 18 times a year.

DYNAMITE
730 Broadway
New York, NY 10003

"Bummers"—a page of things you love to hate—is a regular feature. Also in each issue is "Good Vibrations"—straight talk and solid advice. Stories on fads, fashions, and superstars are in each issue. Published every month.

EBONY JR!
820 South Michigan Avenue
Chicago, IL 60605

Stories about black history and outstanding blacks (kids and adults) are a big part of this magazine. Regular features are "Metric Madness" (about the metric system), "Art Gallery" (art by kids), and "Ink Links" (tips on how to be a better writer). Published 10 times a year.

FOXFIRE
c/o Foxfire Fund
Route 1
Rabun Gap, GA 30568

In 1966 a teacher and 140 kids set out to write a magazine. Today that magazine, *Foxfire,* is still going strong. It is all about life in the Appalachian Mountains of northeast Georgia. The students are always searching for interesting stories. Sometimes the stories are about things of the past like blacksmithing and log cabin building. Other articles are about special people—how they lived many years ago and how they live today. Published 4 times a year.

KIND
2100 L Street N.W., Room 200
Washington, DC 20037

This magazine is dedicated to animals. It tells you about everything from dogs and cats to turtles and elephants. Every month there is a hard question for kids to answer. One question was: People use the skins of fur animals such as beaver, mink, and muskrat to make coats. Do you think this is good or bad? Why? Many kids answered that question. Most of them said it was wrong to kill the animals. Published 6 times a year.

MAD
485 Madison Avenue
New York, NY 10022

Mad is the craziest magazine on the stands. It pokes fun at everything and everybody. Almost all the articles are done in cartoon form. Mad and its "usual gang of idiots" will always make you laugh. Published every month.

NATIONAL GEOGRAPHIC WORLD
17th and M Streets, N.W.
Washington, DC 20036

Many kids say this is one of the best magazines you can buy. It covers animals, sports, outdoor activities, ecology, science, and much more. One very popular feature is "Kids Did It!" which tells about talented kids and the things they do. One issue told about a 10-year-old girl who has 416 trophies for baton twirling. Another issue featured 2 boys who built a house of cards from 1,820 playing cards (32 decks). And don't forget the group of kids who run a teenage disco in Albuquerque, New Mexico. Published every month.

OWL MAGAZINE
59 Front Street East
Toronto, Ontario M5E 1B3
Canada

What is thunder and lightning? What should you do if caught in a thunderstorm? A recent issue of *Owl* answered those questions. This magazine is loaded with nature and animal stories, but it also has articles on subjects like spaceships and pyramids. Kids are invited to send in drawings, jokes, and questions, which are put into an "All Your Own" section. Published in Canada 10 times a year.

RANGER RICK'S NATURE
MAGAZINE
1412 Sixteenth Street, N.W.
Washington, DC 20036

In every issue of this magazine there is a story about Ranger Rick and his friends in the Deep Green Wood. They are always faced with a special problem about nature or animals. You may be surprised to learn how they solve some of those problems. Also in the magazine: "Ollie Otter's Fun Pages," posters, questions from readers. The pictures—full of many beautiful colors—will amaze you. Published every month.

SEVENTEEN MAGAZINE
Box 100
Radnor, PA 19088

Teenage girls read this magazine. It tells them about health and beauty. It also covers sports, careers, and travel. "Mini-Mag" is a regular feature containing many short articles. In a recent issue "Mini-Mag" covered daydreams, babysitting, mathophobia (hating math), taking care of a cat. Published every month.

TEEN
6725 Sunset Blvd.
Box 3297
Los Angeles, CA 90028

Teen is another good bet for girls. It's full of top-notch articles on beauty and fashion. Many girls send questions to "Dear Jack," "Dear Jill," and "Dear Doctor." The "Flea Mart" section lists many items to buy. In it are jewelry, posters, and clothes. Published every month.

TIGER BEAT
105 Union Avenue
Cresskill, NJ 07626

All the latest news on your favorite stars is in *Tiger Beat*. A large number of color pinups fills every issue. Have a secret wish that a special star could make come true? Then write to "The Treasure Chest" column. Another popular column is "The Tale End—The Latest Word in Gossip." Published every month.

STONE SOUP, THE MAGAZINE BY
CHILDREN
P.O. Box 83
Santa Cruz, CA 95063

All of the stories, poetry, and book reviews in this publication are written by kids. They even draw all of the pictures. Most of the kids are 6 to 12 years old. Some recent stories were "A Lonely Night in the Woods" and "The Alive Cloud." Published 5 times a year.

THREE-TWO-ONE CONTACT
E=MC Square
P.O. Box 2934
Boulder, CO 80321

Even if you hate science, this science magazine will turn you on. It covers everything from hiccups and tornadoes to *Star Trek*. Every month there is a new experiment—such as "How to Predict a Snow Storm." Another regular column is "Busy Bodies," which gives interesting facts about your body. One month this column discussed hair. It told how hair grows and what makes it curly, and featured famous hairdos like the ponytail and the afro. Finally, it gave a recipe for an egg rinse to make hair healthy and shiny. Published 10 times a year.

> YOUNG ATHLETE
> P.O. Box 246
> Mt. Morris, IL 61054

What's going on in the world of sports? *Young Athlete* will keep you up-to-date on all the latest news. Every sport you can think of appears sometimes in this magazine. There are interviews with big-name stars like Pete Rose, Bruce Jenner, and Magic Johnson. *Young Athlete* even interviewed The San Diego Chicken! (He cheers for the Padres baseball team.) One of the questions: Does it ruffle your feathers when people say you bother the players? The Chicken replied, "I don't listen to that kind of cheap chirping. However, I can't do the Disco Duck when the bases are loaded. The players get a little ticked off." Published 6 times a year.

Poetry from Around the World

THE LIFE OF A PIECE OF GRASS

I am a seed
All cuddled up so tight
Hoping to be released before tonight

Here I go
Down, down, down
Straight into the dark black
    spooky ground

I am popping
Here I go
I am almost about to grow

I see the sun
Up there so bright
Boy I can't wait until tonight

Good night
See you tomorrow
I have to get up at 7:00 so they can
    watch me grow

Ahh morning
I can't wait
To see everybody look at me so straight
Here they come
To look at me
They will be so happy and dance
    with glee

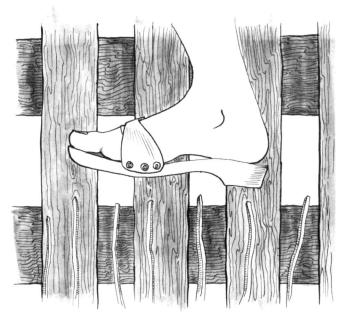

They stepped on me
I am about to die
Here I go to the great grass patch
    in the Sky.

Jeff Beir, 11, U.S.A.

WHEN . . .

When will the world find peace,
When will the day finally come,
When we will not have to be
Afraid any more?
How many are losing their lives
    today?
My heart is beating
Thinking of it.
Maybe you are falling
My dear brother,
While I am dancing.

Laura, 10, U.S.A.

LONELY OLD MAN

Who are you, lonely old man,
Your eyes don't shine,
Your feet don't dance
Your face is full of lines
Your beard is a jungle,
It shouldn't be,
Old man, you are all alone.
Your eyes look without seeing.
No one comforts you,
No one smiles at you,
No one holds your hand,
No one loves you.
Come on, take my hand,
You're not alone anymore, old man.

Karen, 12, Trinidad

403

THE LAND IN MY MOTHER

They all say
when I was in my mother's body
she ate a lot of watermelons.
An army of watermelon seeds came
    into the land
inside her body.
It was small and seeds got stuck
    to the face
of the baby which was I.
That's why I have so many freckles.
I'll get into my mother's body again
and let her eat a lot of lemons
    this time.
Then I'll be fair-skinned
and smelling good without any
    perfume.

Hashimoto Natsue, 10, Japan

(UNTITLED)

If I could rule the world for a day
These are the things I would like
    to say
Peace should reign all over the land
And money should be thrown out of
    every hand
For money is the cause of every hassle
Wherever it may be, in a hut or a castle
I would look for a planet
Where we could dwell
So the children of our world
Could be free to yell
If I could have ruled the world
    for a day
These are the things I would have
    had to say.

Corinne Rowlands, 12, Australia

404

(UNTITLED)

If your friend is hungry or
   thirsty,
Give him your share.
If your friend is in want of love,
Love him.
If your friend is in want of home
   and clothes,
Give him a cottage and clothes.
If your friend is lonely,
Keep him company.
If your friend is lying,
Silence him.

If your friend calls to you,
Listen to him.
If your friend is laughing,
Laugh with him.
If your friend is crying,
Cry with him.
If your friend is ill,
Fetch help.
If your friend dies,
Don't forget him.

Paula Lagerstam, 15, Finland

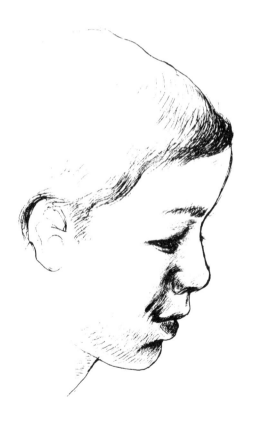
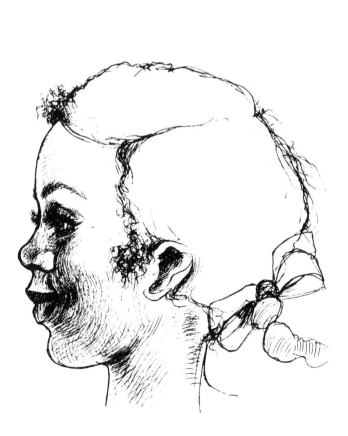

Theater Street

Back in the 1700s, the Russians fell in love with ballet. They didn't create it—the French did—but they probably did more than any other nation to make the ballet great.

The first Russian ballet students were 24 children of servants and serfs. (Serfs were men and women forced to spend their lives working for landowners.) They studied at the Winter Palace, one of the homes of the rulers of Russia, in St. Petersburg (now called Leningrad).

Slowly the ballet school became great. When they grew up, many of its students joined the Kirov Ballet, so it became known as the Kirov School. Its rival was the Moscow Ballet School, whose dancers went on to dance with the Bolshoi.

The school's teachers changed the ballet in many ways. One of them, Charles Louis Dedelot, figured out some stage magic that fascinated audiences of the 1800s. He attached dancers to wires that lifted them high in the air. The dancers seemed to be flying. This trick is still used in theater.

Some famous dancers learned their art at the Kirov Ballet School. Among them were Anna Pavlova, Vaslav Nijinsky, and Rudolph Nureyev. Nureyev was 17, very old, when he was accepted. (Most students are about 8 when they enter the school.) Several well-known choreographers, who arrange dances for the ballet, were also Kirov School students. One is George Balanchine, choreographer with the New York City Ballet.

A great Russian ballerina, Tamara Karsavina, wrote about her life as a student at the Kirov School in a book called *Theater Street*. Tamara, nicknamed Tooska,

was a student in the early 1900s. The students liked to imitate the adult ballerinas, whom they admired. When the teacher left the room, the girls would take a long run and leap on the piano, imitating the leaps ballerinas made into a male dancer's arms.

Once Tamara was punished for sticking her friend Lydia's head in a pail of soapy water. Lydia thought it was funny; the teacher who saw it happen didn't. Tamara was not allowed to go the theater for a time.

The students had a name for teachers they didn't like—"toads." One teacher whom they liked was small and round. The girls called him "bi-ba-bo," Russian for rubber ball.

As a student, Tamara danced several small parts. She became a very good dancer. One teacher gave her pluses after her A grades. An older dancer, Preobrajenskaya, took an interest in her. As Tamara waited in the wings to go on stage, Preobrajenskaya would say, "Now, young beauty! Step off! Fire away! Control your arms if you don't want a partner minus a few teeth!"

After Tamara graduated from the school, she went on to become a famous prima ballerina.

Today the Kirov School is in many ways the same as it was when Tamara went there. It is an honor to be selected by the school. Only one child in 30 who tries to get in is chosen. Most children are 9 or 10 when they apply. For 2 days they are examined, questioned, and judged. Judges look for certain body types with long legs and arms. How good is the child at turning the leg out at the hip? How high can the child jump? How healthy is he or she? How smart? How athletic?

Once children are accepted at the Kirov, those who don't live in Leningrad come to live at the school. From then on, it's 8 years of hard work. Dancing. Studying languages, math, science, acting. More dancing. Learning to play a musical instrument. More dancing. Every day, 3 to 4½ hours are spent practicing dancing. In the first year, children learn the 5 ballet positions standing at the barre, a long railing. They learn ballet movements—pliés, battements, ronds de jambe, relevés. It takes a long time for girls to be ready to wear toe shoes, and it's thousands of hours of sweat and sore muscles later before they are ready to graduate.

Most students go on to dance with ballet companies in the U.S.S.R. The best are chosen to dance with the Kirov; others go to smaller companies. Ballet dancers in the U.S.S.R. live very good lives. They are given beautiful apartments and country houses, and are allowed to travel to foreign countries to dance. The Kirov Ballet School has changed a lot since 1738, when 24 poor children became its first students.

An interesting recent development is that many Russian ballet dancers have defected from the U.S.S.R. because of lack of freedom there. Some have come to live in America, where they feel they can better express themselves personally and artistically.

Choosing a Clara for The Nutcracker

Who will get to be Clara? She's the girl who falls asleep to dream of the Land of the Sweets in *The Nutcracker,* the famous ballet. She's the star who dances with the Nutcracker Prince. She's the child whose dreams turn real. Every year at the School of American Ballet, girl students try out for the part. Two are chosen. Boys try out for Fritz, Clara's troublemaker brother, and for the Nutcracker Prince, who gets to kill the Mouse King with his sword.

If a student isn't picked for a main part, there are other roles—mice, angels, the bunny, a dancer in the party scene. In the New York City Ballet version of *The Nutcracker* there are 82 child dancers. (Adults are in the ballet, too—150 of them.) The 82 children are divided into 2 groups and each group dances in half of the performances. That's so one group doesn't have to dance too often. Auditions are held in early November. The children

are nervous. Who will be picked? What parts will they get?

The ballet is based on a fairy tale by A.E. Hoffman. The music was written by Peter Ilich Tschaikovsky, a Russian composer. Each choreographer, or dance arranger, makes up his own version. The New York City Ballet version was created by George Balanchine.

The ballet begins at a Christmas party. Clara is given a wooden nutcracker as a present by Drosselmeyer, an old man who has something magical about him. Clara falls asleep. Her dreams turn real on the stage. The nutcracker becomes a prince. He fights the evil Mouse King and kills him. Then the prince and Clara enter the Land of Sweets, where they sit on thrones. Before them, wonderful dances are performed—The Waltz of the Flowers, The Dance of the Sugar Plum Fairy. And then, of course, Clara wakes up.

Suzanne Farrell, a principal dancer at

Young Katharine Healey and Peter Boals in the New York City Ballet production of *The Nutcracker*. *Martha Swope, courtesy New York City Ballet)*

the New York City Ballet, was in *The Nutcracker* when she was a student at the school. Patricia McBride was, too. And so was Edward Villella, who entered the school when he was 9. In 1978 red-haired Katharine Healey, then 9, danced Clara. She also starred as a figure skater in Superskates V.

The School of American Ballet is where dancers are trained for the New York City Ballet. Most children are about 8 when they try out for the school. About one child out of every 10 gets in. Students work their way up through 11 divisions, from beginner to advanced. Their leotard colors tell their division. At the school, children learn ballet, discipline, manners, acting. For regular studies they go to the Professional Children's School.

Children from the school are given parts in other ballets. In *Circus Polka,* 54 little girls play the part of trained elephants. In another ballet they dance as toads—warts and all. And there are *Coppélia, Harlequinade,* and *Don Quixote.* But the big one, of course, is *The Nutcracker.*

Filmmaking at the Yellow Ball Workshop

Strange stars and planets drift in space. There is a burst of smoke from the planet Aros, and a silver rocket leaps with a roar into the sky. Its exhaust spells out THE AMAZING COLOSSAL MAN. The space ship lands on earth, and a crowd of curi-

ous earthlings gathers around the strange object. Suddenly, the door opens and the creature from Aros appears. He is huge and frightening. The earth people scream and fall over each other in their attempt to escape. The creature follows them. He presses between buildings, his huge size causing them to collapse. A woman faints. The earthlings call an emergency meeting.

That's only part of what happens in *The Amazing Colossal Man*, the first movie made at the Yellow Ball Workshop in Lexington, Massachusetts. The movie was made by 12 kids, who ranged in age from 5 to 12. The students thought up the story and wrote the script, then created the art and did all the camera work. Finally, they edited the film and added sound.

The Yellow Ball Workshop has been around since 1963. It is run by Yvonne Anderson, who has helped kids make over 200 films. These cartoon movies—called animated movies—have won many awards.

At the workshop kids learn different art forms. They work with cut-outs and flip cards. They make papier maché characters and sets. And that's only the beginning. After finishing all the art work, the kids make everything come to life on the screen.

Adults are saying wonderful things about the workshop films. "Without any exaggeration, these are about the best animated films made anywhere today," said a newspaperman. A magazine writer said, "I have never seen such imaginative films come from the hands of young filmmakers. These leave everyone wanting to rush out and make a film."

The Yellow Ball Workshop has many films that schools can rent. Here are just some of them: *Bag 5* (by kids 9 to 13), *Cinder City* (by kids 6 to 16), *I'm Me* (by kids 9 to 13), and *Plum Pudding* (by kids 11 to 18).

Wish your school had a class in filmmaking? Many schools do. Try to get some teachers interested in starting up a class. Ask them to rent a few films from the Yellow Ball Workshop. One very popular film is *Let's Make a Film*. It shows all the steps that kids go through in making a film. The workshop also sells a wonderful book, *Make Your Own Animated Movies*. Write to Yellow Ball Workshop, 62 Tarbell Ave., Lexington, Massachusetts 02173.

Making films is a great way to express yourself. As Yvonne Anderson says: "A large part of our work at the Yellow Ball Workshop has been with people between the ages of 5 and 18. This has been exciting. We have had fun, and we have found our students to be serious, hard-working artists who have contributions to make. People of this age have special qualities."

Behind the Scenes with The Little Rascals

From 1922 to 1944, 221 *Our Gang* comedies were made. Shown in movie theaters, they were a huge success. Audiences loved the *Our Gang* kids— Alfalfa, with his squeaky voice, and Darla, the Little Sweetheart, and Stymie, with his derby hat, and . . . The same movies are now being shown on television as *The Little Rascals*. Audiences still love them.

Darla Hood spoons out lemonade to other *Our Gang* kids. *(From MGM's Our Gang comedy "Waldo's Last Stand,"* © *1940 Loew's Inc.)*

What was it like for those children when they made movies? Some were so young they didn't realize they were in movies. For instance, Spanky MacFarland thought all children grew up as movie actors. The kids did not have to memorize whole scripts. Instead, they were fed their lines 3 or 4 at a time. If they made up lines that fitted in, that was okay. Some of the best stuff in the comedies was created by the children. If they did a good job of acting, they were rewarded with ice cream. A Good Humor ice cream truck was on the movie lot all the time.

Here are some terms describing "bits" the kids did:

"108"—a stagger, then a fall.

"Burn"—being angry.

"Slow burn"—slowly getting angry.

"Take"—an exaggerated expression.

"Taking it big"—a slow build to a full, big-eyed expression showing the actor knows what's happening.

"Fig bar"—acting coy and embarrassed.

The kids weren't too friendly with each other away from the set. Part of the reason was that they competed for lines. If a kid flubbed his lines, another kid might get them. When a child started misbehaving on the set, the director might turn and yell, "Bring the mother!" The child's mother was then supposed to make him behave.

When the children were acting, their ice cream cones were made of potatoes and cotton whipped together—so they wouldn't melt under the lights. Behind most of the scary stunts were tricks that made them safer than they seemed. In a runaway car scene, a hidden prop man did the actual steering; the steering wheel the kids were holding wasn't attached to the car wheels. The haystack they drove into was actually a tunnel covered with hay.

The kids often had a good deal of fun. The comedians Laurel and Hardy would come from the lot where they were making a movie to visit and joke. They had a funny little car for just that purpose. Laurel wore a derby like Stymie's and helped Darla make mudpies.

Some of the Actors

Stymie Beard (Matthew Beard, Jr.), born 1925. First picture, *Teacher's Pet*, at age 5. Was in 36 *Our Gang* comedies over 5 years. The studio tested 350 kids for the part, then Stymie came on stage and rolled his eyes. That was it—the part was his. His nickname, Stymie, was given him because he was always into things. Every day before shooting began, Stymie had to have his head shaved at the studio barber shop. He was bald—under his famous derby hat—in the show. Once he had to eat dozens of artichokes for a scene. He could never stand them afterwards. But mostly he loved being in *Our Gang*. The money he made helped support 13 brothers and sisters. When he grew too big for the part, he was replaced by Buckwheat. Matthew Beard died in 1981.

"Chubby" Chaney (Norman Myers Chaney), born 1918. First picture at age 11. Was in 18 *Our Gang* comedies over 2 years. When Joe Cobb got too old for the part, a nationwide contest was held to pick a new fat boy. About 20,000 kids competed. When the casting director told him he had won, Norman said, "Mister, are you just kidding me because I'm fat?" Chubby was a funny kid with a friendly personality. He was 3 feet 11 inches tall and weighed 113 pounds.

Jackie Cooper, born 1922. First picture, *Boxing Gloves*, at age 6. Was in 15 *Our Gang* comedies over 2 years. He began with *Our Gang* at a salary of $40 a week. His memory for lines was fantastic. In 1930, in *Teacher's Pet*, he was supposed to cry. To get him to do it, the director said he was going to shoot the *Our Gang* dog. Jackie didn't believe him. Then the director had a policeman pretend to arrest Jackie's mother. That didn't work either. Finally the director said he was firing an assistant director Jackie liked. That did it—Jackie started to sob. Someone from another movie studio saw the scene and wanted Jackie to star in the movie *Skippy*. Jackie was released from *Our Gang* to play the part, which was based on a comic strip character. That was the beginning of Jackie's career as a kid actor in long movies. He made more than a million dollars at it. One of his most famous movies was *The Champ*, with Wallace Beery. He was so good, people claimed he was an adult midget playing a kid's part. (This movie was remade in 1979, with Ricky Schroeder in the role Jackie had in the original.) Jackie is now a movie director. He likes to race cars, fly airplanes, and sail boats, as well as box, cook, and play the drums.

Mickey Gubitosi (Michael James Vincencio Gubitosi, later Robert Blake), born 1933. First picture, *Boy Scouts*, at age 5. Was in 40 *Our Gang* comedies over 5 years. A whiny, awful kid in the series, Mickey was naturally a grouch. When he was 2, he had been in an act with his father and sister on stage. It flopped. His parents sent him out in the morning to steal bottles of milk from doorsteps. As a grown-up, he said of his *Our Gang* acting, "I wasn't a child star. I was a child laborer. In the morning my mother would deliver me like a dog on a leash. . . . My father . . . just hung around the house singing Caruso records and wearing a cape. . . . I didn't like it [acting]. It was no kind of life. Forcing a kid to become a performer is one of the worst things that can happen to a child. It's turning them into adults when they're still youngsters." Later, with a new name—Robert Blake—Mickey played Little Beaver in the western series *Red Ryder*.

Darla Jean Hood (Dorla Jean Hood), born 1931. First picture *Divot Diggers* at age 4. Was in 50 *Our Gang* comedies over 6 years. When Darla was 4, her singing and dancing teacher in Oklahoma City took her to New York. At the Edison Hotel, the band leader asked Darla to sing and lead the orchestra. A casting director from *Our Gang* was in the audience. He gave Darla a screen test, then signed her up. She played the "Little Sweetheart." In the comedies, she was supposed to be in love with Alfalfa, but actually had a crush on Spanky.

Every Christmas the studio gave each *Our Gang* actor a present. One year, Darla asked for a dollhouse. Instead she got a room-sized playhouse with child-sized furniture in it. She and her friends turned it into a clubhouse.

As an adult, Darla has played roles in commercials. She was the voice for the Tiny Tears doll. Once she was asked to play a sore toe. When she asked the commercial director whether it was the right or left, he took her seriously and went to find out. She got fan mail from kids who thought she was still a little girl. Some kids wanted to marry her when she "grew up." She died in 1979.

Farina Hoskins (Allen Clayton Hoskins, Jr.), born 1920. First picture at age 1. Was in 105 *Our Gang* comedies over 9 years. Farina was discovered in Watts,

the black section of Los Angeles. He was in more *Our Gang* comedies than anyone else. A cute kid, his hair in pigtails, he could turn on tears in seconds. When the scene was over he would turn them off. After leaving *Our Gang*, he stayed in show business for a while, then started working to help the handicapped. In 1975 he was elected to the Black Filmmaker's Hall of Fame. He died in 1980 at age 59.

Spanky MacFarland (George Robert Phillips MacFarland), born 1928. First picture, *Free Eats*, at age 3. Was in 95 *Our Gang* comedies over 11 years. He was a 3-year-old model in Dallas, Texas, when his aunt mailed a photo of him to the *Our Gang* studios. It got him a screen test. This was unusual, because every month adults sent about 1,000 kid photographs to the studio, all wanting to get their kids in *Our Gang*. Only one or 2 kids were hired every year. Spanky was a natural, a genius. His name came from his mother's saying to him, "Spankee-spankee, mustn't touch." Spanky was a scene stealer with his cute round face and big cap. "Okay, toots," he'd say when he was ready for a scene to start. He also was in trouble a lot for swearing.

Alfalfa Switzer (Carl Switzer), born 1927. First picture, *Beginner's Luck*, at age 7. Was in 61 *Our Gang* comedies over 6 years. With his brother Harold, Carl Switzer sang at auctions in Illinois, his home state. Then his family came to visit California. It was impossible to get an audition for Carl and Harold for *Our Gang*. No one without a pass could get past the studio gates. So the 2 boys went to the *Our Gang* cafe, outside the gates, where the cast ate. At noon, Carl and Harold marched in and sang. Everyone loved their act, and they were given parts in the series. They were called the "Arizona Nightingales." Harold's nickname was "Slim" or "Deadpan." It was Carl who became famous—as Alfalfa, the kid with the squeaky singing voice, the cowlick that stood up straight on his head, his bug-eyed double take. (The cowlick had to be waxed to stick up that way.) Alfalfa was a big tease on the set. Once he messed up 32 takes of one scene of the kids hanging on the back of a truck. Darla passed out from exhaust fumes and she had to be taken to the hospital.

Buckwheat Thomas (William Henry Thomas, Jr.), born 1931. First picture, *For Pete's Sake*, at age 3. Was in 93 *Our Gang* comedies over 10 years. His mother got him into the studio so he could audi-

tion. For a while it was hard to tell if he was a boy or girl. (Others who played the part, Carlena Beard and Willie May Taylor, were girls.) He charmed everyone with his big eyes and great smile. Though he was shy, he loved acting in *Our Gang*. He died in 1980.

This article is based on material from the book Our Gang: The Life and Times of the Little Rascals *by Leonard Maltin and Richard W. Bann (New York: Crown Publishers, 1977). The book gives summaries of the* Our Gang *comedies and more information about the actors.*

Nathaniel Field—Kidnapped!

In 1600, 12-year-old Nathaniel Field was kidnapped from school and taken to a room at the Blackfriars Theater. There he was locked up with 6 other boys who had been kidnapped, too. Their kidnapper, Henry Evans, yelled at them when they complained about what had happened to them. He said he would whip them if they weren't quiet.

What Evans had done was legal in those days. He had taken the boys to be actors in his theater company, Children of the Chapel. However, Evans made a mistake. One of the boys he had taken, Thomas Clifton, was the son of a rich and powerful man. When Evans refused to give Thomas up, Clifton got Evans into big trouble. Evans was tried by the Star Chamber, a kind of court. He was told he could have nothing more to do with the Children of the Chapel. Thomas went back home. Nathaniel and the other boys stayed with the theater company.

Boy actors were popular in England then. Plays were written just for them by

famous writers, and people paid to see them act.

Blackfriars was a private theater, and tickets cost more than at public theaters. Shows were held indoors, sometimes at night by candlelight. Theaters were different from those of today. Like most, Blackfriars was a large hall with no stage or curtain. The actors put on plays at one end of the hall.

The show began with music. The boys sang, danced, and played flutes, violins, and other instruments. Then the play itself started. Plays were about adults, though there were some children's parts. Names of some of the plays were *Sir Giles Goosecap, All Fools, The Case Is Altered, May Day, Eastward Ho!* and *Cynthia's Revels.*

Twenty boys were in the Children of the Chapel. In 1601 they put on a play for Queen Elizabeth. Soon they became famous. They were so good that adult actors were jealous. Besides, writers for boys' companies took jabs at adult theater through nasty lines in their plays. Nathaniel starred in such a play, called *Poetaster*. The playwright was Ben Jonson, whose works are still read today.

Even William Shakespeare, the greatest writer of plays of all time, was jealous. A "war of the theaters" was begun. The weapons were words. In a play put on at his theater, the Globe, Shakespeare wrote lines making fun of boys' theater. In one, he called the boys "little eyeasses" (baby birds) "that cry out." He had another actor say that it wasn't a good idea for writers for boys' theater to make fun of adult companies. After all, the boys might grow up to be adult actors.

One actor did not grow up. That was Salathiel Pavy. He had joined Blackfriars about the same time as Nathaniel, at the age of 10. Sal was very good at playing old men. When he died, in 1603, Ben Jonson wrote about him, saying Sal was "the stage's jewel" who had died when "scarce thirteen." He praised Sal for acting the part of an old man so well that audiences thought he *was* an old man.

When Nathaniel Field grew up, he joined Shakespeare's company, The King's Men. Some of his friends in Blackfriars did, too. Field also wrote 2 plays—*A Woman Is a Weathercock* and *Amends for Ladies*.

Pantomime

Pantomime is a kind of acting. But you never talk. Everything you wish to "say" has to be expressed with different parts of your body.

You already use pantomime in much of your everyday life. Put your finger silently up to your lips. You are telling someone, "Be quiet." When you stomp your foot on the ground you are really saying. "I am angry." Also, you have proba-

bly played the game called "Charades," in which you have to act out words without speaking. Usually charade players act out names of television shows, movies, or books.

You may be surprised to see how well you can express yourself without talking. There are many different things you can show just by using your mouth. Here are just a few:

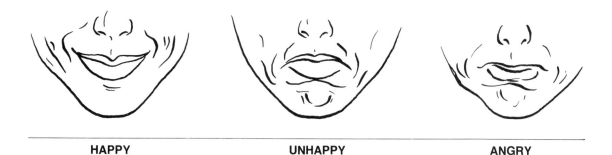

HAPPY   **UNHAPPY**   **ANGRY**

Here are a few good tips to remember when you are doing pantomine:

1. Never speak.
2. Remember to leave space between your fingers when you are holding an imaginary thing. If you are drinking from a glass, your hand will be curled but not closed. Practice with a real glass so you can see how wide open to leave your fingers.
3. If you are acting out a little play, don't forget about the imaginary scenery. You don't want to walk through a closed door!
4. Practice with a friend. A partner can easily see the mistakes you make.
5. Don't be shy. Pantomime is lots of fun. Clowns and magicians use it all the time. It takes practice to be good, but it is not hard to learn.

Here are a few good exercises:

Warm-up Exercises

1. Using only your face, pretend that you are HAPPY. Try being SAD. A couple more: ANGRY, SURPRISED. Practice in front of a mirror until you get it right.
2. Using all of your body, pretend you are COLD. Hints: Use your hands to lightly rub and slap your arms to show you are trying to get warm. You should shiver a little. Don't forget your face. You might want to make your teeth chatter. It might be easier if you imagine that you are outside in the snow. Think snow!

Short Pantomimes

1. Polish your shoes.
2. Fly a kite.
3. Pretend you are a monkey.

A Skit

Pretend you are in a parade. What would you like to be? You might be a

A kid gets ready for the pantomime act in a free performance in Mexico City. *(Martin Pendl, courtesy United Nations)*

clown, a majorette, a cowboy, a dancer, a trombone player, a policeman. After you pick a person, think very carefully about how that person acts. Then see if you can do it in pantomime. For extra fun, see if you can be all of them! After being a clown, for instance, turn away from your audience and wait a few seconds. Then turn back and be someone else. Or get some of your friends to do the skit with you. To really "set the scene," play some marching music.

Most people who do pantomime do not wear fancy costumes. They wear very simple clothes. There is a good reason for this. They want the audience to pay attention to their movements, not to their clothes. Also, mimes often wear white face makeup. This makes face movements easier to see.

Want to learn more about pantomime? Here are some good books:

Books

Vernon Howard, *Pantomimes, Charades, and Skits* (New York: Sterling Publishing, Co., 1977).

Kay Hamblin, *Mime: A Playbook of Silent Fantasy* (New York: Doubleday and Co., Inc., 1978).

Codes

Want to send secret messages to your friends? Or keep a diary that no one else can read? Then you might like to learn one or more of the following codes.

The Ring-a-Ling Code

Here is a code that is easy to learn. If you need help, all you need to do is look at a telephone dial. The code is based on the way the letters and numbers are grouped together. The groupings are the same for the regular dial and the push-button phone.

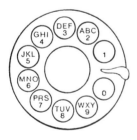

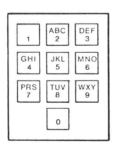

Look at how the *A*, *B*, and *C* are set above the number 2.

Want to write the letter *A* in code? Use a 2 and put a line over it that slants up and to the left. It will look like this: `2. Want to write a *B* in code? It should also be a 2, but the line above it will be straight up and down. And a *C* will be a 2 with a line that slants to the right: ´2. The same rules should be used for all groupings on the dial.

The secret code for the word "candy" is 2 2 6 3 9.

Can you figure out what this says? 6 3 3 8 6 3 2 8 8 4 3 7 2 7 5.

IMPORTANT: The only letters missing from the dial are *Q* and *Z*. Also, the numbers 0 and 1 have no letters. So go ahead and match them up. You can let 0 become the secret code for *Q*, and 1 can stand for *Z*. The word zebra would be: 1 3 2 7 2.

The Pigpen Code

This code was used by prisoners in the Civil War. First draw 2 tick-tack-toe boards and 2 large *X*'s. Then put in all the letters of the alphabet. Only 2 groupings will use dots.

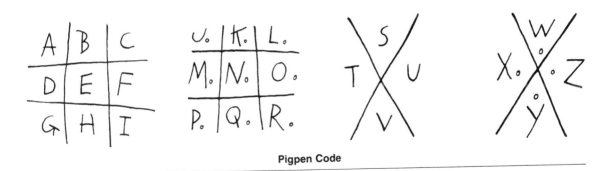

Pigpen Code

Think of each letter as living in its very own "pigpen." The letter *B* has a pen with 3 walls: ⊔ . The letter *L* lives in a home that has a dot: ⌞ . The letter *O* is written like this: ⊏ . And <u>*W*</u> looks like this: ∨ . The word *Blow* would be:

⊔⌞⊏∨

Julius Caesar Code

The great Roman ruler Julius Caesar used this code to send secret war messages. It is called a "shift code." It works

in. Put in *A*, *B*, and *C*—the only letters you were missing.

Want to write the word "dog" in code? Look in the first row for *D*. Then look right below it for the code letter. It is a *G*. Do the same for *O* and *G*. The code word for dog is: GRJ. See if you can figure out what this says: FRGHV DUH IXQ.

You can change your code as much as you like. Just change the key number and shift the alphabet in the same way. If your key number is 4, your second line will start with an *E*.

A B C D E F G H I J K L M N O P Q R S T U V W X Y Z

D E F G H I J K L M N O P Q R S T U V W X Y Z A B C

Julius Caesar Code

by using the alphabet and a "key" number.

Caesar's key number was 3. Here's how he did it. First, write all the letters of the alphabet. Then set your pencil on letter *A* and move the pencil 3 places to the right. You will end up on letter *D*. You will now "shift" the alphabet. Under the letter *A*, put a *D*. Then continue to write the rest of the alphabet in the second row. When you get to Z you will still have 3 spaces to fill

Morse Code

An American named Samuel Morse invented this code. It is used to send messages by telegraph and radio. Using a special key, a person can click out dots and dashes that stand for letters of the alphabet. A dot is a click followed by a short rest. A dash is a click followed by a longer rest.

The time between clicks for a dash is

about 3 times as long as the time for a dot. You don't need a special key to use Morse code; just tap your fingers. You might want to blow a whistle or ring a bell. Some people like to write it out.

A · —	J · — — —	S · · ·
B — · · ·	K — · —	T —
C — · — ·	L · — · ·	
D — · ·	M — —	U · · —
E ·	N — ·	V · · · —
F · · — ·	O — — —	W · — —
G — — ·	P · — — ·	X — · · —
H · · · ·	Q — — · —	Y — · — —
I · ·	R · — ·	Z — — · ·

Morse Code

Semaphore Code

Boy Scouts always learn this code. You can spell out messages by holding your arms in different positions. For example, to show an *R* hold both of your arms straight out at your sides, level with your shoulders. Flags are often used to send messages at a great distance. At night you can hold flashlights to make the message easier to see. There are many wonderful books about codes. If you want to read more about them, here are 2 very good books to get at your library.

Books

Sam and Beryl Epstein, *The First Book of Codes and Ciphers* (New York: Franklin Watts, Inc., 1956).

Walt Babson, *All Kinds of Codes* (New York: Four Winds Press, 1976).

Kimmies Harp Boontling

In Boonville, a small town in California, most of the people speak 2 languages. One of the languages is English. The other is Boontling. Boonters (people of Boonville) made up the language about 100 years ago. There are several stories about how it first came about. One story has it that Boontling was a secret language the children created. Another story says that mothers made it up to confuse their kids. And the most popular story tells how men of Boonville invented Boontling to keep things from their wives and children. Now Boonters speak Boontling so strangers won't know what they're saying.

Many of the words in Boontling come from people's names. Bill Nunn is the

word for syrup, for instance. Why? Because a man named Bill Nunn was so fond of maple syrup that he poured it on almost all his food.

The children of Boonville learn Boontling in school. Some language experts have traveled to Boonville to study the language. A dictionary of 1,000 Boontling words has been published. Here are some of them.

Word in Boontling	Meaning in English
ab	crowd into line
bahl	good
Bill Nunn	syrup
boo	potatoes
briney	ocean
briney glimmer	lighthouse

Semaphore Code

Word in Boontling	Meaning in English
Buckey Walter	telephone
Charley Ball	embarrass
cloudy	foot
codgy	early
cuttin buckeye	taking it easy
dee	day
dehig	cheat
doolsey	sugar
dumplin dust	flour
easter	egg
French boos	French fries
gorms	food
harp	talk
heese	high school
high heeler	judge
hob	dance
hoot	laugh
kimmies	people
mosh	car

Word in Boontling	Meaning in English
nonch	bad
nook	home
pike	drive
shoveltooth	doctor
slif	a little
tidrey	get together
tidric	time
tweed	little kid
wee heese	elementary school

A Little Story in Boontling . . .

Before we pike the mosh to the wee heese, let's go get some gorms. I'd like some French boos, without Bill Nunn. We can harp a slif with the shoveltooth. If you don't Charlie Ball me by acting like a tweed, we'll have a bahl tidric.

Words in Other Languages

How do you say hello to people who speak no English? It's easy. You say hello in *their* language. That shows you're friendly. Here are 4 handy words to know in 7 languages. To learn more, read a foreign-language dictionary or get a friend who knows a foreign language to teach you. Or watch TV programs in that language. Or learn from phonograph records that teach it.

The Language	The Words			
	hello	good bye	please	thank you
French	bonjour (boh-ZHOOR)	au revoir (OH ruh-VWAHR)	s'il vous plait (seel voo PLEH)	merci (mehr-SEE)
Spanish	buenos dias (BWEH-nohs DEE-ahs)	adios (ah dee-OHS)	por favor (POHR-fa-VOHR)	gracias (GRAH-see-uhs)
Italian	buon giorno (BWAWN JOHR-noh)	arrivederci (ah-ree-vay-DAYR-chee)	per favore (payr fah-VOH-ray)	grazie (GRAH-tsyay)

The Language   **The Words**

	hello	good bye	please	thank you
Russian	zdravstvuite (ZDRAH-st'eh)	do svidanya (duh sv'i DAH-n'uh)	pozhaluista (puh-ZHAHL-stuh)	blagodaryu (bluh-guh-duh-R'OO)
Esperanto (**world language**)	bonan matenon (BOH-nahn mah-TEH-nohn	adiau (ah-DEE-ow)	bonvole (bohn-VOH-leh)	dankon (DAHN-kohn)
Swahili	salam alekum (SAH-lahm ah-LEH-koom)	kwaheri (kwah-HEH-ree)	tafadhali (tah-fahd-HAH-lee)	asante (ah-SAHN-teh)
Japanese	ohayō (oh-hah-YOH)	sayonara (sah-yoh-nah-ruh)	kudasai (koo-dah-sahee)	arigatō (ah-rih-gah-TOH)

Index